A Common Life

A Common Life

FOUR GENERATIONS
OF AMERICAN
LITERARY FRIENDSHIP
AND INFLUENCE

David Laskin

UNIVERSITY PRESS OF NEW ENGLAND
Hanover & London

UNIVERSITY PRESS OF NEW ENGLAND
Hanover, NH 03755

First UPNE paperback edition 1996.

Originally published in hardcover by
Simon & Schuster, Inc. in 1994.
Reprinted by arrangement with
Simon & Schuster, Inc.

Printed in the United States of America
5   4   3   2   1

CIP data appear at the end of the book

The author gratefully acknowledges permission from the following sources to reprint material in their control:

Isabel Bayley, Literary Trustee for the Estate of Katherine Anne Porter, for quotations from unpublished letters by Katherine Anne Porter.

The Estate of Elizabeth Bishop, Vassar College Library, and the Harry Ransom Humanities Research Center at the University of Texas at Austin for quotations from the unpublished letters of Elizabeth Bishop, copyright © 1994 by Alice Helen Methfessel.

Harvard University Press for material from Henry James Letters, edited by Leon Edel, copyright © 1984 by Leon Edel, editorial; copyright © 1984 Alexander R. James, James copyright material.

Houghton Library, Harvard University, and Frank Bidart, literary executor for Robert Lowell, for quotations from unpublished letters and poems of Robert Lowell.

Farrar, Straus & Giroux, Inc., for excerpts from The Complete Poems 1927–1979 by Elizabeth Bishop, copyright © 1979, 1983 by Alice Helen Methfessel; excerpts from Day by Day, copyright © 1977 by Robert Lowell; excerpts from The Dolphin, copyright © 1973 by Robert Lowell; excerpts from For Lizzie and Harriet, copyright © 1973 by Robert Lowell; excerpts from For the Union Dead, copyright © 1964 by Robert Lowell and copyright renewed © 1992 by Harriet Lowell, Sheridan Lowell, and Caroline Lowell; excerpts from Life Studies, copyright © 1959 by Robert Lowell and copyright renewed © 1987 by Harriet Lowell; excerpts from Near the Ocean, copyright © 1967 by Robert Lowell; excerpts from the letters of Eudora Welty from Author and Agent by Michael Kreyling, Eudora Welty letters copyright © 1991 by Eudora Welty.

Harcourt, Brace & Company for material from the Melville Log: A Documentary Life of Herman Melville 1819–1891 by Gay Leyda, copyright 1951 and renewed 1979 by Gay Leyda.

Charles Scribner's Sons, an imprint of Macmillan Publishing Company, for material from A Backward Glance by Edith Wharton, copyright 1933, 1934 by The Curtis Publishing Company, renewed 1961, 1962 by William R. Tyler; material from The Letters of Edith Wharton, edited by R. W. B. Lewis and Nancy Lewis, copyright © 1988 by R. W. B. Lewis, Nancy Lewis, and William R. Tyler; material from Henry James and Edith Wharton: Letters: 1900–1915, edited by Lyall H. Powers, copyright © 1990 by Lyall H. Powers.

Yale University Press for material from The Letters of Herman Melville, edited by Merrell R. Davis and William H. Gilman, copyright 1960 by Yale University Press.

To the memory of my friend
ANN STEWART TAYLOR

Acknowledgments

I WAS LUCKY to have the help of so many of the friends, acquaintances, and biographers of the eight friends I wrote about, as well as scholars in the field. My conversations with these people were the most pleasurable, and most rewarding, part of my research. I would like to thank Daniel Aaron and Cleanth Brooks for pointing me in the right direction. Marcella Comès Winslow, Frank Bidart, Helen Vendler, Lloyd Schwartz, James Merrill, Richard Wilbur, Philip Booth, Richard Tillinghast, and Ruth Vande Kieft were uncommonly generous with time, memories, and insights.

I want to thank Stanley Kunitz, Joseph and U. T. Summers, John Malcolm Brinnin, Elizabeth Hardwick, Anthony Hecht, Dana Gioia, Jonathan Galassi, and Robert Shaw for sharing their recollections of Robert Lowell and Elizabeth Bishop.

David Diamond, William Jay Smith, Michael Seide, Calvin Skaggs, Joan Givner, Tim Seldes, Seymour Lawrence, Michael Kreyling, E. Barrett Prettyman, Jr., Norman McMillan, Elizabeth Spencer, Ronald Sharp, Paul Porter, and Eleanor Clark answered many questions about Katherine Anne Porter and Eudora Welty.

My own friends and friends of friends were a rich and sometimes surprising source of information, clues, clippings, accommodations, and support. Many helped without even knowing it. In particular I'd like to thank Joyce Hartsfield and Regis Obijiski, Jim Witkin and Nancy Flickinger, Jenny Whitman and David Foster, Lisa Guerrero, Phil Patton, Karen Pennar, Emily Harris, Sue Bryson, David Low, Holly Hughes, Linda Corrente, and Debbie Mayer.

Nancy S. MacKechnie at the Vassar College Library, Cathy Henderson at the Harry Ransom Humanities Research Center at the University of Texas at Austin, Dr. Blanche Ebeling-Koning at McKeldin Library at the University of Maryland, and the staffs of Houghton Library at

Harvard and Beinecke Library at Yale facilitated my archival research. I thank all of them for their interest, efficiency, and grace under pressure. The Poets and Writers Information Center made tracking down writers a good deal easier.

I'm grateful to Alice Methfessel, Elizabeth Bishop's literary executor; Isabel Bayley, Katherine Anne Porter's executor; and Frank Bidart, Robert Lowell's executor, for permission to quote from letters.

Anyone writing about Henry James owes a tremendous debt to the life's work of Leon Edel, whose five-volume biography of James and whose editions of James's letters and short stories are stunning monuments to both of them. R. W. B. Lewis's biography of Edith Wharton and the volume of Wharton's letters that he edited with Nancy Lewis are also indispensable texts. Lyall H. Powers did an admirable job of editing and annotating the complete correspondence between James and Wharton, which I found tremendously useful. I also must acknowledge a considerable debt to David Kalstone's *Becoming a Poet,* which covers the literary friendship between Lowell and Bishop with great sensitiveness and insight.

My agent, Diane Cleaver, believed in the project from the very first, helped me formulate the shape and style of the book, and matched me up with a superb and enthusiastic editor, Bob Bender of Simon & Schuster, who has guided the book through to publication with uncommon kindness and wisdom. I count myself extremely lucky to have fallen into both of their hands. Thanks also go to Johanna Li at S & S.

I'm grateful for the support and patience of my family—parents, brothers, sisters-in-law, parents-in-law, and more distant kin. My mother, Dr. Leona C. Laskin, answered medical questions. My children, Emily, Sarah, and Alice, allowed me to work at home in relative peace, delighted me with their questions about "my" writers, and were the only ones to express unalloyed admiration for the size of the manuscript.

Finally, I want to thank my wife, Kathleen O'Neill, who has, over the years, become my ideal audience of one as well as so much more.

Contents

"Life in common among people who love each other is the ideal of happiness."

—GEORGE SAND,
Histoire de Ma Vie

Introduction

> *Friends do not live in harmony merely, as some say,*
> *but in melody.*
>
> —HENRY DAVID THOREAU,
> *A Week on the Concord*
> *and Merrimack Rivers*

"HE WAS POOR, he was solitary, and he undertook to devote himself to literature in a community in which the interest in literature
was as yet of the smallest," the young, suave, freshly expatriated
Henry James wrote of the strange, sequestered apprenticeship of
Nathaniel Hawthorne. "[E]very man works better when he has
companions working in the same line."[1] James spoke from experience for he himself was just reaping the benefits of keeping company with the leading lights of literary London. In fact, his
pronouncement fits more or less snugly all of the writers whose
friendships I consider in this book. Nathaniel Hawthorne and
Herman Melville, Henry James and Edith Wharton, Katherine
Anne Porter and Eudora Welty, Elizabeth Bishop and Robert Low-

ell: four friendships spanning most of the history of American literature that yielded immeasurable riches to eight of our most important writers. Each of the friends did indeed work better knowing that a like-minded companion was working "in the same line." But these distinguished friendships were far more than professional associations: Their influence seeped all the way down to what James called "the deeper & darker and the unapparent, in which things *really* happen to us . . ." For at least one friend in each pair, the friendship stood as one of life's central, defining experiences—a beacon, a mirror, a challenge, a door opening into a new world, a model for how to live and work, a precious source of support and approval and inspiration.

When I set out to write this book, I chose these four particular friendships because of the importance of the writers and because of their common participation in the great tradition of American literature. Hawthorne and Melville, of course, stood near the headwaters of that tradition. But for each succeeding generation, the works of their predecessors were sacred texts, to be studied, absorbed, criticized, in some cases forcefully rejected. James was Hawthorne's uneasy heir. Robert Lowell reached out in his first volume for the mantle of Melville and Hawthorne, and he wrestled, reverently, with these literary fathers all his life. Bishop is kin to Welty in submerging herself unaccompanied in the river of experience, in feeling most alive and most herself when she is floating along the margins of the human communities she belongs to but never fully belongs in. Both women adopted Hawthorne's stance of the hidden observer, a stance that suited James as well. Porter harks back to Melville in her most famous book, a shipboard epic of good and evil, in which history grinds through the aspirations of individuals and disparate factions are forced to join hands in a temporary community. Porter also, like Wharton and James, probes the makeshift but severe strictures of American social life—the customs of the country that seem to change generation by generation, in the process casting up victims gasping on the sand. The idea of defining, discovering, or recovering one's true home and one's true self through travel or residence abroad is another shared theme—Melville in *Typee* and *Redburn* and later in a special sense in *Moby-Dick;* Hawthorne in *The Marble Faun;* James and Wharton throughout their careers; Porter in the Mexico stories, in "Holiday," and *Ship of Fools;* Bishop in nearly everything she wrote; Lowell in *History* and *The Dolphin,* and even

Welty in such stories as "The Bride of the Innisfallen" and "Music from Spain."

As writers, as Americans, these eight make sense together. But I must confess that I chose them in part because they are some of the writers who have most fascinated me. The very fact that such great seminal American writers were friends at all remained a perpetual source of wonder as I wrote the book. How extraordinary that Nathaniel Hawthorne and Herman Melville, founding fathers of American prose fiction, should have been neighbors in the Berkshires for a year—and that their intense, impassioned relationship should have coincided exactly with the composition of *Moby-Dick*. How wonderful that James and Wharton engaged in intimate intrigues that were as complicated, secretive, and delicate as anything they wrote about in their novels—and that they laughed so much when they were together. How strange that the extravagant, flamboyant southern belle Katherine Anne Porter should have launched the career of the shy, watchful, carefully guarded Eudora Welty. How *unlikely,* as Elizabeth Bishop loved to say, that she, perhaps the quietest and most modest American poet of the century, should have been the dearest friend of the aggressive, ambitious, nakedly confessional, megalomaniacal Robert Lowell. I knew and loved all eight of these writers as individuals. But the new insights I gained by rereading them as *pairs* amazed me.

I began with the impulse to illuminate my amazement—to tell the stories of the friendships, to recapture the past, to tease out the hidden dramas and the literary crosscurrents, to steep myself in the feeling of *being there* on the slopes of Monument Mountain, where Hawthorne and Melville met, or on the wide sand beach at Rio where Bishop witnessed Lowell unravel into madness. The "germ" of the book, to use James's term, was my desire to imagine the exact texture of connectedness that existed between James and Wharton on the day when they drove together deep into the English countryside until they arrived at the moated, crumbling towers of Bodiam, and he turned to her as they sat before this perfect vision and said, "Summer afternoon—summer afternoon; to me those have always been the two most beautiful words in the English language."

Each of the friendships has its own epiphanic moments—and my idea was to try to find them and then to string them together as so many luminous pearls. Yet I discovered, as I brought more and more of the stories to light, that a common thread unspooled from the essential fact of nationality. These eight friends were not only colleagues working "in the same line" but American comrades devoting themselves to literature in communities in which interest in literature was either of the smallest, as James noted of Hawthorne's Salem, or at least small enough to make the sympathy and support of another great writer extremely welcome. The comparative shortness of American history and the fluidity of our young literary tradition, the absence of an official court culture or noble patrons, the immense size of the country and the length of the shadow cast by Europe: These abstract "global" conditions of our national culture stamped each of the friendships with the same watermark. There were, I found, surprising echoes and correspondences from generation to generation. Themes and issues repeated in the lives and the works. Related attitudes and responses. Parallel desires and betrayals. I was dealing with four great American literary friendships—with equal emphasis on each of the adjectives.

The lack of the "comfort and inspiration of belonging to a class," as James put it, has been both a curse and a blessing for American writers. Without the well-worn path from Eton or Harrow or Winchester to Oxford or Cambridge to literary London (or one of its outposts) that English writers have commonly taken, American writers have been forced to strike out on their own—making a whaling ship their Yale and Harvard, as Melville did, or holing up for a decade in a chilly upstairs bedroom in one's mother's house, as Hawthorne did, or going abroad for "impressions" and "experience" as James and Wharton did, or running through a string of marriages and journalism jobs, as Katherine Anne Porter did, and so on. The blessing is the newness, the adventure of being the first, the shivering *strangeness* of finding one's own way through alien virgin territory. The curse, of course, is the toll such pioneering takes: the loneliness, the alienation, the drain of drawing continually on the self's precious account, the bruising struggle to create without recognition, sympathy, or return.

That's where the friendships come in. The eight friends I am writing about were lucky enough to find each other at critical moments in their literary careers. In each case, the friendship came as a revelation of new possibilities at the first flush of artistic maturity or it furnished an affirmation of commitments that had been eroded by doubt. In each case, admiration (or at least a fascinated appreciation) for the other's work came first and smoothed the way to the personal bond. The friendships threw open windows, let in shafts of light and rushes of fresh air.

Melville encountered Hawthorne (the man and his work) a few months after starting *Moby-Dick,* and the "shock of recognition" that passed between them altered the course of this masterpiece. Wharton was nearing forty when she met James and he implored her to "DO NEW YORK!": Though she bridled at his unsolicited advice, three years later she scored her first major artistic and commercial success by doing New York in *The House of Mirth.* Eudora Welty was living at home with her mother in Jackson, Mississippi, during the Great Depression and writing weird, brilliant short stories that no New York publisher would touch when her fellow-southerner Katherine Anne Porter read her work and invited her to come visit her in Baton Rouge. Porter, herself at the height of her literary powers, took Welty under her wing, helped her get fellowships and an invitation to Yaddo (the artists' colony in Saratoga Springs), and, most important of all, wrote the introduction to the collection of stories that Doubleday, Doran finally agreed to publish. Lowell and Bishop had both published first books of poetry to considerable acclaim (and in Lowell's case instant celebrity) when they met in New York and instantly hit it off; their deepening friendship, which teetered on the brink of a love affair and even marriage, challenged Bishop to reexamine her sense of vocation and eventually to open herself emotionally in her verse. It provided Lowell with a safe haven from the violence of his domestic life and the nightmare of his incurable madness.

These four friendships clicked into place at once, as close friendships so often do. "I met Melville, the other day, and liked him so much that I have asked him to spend a few days with me," Hawthorne wrote a college friend of his after the famous hike up Monument Mountain, and the others felt much the same way after their first encounters. They recognized each other instantly as allies and freely helped each other in whatever ways they could. The friends boosted each other's careers, shared contacts and editors, wrote reviews and jacket blurbs for each other's books, pulled strings and rolled logs for each other, steered appointments, awards, and book contracts each other's way. They were perhaps the ideal readers of each other's work—the reader who could see deepest down into the well of creation. "He could never wholly overcome the longing, not to be bought by the many but at least to be understood by the few," Wharton once wrote of James.[2] This was the kind of rare, supreme understanding the friends gave each other. For a writer, there is no greater gift.

"The essence of friendship is entireness, a total magnanimity and trust," wrote Emerson. "It must not surmise or provide for infirmity. It treats its object as a god, that it may deify both."[3] Each of the friendships aspired, at least for a time, to this exalted state. The depth of the friends' longing for support and companionship, the pleasure of finding these boons in a gifted and sympathetic colleague made these four friendships extremely intense—and also at times extremely tense. Melville's heated devotion to Hawthorne was just a whisker shy of the erotic, and Hawthorne probably recoiled from the younger man's celebration of their "infinite fraternity." James seethed with envy over Wharton's popular success (coming as it did on top of her already sizable trust fund) and he deeply resented her charitable meddling in his own finances. Welty grew frantic while waiting for Porter to write the introduction to her book, and Porter was furious when Welty published a two-part essay on the short story that failed to mention her. Bishop was appalled when Lowell lifted a passage from her most anguished letter and "versed" it, practically verbatim, into one of his sonnets. And so on. Literary friends are notorious for their malice and jealousy (Oscar Wilde once called friendships between writers "mixing the poisoned cup")—and these eight, despite their real affection for each other, did not always resist the temptation to proffer the cup. The serenity of summer afternoons was punctuated by literary slaps, jabs, sharp knives expertly inserted into exposed backs, and a fair amount of rather nasty gossip.

Each friendship vibrated between frequencies of love and jealousy, support and resentment, reverence and disgust, admiration and anger, passion and skepticism, idealism and disappointment. But isn't this in the very nature of friendship? The shared understanding that brings friends together also makes them compete: They know each other too well; they want the same things; they compare themselves to each other—and the friend who comes up short (or perceives it that way) lashes out at the friend who comes out on top. Friendships lack the totality of marriage, but perhaps they involve as much or more risk—the risk of unveiling one's emotional needs and sometimes one's darkest secrets to another person, of exposing oneself to humiliation or rejection, the risk of negotiating the straits of a relationship that admits affection but not sex, loyalty but not exclusivity, intimacy coupled to the constant threat of betrayal. Literary friendships are especially dangerous because the betrayals, like the loyalties, may be exhibited in public.

Our close friendships, as these eight revealed to me again and again, are full of complexities and contradictions. Melville's letters to Hawthorne radiate heat; yet to a common friend Melville complained of Hawthorne's bloodlessness. James felt it necessary to masquerade as the *victim* of Wharton's "rushing, ravening" hospitality, rather than the willing beneficiary of her car and country house. Welty can laugh about Porter's follies in private, but becomes furious when anyone attempts to quote her on this subject. Lowell and Bishop adored each other and exchanged reams of brilliant letters; yet whenever they met she drank herself into a stupor and he spun into a manic attack. These four friendships were fascinating and often bizarre. But I think their strangeness is illuminating of the writers' lives and work, and, at a deeper level, of the issues and patterns that shape all great friendships.

Welty wrote in an essay on Willa Cather, "The events of a story may have much or little to do with the writer's own life; but the story *pattern* is the nearest thing to a mirror image of his mind and heart."[4] I have tried to approach the heart of the four friendships by uncovering these "story patterns," especially in the works the authors wrote about, for, or under the influence of the friend. Which is not to say that I rifle through the works for hidden keys and clues to the authors' lives (and vice versa). A literary text, no matter how autobiographical, does not "explain" its creator's psychology or motivation any more than biographical details define the meaning of a text. To say that *Ethan Frome* is bleak because Wharton was desperately unhappy in her marriage when she wrote the book does violence both to the novel and to the inner life of its author. To assert that Hollingsworth in *The Blithedale Romance is* Melville is to reduce Hawthorne's satire to crankiness. On the other hand, it is obviously absurd to seal off the life and the work in separate chambers. The life may not be the map's legend to the work, but surely it furnishes one essential context. We blind ourselves needlessly if we ignore this context.

When I do examine particular stories or poems for insights into the authors' minds and hearts, I look for sanction in their letters, memoirs, or stray remarks. Eudora Welty admitted to interviewers that she drew on her mother's family background in *The Optimist's Daughter,* and friends of Welty (including Porter) noted that this novel was her most "confessional." James's comment to Wharton that his story "The Velvet Glove" "reeks of you" throws the door wide open to the biographer. Book dedications (most famously Melville's dedication of *Moby-Dick* to Hawthorne; most perplexingly Lowell's dedication of *Imitations,* his volume of very loose verse translations, to Bishop), prefaces (Porter's introduction to Welty's first volume of stories), and critical essays (Melville's "Hawthorne and His Mosses," Lowell's review of Bishop's first volume of poems) open still other avenues of conjecture.

Questions of literary influence between the friends, I discovered, are just as vexed as the relationships between art and life—and for much the same reasons. It is well known that Melville was devouring Hawthorne's stories during the writing of *Moby-Dick,* and that Hawthorne's "power of blackness" transformed the story of the whale. And it is pretty clear that Wharton was thinking a good deal about James when she wrote *The Age of Innocence* just a few years after the Master's death. But as I worked my way deeper into my book, I came to feel that literary influence depended more on the way I *read* the friends' works than on the way they were *written.* Lowell's *Life Studies* colored my responses to Bishop's *Questions of Travel.* Porter's "The Jilting of Granny Weatherall" and "Theft" changed the way I read Welty's "Death of a Traveling Salesman" and "A Piece of News." *Delta Wedding* looked different in the light of "The Old Order," and so on. The friendship itself became part of my experience of the texts. The same may well happen to readers of this book.

As my book took shape and the patterns of art and life and influence emerged more sharply, I noticed more and more parallels in the "structures" of the friendships. The same or related themes surfaced in generation after generation. The conflicting claims of the domestic and the strange. Tension between love affairs, marriages, and the friendship. The loneliness of the writer's life. Competition over money and fame. The exchange of gifts, both material and literary. Mental and physical illness. Questions of travel and expatriatism. These issues arose in one form or another in all four of the friendships; and all eight friends wrestled with these issues in their most important and characteristic works. Melville's *Pierre,* Hawthorne's *The Blithedale Romance,* all of

James's late novels, Wharton's *The House of Mirth* and *The Age of Innocence* as well as many stories, Porter's "Rope," "That Tree" and "Old Mortality," Welty's *The Optimist's Daughter*, Lowell's *Life Studies*, Bishop's *Questions of Travel:* These works bristle with insights into the passions and preoccupations of their creators and resonate most marvelously with each other. In some cases, the authors' passions took fire from the friendship itself. But in all cases, the works illuminate the depths of the friendship just as the friendship illuminates the mysteries of the work.

A stronger and most focused beam shines forth from the letters, reviews, jacket blurbs, introductions, and eulogies that the friends wrote for each other. "Friendship lives, as do we ourselves, in an ephemeral world," wrote Welty in the introduction to her anthology of friendship. "How much its life depends on the written word."[5] The abundance and the beauty of the words these writers shared with each other rescue their friendships, far more than other "normal" friendships, from the whims of the ephemeral. For each pair of friends, I take a careful look at all the various words on which the life of the friendship depended.

At some point during my three-year immersion in this book, I began to see the friendships not only as windows on the lives and works of eight of our most eminent writers, but also as a magical, golden frame through which the light of American literary history, indeed of American history itself, shone in tantalizing new patterns. War—the Civil War, the two world wars, and the Vietnam War; politics; the proliferation of technology; race and class relations; gender relations and feminism; economic booms and busts; the place of New York City in American letters; literary relations between North and South, New World and Old; the vagaries of the tastes of the American reading public: All of these events and issues struck me as newly and strangely significant in the light of how they affected "my" friends. One can get carried away with this and end up with "a virtuoso's collection" (as Hawthorne called one of his sketches) in which great historical and literary objects, figures, and symbols are wrenched from their context and reduced to an assorted heap of curiosities. I have tried to strike a balance in this regard, mentioning events from history as they affected the lives of the friends.

I admit that my choice of these eight writers was, to some extent, arbitrary, dictated as it was by their literary stature and by the importance of the friendship in their lives or works or both. But once I had the group assembled, I began to see remarkable correspondences and coincidences. I had selected a representative from each generation of American literary history from the mid-nineteenth to the midtwentieth century: Hawthorne was born in 1804, Melville in 1819, James in 1843, Wharton in 1862, Porter in 1890, Welty in 1909, Bishop in 1911, Lowell in 1917. All of the writers, with the exception of Henry James (and possibly Katherine Anne Porter), had ancestors who had fought in the American Revolution, and James's grandfather emigrated from Ireland in 1789 as a direct consequence of the revolution. I had managed to achieve a perfect balance of men and women and a nice symmetry in covering one friendship between two men, one between two women, and two mixed gender friendships. Aside from Hawthorne, all my writers lived in and wrote about New York at some point in their literary careers.

Social and professional connections between the writers and between the generations of writers abounded. Robert Lowell's ancestor James Russell Lowell knew both Hawthorne and Henry James, and James's father knew Hawthorne as well. Melville was born into the same upper-middle-class New York circle as Edith Wharton and his mother was related through the Van Rensselaers to Wharton's lifelong friend Walter Van Rensselaer Berry. Katherine Anne Porter met Lowell when he was still in college and they remained friendly from then on; they were more intimately connected through the poet Allen Tate, who was one of Lowell's early mentors and who had a brief affair with Porter. Lowell's best male friend, Peter Taylor, was also a friend of Eudora Welty. Bishop and Porter were connected through the Library of Congress, where both of them worked for a time. Bishop and Welty lunched together in New York once and exchanged a couple of notes praising each other's work. And so on and on. My book turned out to be yet another illustration of how "everything connects"—especially everything literary and American. I have traced these connections as seemed worthwhile in the three brief "Intergenerational" sections placed between the main chapters on the four friendships.

Although women's issues or homosexuality figure in one way or another in all four relationships, my choices, I admit, are otherwise woefully mainstream in terms of class, race, religion, and ethnic background: All eight writers were "old stock" WASPs (Porter and Lowell converted to Catholicism, but Lowell later rejoined the Protestant fold) with admixtures of Scotch-Irish, French Huguenot, and Swiss (Welty's father's side). Friendships between American writers of other races, classes, and ethnic backgrounds is a field wide open for future exploration.

The connections between my eight, as I hope the pages that follow will make clear, run far deeper than their membership in the same social and literary circles. Together, generation by generation, these friends bored deep into the core of what it means to be American. Indeed their friendships themselves are part of the core: Melville expostulating to Hawthorne about providence, futurity, and annihilation among the bleak sand hills of Liverpool; James roping in "a huge netful of impressions" while cruising through western Massachusetts in Wharton's car; Katherine Anne Porter setting her seal of approval on the first story collection of her fellow southerner Eudora Welty; Bishop on the rocky shore of Stonington, Maine, chatting about Marianne Moore's excursions to the zoo while Lowell floundered with a marriage proposal. Each of these moments strikes me as quintessentially American. In their exchanges, alliances, admirations, and generosities, these eight friends partake of something large and free and original.

The breath of American innocence rises from all of these relationships, and the shadow of American blackness falls over them. Each of these writers was, as Edith Wharton said of Henry James, "a solitary who could not live alone."[6] Hence the urgencies and tensions of their friendships. Their need for each other was very great, and so was their disappointment when the friendship failed. Hawthorne shrank from Melville's fervor. James despised and envied Wharton's wealth. Porter suffered from Welty's success. Bishop railed against Lowell's predations. Because of their passionate admiration for each other's works, these friends turned to each other passionately, even desperately, for understanding. But could anyone ever understand enough?

As American artists, each pair of friends fed the sacred flame of the American literary tradition and each generation received the flame, consciously, deliberately, from their ancestors and passed it down to their heirs. "My Friend is not of some other race or family of men," wrote Thoreau, "but flesh of my flesh, bone of my bone. He is my real brother. I see his nature groping yonder so like mine."[7] In this sense, this book of four American literary friendships is really the chronicle of four generations of the same enduring family.

PART ONE

Nathaniel Hawthorne
and
Herman Melville

Why does Hawthorne give us the afternoon hour later than anyone else?—oh late, late, quite uncannily late, as if it were always winter outside?

—HENRY JAMES, *lecture on Balzac*

Our noblest example of ambition was a writer who never claimed he was the best writer alive, yet may have reached it: Melville.

—ROBERT LOWELL *to an interviewer*

ONE

Turkey and Thunder

*So far as I am a man of really individual attributes I
veil my face; nor am I, nor have I ever been, one of
those supremely hospitable people who serve up their
own hearts, delicately fried, with brain sauce, as a
tidbit for their beloved public.*

—NATHANIEL HAWTHORNE, *"The Old Manse"*

*Appalling is the soul of a man! Better might one be
pushed off into the material spaces beyond the utter-
most orbit of our sun, than once feel himself fairly
afloat in himself!*

—HERMAN MELVILLE, *Pierre*

IT IS FITTING—indeed, emblematic, to use a word they both
loved—that Nathaniel Hawthorne and Herman Melville met on a
mountainside. Actually, "mountain" is not entirely accurate, for at
1700 feet, Monument Mountain in the Berkshire Hills of western
Massachusetts is hardly monumental. The ascent (which hikers
can still make) requires scarcely an hour. Yet Monument's flanks
are steep and strewn with pale quartzite crags where peregrine
falcons once nested; its trails wind through stands of birch, hemlock, oak, white pine, and tangles of white- and pink-flowering
mountain laurel; its rocky summit affords distant vistas of undu-
lating ridges and valleys; its history holds a dark legend of an
Indian girl's suicide. These days the buzz of automobile traffic

27

along busy Route 7 penetrates deep into the forest. But back on what one biographer terms that "legend-encrusted" Monday, August 5, 1850, the silence of the "heathen wilderness" had not yet been broken by the combustion engine. The dense, mysterious, primeval gloom that broods over the forest scenes of Hawthorne's "Young Goodman Brown," "Roger Malvin's Burial," and his just-published *The Scarlet Letter* instantly enveloped the party of literary hikers. The day was warm and close. Clouds were massing in the south, and distant thunder rumbled ominously down the valleys. But Hawthorne and Melville and their distinguished companions—poet and physician Oliver Wendell Holmes (father of the jurist); New York editor Evert A. Duyckinck; Boston publisher James T. Fields and his wife; and a few others—had their hearts set on revelry and ignored the stormy portents.

Duyckinck's account of the outing in a letter written to his wife the next day is considered the most reliable:

> Hawthorne and myself [were] in advance, talking of the Scarlet Letter. As we scrambled over rocks at the summit which surveys a wide range of country on either side, a black thunder cloud from the south dragged its ragged edges toward us—the thunder rolling in the distance. They talked of shelter and shelter there proved to be though it looked unpromising but these difficulties, like others, vanish on trial and a few feet of rock with a damp underground of mosses and decay actually sheltered publisher Fields curled whiskers, his patent leathers and his brides delicate blue silk. Dr Holmes cut three branches for an umbrella and uncorked the champagne which was drunk from a silver mug. The rain did not do its worst and we scattered over the cliffs, Herman Melville to seat himself, the boldest of all, astride a projecting bowsprit of rock while Dr Holmes peeped about the cliffs and protested it affected him like ipecac. Hawthorne looked wildly about for the great carbuncle. Mathews [another New York literary luminary] read Bryant's poem. The exercise was glorious. We shed rain like ducks.[1]

The damp group descended without incident, despite the Champagne (which Fields remembered as "a considerable quantity"), and repaired to the nearby house of Dudley Field to sit down to a monumental midafternoon Victorian "dinner," "a three hour's business from turkey to ice cream," as Duyckinck told his wife, "well moistened by the way." But the day's revels were not over yet, as Duyckinck continued, groaning: "It was a merciless thing to get us off from such a dinner in the afternoon to the Ice Glen, a break in one of the hills of tumbled huge, damp, mossy rocks in whose recesses ice is said to be found all the year round. . . ." Fields recollected that on this outing, "Hawthorne was among the most enterprising of the merrymakers; and being in the dark much of the time, he ventured to call out lustily and pretend that certain destruction was inevitable to all of us."[2] Thus in a damp cavern of Massachusetts a glimmering comic prefiguration of the dreadful encounter in the Roman catacombs on which the plot of *The Marble Faun*, published a decade later, hangs.

Though there is no record of whether Hawthorne and Melville were thrown together much that day, clearly they impressed each other favorably, despite their considerable differences in temperament, style, and character. Two days later, Hawthorne wrote to his college friend Horatio Bridge, "I met Melville, the other day, and liked him so much that I have asked him to spend a few days with me."[3] Melville was, if anything, even more favorably disposed—and so began one of the most important, and puzzling, friendships in American letters.

On the face of it, the events of that early August day seem unexceptional, even a touch absurd. Here were two comfortably established literary gentlemen and their cronies on summer vacation. Hawthorne and Melville, husbands and fathers both, presided over two utterly conventional middle-class households (Melville's even included his mother and unmarried sisters). The Champagne and turkey, the poetry reading and ice cream, the innocent outdoor frolics on mountain and glen—such were the trappings of midcentury bourgeois leisure. And yet, despite the quaint Currier and Ives homeyness of it all, an aura of myth incandesces around the occasion. Hawthorne and Melville loom over our national literature as primordial gods, titans who seized their fire straight from heaven and enshrined it within the giant pillars of the first true temple of American literary art. The fact that these strange, obsessed, demonically imaginative men lived, for a little more than a year, six miles apart in the bucolic Berkshire countryside, that they read and wrote about each other's books, that they corresponded and gathered regularly to drink brandy and gin and port and smoke cigars and speak of time, eternity, and book publishers strikes us today, nearly a century and a half later, as little short of miraculous.

The friendship that sprang up on Monument Mountain was brief, intense, and passionate. Some critics have compared it to an earthquake that altered the map of American literature. Every letter they wrote, every reference they made to each other in journals or reviews, every twist and turn of possible literary influence has been tracked down, speculated about, debated. The crust of legend has grown so thick there is no longer any hope of scraping it clean. To students of American literature, the friendship between Melville and Hawthorne is as charged with meaning as if it were itself a sacred text. And yet, when we read their letters, visit the homes where they lived and met, climb the hills they knew, study portraits of their wives and children and in-laws, we plummet at once from the celestial to the quotidian. From Ahab's apocalyptic doom and the scarlet flames of Hester Prynne's embroidered *A* to literary picnics and cramped front parlors. In our minds, their images shimmer. The mountain and the thunderstorm; the ascent through the brooding forest; the shining banquet of fraternity and the dark, threatening cavern—these were the emblems of their friendship as much as the humble turkey, ice cream, and Champagne they consumed together that day.

In a way, their friendship itself is emblematic—certainly it foreshadows the loyalties and conflicts that shaped the three other friendships considered in this book. Hawthorne and Melville, arising at the source, stand as archetypes for how American writers have related to each other ever since. Gods and men. Emblems and flesh-and-blood historic figures. In considering their friendship, one needs to give both the turkey and the thunder their due.

Perhaps it was a coincidence that the friendship came at pivotal moments in both of their careers. But it's also possible that the friendship blossomed *because* they both stood at critical turning points. Hawthorne, at forty-six, had finally attained that peak that all writers dream of: simultaneous commercial and critical success. *The Scarlet Letter*, published on March 16, 1850, made Hawthorne famous, and if not rich, at least far more comfortable than he had been for years. The reviews were little short of rapturous; sales were brisk, impelled in part by the book's racy subject—adultery, the subject that would obsess Henry James at the end of his life. Hawthorne was decidedly no longer "the obscurest man of letters in America," as he dubbed himself in his preface to the 1851 edition of *Twice-Told Tales*. Rather, as Melville wrote of him with a stab of envy, "this N.H. is in the ascendant. My dear Sir, they begin to patronize."[4]

His success had been a long time in coming. A native of Salem, Massachusetts, and the scion of two "stern and black-browed" prominent Puritan families (his great-great grandfather John Hathorne—the author added the "w"—was one of the judges during the notorious witch trials), Hawthorne had grown up in the painfully dependent role of the "poor relation." He was not quite four years old when his father, a sea captain, died in Surinam of yellow fever. Captain Hathorne's widow, the former Elizabeth Manning, was left with three young children (Nathaniel had an older and a younger sister) and $296.21 after the creditors were paid off.[5] She had little choice but to return to her father's house. Luckily, Richard Manning, the proprietor of the Boston and Salem Stagecoach line, was "in comfortable circumstances" in Salem, as Hawthorne's sister Elizabeth wrote years later, and his daughter and her fatherless children were "abundantly cared for" though in somewhat cramped quarters (eight aunts and uncles were in residence when they moved in).

Hawthorne spent much of his childhood in the Manning house on Herbert Street (sharing a bed with his uncle Robert, who was twenty years his senior), and after graduating from Bowdoin College in 1825, he moved back there to live for a decade with his mother and sisters. Lack of funds and lack of firm plans partly motivated the return home. But Hawthorne was hardly the typical graduate biding his time under the parental roof: His return home was a deliberate withdrawal from the world, an immurement in "dark seclusion," as he recollected later, in an "atmosphere without any oxygen of sympathy." He had in a sense given himself a prison sentence that would endure until he had mastered the craft he had chosen, or, rather, that had chosen him—the writing of fiction. During his twenties and early thirties, he lived and wrote in a small room under the eaves, steeping in the strange vapors of his imagination, seeing no one aside from his mother and sisters for weeks on end, sometimes emerging onto the street only after dusk. "If ever I should have a biographer, he ought to make great mention of this chamber in my memoirs," Hawthorne wrote after revisiting the attic room years later, "because so much of my lonely youth was wasted here, and here my mind and character were formed."[6] "Wasted" is an exaggeration for some of Hawthorne's most powerful and disturbing stories grew like mushrooms in his dark seclusion, including "My Kinsman, Major Molineux," "Roger Malvin's Burial," "The Gentle Boy," and "Young Goodman Brown" (*Fanshawe*, an early novel that Hawthorne later disavowed, was published in 1828, though some of it may have been written when Hawthorne was in college). He also exaggerated the loneliness of his "castle dismal," for he maintained close ties with college friends throughout this period and ventured forth on occasional trips through New England.

In 1837, Hawthorne assembled the first edition of *Twice-Told Tales* from previously (and anonymously) published stories. Henry Wadsworth Longfellow, a college classmate, hailed Hawthorne in a famous review as a "new star" rising in the heavens and proclaimed that his "little book" came "from the hand of a man of genius."[7] Hawthorne, having inaugurated what he called his "intercourse with the world," considered his prison term filled. And yet hardly a soul took notice. As he wrote in the preface to *The Snow Image and Other Twice-Told Tales,* his first books circulated among "a very limited circle of friendly readers." "Was there ever such a weary delay in obtaining the slightest recognition from the public, as in my case?" he demanded. "I sat down by the wayside of life, like a man under enchantment, and a shrubbery sprung up around me, and the bushes grew to be saplings, and the saplings became trees, until no exit appeared possible, through the entangling depths of my obscurity."[8]

In the 1851 preface to *Twice-Told Tales,* Hawthorne acknowledged, derisively, that "on the internal evidence" of his stories he had come "to be regarded as a mild, shy, gentle, melancholic, exceedingly sensitive, and not very forcible man"— and, indeed, he has never shaken off this shrinking, veiled image. It is hard to resist the temptation of viewing Arthur Dimmesdale in *The Scarlet Letter* as a self-portrait of his creator: "He was a person of very striking aspect," writes Hawthorne of the adulterous minister, "with a white, lofty, and impending brow, large, brown, melancholy eyes, and a mouth which, unless when he forcibly compressed it, was apt to be tremulous, expressing both nervous sensibility and a vast power of self-restraint. Notwithstanding his high native gifts and scholar-like attainments, there was an air about this young minister,—an apprehensive, a startled, a half-frightened look,—as of a being who felt himself quite astray and at a loss in the pathway of human existence, and could only be at ease in some seclusion of his own."[9]

Contemporary accounts, photographs, and paintings lend some—but only some—credence to the resemblance. Like Dimmesdale, Hawthorne was diffident and ill at ease with his fellowman. He was also "a person of very striking aspect"—an exceptionally handsome man, with classic features, a lofty forehead, thick dark hair and brows, and deep-set gray eyes that he habitually averted from the gaze of others. Anthony Trollope supposedly said Hawthorne was "the handsomest Yankee that ever walked the planet," and Duyckinck, waxing poetic, called him "a fine ghost in a case of iron."[10] Others noted a feminine aspect in his appearance and manner—his blushes, his trembling hand, his constrained, hesitating conversation, and the long silences he kept in company. Many found this manner enchantingly Byronic; but Henry James's father was one who did not succumb to Hawthorne's charms: "Hawthorne isn't to me a prepossessing figure," he wrote after dining with him one night at a Boston club, "nor apparently at all an *enjoying* person in any way: he has all the while the look . . . of a rogue who suddenly finds himself in a company of detectives. . . . I felt him bury his eyes in his plate and eat with such voracity that no one should dare to speak to him."[11]

Hawthorne's letters, prefaces, sketches, and his lighter fictions reveal many sunnier character traits—a bluff manly loyalty to friends; a stiff backbone in battling enemies; an abiding tenderness for his wife and children; an adroitness at political maneuvering; a healthy cynicism about publishers, book reviewers, and the tastes of readers; a genial, if somewhat prudish, appreciation for painting, sculpture, and travel; a sense of humor now playful, now sharply sarcastic; a keen eye for feminine beauty. Henry James, in his influential critical biography of Hawthorne, scoffs at the stereotype of the dark, secretive, guilt-tormented Hawthorne: "The general impression of this silence-loving and shade-seeking side of his character is doubtless exaggerated, and, in so far as it points to him as a somber and sinister figure, is almost ludicrously at fault. . . . The qualities to which the Note-Books most testify are, on the whole, his serenity and amenity of mind."[12] And yet for all this, it is impossible to dispel all the shadows that have gathered around Hawthorne.

Philip Rahv, in a seminal essay, asserts that the "problem of sin" in Hawthorne's writings is actually a cover for the deeper "problem of experience"—a conflict between his desire for an active passionate life and "a fear of life induced by narrow circumstances and morbid memories of the past." Rahv believes that Hawthorne embodied this conflict most dramatically in the figure of the "dark lady" that runs through his fiction—Hester Prynne in *The Scarlet Letter;* Beatrice Rappaccini; Zenobia in *The Blithedale Romance;* and Miriam in *The Marble Faun*—all beautiful, raven-haired, intensely erotic, and fiercely independent women whom Hawthorne felt compelled to destroy.[13] There is a good deal to this. A legend has grown up, partly fostered by Melville, that Hawthorne concealed some deep, dreadfully significant secret—incest? sexual perversion? abiding guilt over some unfathomable, unpardonable sin? The poisonous erotic perfume that arises from Professor Rappaccini's garden hangs heavy over many of Hawthorne's creations—and seeps into his private life as well. Whether he harbored one shocking all-explaining secret, or many subtler shaming evasions, the man who imagined the whole earth as "one stain of guilt, one mighty blood-spot" of sin in "Young Goodman Brown" and who created such diseased, tormented figures as the masturbatory Roderick Elliston with his "bosom serpent" ("It gnaws me! It gnaws me!") and the morose Parson Hooper who hides his face and his "secret sin" behind a black veil—such a man cannot have had a clear or easy conscience. "What is Guilt? A stain upon the soul," opens the sketch "Fancy's Show Box," and we know at once that this can only have come from the pen of Hawthorne. Even James acknowledges that to Hawthorne, as to his Puritan ancestors, "the consciousness of *sin* was the most important fact of life."[14] "This shy distrustful ego," Robert Lowell conjures up his shade in the commemorative poem "Hawthorne," "furtive, foiled, dissatisfied. . . ."

And yet strangely enough, Hawthorne had a blissful marriage—"the happiest marriage, very likely, enjoyed by any major American writer," according to one biographer.[15] He met his future wife in 1837, the same year *Twice-Told Tales* appeared. Sophia Peabody, an intelligent, learned, but sickly and no-longer-youthful woman from a bookish Salem family, was not considered marriageable, even by herself. Chronic migraine headaches had strung her nerves so unbearably tight that she could not stand the sounds of silverware clinking against the dinner plates. But despite her infirmities, Sophia Peabody proved to be a robustly devoted wife to Nathaniel Hawthorne—once they finally got around to marrying. Two constrained, vacillating years passed before Hawthorne proposed, and then the engagement dragged on for three more years (in secret, naturally). When they wed at last in 1842, Nathaniel was thirty-eight, Sophia thirty-three. It was, by all accounts, a perfect match in body and soul. Sophia was the model, prefeminist writer's wife—intelligent enough to appreciate, indeed adore, her husband's work yet never envious of his success, unwavering in her faith in his genius, assiduous in arranging the best possible working conditions for him, uncomplaining about the vicissitudes of the literary life (Hawthorne uprooted his family repeatedly during the twenty-two years of his married life, never occupying the same house for more than four years—a restless precedent that Katherine Ann Porter, Elizabeth Bishop, and to a lesser extent Henry James, Edith Wharton, and Robert Lowell later followed).

The Hawthornes' main trouble in the first years of their marriage was money—"pecuniary botheration," as Hawthorne called it. After the wedding the couple set up housekeeping in the famous Old Manse at Concord, Massachusetts, where their neighbors included Emerson (who once lived in the house and wrote glowingly of watching the "Assyrian dawn and Paphian sunset" there), Thoreau, and Margaret Fuller. Hawthorne was too ecstatic over the pleasures of married life to work much at first, and what he did write fetched little money, which he had to pry slowly and painfully from the tight fists of magazine publishers. Only three important stories came out of the three happy years in the Old Manse ("the calm summer of my heart and mind" Hawthorne called this period)—"The Birthmark," "The Artist of the Beautiful," and "Rappaccini's Daughter." By the winter of 1844–45 he was forced to borrow to provide "even for the day's wants," as he wrote his wife. When the owner of the Old Manse returned to take possession in October 1845, the Hawthornes, with only ten dollars of ready cash, decamped for Salem. Now forty-one years old, with a wife, a baby daughter, and another child on the way, Nathaniel Hawthorne was living once again in the room under the eaves on Herbert Street where he had "wasted" his lonely youth. He did not, however, lack prospects.

Despite his shyness, Hawthorne was well connected politically with the Democratic Party, and his connections paid off handsomely in March 1846 when, after much wrangling and lobbying, he was appointed surveyor of the customhouse of the port of Salem, a position that paid $1200 per year for three and a half hours a day of work. His three-year tenancy in office, during which he wrote very little, ended in a blaze of controversy in 1849 when the newly elected president, Zachary Taylor, replaced him with a member of his own Whig Party. Hawthorne tenaciously and bitterly fought the ouster, defending himself in the local press against scurrilous charges of corruption and favoritism. News of the battle spread far beyond Salem—"Mr. Hawthorne's name is ringing throughout the land," Sophia wrote her mother[16]—and newspapers in Boston and New York took his side. But the Whigs prevailed, and Hawthorne once again faced serious pecuniary botheration.

Out of this debacle came *The Scarlet Letter*. Hawthorne began the novel shortly after his dismissal, working quickly, even compulsively, writing "immensely," as Sophia put it, both morning and afternoon, which he had seldom done before. The young Boston publisher James T. Fields convinced Hawthorne to let him see the partial manuscript during the winter of 1849 and instantly agreed to publish it. The book was completed on February 3, 1850 and issued by Ticknor, Reed & Fields the following month, running through its first edition of 2,500 copies in ten days, its second edition of 2,500 in a few months, and requiring a 1,000-copy third edition in September (Henry James, seven when the book appeared, remembered hearing his elders speak of it with a shiver of moral dismay). Hawthorne had turned his bitter political defeat into literary triumph. *The Scarlet Letter* was recognized immediately as a masterpiece. An "instant classic" (Henry James called it "a literary event of the first importance . . . the finest piece of imaginative writing yet put forth in the country"),[17] the novel has never slipped from the summit of Parnassus.

Hawthorne shot *The Scarlet Letter* into the world like an arrow tipped with a barbed and poisoned head. In "The Custom-House," the memoir/sketch/diatribe with which he introduced his Puritan romance, Hawthorne took his sweet revenge on his local enemies. It is one of the most lethal pieces of social and political vituperation in American letters, as ferocious as Norman Mailer, as funny as Mark Twain. "The Custom-House" roasts Salem and Salemites, officers and hangers-on past and present of the customhouse, local politicians, and even the dour Puritan ancestors who planted the Hathorne family in the town in 1630 and engendered the author's "unjoyous attachment" to the place. Salem, be-numbed by "the chilliest of social atmospheres," comes off as a hideous backwater, a moribund, depressing, decaying port with "few or no symptoms of commercial life." Hawthorne's fellow customhouse officers are a bunch of decrepit, petty, torpid old men who spend their days snoozing, gossiping, and siphoning money from the government. He reports with some pride that as surveyor he was "guilty" of "abbreviating the official breath of more than one of these venerable servants of the republic," most of whom dropped dead promptly after being fired "as if their sole principle of life had been zeal for their country's service; as I verily believe it was."[18] As for the controversy surrounding his own official termination, he dismisses it with a sharp swipe of the pen: "In view of my previous weariness of office, and vague thoughts of resig-nation, my fortune [in being thrown out] somewhat resembled that of a person who should entertain an idea of committing sui-cide, and, altogether beyond his hopes, meet with the good hap to be murdered."[19] In "The Custom-House" Hawthorne strips off his customary black veil, steps out of the shadows, and gives his adversaries a sound thrashing with his bare fists.

"My preliminary chapter has caused the greatest furor that has happened here since witch-times," Hawthorne wrote his old friend Bridge from Salem after *The Scarlet Letter* appeared. "If I escape from town without being tarred and feathered, I shall con-sider it good luck. I wish they would tar and feather me; it would be such an eminently novel kind of distinction for a literary man."[20] Unlike the character Major Molineux, Hawthorne did not wait for this novel distinction to befall him. He left Salem voluntarily in the damp spring of 1850, and after paying some visits to friends and relations in Portsmouth, New Hampshire, and Boston, he moved his family west across the width of Massachu-setts to settle, at least for a while, in a cramped red farmhouse overlooking a picturesque lake outside of Lenox.

And so Nathaniel Hawthorne, at the height of his fame and his artistic powers, came to dwell in the Berkshires and found himself, on that memorable Monday in August, on the slopes of Monument Mountain in the company of Herman Melville.

Melville, who had turned thirty-one four days before meet-ing Hawthorne, also stood at the peak of his literary powers. But unlike Hawthorne, Melville attained this peak only by killing his commercial and critical success. The two writers intersected at a point where their careers were moving rapidly in opposite directions.

Fame and a certain amount of fortune had come quickly, and seemingly effortlessly, to Melville as soon as he began writing. His first volume, *Typee,* based on his actual adventures with a primitive tribe in the South Sea Islands, was an instant best-seller when it was published in 1846 and it gained Melville a dubious notoriety as "the man who lived among the cannibals." *Omoo, Mardi, Redburn,* and *White-Jacket* followed swiftly, and, with the exception of the dreamily allegorical *Mardi,* the books sold well and received considerable, if not uniformly enthusiastic, critical attention. (Hawthorne, reviewing *Typee* for the *Salem Advertiser,* praised this production of "a young and adventurous sailor" as "lightly but vigorously written. . . . The narrative is skilfully managed, and in a literary point of view, the execution of the work is worthy of the novelty and interest of its subject."[21]) Melville's youthful vault into literary eminence set the pattern for a host of American followers, including Henry James, F. Scott Fitzgerald, Carson McCullers, Robert Lowell, Norman Mailer, and Truman Capote.

Melville also pioneered the American tradition of the literary crack-up. By the summer of 1850, he was edging toward an abyss into which his reputation, his solvency, his peace of mind, his physical health, and very nearly his sanity were to plunge. *Moby-Dick,* the masterpiece with which he wrestled during 1850 and 1851, received mixed reviews and disappointingly sluggish sales (three years after publication only 2,390 copies had been sold, while *The Scarlet Letter* sold 2,500 in ten days). But its successor, *Pierre,* published in 1852, was a disaster, universally (and deservedly) slashed and shunned. Melville never recovered from these blows. In 1857, after the publication of *The Confidence-Man,* he fell silent as a writer of fiction—a silence that he maintained until his death in 1891 (his volumes of poetry raised barely a whisper of attention in his lifetime). In the eleven years during which he tried to earn his living as a writer, Melville had published ten substantial volumes of fiction. Crack-up or burnout? It's hard to say.

Melville's friendship with Hawthorne is all the more fascinating because it coincided with the first tremors of his collapse.

Indeed, some biographers *blame* the collapse on Hawthorne, although this has stirred considerable controversy.

Like Hawthorne, Melville was born into an old and distinguished family in decline, only in Melville's case, the decline was far more precipitous. The Melvilles—or Melvills, as the family usually spelled it in America—traced their ancestry back to Scottish nobility and French Huguenots. His mother, Maria, was a Gansevoort, one of the old Dutch patroon families that dominated the Hudson Valley and intermarried with the Van Rensselaers and the Ten Eycks. (In her memoirs, Edith Wharton identifies the Van Rensselaers as one of the very few "good" New York families that "could show a pedigree leading back to the aristocracy of their ancestral country." Wharton mentions Melville briefly while explaining the almost complete absence of writers from her parents' social circle in the 1860s: "As for Herman Melville, a cousin of the Van Rensselaers, and qualified by birth to figure in the best society, he was doubtless excluded from it by his deplorable Bohemianism, for I never heard his name mentioned, or saw one of his books."[22]) Both of Melville's grandfathers served memorably in the American Revolution: Major Thomas Melvill, his father's father, had taken part in the Boston Tea Party (as did Wharton's great grandfather Major-General Ebenezer Stevens, who went on to play a prominent role in the defeats of General Burgoyne and Lord Cornwallis); and his mother's father, General Peter Gansevoort, valiantly defended Fort Stanwix. In *Pierre,* Melville makes a lot of noise about the heroic exploits of his grandfather and describes his sword as a kind of sacred talisman. Elsewhere in his fiction he keeps his noble pedigree buried.

The match between the handsome, charming Allan Melvill and the proud aristocratic Maria Gansevoort seemed propitious. Allan ran a business importing French millinery and when Herman, their third child, was born in 1819, the family was living in outward prosperity at 6 Pearl Street in lower Manhattan. Additional children (eventually there would be eight in all, four sons and four daughters) necessitated moves to larger houses uptown, first on Bleecker Street and then, in 1828, at 675 Broadway (just two blocks from where Henry James was born in 1843). The Melvills were "qualified by birth," as Wharton put it, to take their place in the patrician society then residing around Astor Place. But Allan Melvill was cursed—with bad luck or bad business sense or both. The millinery business failed and his next venture, a dry goods store, went so poorly that he was forced to borrow thousands of dollars from his father and in-laws. In 1830 Allan Melvill, bankrupt, moved his family to Albany and there he died in January 1832, massively in debt and raving mad—"deprived of his intellect" as his wife put it. Herman, at age twelve, was hurled overnight from a life of at least illusory well-being and high social standing to a marginal existence "on or just over the edge of poverty."[23]

Melville and Hawthorne shared the pain and hardship of losing their fathers during childhood, and a yearning for fatherly love and guilt over paternal death haunts both of their fiction—most memorably in Hawthorne's "Roger Malvin's Burial" and Melville's *Pierre* and, more obliquely, in "Bartleby, the Scrivener." The early loss of a parent is a common thread that connects many of the lives in this book: Wharton's father died when she was twenty; Katherine Anne Porter was not yet two when her mother died and her father, emotionally withdrawn and shiftless, turned his children over to his mother; Elizabeth Bishop never knew her father, who died of Bright's disease when she was eight months old, and she was left a virtual orphan at age five when her grief-stricken mother was permanently institutionalized; Eudora Welty's father died of leukemia when she was twenty-two, which bound her evermore to her mother's side. Of the eight literary friends, only Henry James and Robert Lowell had both their parents into adulthood. A good case could be made with the other six for tracing the impulse to write to the early loss of a parent and the attendant decline in social and financial status.

But father loss devastated Melville far more than any of the others. In effect, it terminated his childhood and thrust him into the working world. Through his teens he took a succession of odd jobs, clerking in the New York State Bank and later in his brother's cap and fur store, which also went bankrupt. In 1839, at age nineteen, he shipped out as a common sailor—a cabin boy—on a merchant ship crossing to Liverpool (the voyage he re-created in *Redburn*), and two years later, more or less out of desperation, he went to sea again, this time on a whaling ship bound for the South Seas. Melville's extraordinary experiences over the next four years would supply the raw material for all of his novels up to *Pierre*: the wretched conditions aboard the *Acushnet* that prompted him to jump ship at the island of Nukahiva in the Marquesas and live for a month with the Typee tribe (*Typee*, 1846); his participation in a mutiny aboard an Australian whaler and his beachcombing on Tahiti and Eimeo (*Omoo*, 1847); his signing on with the Nantucket whaler *Charles and Henry* in 1842 (*Moby-Dick*, 1851), and his discharge, six months later, at Hawaii, where he worked for a time setting pins in a bowling alley; his enlistment in the U.S. Navy aboard the frigate *United States*, on which he sailed from Honolulu, around Cape Horn, and finally back to Boston (*White-Jacket*, 1850), where he was discharged on October 14, 1844—a sunburned, sea-toughened, twenty-five-year-old salt with only his meager sailor's pay in his pocket, but vast passions and hopes.

"From my twenty-fifth year I date my life," Melville later wrote Hawthorne. "Three weeks have scarcely passed, at any time between then & now, that I have not unfolded within myself." His twenty-fifth year did indeed mark an absolute division in his life: Melville ended his adventures at sea and opened the dark volume of the inner life. Settling down in his mother's house in Lansingburgh, north of Albany, he began to write about what he had done and seen while traveling around the world. Melville seems to have turned to writing not out of any sense of mission or to fulfill a long-held desire, as Hawthorne did, but rather because he had something to write about—and nothing else to do. He was one of the first Westerners to "bring the news" from the South Seas, as John Updike notes, "and still among the best."[24] He completed *Typee* fairly rapidly during the winter and spring of 1844–45, and his older brother Gansevoort, in London as the secretary of the American legation, sold the manuscript to John Murray (the son of the famous John Murray who published Byron's work) for £100. Murray brought the book out in England in February 1846, and Wiley & Putnam issued the American edition a month later. The reviews were almost uniformly favorable, and in some cases ecstatic. Sales on both sides of the Atlantic were good, and a renewed surge of interest broke in July when Toby Greene, Melville's companion in the Marquesas Islands, testified in a letter to the editor of the *Buffalo Commercial Advertiser* to "the entire accuracy of the work." There is a story, perhaps apocryphal, that Melville was hoeing in his mother's garden that summer when a stranger approached the house and asked for the signature of the celebrity author. Melville was splendidly launched.

If the man veiled behind the fictions of Nathaniel Hawthorne comes across as creepy, furtive, and guilt obsessed, Melville in his early narratives strikes us as a hasty, high-spirited, opinionated, extravagant fellow, always eager to grab us by the lapels, sit us down, and enchant us with his adventures (some of which were in fact not his at all, but "yarns" borrowed from other sea writers). A natural democrat, this young Melville instinctively sides with the "people" (the common sailors) against the officers, the natives against the missionaries, with life and youth and manly strength and beauty against authority, hypocrisy, "niceness," refinement, and bigotry. He is a freewheeling freethinking pure product of America, fit to keep company with Walt Whitman (his exact contemporary) if only Whitman would forsake the open road and take to the sea. Though Melville deplores the hardships of shipboard life, he celebrates the "fellow-feeling" that springs up between men who are "all employed at the same common business; all under lock and key; all hopeless prisoners like myself; all under martial law; all dieting on salt beef and biscuit; all in one uniform, all yawning, gaping, stretching in concert."[25]

He loves his comrades, tolerates their foibles, and admires their supple vigor with hardly a murmur of complaint at being deprived of the company of women. It is Melville's genius, in these early works, to make his readers his instant and confidential friends—to put *us* in the ranks of his fellow sailors. As Harry Levin puts it, "To enter into direct relations with his audience, on the basis of an informality which soon becomes an intimacy, is Melville's arresting gift as a *raconteur*."[26] "Six months at sea!" he opens *Typee,* buttonholing us like a sideshow barker. "Yes, reader, as I live, six months out of sight of land . . ." "Call me Ishmael," he commands us brusquely in perhaps the most celebrated opening line in American literature. John Updike writes of the "assured, playful, precociously fluent, and eagerly pitched voice of the sea novels"—and even allowing for rhetorical flourishes and authorial exaggerations, these traits can safely be ascribed to the young Melville himself. The man radiates exuberance. The thousands of pages seem to shower from his brain in quick, drenching torrents.

On the strength of his reviews and royalties for *Typee,* and the fair prospects of his second book, *Omoo,* Melville proposed marriage to Elizabeth Shaw in the summer of 1847. It was a match thoroughly in keeping with his return to staid respectability. Elizabeth—or Lizzie, as her family called her—was the daughter of Lemuel Shaw, the chief justice of the Massachusetts Supreme Court and one of Melville's father's closest friends. Unlike the unsteady and unlucky Allan Melvill, Lemuel Shaw was a man of strict sobriety, dignity, and solid wealth (he was worth more than three hundred thousand dollars at his death)—a true Bostonian of the old school. His daughter, Elizabeth, seems to have been cut from the same cloth. Certainly her letters reveal far greater concern with housekeeping, meals, comfort, and social obligations than with literature—in marked contrast to Sophia Hawthorne, whose wifely existence revolved solely around what her husband wrote. "The truth is, my wife, like all the rest of the world, cares not a fig for my philosophical jabber," Melville wrote in "I and My Chimney," a heavily satirical sketch which has the ring of psychological if not literal truth.[27] But though Elizabeth Shaw may have been too conventional in outlook and too limited in experience to fathom Herman Melville's depths, she nonetheless accepted his proposal. They were married in Boston on August 4, 1847, and after a rather strenuous honeymoon journey through New Hampshire, Montreal, and Quebec, the couple settled down in Manhattan. Herman's younger brother Allan was also married that year to a fashionable New York heiress named Sophia Thurston. The families of the two Melville brides contributed enough money for the brothers to purchase a house, at 103 Fourth Avenue, not far from where the Melvills had lived in the 1830s. In an arrangement that most people would find suffocating today, the brothers and their new wives were joined by Mrs. Melville and her four unmarried daughters. Before long, each of the brothers fathered a child (Herman and Lizzie's son Malcolm was born in February 1849), adding a new layer of responsibility—and noise—to the household.

Melville set out manfully to discharge the duties of husband, son, and father. During the summer of 1849, he worked furiously to recoup the losses of the ambitious but unreadable *Mardi* by writing not one, but *two* commercial sea stories—"two jobs," as he described *Redburn* and *White-Jacket* in a letter to his father-in-law, "which I have done for money—being forced to it, as other men are to sawing wood." He confessed in the same letter that "so far as I am individually concerned, & independent of my pocket, it is my earnest desire to write those sort of books which are said to 'fail.'—Pardon this egotism."[28] Melville was indeed unfolding within himself at a furious pace. Now a fully established literary gentleman, he fell in with the circle of New York writers revolving around Evert Duyckinck. Though Duyckinck continued to regard Melville as something of a natural wonder—the amazing scribbling sea salt—he gladly let him borrow volumes of philosophy and religion from his extensive library, introduced him to his friends, encouraged him to write in a distinctively American style, and published his sketches and reviews in his two magazines, the well-respected *The Literary World* and the satirical *Yankee Doodle,* an early attempt at an American *Punch.* Melville also began to immerse himself in Shakespeare during this period.

In the winter of 1849, he traveled to Europe, ostensibly to arrange British publication of *White-Jacket,* but incidentally for a well-deserved vacation. His tour was extremely rapid by the standard of the day, just a month on the Continent to whirl through Paris, Brussels, Cologne, and the Rhine Valley. By February 1850, he was back in New York and embarked on his next literary voyage—*Moby-Dick.* The new work progressed fairly smoothly, at least in its initial stages, and by May 1, 1850, he was able to write to Richard Henry Dana, Jr. (whose *Two Years Before the Mast* Melville greatly admired), "I am half way in the work. . . . It will be a strange sort of a book, tho', I fear; blubber is blubber you know; tho' you may get oil out of it, the poetry runs as hard as sap from a frozen maple tree. . . . Yet I mean to give the truth of the thing, spite of this."[29]

That summer, Melville transported his family and his manuscript from Manhattan to the Berkshires—or "Berkshire" as he called the region—for vacation. He was familiar with the rural, gently mountainous countryside for he had spent the summer just after his father's death at Broadhall, his uncle Thomas Melvill's farm in Pittsfield, and in 1837 he had taught school for a term just three miles away. It was to Broadhall that Melville returned now. His uncle had died since he had last visited the place, and his cousin Robert was now running the stately old farmhouse as an inn (in fact, he had already sold it, but was keeping it going for one last season). Duyckinck, who came up at the beginning of August as Melville's guest, described Broadhall to his wife as "quite a piece of mouldering rural grandeur"—an impression that holds true today, despite the numerous renovations and expansions that have transformed the original house into the Pittsfield Country Club. Though documentation is scanty, it seems likely that Melville intended to stay in Berkshire only for the summer. In fact, he and his family remained for thirteen years.

We can only speculate about what impelled the move. There

are threads of circumstances that tempt us to weave a pattern. In August, Melville met Hawthorne on Monument Mountain. A month later, he borrowed three thousand dollars from his father-in-law to buy a 180-acre farm adjoining Broadhall and situated six miles from Hawthorne's little red farmhouse at Lenox. In the days between the meeting and purchase, he read much of Hawthorne's story collection, *Mosses from an Old Manse,* and published a rapturous anonymous appreciation of the author and his work in Duyckinck's *The Literary World.* And meanwhile, his novel-in-progress, when he had time to pick it up, began to acquire a vastly darker tone and deeper vision than anything he had written before. As John Updike puts it, Melville "thoroughly revised the whaling story" after meeting Hawthorne, "making of it the elaborate, symbolic, rhapsodic, pessimistic volume of wonders it became."[30] It would be wrong to draw one straight line connecting all of these momentous events in Melville's life—the friendship, the purchase of Arrowhead (as he named the farm), the book. But the correspondences are impossible to ignore. Whether the farm, the book, the friendship came together in a rush as a single expression of Melville's creative unfolding or whether the farm and the book flowered out of a seed planted by Hawthorne, we'll never know. It's enough to say that these events were transpiring simultaneously, and together they ushered Melville into a new region of the imagination.

TWO

Fire Worship

> We live in dead men's houses ... as in this of the
> Seven Gables. ... The house ought to be purified
> with fire,—purified till only its ashes remain.
>
> —NATHANIEL HAWTHORNE,
> The House of the Seven Gables

> By marriage, I might contribute to the population of
> men, but not to the census of the mind. The great
> men are all bachelors, you know. Their family is the
> universe ...
>
> —HERMAN MELVILLE, Pierre

MELVILLE WAS HIGHLY PRIMED for the intense, passionately admiring bond that he quickly forged with Hawthorne. Overshadowed by his glamorous brother Gansevoort (the family's pet) and
deprived of his father at the threshold of manhood, Melville fixed
a very high value on the love and approval and companionship of
a male chum. Exalted buddy relationships figure prominently in
Melville's novels, as many critics have pointed out: Tommo, the
narrator of *Typee,* has his shipmate Toby and, on Nukahiva, a
devoted native body servant named Kory-Kory; in *Omoo* there is
also a white and a native buddy—Dr. Long Ghost and Poky; the
narrator of *White-Jacket* is starry-eyed in his hero worship of Jack
Chase, the "frank and charming," handsome, wise, poetry-loving,

left-wing, brown-bearded first captain of the top; and in *Moby-Dick,* Ishmael and the tattooed Polynesian "cannibal" Queequeg initiate their bosom friendship by sleeping together in a comic scene that has spawned reams of commentary. "I felt a melting in me," Ishmael writes as he gazes fondly at the "hideously marred" face of his newfound friend. "No more my splintered heart and maddened hand were turned against the wolfish world. This soothing savage had redeemed it."[1]

This melting, soothing redemption was for Melville the special balm of male friendship. In a pre-Freudian age, he could yearn for such a friendship and fantasize about it without worrying about homosexuality. Indeed, Melville is so relaxed about the sexual implication of male bonding that he turns it into a joke, describing the friendship between Ishmael and Queequeg as a marriage "consummated" by their sharing a bed: "How it is I know not; but there is no place like a bed for confidential disclosures between friends. Man and wife, they say, there open the very bottom of their souls to each other; and some old couples often lie and chat over old times till nearly morning. Thus, then, in our hearts' honeymoon, lay I and Queequeg—a cosy, loving pair."[2] It seems inconceivable that a man tormented by guilty, frustrated homosexual urges, as some critics have made Melville out to be, could have written this. On the other hand, he would not have put this "cosy, loving" male pair in bed together had the idea not appealed to him: Such a scene is unthinkable in Hawthorne. At the time he met Hawthorne, Melville was perfectly aware of his longing for a bosom male friend and seemed to be utterly unembarrassed by it. He saw nothing amiss in usurping the marriage bed, albeit comically and symbolically, as the arena for "confidential disclosures between friends." Indeed, friendship, in his mind, offered a welcome refuge from the tyrannies of marriage.

Hawthorne eminently fit the bill of Melville's ideal male friend. Fifteen years Melville's senior, he was a kind of literary land-bound New England Jack Chase—still handsome at forty-six, clear-eyed and fine-featured, highly accomplished, increasingly respected, admirable in every way. Even before he had read much of his work, Melville seized on Hawthorne as his model and his forerunner in American letters. Here, far more than the lumbering James Fenimore Cooper or the smooth patrician Washington Irving, was an American writer he felt inspired to follow. To have such a man as a neighbor, a friend, a fellow toiler, and a literary admirer answered many, many prayers. As the editors of the definitive Northwestern–Newberry edition of Melville's works write, "As a connoisseur of manly beauty from his sailing and island-hopping years and now almost frantic to validate his exalted new self-estimate by identifying another American fellow writer as comparably great, Melville beyond any doubt decided Hawthorne was the most fascinating American he had ever met."[3]

Hawthorne's feelings for Melville were more muted and more veiled, but he was at the very least happy to accept the homage of his younger colleague. Theirs was from the start a true literary alliance, rooted in a shared appreciation of each other's writing and a shared desire to have their books compared and their names associated in the minds of readers. Comradeship in letters— the joy of finding another writer who speaks and understands one's language, an ally who can serve as the ideal audience of one—would, in the coming generations, inspire and sustain the friendships between Katherine Anne Porter and Eudora Welty and Robert Lowell and Elizabeth Bishop, though not, as we'll see, the Henry James–Edith Wharton connection, which flourished *despite,* not because of, their work.

On Melville's side, admiration for Hawthorne the writer sprang up almost simultaneously with affection for Hawthorne the man. By a strange coincidence, his aunt Mary Ann gave him a copy of Hawthorne's *Mosses from an Old Manse* just a few weeks before the Monument Mountain picnic, and Melville probably read at least some of the stories immediately beforehand. We know from a famous allusion to "my fine countryman, Hawthorne of Salem" in *White-Jacket* that Melville was already aware of Hawthorne's status and familiar with his writing. But the *Mosses* penetrated his imagination as no other work had done. Six days after meeting the author of the stories, Melville sat down in the garret of Broadhall at his uncle's old desk, which was stained with chicken droppings from long storage in a corn loft, to write the extraordinary hymn of praise he titled "Hawthorne and His Mosses."[4] Part sketch, part critical reappraisal, part Whitmanesque proclamation of America's claim to literary greatness, part fictionalized autobiography, "Hawthorne and His Mosses" has the buoyant, rolling enthusiasm of Melville's early sea narratives, though the whole composition is shadowed by the dark cloud of his looming maturity. It is one of the most electrifying accounts ever written of the "shock of recognition" running from one great literary mind to another.

The piece appeared anonymously in Duyckinck's *Literary World* on August 17 and 24 under the subtitle "By a Virginian Spending July in Vermont," but the lake and mountain scenery and the "papered chamber in a fine old farm-house" mentioned in the first paragraph are easily recognizable as Broadhall and its Berkshire environs. Perhaps the use of a fictitious narrator freed Melville's imagination or allowed him to speak more feelingly from the heart. Whatever stimulus propelled the piece, it was clearly a powerful one, for "Hawthorne and His Mosses" is itself a glorious work of literature, shot through with rhetorical flashes worthy of Shakespeare (who is invoked frequently as a fit standard of comparison for Hawthorne). Among its more memorable phrases are: "His wild, witch voice rings through me," "infinite obscure," "axis of reality," "sane madness of vital truth," "literary flunkeyism." The piece hauled around the prevailing critical winds on Hawthorne, blasting the contemporary view of him as a "pleasant writer, with a pleasant style . . . a sequestered, harmless man" and deifying him as the master of "mystical blackness . . . ten times black . . ." and the possessor of "a great, deep intellect, which drops down into the universe like a plummet." The oft-quoted seminal sentence, one of the essential articles of America's literary constitution, is worth quoting yet again: "Certain it is . . . that this great power of blackness in him derives its force from its appeal to that Calvinistic sense of Innate Depravity and Original Sin, from whose visitations, in some shape or other, no deeply thinking mind is always and wholly free."[5] Such visitations were to descend, in some shape or other, on James, Wharton, Porter, Welty, and Lowell. Of the eight friends, only Bishop, possibly, warded off the power of blackness; but she had other demons to plague her.

"Hawthorne and His Mosses" proclaims that an American writer can be as great as Shakespeare and crowns Hawthorne as the writer who has come closest to attaining that pinnacle—"the American, who up to the present day, has evinced, in Literature, the largest brain with the largest heart."[6] But the piece is almost as much about Melville and his current aspirations as it is about Hawthorne and his past accomplishments. "Hawthorne and His Mosses" draws a detailed map of the terrain that Melville himself was about to traverse, both in his work and in his friendship with Hawthorne. It was this very "power of blackness" that was to make *Moby-Dick* so vastly different from anything Melville had produced before. Ahab's declaration, "I am darkness leaping out of light," comes straight out of Hawthorne—though Hawthorne would have had him gliding, flitting, or stealing out of light. When Melville declares that "Shakespeares are this day being born on the banks of the Ohio" and when he describes the "American genius" as an "explosive sort of stuff [that] will expand though screwed up in a vice, and burst it, though it were triple steel," he is really speaking of himself and the book then exploding out of him.

He all but thrusts himself into the piece when he tells his readers that to "confess" Hawthorne's genius is to "brace the whole brotherhood" of writers: "For genius, all over the world, stands hand in hand, and one shock of recognition runs the whole circle round." Surely he himself belongs in this circuit. Just as he argues that Marlowe, Webster, Ford, Beaumont, and Jonson shared the genius of Shakespeare, so he implies that he can claim a share in Hawthorne's genius: They breathe the same crystalline air of new creation. The comparison with Elizabethan England was, in fact, preternaturally intuitive for the American renaissance was coming into full flower even as he wrote this, with *The Scarlet Letter, Moby-Dick, Walden,* and *Leaves of Grass* all published in a five-year span. Melville's prediction that "political supremacy among the nations" awaited America at the close of the century was also eerily correct.

Finally, at the personal climax of the piece, Melville breaks into the language of sexual ravishment:

> To what infinite height of loving wonder and admiration I may yet be borne, when by repeatedly banqueting on these Mosses, I shall have thoroughly incorporated their whole stuff into my being—that, I can not tell. But already I feel that this Hawthorne has dropped germinous seeds into my soul. He expands and deepens down, the more I contemplate him; and further, and further, shoots his strong New-England roots into the hot soil of my Southern soul.[7]

Such a passage would probably provoke a sexual harassment suit today—though the editorially timid Duyckinck let it stand unchanged in 1850. Each literary period has its own characteristic register of metaphor. Animals, prisons, armed combat, fire, water, and drugs are the images of love in Lowell and Bishop. James and

Wharton used the language of finance to write of sexual relationships—interest, pay, owe, value, sacrifice. Melville used the language of eating and fertilization to write of literary creation and literary comradeship. The same erotic charge runs through many of the letters he addressed to Hawthorne over the next year. The same panting hyperbole, shading between the lofty and the comic, informs the chummy passages of *Moby-Dick* ("Come; let us squeeze hands all round; nay, let us all squeeze ourselves into each other; let us squeeze ourselves into the very milk and sperm of kindness").[8] Melville was stirred "to his very bones," as he puts it, by the immensity of encountering Hawthorne, the work and the man, at this turning point in his career. The germinous seeds that Hawthorne dropped into his soul erupted over the course of that year into *Moby-Dick* just as, more than one hundred years later, during the summer of 1957, the verse and friendship of Elizabeth Bishop catalyzed Robert Lowell's breakthrough in *Life Studies*.

There is no denying that Melville's feelings were "warm." Hawthorne excited him in every way. Desire figured immensely in this relationship—and who can precisely analyze the "purity" or "impurity" of desire? What is even more striking than the erotic imagery of "Hawthorne and His Mosses" is the fact that Melville was instantly conscious that this artistic fertilization was taking place inside him. It is a sign of the pitch he was working at just then.

Other literary friendships have commenced with a glowing written tribute or perceptive review. Porter launched Welty's career by contributing an introduction to her first collection of stories; Lowell wrote a brilliant and influential review of Bishop's first volume of poetry right around the time they met; Emerson authorized the publication of his famous letter praising Whitman's *Leaves of Grass;* James circulated shrewd critiques of Wharton's early novels and stories to friends they knew in common and dispensed unsolicited advice to Wharton herself. But for sheer passion and grandeur, Melville's "Hawthorne and His Mosses" has never been surpassed. Melville claims in the piece that he wrote it in two days, confessing that only after his first writing session did he read the very fine (and exceedingly black) "Young Goodman Brown." "Hawthorne and His Mosses" radiates a white heat of inspired appreciation—indeed, it remains, still, as fresh and vivid as if it had been written yesterday. The actual relationship that ensued could not possibly live up to the extravagant hopes and immodest demands of the piece. In a way, the friendship was doomed from the start.

The publication of Melville's essay pitched the Hawthorne household into a fever of gratitude, pride, and speculation about the identity of the exceedingly perceptive Virginian. "I cannot speak or think of any thing now but the extraordinary review of Mr Hawthorne in the Literary World," Sophia wrote to Evert Duyckinck at the end of August. "The Virginian is the first person who has ever in *print* appreciated Mr Hawthorne. . . . Who can he be, so fearless, so rich in heart, of such fine intuition?" And to her mother: "Do not wait an hour to procure the two last numbers of 'The Literary World,' and read a new criticism on Mr. Hawthorne. . . . At last some one dares to say what in my secret mind I have often thought—that he is only to be mentioned with the Swan of Avon; the great heart and the grand intellect combined."[9] Hawthorne himself, more restrained and modest, confessed to Duyckinck that he read the piece "with very great pleasure. The writer has a truly generous heart. . . . But he is no common man; and, next to deserving his praise, it is good to have beguiled or bewitched such a man into praising me more than I deserve." In the same letter, Hawthorne warmly praised Melville's early novels, copies of which Duyckinck had sent him up from New York two weeks earlier: "I have read Melville's works with a progressive appreciation of the author. No writer ever put the reality before his reader more unflinchingly than he does 'in 'Redburn,' and 'White Jacket.' 'Mardi' is a rich book, with depths here and there that compel a man to swim for his life. It is so good that one scarcely pardons the writer for not having brooded long over it, so as to make it a great deal better."[10]

Though Hawthorne was not so moved by Melville's work as to dash off an essay about his "progressive appreciation," he certainly felt disposed to deepen his acquaintance with the younger writer. The men spent several days together in early September, first at Lenox and then at Broadhall, and possibly exchanged another visit a few weeks later. Sophia, keeping a close eye on the developing friendship, warmed steadily to Melville, especially after she discovered that he was the mysterious Virginian. Sophia's letters to her family are worth quoting at length for they are the only firsthand accounts of these early encounters. She confesses to her mother after the September 3 visit that she and Mr. Hawthorne were both surprised to find Mr. Melville so "very agreeable and entertaining. . . . A man with a true, warm heart, and a soul and an intellect,—with life to his finger-tips; earnest, sincere, and reverent; very tender and *modest*. And I am not sure that he is not a very great man; but I have not quite decided upon my own opinion." Having praised his character and his "keen perceptive power," she turns to his physical appearance, which she finds somewhat wanting:

> What astonishes me is, that his eyes are not large and deep. . . . They are not keen eyes, either, but quite undistinguished in any way. His nose is straight and rather handsome, his mouth expressive of sensibility and emotion. He is tall and erect, with an air free, brave, and manly. When conversing, he is full of gesture and force, and loses himself in his subject. There is no grace nor polish. Once in a while, his animation gives place to a singularly quiet expression, out of these eyes to which I have objected; an indrawn, dim look, but which at the same time makes you feel that he is at that instant taking deepest note of what is before him. It is a strange, lazy glance, but with a power in it quite unique. It does not seem to penetrate through you, but to take you into himself.[11]

In another letter, possibly written to her sister, Sophia speaks of her joy in learning that Melville was the author of "Hawthorne and His Mosses":

> I had some delightful conversations with him about the "sweetest Man of Mosses" after we discovered him to be the author of the Review. One interview we had upon the Verandah of Chateau Brun [the red farmhouse] in the golden light of evening twilight, when the lake was like glass of a rose tint . . . Mr. Melville and I went out to sit in the light of the setting sun. He said Mr. Hawthorne was the first person whose physical being appeared to him wholly in harmony with the intellectual & spiritual. He said the sunny hair & the pensiveness, the symmetry of his face, the depth of eyes, "the gleam—the shadow—& the peace supreme" all were in exact response to the high calm intellect, the glowing, deep heart—the purity of actual & spiritual life. *Mr.* Melville is a person of great ardor

& simplicity. He is all on fire with the subject that interests him. It rings through his frame like a cathedral bell. His truth and honesty shine out at every point.[12]

Sophia notes with approval that Melville, while a guest in their house, was "very careful not to interrupt Mr. Hawthorne's mornings," but let him work in peace. After Hawthorne had finished his day's writing, the friends spent the afternoon tramping and chatting—or rather, Melville talked "to a great extent" while Hawthorne maintained a "great but hospitable silence." Melville told Sophia that "sometimes they would walk along without talking on either side, but that even then they seemed to be very social." She concludes with the glad news that Melville has just bought Arrowhead, "So we shall have him for a neighbor."

Given Melville's enthusiasm for male comradeship and Hawthorne's temperament, we tend to think of their relationship as a stag affair—Ishmael and Dimmesdale roaming through the dark forests, expostulating on guilt and sin and retribution, raging over the black heart of man, the wolfish world and the appalling indifference of nature. But, in fact, as Sophia Hawthorne's letters show, the friendship really touched the entire family. Melville, in his visits to the Hawthornes' red farmhouse, evidently spent as much time with Sophia as with Nathaniel and developed a cordial relationship with her based on their shared devotion to Hawthorne and his work. When Hawthorne later came to stay at Arrowhead in March 1851 he brought along his seven-year-old daughter, Una; and years later his son, Julian, recorded his fond memories of "Mr. Omoo," as the children called Melville, entertaining the family with his playacting and his "tremendous stories" about his adventures in the South Sea Islands. Julian also recalled riding on the back of Melville's Newfoundland, which often accompanied its master to Lenox (the Hawthornes did not have a dog of their own).[13] There is no record of any contact between the wives or of Lizzie Melville's impressions of Hawthorne.

Melville once told his sister Augusta that the Hawthornes were "the loveliest family he ever met with, or anyone can possibly imagine." The editors of the Northwestern–Newberry edition of Melville's work attribute at least some of this enthusiasm to Melville's admiration for "how Sophia subordinated everything else to the needs of her husband, whom she quite literally worshipped."[14] Melville himself received no such reverence at home, at least from his wife. Documentation in letters and journals is scanty; but hints and asides in Melville's fiction suggest that he had a profound ambivalence about his marriage and family life, an ambivalence that seems to have played an important role in his friendship with Hawthorne. "Melville, lured by cosmic enigmas and hounded by mundane worries, has sea-dreams at home and land-dreams on shipboard," writes Harry Levin in his seminal study, *The Power of Blackness.* "The familiar and the strange change places, just as night and day reverse themselves in the antipodes."[15] Henry A. Murray goes even further in his valuable introductory essay on *Pierre,* pointing to an "uncompromising dichotomy" in Melville's work between sea and land, open space and closed space (especially in cities), freedom and slavishness, adventure and family obligations, danger and domestic comforts, the heart and the head, passionate thought and conventional commonplace, and so on. "Over and over again, in multifarious rhetorical forms, Melville contrasts these two clusters of value," says Murray, "and always champions the former," though he acknowledges its potential dangers.[16]

The sea and land dreams flash to the surface in his novels as reveries, asides, poetic expostulations. In *White-Jacket,* he writes, swaggering on board the man-of-war, that "of all chamber furniture, best calculated to cure a bad temper, and breed a pleasant one, is the sight of a lovely wife."[17] In *Moby-Dick* he has Ishmael conclude in midvoyage that "attainable felicity" cannot be found "anywhere in the intellect or the fancy; but in the wife, the heart, the bed, the table, the saddle, the fire-side, the country."[18] Yet at the start of the voyage, just as the *Pequod* clears Nantucket harbor and "plunges like fate into the lone Atlantic," Melville turns around to ponder the secret treachery of "The Lee Shore" and to acknowledge, in his own voice, the irresistible sway of the open sea: "But as in landlessness alone resides the highest truth, shoreless, indefinite as God—so, better is it to perish in that howling infinite, than be ingloriously dashed upon the lee, even if that were safety!"[19] In *Pierre,* he formulates the conflict even more explicitly:

> Weary with the invariable earth, the restless sailor breaks from every enfolding arm, and puts to sea in height of tempest that blows off shore. But in long night-watches at the antipodes,

how heavily that ocean gloom lies in vast bales upon the deck; thinking that that very moment in his deserted hamlet-home the household sun is high, and many a sun-eyed maiden meridian as the sun. He curses Fate; himself he curses; his senseless madness, which is himself. For whoso once has known this sweet knowledge, and then fled it; in absence, to him the avenging dream will come.[20]

For Melville, the tensions between "the wife, the heart, the bed" and "the howling infinite" became acute after his move to Pittsfield. Now married three years and the father of a toddler son, living far inland and working under the strain of sizable debt to his father-in-law, he felt oppressed as never before by the heaviness of domestic life. Melville truly loved Arrowhead—the mellow old farmhouse with its snug low-ceilinged rooms and massive central fireplace; the bare, square, upstairs corner room where he wrote facing north to a distant view of whale-backed Mount Greylock; the barn which he dutifully visited each morning and afternoon to feed his horse and cow; the deep green fields studded with spreading pines; the famous "piazza" that he built on himself. Yet he also, increasingly, felt both isolated and cramped in the "daughter-full" house (his mother and four sisters had moved up from Manhattan and every two years another baby was born, for a total of four, two sons and two daughters, by 1855). Melville vented some of his frustration in a sketch published in 1856 called "I and My Chimney." The piece is usually read as a bit of whimsy and mockery, but in fact, as John Updike points out, beneath the "thin and facetious disguise" it is "a harrowing revelation of Melville's domestic attitudes."[21] The house, clearly recognizable as Arrowhead, is a war zone between a harridan wife of "unwarrantable vitality" and the battle-fatigued, henpecked, pipe-smoking narrator. Having "stripped" her husband "by degrees of one masculine prerogative after another," this meddlesome woman now launches a campaign to take down the house's huge, tapering, central brick chimney ("a phallic symbol of male independence," according to Updike) in order to open up a grand entrance hall. With "both wife and daughters ever at . . . elbow and ear," the narrator feels like a virtual prisoner in his own home—spied upon, badgered, nagged, and threatened by a cabal of powerful females.

The situation is strangely reminiscent of Elias Canetti's *Auto-Da-Fe* in which an elderly, fanatically bookish gentleman is turned out of his own precious library by the crafty, greedy peasant housekeeper he has been tricked into marrying. In one particulary gruesome passage, Melville's narrator describes how his wife reads to him "with a suppressed emphasis" a newspaper story about "some tyrannic day-laborer, who, after being for many years the Caligula of his family, ends by beating his long-suffering spouse to death, with a garret door wrenched off its hinges, and then, pitching his little innocents out of the window, suicidally turns inward towards the broken wall scored with the butcher's and baker's bill, and so rushes headlong to his dreadful account."[22] This is not the fantasy of a happily married man. "I and My Chimney" is clearly fabricated in many particulars (Lizzie Melville insisted that the wife in the sketch was actually her mother-in-law, "who was very vigorous and energetic about the farm," and that "the proposed removal of the chimney is purely mythical") and it's also quite funny, in a black humorous sort of way. Yet the sketch reflects Melville's real torment and rage about his domestic situation, as does *Pierre*, but even more horrifically. For Melville, the land dream had become a nightmare.

The Hawthorne household at Lenox must have struck Melville as a blissfully safe harbor from the pressures he endured at Arrowhead: Here the male writer was the domestic god, the wife was the adoring high priestess of his cult, and the house was unencumbered by needy relatives and in-laws except for brief interludes. The chimney of the red farmhouse was safe. But for all the snug comfort and warmth it radiated, it was a real chimney and the fire that spiraled smoke up into it was hot and dangerous. In "Hawthorne and His Mosses" Melville quotes appreciatively this passage from Hawthorne's sketch "Fire Worship" about the violent side of the household fire:

> Nor did it lessen the charm of his soft, familiar courtesy and helpfulness, that the mighty spirit, were opportunity offered him, would run riot through the peaceful house, wrap its inmates in his terrible embrace, and leave nothing of them save their whitened bones. This possibility of mad destruction only made his domestic kindness the more beautiful and touching.[23]

The "Fire Worship" sketch reflects the genial, tender, gentle side of the "Man of Mosses," but in its heart it conceals a horror of "mad destruction." It was this very fusion of the domestic and the terrible in Hawthorne's fire worship that Melville found so enormously appealing. Melville also engaged in fire worship, but his version blew him out of the house and into the fierce elemental maelstrom of *Moby-Dick*. In "The Candles" chapter, Ahab worships fire by shrieking his defiance—"blood against fire!"—at the eerie white flame of the corpusants, globes of electrical energy that gather in the spars of a ship:

> Oh! thou clear spirit of clear fire, whom on these seas I as Persian once did worship, till in the sacramental act so burned by thee, that to this hour I bear the scar; I now know thee, thou clear spirit, and I now know that thy right worship is defiance.[24]

Though Hawthorne was possessed of a kind of moral X-ray vision that revealed to him the spark of death in the cheery parlor fire, the skull beneath the skin, and "in every bosom, the deep mystery of sin," he remained resolutely land bound, both in reality and in imagination. Neither his seagoing ancestors, his longtime residence in a port town, nor his friend Herman Melville inspired Hawthorne to venture forth onto "the howling infinite": In fact, he embarked on an ocean voyage only once in his life, after he was well advanced in middle age. He preferred to spend his days sequestered and sheltered by his hearthside—or rather hearthsides, for Hawthorne, despite his homing instinct, moved restlessly from house to house throughout his married life. "I do not take root anywhere and never shall," he once wrote a friend.[25] Melville, paradoxically, scarcely budged once he settled into life on dry land, remaining at Arrowhead for thirteen years and then keeping the same Manhattan address for the final twenty-eight years of life. Nevertheless, in imagination, the centripetal Hawthorne "never left home," as Levin points out, while Melville was cast centrifugally "far into the night." Theirs was the classic attraction of opposites. To quote Levin once more:

> Melville, as an outdoor man, was intrigued by the indoor cast of Hawthorne's writing, by its interiors rather than its landscapes. . . . [Hawthorne's] journey ends in a house and within a locked room. . . . But this does not mean that he has never

adventured; for there can be cosmic adventure in introspection, as much as in exploration.[26]

The homebound Eudora Welty concludes her memoirs with exactly the same claim: "A sheltered life can be a daring life as well. For all serious daring starts from within."

While visiting at Lenox, Melville had a chance to witness Hawthorne's serious daring close up and he found it intoxicating—replete with possibilities for himself and his art. On the few occasions when he had Hawthorne to Arrowhead, Melville was eager to extract him from the polite feminine bustle downstairs and get him outside for a long walk in "the infinite air," out to the barn, or upstairs to the exclusively male bastion of his study. Friendship with Hawthorne, with the Hawthornes, gave Melville some of the higher truth and free camaraderie of "landlessness" without setting sail. The friendship opened a chamber outside the confines of his fraught marriage where he could sit by the fire with a bosom friend, smoking and drinking and indulging in what he self-mockingly called "ontological heroics." Here was a different mode of fire worship—calmer and quieter and more companionable than Ahab's, but in thrall, nonetheless, to the knowledge that the mild household god of the hearth was also the wild agent of the apocalypse "who loves to riot through our own dark forests and sweep across our prairies," as Hawthorne writes in "Fire Worship," "and to whose ravenous maw, it is said, the universe shall one day be given as a final feast."[27] With Hawthorne as his companion, Melville could bring the familiar and the strange into alignment, at least for a time.

After Hawthorne went home to the little red farmhouse in Lenox, Melville let the fumes of cigar, wood smoke, and brandy clear from his brain and then he sat down again in the solitude of his north-facing study to incorporate the "heroics" of their encounters into *Moby-Dick*. We have no way of knowing what sort of book *Moby-Dick* would have been had Melville never read *Mosses from an Old Manse* and struck up a friendship with its author during the summer of 1850. Certainly a *different* book— but in what way? One of the central tenets in Melville studies—an idea so often repeated that most take it as established fact—is that *Moby-Dick* started out as a semiautobiographical sea narrative, in the manner of *Redburn* and *White-Jacket,* and then underwent a complete overhaul after Melville met and read Hawthorne. Since no dated manuscripts or letters exist to support this idea, we must turn to the text itself—and the text opens deep and fertile ground for speculation. *Moby-Dick* is indeed radically different from anything Melville had written before—but it is also radically different from anything in Hawthorne. For starters, there are no women, the sine qua non of Hawthorne romances. There is no secret crime or sin motivating the story. Guilt and evil in *Moby-Dick* are not interpersonal but cosmic, elemental. None of the characters in *Moby-Dick,* with the exception of the conscience-stricken Starbuck, is conceivable in a Hawthorne story.

Ahab, the book's hero, is, on the face of it, the least Hawthornian figure of all, and yet "hark ye yet again," as Ahab himself commands Starbuck, "the little lower layer." Beneath their sneaking and shrinking and weird sexual dementias, aren't many of Hawthorne's males possessed of the same mania as Ahab—the obsessive need to fathom, master, and control nature? Ahab acts out of a frenzied desire to "strike through the mask" of nature: He risks everything, including his life and the lives of his crew, in his quest to destroy the "inscrutable malice" of the white whale. But consider the Faustian machinations that impel so many of Hawthorne's heroes: Aylmer's fiendish attempt to gain "ultimate control over nature" by excising his wife's birthmark and thereby re-create her without the taint of mortality; Rappaccini's willingness to sacrifice human life, even his own daughter, "for the sake of adding so much as a grain of mustard-seed to the great heap of his accumulated knowledge"; Chillingworth's consuming desire to know the truth about his wife's adultery so he can triumph over her sexual partner; Ethan Brand's monomaniacal pursuit of "the unpardonable sin," in the course of which he turns himself into "a cold observer, looking on mankind as the subject of his experiment" and willing to corrupt and destroy anyone for the sake of knowledge. Hawthorne by temperament was drawn to scientists, ministers, doctors, and artists (Brand, the lime burner, is an exception); Melville, because of his youthful experience, chose a sea captain for his Faust. But the same fevered blood courses through their heroes' veins.

Certainly, Melville has twisted many other literary influences into Ahab as well—the rhetoric of Shakespeare's Lear and Milton's Satan, strands of Carlyle, Byron, and Coleridge, echoes of the Bible funneled into a raging Gnosticism; but the impact of Hawthorne is undeniable. The moral profundity of *Moby-Dick*, its powerful use of symbol, and, of course, its darkness and sense of universal doom have all been laid at Hawthorne's feet. But surely the conception of Ahab's character arose, at least in part, from the flames of fires that Melville and Hawthorne worshiped together that year.

Perhaps all of us have our versions of land dreams and sea dreams. And perhaps all of our best friendships stand on the middle ground between these dreams, merging and reconciling the familiar and the strange. We welcome a bosom friend to join us on the serious daring of our adventures, while we must shun the company of wife, husband, parent, and child. "It must be hard for man to be an uncompromising hero and a commander among his race, and yet never ruffle any domestic brow," writes Melville in *Pierre*.[28] Once family enters in, the adventure ceases to be heroic. Certainly this merging of the familiar and the strange played a role among all the literary friends considered in this book.

For James and Wharton, Europe took the place of the "howling infinite" of Melville's sea—it was a "corrupt" passion they shared, as James wrote her, "dans le fond de la nature & jusque dans le sang" [at the bottom of our nature and even in the blood];[29] for Porter and Welty the strange was the very fact of being simultaneously Southern "ladies" and serious artists; Bishop pursued the strange in endless exotic travel, and paradoxically discovered that home was the strangest place of all; Lowell repeatedly abandoned wife, home, and child in violent bouts of madness and in his compulsive love affairs, and then repeatedly slunk back again. For all of these friends, their land dreams and sea dreams meshed and overlapped. Each pair practiced fire worship side by side. In this, as in much else, the Melville–Hawthorne friendship was the forerunner—a "type" as they would have said. It's not that they invented this aspect of friendship, but rather, in our literary tradition, they were among the first to find words for it. Their friendship, like their writing, is scripture.

THREE

Infinite Fraternity and the Negatives of Flesh

This book-making life is certainly an unwholesome one, since it creates such a tendency to make itself the subject of discussion.

—NATHANIEL HAWTHORNE *to Evert Duyckinck*

I had promised myself much pleasure in getting [Hawthorne] up in my snug room here, & discussing the Universe with a bottle of brandy & cigars.

—HERMAN MELVILLE *to Evert Duyckinck*

ALL TOLD, Hawthorne and Melville were neighbors in the Berkshires for only fifteen months, but they managed to pack a good deal of friendship into this short span of time. Melville kept the temperature of their relationship high. If he was, as one critic writes, "the aggressive suitor in their literary courtship," Hawthorne was at least willing to be wooed.[1] Judging from what scant evidence we have, Hawthorne seems to have thawed a bit in Melville's company. He probably had some trouble with the concept of shooting strong roots into the hot soil of Melville's soul; yet once the summer picnic season ended and damp, drizzly November closed in on the Berkshires, Hawthorne must have welcomed the companionship of a talented and ardently admiring younger colleague. Adept at ridding himself of unwanted company, he showed no signs of seeking to evade the squeeze of Melville's hand. Hawthorne did not crave a bosom friend the way Melville did: His wife and children satisfied his immediate emotional needs, and he was deeply loyal to a couple of old college friends, including Horatio Bridge and Franklin Pierce (soon to be elected president). But he enjoyed Melville's attention and appreciated his status. Here was a rising literary ally, well connected with the newly powerful New York publishing world and willing, indeed eager, to place an ecstatic review of his work in an influential journal. From Hawthorne's point of view, Melville was entertaining in the parlor, playful with the children, considerate of the wife, and passionately devoted to his work. So what if his reckless, extravagant way of expressing himself was a touch embarrassing? For Hawthorne, in the winter of 1850–51, friendship with Melville was hard to resist.

The surviving records cast but tantalizing flickers of light on their encounters. On January 22, Melville, "after a long procrastination," paid a visit to Hawthorne at Lenox and found him "buried in snow," as he wrote Duyckinck "& the delightful scenery about him, all wrapped up & tucked away under a napkin, as it were."[2] "We gave him cold chicken," Sophia recorded primly in her diary. Hawthorne supplemented the meager meal by making a gift of the first and second series of his *Twice-Told Tales* and by promising to visit Arrowhead. Four days after Melville's departure, Hawthorne completed *The House of the Seven Gables*, so it would seem likely that the friends talked about that novel as well as Melville's work in progress. Melville, back at Arrowhead, delved into Hawthorne's stories and set down his opinion of them in a letter to Duyckinck:

> They far exceed the "Mosses" [a flat contradiction of what he had said in "Hawthorne and His Mosses"]—they are, I fancy, an earlier vintage from his vine. Some of those sketches are wonderfully subtle. Their deeper meanings are worthy of a Brahmin. Still there is something lacking—a good deal lacking—to the plump sphericity of the man. What is that?—He doesn't patronise the butcher—he needs roast-beef, done rare.[3]

Melville seems to be speaking here of Hawthorne the writer—but his remarks pertain equally to the man. There *is* something bloodless and waxen about Hawthorne: Melville puts his finger on it in the phrase "He doesn't patronise the butcher." "Hawthorne and His Mosses," written before Melville really knew Hawthorne or his work very well, is pure praise. It's interesting that a shade of disappointment, even aversion, fell over Melville after he got to know Hawthorne better. Clearly, he was not so ravished by Hawthorne's wild witch voice as to take leave altogether of his senses, or his sense of humor.

On March 12, Melville turned up at Lenox again to invite the entire Hawthorne family to come visit Arrowhead. Sophia, ever mindful of the larder, noted in her diary that "he was entertained with Champagne foam—manufactured of beaten eggs, loaf sugar, & champagne—bread & butter & cheese. My husband concluded to go with Una."[4] The following day, father and daughter set off in a snowstorm for Pittsfield, where they remained two days as Melville's guests. Melville had already promised Hawthorne that he would not have to stand on ceremony at Arrowhead. "Do not think you are coming to any prim nonsensical house," he wrote before the visit. "You may do what you please—say or say *not* what you please. And if you feel any inclination for that sort of thing—you may spend the period of your visit *in bed,* if you like—every hour of your visit."[5] Hawthorne was evidently out of bed long enough to repair with Melville to the barn, where they smoked cigars for hours on end and talked metaphysics. Una, presumably, was entrusted to the care of the womenfolk.

"I write you from the house of our friend Herman Melville," Hawthorne wrote Duyckinck on March 14, "and have only to glance my eye aside to obtain a fine snow-covered prospect of Graylock." He commended Melville in the same note for making himself and his friends "snug and comfortable."[6] As further evidence of *how* snug and comfortable, Hawthorne mentioned in a letter to another friend that Melville "is an admirable fellow, and has some excellent old port and sherry wine."[7] Drinking was also much on Melville's mind in connection with the friendship. "We will have mulled wine with wisdom, & buttered toast with storytelling & crack jokes & bottles from morning till night," he wrote Hawthorne in anticipation of a visit.[8] (The fumes of alcohol and tobacco also pervaded future generations of literary encounters, although starting with James and Wharton, cigarettes replaced cigars. Strong liquor, however, continued to flow freely, sometimes too freely, down the years—only Wharton, of the eight friends, did not imbibe.) In April, Melville transported a bedstead and clock to Lenox for the Hawthornes, and Nathaniel gave him a copy of the just-published *The House of the Seven Gables,* which he read in a day. The visits tapered off in the spring. Between getting in the crops on the farm and trying to finish *Moby-Dick,* Melville was understandably exhausted.

There was another flurry of visits in August, when Sophia Hawthorne was away with Una, and Nathaniel was left in Lenox in charge of Julian. Melville makes a couple of fleeting appearances in Hawthorne's journal from that month, starting on August 1: "After supper, I put Julian to bed; and Melville and I had a talk about time and eternity, things of this world and of the next, and books, and publishers, and all possible and impossible matters, that lasted pretty deep into the night, and if the truth must be told, we smoked cigars even within the sacred precincts of the sitting room."[9] A week later, Melville was back, with the Duyckinck brothers, and the men, along with Julian, rode off to visit the Shaker village at Hancock. Afterward, as Hawthorne confides in his journal, he felt "constrained by the necessity of the case" to invite the party back to the red farmhouse for tea, though "with many doubts as to the result." Since there was scarcely any food in the house, Hawthorne had to go next door to borrow some provisions and then beg his cranky cook to improvise a meal: "Tea, bread and butter, dropt eggs, little bread-cakes, raspberry jam," he records in the journal; "and I truly thanked Heaven, and Mrs Peters [the cook], that it was no worse! After tea, we had a smoke and some pleasant conversation; and at ten o'clock the guests departed. . . . It was a most beautiful night, with full, rich, cloudless moonlight, so that I would rather have ridden the six miles to Pittsfield, then have gone to bed."[10] A rather extraordinary admission, this, for the nervous, homebound Hawthorne. In his next journal entry, he notes that Julian told him that he had so enjoyed the previous day's expedition that "he wanted to go again, and that he loved Mr Melville as well as me, and as mamma, and as Una."[11]

Hawthorne, even in his journal, says nothing about his own feelings toward Mr. Melville. We have to read heavily between the lines about the tea and jam and cigar smoke to surmise that Hawthorne, like his son, found Melville's company stirring and that his uncharacteristic urge to ride off into the night had as much to do with his inspiring companion as with the rich moonlight. Sophia, as usual, reveals far more vividly than her husband what a visit from Melville looked and felt and sounded like. "Nothing pleases me better," she wrote her sister, "than to sit & hear this growing man dash his tumultuous waves of thought up against Mr Hawthorne's great, genial, comprehending silences—out of the profound of which a wonderful smile, or one powerful word sends back the foam & fury into a peaceful booming, calm—or perchance not into a calm—but a murmuring expostulation—for there is never a 'mush of concession' in him. Yet such love & reverence & admiration for Mr Hawthorne as is really beautiful to witness—& without doing anything on his own part, except merely *being,* it is astonishing how people make him their innermost Father Confessor."[12]

Melville kept no journal and wrote no letters to other friends or family members about his visits with Hawthorne; but his "love & reverence & admiration" as well as his "foam & fury" reverberate through the extraordinary series of letters that he began to send to Hawthorne starting in January 1851. Letters are the soul of a literary friendship, but in this case, we are privy to only half a soul, since Melville destroyed Hawthorne's letters to him. This lacuna is all the more maddening since Melville's letters to Hawthorne rank with the most magnificent in the literature. Certainly, they blaze out in the volume of his collected letters for their spirit, their range of ideas, and their emotional nakedness. Only in his letters to Hawthorne did Melville attempt to "strike through the mask," as Ahab puts it, and delve down into "the little lower layer." It was the one moment in his epistolary career when he really seemed to be *living* in and through his letters. Melville wrote to Hawthorne of topics that were uppermost in his mind—their books, the farm, fame, fortune, the deity, politics, reputation—but whatever his ostensible subject, he was always fundamentally writing about himself, indeed laying his heart and soul bare as before his "innermost Father Confessor." Occasionally in their correspondences, James and Wharton, Porter and Welty, Bishop and Lowell met each other on the highest ground of honesty and eloquence. But Melville in writing to Hawthorne never came down from the mountaintop.

The letters have been quoted and analyzed many times before, and there is no need to cover this terrain again inch by inch. Their climaxes—the peaks and pinnacles of the summit—are almost as familiar as the great rhetorical flights of *Moby-Dick*. There is Melville's wry commentary on *The House of the Seven Gables:* "There is old china with rare devices, set out on the carved buffet; . . . there is a smell as of old wine in the pantry; and finally, in one corner, there is a dark little black-letter volume in golden clasps, entitled 'Hawthorne: A Problem.' "[13] There is his harrowing speculation on "the Problem of the Universe": "As soon as you say *Me,* a *God,* a *Nature,* so soon you jump off from your stool and hang from the beam." There is his famous distillation of the "grand truth about Nathaniel Hawthorne. He says NO! in thunder; but the Devil himself cannot make him say *yes.*"[14]

There is his bitter aphorism on the consequence of telling the truth in art: "Truth is the silliest thing under the sun. Try to get a living by the Truth—and go to the Soup Societies."[15] And the lament about the wretchedness of his working conditions: "The calm, the coolness, the silent grass-growing mood in which a man *ought* always to compose,—that, I fear, can seldom be mine. Dollars damn me; and the malicious Devil is forever grinning in upon me, holding the door ajar. . . . What I feel most moved to write, that is banned,—it will not pay. Yet, altogether, write the *other* way I cannot. So the product is a final hash, and all my books are botches."[16] Despairing over the prospects for enduring literary success, he demands, "What's the use of elaborating what, in its very essence, is so short-lived as a modern book? Though I wrote the Gospels in this century, I should die in the gutter."[17] A propos of Hawthorne's "Ethan Brand," the story of the lime burner who discovered that the "unpardonable sin" was to sacrifice the heart to the intellect, he declares his own emotional allegiance: "I stand for the heart. To the dogs with the head!" And as he nears the end of *Moby-Dick* he offers this astonishing artistic self-assessment: "But I feel that I am now come to the innermost leaf of the bulb, and that shortly the flower must fall to the mould."[18]

Such passages shed a brilliant light on Melville's state of mind at the time he wrote his masterpiece. But let us linger over more intimate moments in the letters—his flights into fantasy, the choice of images, the eddyings of tone. Read in sequence, the letters form a recurrent tidal pattern of advances and withdrawals,

revelations and denials, solicitations and apologies. One can practically see Melville at his desk, scribbling away in a passion of
communion and then pulling up abruptly, hot in the face with
embarrassment over what he has written. Again and again, he
imagines himself cloistered with Hawthorne in some private paradise of brotherly comradeship. "I keep the word 'Welcome' all
the time in my mouth, so as to be ready on the instant when you
cross the threshold," he writes eagerly in the first surviving letter
about a promised visit to Arrowhead.[19] In June, feeling knocked
out by farm work and disgusted by his working conditions (the
"dollars damn me" mood), he longs for an eternal reward of wine
and Hawthorne:

> If ever, my dear Hawthorne, in the eternal times that are to
> come, you and I shall sit down in Paradise, in some shady
> corner by ourselves; and if we shall by any means be able to
> smuggle a basket of champagne there (I won't believe in a
> Temperance Heaven), and if we shall then cross our celestial
> legs in the celestial grass that is forever tropical, and strike our
> glasses and our heads together, till both musically ring in con-
> cert,—then, O dear fellow-mortal, how shall we pleasantly
> discourse of all the things manifold which now so distress
> us. . . .[20]

The images of eating and drinking that biographer Edwin
Haviland Miller points to in "Hawthorne and His Mosses" crop
up again in the oral fixation of these letters.[21] Fertility images also
abound. The "germinous seeds" of the essay have sprouted here
into fresh green shoots and thickets and clustering fruits of metaphor: the "silent, grass-growing mood" of creation; the shady
corner carpeted in "forever tropical" grass on which the friends
will recline in paradise; the grapes that will yield the "champagne
hereafter." "I thank you for your easy-flowing long letter . . .
which flowed through me, and refreshed all my meadows,"
Melville wrote on another occasion, mingling the metaphors of
drinking, vegetative growth, and fertility.[22] The letters express
Melville's literal thirst for this friendship: his desire to drink with
and drink in Hawthorne.

Yet the fantasies of comradeship and the strong desires
from which they spring also embarrass Melville. Again and again,

after exposing his tender sensual wishes, he takes cover behind bluff manly jests and defensive shrugs. "Don't trouble yourself . . . about writing; and don't trouble yourself about visiting," he tells Hawthorne a few sentences after the fantasy of the Champagne hereafter; "and when you *do* visit, don't trouble yourself about talking. I will do all the writing and visiting and talking myself." "This is rather a crazy letter in some respects," he apologizes in another letter.[23] It's as if Melville abruptly awakes from his dream of fellowship to a troubling image of Hawthorne's reading the letter and recoiling from it in disgust. He reminds one of Hawthorne's Feathertop—an elegant gentleman fabricated by a witch out of sticks and scraps who perceives "the sordid patchwork of his real composition" when he looks at himself in a mirror: The illusion is shattered and he turns back into a scarecrow. Self-consciousness is crushing.

All of these images, postures, fantasies, and needs climax in the famous letter of November 17, 1851, the "Farewell Letter" as some call it. Melville had finally driven *Moby-Dick* "through the press," as he wrote, having worked and slaved on it for a month in New York and then, when he could stand the summer heat and dust of the city no longer, back in Pittsfield. The book was published first in London as *The Whale*, in mid-October, and a month later in New York with the "better *selling* title," as Melville hoped, of *Moby-Dick*. Both editions bore the sonorous dedication:

IN TOKEN
OF MY ADMIRATION FOR HIS GENIUS,
This Book Is Inscribed
TO
NATHANIEL HAWTHORNE.

Hawthorne read the epic with remarkable speed, given its length and difficulty, and instantly wrote Melville what must have been a hymn of praise for the letter inspired a rapturously appreciative reply. Melville opens the reply by asserting that "I don't think I deserve any reward for my hard day's work" beyond "my peace and my supper"—a fact that makes Hawthorne's "joy-giving and exultation-breeding letter" all the more welcome—"the good goddess's bonus over and above what was stipulated for." He continues, warming to this theme:

Appreciation! Recognition! Is love appreciated? . . . I say your appreciation is my glorious gratuity. In my proud, humble way,—a shepherd-king,—I was lord of a little vale in the solitary Crimea; but you have now given me the crown of India. . . .

Melville then backs off for a moment to explain that circumstances prevented him from answering Hawthorne's letter as soon as he read it, and that in the intervening hours, he has lost the savor of his emotion: "In me divine magnanimities are spontaneous and instantaneous—catch them while you can. . . . So now I can't write what I felt." But then he tries to recapture his feeling in the most moving passage in the letter:

> I felt pantheistic then—your heart beat in my ribs and mine in yours, and both in God's. A sense of unspeakable security is in me this moment, on account of your having understood the book. I have written a wicked book, and feel spotless as the lamb. Ineffable socialities are in me. I would sit down and dine with you and all the gods in old Rome's Pantheon. It is a strange feeling—no hopefulness is in it, no despair. Content— that is it; and irresponsibility; but without licentious inclination. I speak now of my profoundest sense of being, not of an incidental feeling.
>
> Whence come you, Hawthorne? By what right do you drink from my flagon of life? And when I put it to my lips—lo, they are yours and not mine. I feel that the Godhead is broken up like the bread at the Supper, and that we are the pieces. Hence this infinite fraternity of feeling. Now, sympathizing with the paper, my angel turns another page. You did not care a penny for the book. But, now and then as you read, you understood the pervading thought that impelled the book— and that you praised. Was it not so? You were archangel enough to despise the imperfect body, and embrace the soul. Once you hugged the ugly Socrates because you saw the flame in the mouth, and heard the rushing of the demon,—the familiar,—and recognized the sound; for you have heard it in your own solitudes.[24]

All the images and fantasies of previous letters are present— the drinking and feasting, the fixation on mouths and lips, the desire to retreat with Hawthorne to a well-stocked paradise (though now he invites the entire slate of Roman gods as well). But Melville now takes a step beyond to claim total union with Hawthorne—a union that will merge them heart and soul with each other and with God: "your heart beat in my ribs and mine in yours, and both in God's." Melville's excited chain of association is incredibly fluid, snaking from pantheism to Christianity to classical Greece to demonology ("the familiar"), and transmogrifying his and Hawthorne's physical presences from lips drinking at the same "flagon of life" to fragments of the Eucharistic Host. Each change of shape fuses the two men more completely into a single being, until they are at last spiritually indistinguishable pieces of the same godhead—literal soul mates. The spell of "infinite fraternity" is broken, or weakened, when Melville has to turn the page, and he retreats from his insistence on fusion to let Hawthorne reassume his separate, but closely related identity: Each man dwells apart in his own solitude, but they hear and recognize together the eerie sound of "the rushing of the demon." These paragraphs truly rival Ahab's mightiest blasts.

And then comes the inevitable retraction, as shame scorches him:

> My dear Hawthorne, the atmospheric skepticisms steal into me now, and make me doubtful of my sanity in writing you thus. But, believe me, I am not mad, most noble Festus. But the truth is ever incoherent, and when the big hearts strike together, the concussion is a little stunning. Farewell. . . .
>
> What a pity, that for your plain, bluff letter, you should get such gibberish!

For the first and only time in his correspondence with Hawthorne, he signs with his Christian name—Herman. But he is still too worked up to quit, and he hits on a strikingly odd new image in his first postscript:

> P.S. I can't stop yet. If the world was entirely made up of Magians, I'll tell you what I should do. I should have a paper-mill established at one end of the house, and so have an endless riband of foolscap rolling in upon my desk; and upon that endless riband I should write a thousand—a million—billion thoughts, all under the form of a letter to you. The divine

magnet is on you, and my magnet responds. Which is biggest? A foolish question—they are *One*.

And yet the final words of this astounding letter are brusque and chilly:

P.P.S. Don't think that by writing me a letter, you shall always be bored with an immediate reply to it—and so keep both of us delving over a writing-desk eternally. No such thing! I sh'n't always answer your letters, and you may do just as you please.

So Melville ends with a bang and then a whimper. The image of the unspooling riband of foolscap suggests a kind of lifeline—an intellectual umbilical cord—connecting the two writers with an endless flow of words: constant one-way communication. The divine magnet is perhaps the most blatantly sexual image in a letter that swoons and sweats with passion. The imagery and tone of this letter, even more than the strong roots and hot soil of "Hawthorne and His Mosses," raise the vexed question of Melville's sexuality: Was Melville's passion for Hawthorne Platonic? Or did he desire, consciously or not, an actual physical union to match his fantasies? Critics and biographers are intensely, vociferously divided on this issue. At one extreme, there is Edwin Haviland Miller, biographer of both friends, who pinpoints the time (mid-September 1851) and the place (the Stockbridge Bowl) where Melville made "advances" to Hawthorne.[25] At the other extreme is Leon Howard, whose respected 1951 biography of Melville holds the homosexual allegations at arm's length, downplays the friendship with Hawthorne, passes by the sexual imagery in the letters and essay, and concludes that the bond with Hawthorne grew from a "desire for companionship which was a strong but by no means abnormal quality of his nature."[26] Melville scholar Harrison Hayford, in a paper entitled "Melville's 'Monody': Really for Hawthorne?," provides a convenient survey of how the major biographers and critics from the past half century line up on the issue of Melville's sexuality: Raymond Weaver (1921, 1928, 1931)—gradually leaning toward the homosexual view; Lewis Mumford (1929)—"staunchly heterosexual"; Lloyd Morris (1927)—"all but overtly homosexual"; Freudian and Jungian psychologist Dr. Henry A. Murray (1949, 1951, 1966)—not homosexual but "very peculiar"; and so on, down to the present with Robert K. Martin (1986)—homosexual in imagination but frustrated in life, and James R. Mellow (1980)—heatedly homoerotic, but probably not to the point of acting on it.[27]

Hayford himself shrewdly points out that "no evidence supports any of these versions, homosexual or heterosexual, apart from identifications conjured from clues in Melville's, and Hawthorne's, works."[28] His essay demonstrates how, over the generations of literary criticism, these "clues" have engendered theories and legends that in turn have calcified into "facts." John Bryant, in his introduction to the recent *A Companion to Melville Studies,* notes that these legends have exerted such sway over our imaginations that now "many think of Melville as a manic depressive homosexual abusing wife and family while pining for blue-eyed Nathaniel Hawthorne."[29]

When we hack away the tangles of literary mythology, we are left with precious few hard substantiated facts. We have certain knowledge only about Melville's heterosexual activity: He married as a young man, fathered a family (his second child, Stanwix, was born four days after *Moby-Dick* was published and three weeks before the "infinite fraternity" letter), and lived with his wife until he died. Everything relating to his homosexuality comes from his fiction. On the evidence of *White-Jacket,* he was aware of the long-standing practice of sodomy on board ships (the oft-quoted sentence reads: "The sins for which the cities of the plain were over-thrown still linger in some of these wooden-walled Gomorrahs of the deep"). And yet this passage leaves no doubt that he was repelled by such acts. It is one thing to admire masculine beauty—as Melville does again and again in nearly all his books, starting with the "Polynesian Apollo" Marnoo in *Typee* and ending with the smooth-faced, blond-haired, "all but feminine" "Handsome Sailor" Billy Budd; but it is quite another thing to want to drag such manly specimens "down into tarry perdition." John Claggart, whose hatred for Billy Budd is fueled by repressed sexual desire, is perhaps the most despicable character in all of Melville. On the surface level, Melville reviles homosexuality in his work.

Other clues in the fiction are fainter. As we've seen, Melville writes humorously, but warmly, about Queequeg and Ishmael's bed sharing in *Moby-Dick* and lingers over a fantasy of intimate male comradeship in the "A Squeeze of the Hand" chapter. In his long poem *Clarel*, written years after the friendship with Hawthorne, Melville describes his hero's ambiguous "courtship" of a shy older man who many critics believe is modeled on Hawthorne. And, of course, there is the sexually charged imagery in "Hawthorne and His Mosses" and the letters we have just examined.

Can we conclude from these passages that Melville was homosexual? Probably not. When Clarel, in silent fantasy, wishes Vine would burst out, "Ah, call me *brother*—" he means just that: brother, not lover. "But for thy fonder dream of love/In man toward man—" Clarel imagines Vine saying to him a few lines later,

> —the soul's caress—
> The negatives of flesh should prove
> Analogies of non-cordialness
> In spirit.[30]

The "negatives of flesh" were an overpowering taboo. Melville's imagination was extraordinarily alive to the sympathy, understanding, and admiration that men can give each other—the "communion true and close" in which male friends find "unspeakable security" and deep "content." His ideal of male friendship was comparable to the ardent comradeship that soldiers speak of in war—a bond "passing the love of woman fond" as Melville writes in *Clarel*, but a bond rarely expressed sexually.[31] It was this bond that Melville sought from and projected onto Hawthorne, and that he fleetingly attained when reading Hawthorne's "joy-giving and exultation-breeding" letter about *Moby-Dick*. Leslie Fiedler claims in a famous essay that *Moby-Dick* is "a love story, perhaps the greatest love story in our fiction . . . ," and that it reflects "the peculiar American form of innocent homosexuality."[32] I think "innocent homosexuality" aptly describes Melville's love for Hawthorne.

"Mentally and sentimentally he needed understanding," Edith Wharton wrote of Henry James after his death. The same was true of Melville, only more so—much more so. Hawthorne's praise of *Moby-Dick* was the richest, deepest lode of understanding Melville had ever received. "Appreciation! Recognition!" he raves in the "infinite fraternity" letter as his gratitude mounts. Melville could only express erotically the ecstasy he felt at being understood by the one person whose appreciation and recognition he most craved. But the origin of the feeling, the force concentrated at the center of his magnet, was art, not eros—or perhaps a convergence of art and eros too deep for us to fathom.

FOUR

The Downlook

Last summer nothing dared impede
the flow of the body's thousand rivulets of welcome,
winding effortlessly, yet with ambiguous invention—
safety in nearness.

Now the downlook, the downlook . . .

—ROBERT LOWELL, "The Downlook"

. . . foes are far more desirable than friends . . .

—HERMAN MELVILLE, Pierre

WHAT RAN THROUGH Hawthorne's mind and heart when he read
Melville's rapturous reply to his letter about *Moby-Dick*? Was it a
coincidence that four days later, in a storm of snow and sleet, the
Hawthorne family moved out of the red farmhouse, boarded the
train in Pittsfield, and crossed the state of Massachusetts once
more to set up a new household in West Newton? Had Hawthorne
been planning the move or was he in fact fleeing Melville's heated
importunities? Again, as with the issue of Melville's sexuality,
critics and biographers split sharply over unanswerable questions.
The "rupture" school (Mumford, Weaver, Lloyd Morris, et al.)
stitches together scraps of supposedly autobiographical passages
in Melville's and Hawthorne's writings to prove that the friends

became estranged after (and some argue *because of*) the "infinite fraternity" letter. They see Hawthorne's hasty departure from Lenox as a deliberate shunning of Melville. In the other camp are the "fact-minded scholars," as Hayford dubs them, who point out that the "rupture hypothesis" not only "lacks the slightest documentary confirmation" but also "flies in the face of the contradictory evidence" in the letters.[1]

A few clear points emerge from the academic muck. Melville himself sensed that he was far more involved in the friendship than Hawthorne was, and he worried, as we've seen, that Hawthorne would take his emotional effusions as signs of insanity. In one letter he imagines Hawthorne recoiling with "a touch of a shrink" from his hearty democratic embrace. A tendency to shrink from physical and emotional contact was a trait Hawthorne shared with many of his male characters (Sophia once said that her husband "hates to be touched more than anyone I ever knew").[2] Certainly everything we know of Hawthorne's temperament suggests that "infinite fraternity" was not his cup of tea. It is probably safe to say that Melville's letter embarrassed Hawthorne a bit, as Melville feared it would. On the other hand, Hawthorne says nothing in his letters or journals from the autumn of 1851 about wanting to escape from Melville; in fact, after the summer he scarcely mentions Melville at all (with one notable exception).

What he *does* write about is his eagerness to get away from the oppressive atmosphere of Lenox and the cramped little farmhouse, which he once called "certainly the most inconvenient and wretched little hovel I ever put my head in."[3] He fumed in his notebook, "I hate Berkshire with my whole soul, and would joyfully see its mountains laid flat";[4] he pined for a cottage near the sea; by the autumn, he and Sophia were bickering with their landlord and -lady. And anyway, the Hawthornes had never intended to settle in Berkshire permanently. All of this, coupled with Hawthorne's innate restlessness, adequately explains his abrupt departure from Berkshire without dragging in Melville at all. As John Updike writes, "Melville came on too strong with his wish to be called 'brother,' but it is unlikely that this was what drove Hawthorne away; the friendship straggled on for years."[5]

It seems that Melville was simply not important enough to Hawthorne to have influenced his decision one way or the other. Hawthorne's destroyed letters to Melville were, in Melville's own words, "plain" and "bluff"—and so possibly were his feelings.

Hawthorne found the younger writer "an admirable fellow," a pleasant drinking companion, a stimulating conversationalist, a good neighbor. He partook happily enough of Melville's sherry and port, but he had no wish to put his lips to Melville's "flagon of life." He never *needed* Melville, or any male friend, in the way Melville needed him. "Between man and man there is always an insuperable gulf," says the sculptor Kenyon in Hawthorne's last romance *The Marble Faun*. "They can never quite grasp each other's hands."[6] Melville, the champion of man-to-man hand squeezing, could never bring himself to believe this. His hopes of closing the insuperable gulf left him vulnerable to perpetual disappointment—and never more vulnerable than he was with Hawthorne. Hawthorne's departure, without, apparently, so much as a farewell letter or an invitation to see him off at the station, only highlighted the imbalance in the relationship. To be rejected would have been less wounding than to be ignored.

Once the Hawthornes left Lenox, the friendship between the men became fragmentary and fitful. Melville wrote Sophia at West Newton in January 1852, thanking her for her "highly flattering letter" praising *Moby-Dick* and expressing his surprise that a *woman* should like the book "for as a general thing, women have small taste for the sea."[7] Hawthorne, meanwhile, had written Duyckinck to chide him for his tepid review of *Moby-Dick* in *The Literary World:* "What a book Melville has written! It gives me an idea of much greater power than his preceding ones. It hardly seemed to me that the review of it, in the Literary World, did justice to its best points."[8] Hawthorne obeyed Melville's injunction not to review the book. The friends had another little flurry of communication the following year over the "Agatha story."

Melville had heard the true story of this forsaken seacoast wife while traveling with his father-in-law to Nantucket, Martha's Vineyard, and the Elizabeth Islands during the summer of 1852. The plight of the woman (who took in a shipwrecked man, married him, and bore him a daughter, only to be abandoned by him twice at long intervals) moved Melville deeply, but he felt that Hawthorne "would make a better hand" than he at writing it down and he turned over the material to him, along with his musings on the subject. Hawthorne evidently toyed with the idea of working up Agatha's story into a novel, but in the end, he chose not to. During a brief visit that Melville paid him at his new home in Concord during the fall of 1852, Hawthorne urged Melville to undertake the tale himself and Melville agreed. But the manuscript of the Agatha story, if indeed there ever was one, has not survived. It's interesting that James, a half century later, gave Wharton the donnée for a story arising from a tangled bit of gossip about some friends of his: Wharton, unlike Hawthorne, kept the gift and used it as the basis for a slender little story called "The Pretext." Lowell, another half century later still, was not so delicate as to wait for literary gifts to be handed over: He took, without asking, Bishop's finest short story and one of her most anguished letters and rewrote them as poetry, and he inserted images from her letters into various poems. Lowell did, in turn, urge on her a donnée for a poem about the political situation in Brazil during the 1960s; but Bishop, following Hawthorne's example, preferred to hatch her own ideas.

The letters that Melville wrote Hawthorne about the Agatha business in 1852, while a good deal calmer and quieter than his outpourings of the previous autumn, certainly show no sign of a rupture. "I shall lay eyes on you one of these days," he promised on October 25, 1852, adding the familiar command to "keep some Champagne or Gin for me."[9] And after the Concord visit he wrote to tell Hawthorne how "greatly" he had enjoyed himself and "hope that you reaped some corresponding pleasure." Melville's equable tone is somewhat deceptive for his affairs had taken a turn for the worse since Hawthorne's departure from Berkshire. The critical reception of *Moby-Dick,* while hardly the universal damnation that legend makes it out to be, was a serious disappointment to Melville, and so were the book's sales. True, a couple of reviewers used the word "genius" in connection with author and novel; but several prominent journals attacked it savagely: "an ill-compounded mixture of romance and matter-of-fact . . . so much trash belonging to the worst school of Bedlam literature" was the judgment of *The Athenaeum; The Albion* concluded that the character of Ahab was "a perfect failure, and the work itself inartistic"; and *The Literary Gazette* warned Melville not to "waste his strength on such purposeless and unequal doings as these rambling volumes about spermaceti whales."[10] Melville by temperament was more likely to brood over the negative notices than bask in the positive, especially since the sales were correspondingly poor.

Hawthorne, by contrast, had enjoyed both good (though not great) press and brisk sales for *The House of the Seven Gables,* which had gone into four printings by September 1851, selling 6,710 copies in its first year (710 more than *The Scarlet Letter* and almost three times what *Moby-Dick* sold in its first three years). Melville was acutely aware of the divergence in their literary fortunes. In June 1851, he wrote Hawthorne that he had just returned from a day trip to New York where "I have seen and heard many flattering (in a publisher's point of view) allusions to the 'Seven Gables.' And I have seen 'Tales,' and 'A New Volume' announced, by N.H. So upon the whole, I say to myself, this N.H. is in the ascendant. My dear Sir, they begin to patronize."[11] N.H. remained in the ascendant when *The Blithedale Romance* appeared in July 1852. Again, Melville took note of his friend's success, this time a touch more bitterly: "This name of '*Hawthorne*' seems to be ubiquitous," he opens a letter composed after returning from his tour of the Massachusetts islands; "it has saluted me vocally & typographically in all sorts of places & in all sorts of ways." And he proceeds to recount them—men and women rushing into parlors wherever he stayed crying "*Hawthorne's* new book!"[12]

The Blithedale Romance, based on Hawthorne's experiences at the Brook Farm transcendentalist Utopian community (where he lived for a year before his marriage), did indeed create a stir when it was published, selling out its first printing of 5,090 copies in a month.[13] But reviews were rather tepid, and interest in the book—Hawthorne's most realistic novel—fizzled quickly. Three years passed between the second and third printings, and then only 536 additional copies were published. *The Blithedale Romance,* lacking the drama and symbolic complexity of *The Scarlet Letter* and the vivid historic details of *The House of the Seven Gables,* marks a sharp aesthetic falling off for Hawthorne. Though James deemed it "the lightest, the brightest, the liveliest" of Hawthorne's "unhumorous fictions,"[14] in fact this story of the romantic entanglements of the Brook Farm colonists is rather lumbering and strained.

Its main interest today lies in Hawthorne's use of a detached unreliable narrator—Miles Coverdale by name, a weak, fussy, rather cold-hearted voyeur who spies on his fellows from a kind of treehouse. James called Coverdale "half a poet, half a critic, and all a spectator"—a formula that applies perfectly to a host of James's own heroes and narrators, from Winterbourne in *Daisy Miller* to the nameless narrator of *The Aspern Papers* to Lambert Strether in

The Ambassadors. Later Eudora Welty made use of a voyeuristic narrator in her seminal early story "A Memory," and characters peep from behind or through "curtains of green" throughout her work. *Blithedale* is also memorable for the voluptuous, mesmerizing character Zenobia, one of Hawthorne's passionate dark ladies, a cousin to Hester Prynne and to Miriam in *The Marble Faun.* Zenobia's commitment to women's rights anticipates the more militant feminism of Olive Chancellor in James's *The Bostonians*—and both women are ultimately, ironically, defeated by the power of love between the sexes. But fascinating as it is from a literary historical perspective, *The Blithedale Romance* has never captured the imaginations of readers the way *The Scarlet Letter* did. "I hope Hawthorne will give us no more Blithedales," his publisher and friend James Field grumbled to a London literary hostess.[15]

The disappointment of *Blithedale,* however, pales beside the outright catastrophe of Melville's *Pierre,* which was published just a few weeks later. "Perhaps, the craziest fiction extant," howled the *Boston Post* in July. ". . . The amount of utter trash in the volume is almost infinite. . . . A thousand times better, had [Melville] dropped authorship with 'Typee.'" "A dead failure," pronounced *The Albion.* "[A]bsurd to the last degree. . . . The author has attempted seemingly to combine in [*Pierre*] the peculiarities of Poe and Hawthorne, and has succeeded in producing nothing but a powerfully unpleasant caricature of morbid thought and passion. . . ." "A bad book!" thundered *The American Whig Review.* "Affected in dialect, unnatural in conception, repulsive in plot, and inartistic in construction."[16] Time has shown the early attackers and misconstruers of *Moby-Dick* to be obtuse fools; but sadly, these first savagers of *Pierre* were on target. *Pierre is* irredeemably wretched. In four hundred fraught, lurid, horrendously overwritten pages, Melville slogs through the ghastly tale of Pierre Glendinning, an aristocratic youth living in splendor in a manor house modeled on Broadhall, who plummets from cloying complacency to abject poverty and woe when he learns that his father had sired an illegitimate daughter named Isabel before his marriage. Pierre, after spending two evenings with his newfound half-sister, decides that the only way he can "save" her is to declare to the world that he has married her—a move that drives his mother insane with rage, breaks the heart of his angelic and beautiful fiancée, Lucy Tartan, and ends in a dangerous illicit erotic entanglement. Pierre and Isabel leave the bucolic countryside and move to a seedy, sinister New York, where Pierre, having been disinherited by his mother, sets up as an author—a tortured starving author in the high Romantic tradition. Several implausible plot twists later, the book ends, like an Elizabethan revenge tragedy, with a pile of corpses: Pierre, imprisoned for the murder of his cousin, has poisoned himself; Isabel, who polishes off the poison, is draped over him; and Lucy (who has moved into the couple's dismal Manhattan lodging) lies at his feet, having dropped dead of shock after learning that Isabel is his half-sister.

Pierre, though far more shrill and hyperbolic than anything Hawthorne wrote, does draw on some of Hawthorne's characteristic motifs and settings: dimly lit interior scenes, revelations of long-buried sins, a dark and a fair heroine, adultery, murder, poison, incest. Yet Melville takes these Hawthornian elements and inflates them into hysterical melodrama. Melville is completely out of his element in *Pierre*—he is "at sea on land," as Updike puts it. Unlike Hawthorne, who usually moves his stories briskly along, Melville has a supreme difficulty getting anything to *happen* in the first two thirds of *Pierre*. The novel is constipated: Melville belabors each incident with heavy foreshadowing, italicizes thoughts and feelings with virulently purple prose, bludgeons us with the moral, and then circles back to strain for even more portentous effects. After a while, one wants to strangle the entire cast of characters. But enough. *Pierre* has suffered from 140 years of justified abuse, and there is no cause to kick it yet again.

Inevitably, given the fact that Melville started the book soon after Hawthorne's departure from Berkshire, critics have scoured it for clues about the friendship. A tradition has grown up identifying the character of Plotinus Plinlimmon with Hawthorne. Described as "a very plain, composed, manly figure" in whose blue eyes "the gay immortal youth Apollo seemed enshrined; while on that ivory-throned brow, old Saturn cross-legged sat," Plinlimmon is the inscrutable "Grand Master" of a literary set in New York and the author of the pedantic philosophial pamphlet "Chronometricals and Horologicals" contrasting Greenwich time (the worldly time of our daily lives) with heaven's time. Pierre becomes haunted by Plinlimmon's face staring at him from across the courtyard of the church turned artists' quarters they both live in, and he imagines that the older man is mocking him for the vanity of his own literary efforts and for his secret life with Isabel: "Vain! vain!

vain! said the face to him. Fool! fool! fool! said the face to him. Quit! quit! quit!"[17] When he encounters Plinlimmon in the flesh, Pierre shrinks from him, unable to return his greeting.

Henry A. Murray, in his brilliant introduction to *Pierre,* argues that Plinlimmon, like Hawthorne, is an intellectual voyeur, a Paul Pry who peeps into Pierre's life without sympathy and thus drives him to distraction: Hawthorne/Plinlimmon's "timid, phlegmatic philosophy," writes Murray, "was Death to Melville's morbidly longing and enthusiastic, but ever-baffled soul."[18] Other critics, noting that the red farmhouse where Isabel lives is an exact replica of the Hawthornes' Lenox "shanty," claim less plausibly that Isabel is a female stand-in for Hawthorne. It is also notable that in the relationship between Pierre and his once-beloved cousin Glen Stanly, Melville depicts the full cycle of male friendship—from the impassioned heights of a "mystical boy-love" (that "revels for a while in the empyrean of a love which only comes short, by one degree, of the sweetest sentiment entertained between the sexes")[19] to bitter disenchantment in early manhood to a violent estrangement that culminates in Pierre's hatred and finally his murder of his cousin. As Miller sums up, "Melville's love for Hawthorne, then, is echoed in the three loves in Pierre's life, Lucy, Isabel, and Glen Stanly."[20]

There is a parallel critical tradition that Hawthorne aired his feelings about Melville in the character of Hollingsworth in *The Blithedale Romance.* Hollingsworth, the burly, muscular, black-browed blacksmith turned social reformer, does indeed resemble Melville physically, and his exalted views on male friendship correspond closely with the emotion of Melville's "infinite fraternity" letter. At a climactic moment in the book, Hollingsworth tries to persuade Coverdale to "be my brother" in his secret "scheme for the reformation of the wicked": "Strike hands with me," he implores Coverdale, "and from this moment you shall never again feel the languor and vague wretchedness of an indolent or half-occupied man. . . . Coverdale . . . there is not the man in this wide world, whom I can love as I could you. Do not foresake me! . . . Will you devote yourself, and sacrifice all to this great end, and be my friend of friends, forever?"[21] Many read this as a sign of Hawthorne's revulsion against Melville's exaltation of male bonding. Yet it's also possible that Hawthorne was poking Melville in the ribs with Hollingsworth—indulging in one of his sarcastic, teasing, inside jokes. Surely Hawthorne, unless he was truly perverse, would not have requested his publisher to send Melville a "presentation copy" of The Blithedale Romance, as he did on July 7, 1852, had he intended Hollingsworth to be a vicious burlesque or attack on his friend.

Whether or not Melville really had Hawthorne in mind when he created Plinlimmon and Glen Stanly or Hawthorne used Melville as a model for Hollingsworth, it is telling that both of them depicted failed male relationships in the books they wrote immediately after their paths diverged. They had taken their own friendship as far as it could go during Hawthorne's last weeks in Berkshire. After the "infinite fraternity" letter there could only be a falling off. To quote Murray once again, Hawthorne and Melville did not have "a quarrel, but an estrangement, and this was so mutually traumatic that each of them felt compelled to write an interpretation, an apologia, a vindication, of his own position."[22] Trauma goes too far; but there was unquestionably tension between the men and between the male characters they both created at this time. Even Melville must have perceived that the fantasy of the endless "riband" of foolscap connecting him to Hawthorne was not only doomed, but also a bit foolish (a word with which he repeatedly lashes Pierre).

Pierre slaughtered what remained of Melville's literary reputation after Moby-Dick. What made the ordeal even more galling to Melville was that he sincerely expected the book to be a popular success. But eight months after the ambitious 2,310-copy first printing, only 283 copies had been sold. Pierre, alas, earned Melville far more scorn and ridicule than money.

Whatever its failings as fiction, however, Pierre is a gold mine of insight into Melville's psychology. Though its plot is obviously invented, Pierre's background and family relationships are patterned closely on Melville's own. Melville reveals here as nowhere else his adoration of and furious disappointment in his father, his pride in his aristocratic heritage, and his despair at having been deprived of its privileges, his mixture of reverence, fear, and contempt for his mother (Mary Glendinning, the mother whom Pierre insists on calling sister, is perhaps the book's most memorable character—a lethally frigid, pride-choked, aging queen bitch; the scene in which she hurls a fork through a portrait of herself was tailor-made for Joan Crawford). Both of Pierre's parents die insane—his mother of "hate-grief," his father of "sin-grief"—a pretty pair. In Pierre Melville displays, even more nakedly than in *Moby-Dick*, his terrifying mood swings and his appalling sense of having been disinherited both materially and spiritually. Shorn of the support of man and God, Pierre rails against the "dreary heart-vacancies of the conventional life," yet he has nothing to replace them with but violence, hatred, and death.

The novel paints a blistering portrait of the artist as a freezing, cramp-backed, hungry, feverish, insomniac, obsessed, and self-loathing young man: The literary profession, Melville concludes bitterly, is "that most miserable of all the pursuits of a man." Women, notoriously absent from *Moby-Dick*, crowd into *Pierre* as predators, victims, sirens, holy innocents: They whip the narrative into a frenzy of guilt, illicit lust, divided loyalties, and betrayals. Yet sex is riddled with conflict. Pierre, on the threshold of manhood, dooms himself to a choice between chastity and incest: His pretense of being his half-sister's husband throws up a "wall of iron" in the center of his life that he can never penetrate. By the end of the book, he declares himself "neuter." But Pierre isn't missing out on much by shunning a "normal" sex life since marriage, according to Melville, is "that climax which is so fatal to ordinary love." Dr. Murray speculates that Pierre, with his domineering mother, emotionally withdrawn father, and predilection for sexless women, may be a repressed homosexual.

Melville wrote *Pierre* under tremendous pressure, and it shows: He started it right after finishing *Moby-Dick* and pushed it through to completion in a black frenzy, desperately hoping to recoup the financial losses of his masterpiece. According to the Melville mythology, he ruined *Pierre* by turning it into a platform from which to scream abuse at the unappreciative critics of *Moby-Dick*, including Duyckinck and his *Literary World*, which is broadly parodied as the inane "Captain Kidd Monthly." It's true that Melville seems to have decided in midstream to make Pierre an author; but this can hardly be said to have spoiled the book since what came before was so awful to begin with. For whatever reason, Melville made a terrible botch of *Pierre* and he would have been far better off had he burned it. But of course this wasn't possible since these pages, dreadful as they were, represented his sole means of making money: The novel, like the doomed book Pierre forced himself to write in Manhattan, was "born of unwillingness and the bill of the baker."

•

Hawthorne's removal from Lenox and the markedly different receptions of *The Blithedale Romance* and *Pierre* during the summer of 1852 drove a wedge between the friends. The wedge widened appreciably when Hawthorne's old college friend Franklin Pierce was elected fourteenth president of the United States that November. Hawthorne had done his bit for Pierce by writing the official campaign biography (about which James noted that "there is nothing particular to say save that it is in very good taste"[23]); and Pierce rewarded him handsomely by giving him the consulship at Liverpool, which, as one biographer points out, was then the "best-paying post in the foreign service, second in prestige only to that of ambassador to Great Britain."[24] Even though Congress promptly slashed his salary by half in a cost-cutting move, Hawthorne still netted between $5,000 and $7,000 a year, a considerable sum in those days and far more than he had ever earned before.[25]

Hawthorne's good fortune excited the jealousy and ambition of Melville and his family. His mother, Maria Melvill, set out at once to milk the Hawthorne connection for everything it was worth, soliciting powerful friends in Albany to write "strong letters" on her son's behalf, which Hawthorne would then present to the president-elect. She wrote confidently to her brother Peter Gansevoort that Hawthorne "will befriend Herman all in his power, and he has a good deal of influence." She explained that she was running this campaign herself because "Herman dislikes asking favors from any one. He therefore postponed writing from time to time, until he became so completely absorbed in this new work . . . that he has not taken the proper, & necessary measures to procure this earnestly wished for office." It's true that the one letter Melville wrote Hawthorne after the election makes no mention of politics. Maria made it clear that her son was in fairly desperate straits:

> Herman would be greatly benefitted by a sojourn abroad, he would then be compelled to more intercourse with his fellow creatures. It would very materially renew, & strengthen both his body & mind. The constant In-door confinement with little intermission to which Herman's occupation as author compels him, does not agree with him. This constant working of the brain, & excitement of the imagination, is wearing

Herman out, & you will my dear Peter be doing him a lasting benefit if by your added exertions you can procure for him a foreign consulship.[26]

The eternal voice of the anxious mother.

Hawthorne did what he could while he was in Washington during April 1853, and for a while it looked as if Melville would get the consulship at Honolulu or at Antwerp, but in the end both posts slipped through his fingers. Wharton, Porter, and Lowell would all, in future generations, use their political and cultural influence to assist their literary friends in need, though none of them commanded as much power as Hawthorne did during the Pierce administration. But even Hawthorne's influence was not strong enough to break Melville's run of bad luck.

On July 6, 1853, Hawthorne crossed the Atlantic for the first time in his life, sailing out of Boston Harbor bound for Liverpool. He had turned forty-nine two days before. In August he took up his official duties ("such as they are," as he wrote sardonically in his notebook), and when he resigned the consulship four years later he had amassed thirty thousand dollars in savings, which spun off enough interest to support the family handsomely for some time. The Hawthornes spent 1858 and half of 1859 traveling on the Continent, mostly in Italy, and then they returned to England in the summer of 1859. In England, Hawthorne settled down to finish *The Marble Faun*, his last romance, which drew heavily on his impressions of Italian art and landscape. The Hawthornes sailed back to Boston in the summer of 1860. They had been abroad for seven years in all.

Melville, meanwhile, had been sinking deeper and deeper into poverty and depression in Pittsfield. The novels that followed *Pierre—Israel Potter* in 1855 and *The Confidence Man* in 1857— were not successful; and though the stories and sketches he published in magazines during 1853–56 (collected as *The Piazza Tales* in 1856) brought in some money (a total of $725 to be exact), the children remembered many suppers of tea and bread.[27] The restless, impetuous, adventure-seeking Ishmael has dwindled down, in a mere two years, to Bartleby, the "pallidly neat, pitiably respectable, incurably forlorn" homeless law clerk who "would prefer not to." "Bartleby, the Scrivener," Melville's masterpiece in short fiction, has the grim, bleak humor of Kafka—the humor of a man who laughs at horrors because he knows there is no other relief from them. Such was the state of Melville's soul in the years after Hawthorne's departure from Lenox.

Madness ran in the Melville family, and it is fairly clear that Lizzie Melville believed her husband to be on the brink of insanity by the mid-1850s. She wrote her father about Herman's physical deterioration (he suffered terribly from sciatica), overwork, and "severe nervous affections," and Lemuel Shaw was alarmed enough by these letters that he advanced his son-in-law yet another sum of money ($1,400 or $1,500 he later recalled) to outfit him for a prolonged restorative tour of Europe and the Middle East. Melville set sail from New York to Glasgow on October 11, 1856, and after wandering for several days through Scotland, Ireland, and the north of England, he turned up in Liverpool. It was here that he and Hawthorne met for the last time.

Both men recorded the occasion in their journals. Here are Melville's terse and rather dreary entries:

> November 9. Rain. Stayed home [at the White Bear Hotel] till dinner. After dinner took steamboat for Rock Ferry to find Mr Hawthorne. On getting to R.F., learned he had removed thence 18 months previous, & was residing out of town.— Spent evening at home.

> November 10. Went among docks to see the Mediterranean steamers. Explored the new docks "Huskisson" &c. Saw Mr Hawthorne at the Consulate. Invited me to stay with him during my sojourn at Liverpool. —Dined at "Anderson's" a very nice place, & charges moderate.[28]

Hawthorne wrote of the meeting with far more color and feeling:

> A week ago last Monday, Herman Melville came to see me at the Consulate, looking much as he used to do (a little paler, and perhaps a little sadder), in a rough outside coat, and with his characteristic gravity and reserve of manner. He had crossed from New York to Glasgow in a screw steamer, about a fortnight before, and had since been seeing Edinburgh and other interesting places. I felt rather awkward at first; because

this is the first time I have met him since my ineffectual attempt to get him a consular appointment. However, I failed only from real lack of power to serve him; so there was no reason to be ashamed, and we soon found ourselves on pretty much our former terms of sociability and confidence. Melville has not been well, of late; he has been affected with neuralgic complaints in his head and limbs, and no doubt has suffered from too constant literary occupation, pursued without much success, latterly; and his writings, for a long while past, have indicated a morbid state of mind. . . . I do not wonder that he found it necessary to take an airing through the world, after so many years of toilsome pen-labor and domestic life, following upon so wild and adventurous a youth as his was.[29]

After the initial awkwardness wore off, Hawthorne invited Melville to stay with him for a few days in Southport, the seaside resort town seventeen miles north of Liverpool where he and his family had recently moved. Hawthorne noted with a little shiver of repugnance that his old friend took with him "by way of luggage, the least little bit of a bundle, which, he told me, contained a night-shirt and a tooth-brush. He is a person of very gentlemanly instincts in every respect, save that he is a little heterodox in the matter of clean linen."[30] Despite the state of Melville's underwear, the visit went well. "An agreeable day," Melville wrote in his entry for November 12. "Took a long walk by the sea. Sands & grass. Wild & desolate. A strong wind. Good talk. In the evening Stout & Fox & Geese. —Julian grown into a fine lad, Una taller than her mother. Mrs. Hawthorne not in good health. Mr H. stayed home for me."[31] Hawthorne's record of this day goes down as one of the finest verbal portraits of Melville ever written:

> . . . We took a pretty long walk, together, and sat down in a hollow among the sand hills (sheltering ourselves from the high, cool wind) and smoked a cigar. Melville, as he always does, began to reason of Providence and futurity, and of everything that lies beyond human ken, and informed me that he had "pretty much made up his mind to be annihilated;" but still he does not seem to rest in that anticipation; and, I think, will never rest until he gets hold of a definite belief. It is strange how he persists—and has persisted ever since I knew him, and

probably long before—in wandering to and fro over these deserts, as dismal and monotonous as the sand hills amid which we were sitting. He can neither believe, nor be comfortable in his unbelief; and he is too honest and courageous not to try to do one or the other. If he were a religious man, he would be one of the most truly religious and reverential; he has a very high and noble nature, and better worth immortality than most of us.[32]

This reads like a farewell salute, but in fact the friends saw each other a few more times before Melville left England bound for Greece and Constantinople. On November 15, they spent the day together in the quaint walled medieval town of Chester ("perfect in its antiquity," James describes it in an early travel essay, and in *The Ambassadors,* he gives Lambert Strether his first taste of Europe here, after hurrying him through Liverpool). Hawthorne noted that they dined on veal pies and damson tarts, drank Bass's ale and stout, inspected the cathedral and the Yacht Inn where Jonathan Swift once stayed, but he made no mention of their conversation. It is clear from Hawthorne's journal entries that in the course of the week he spent with Melville he became increasingly alarmed by his friend's state of mind. "He said that he already felt much better than in America," Hawthorne wrote on November 17; "but observed that he did not anticipate much pleasure in his rambles, for that the spirit of adventure is gone out of him. He certainly is much overshadowed since I saw him last; but I hope he will brighten as he goes onward."[33] Melville, the same day, noted his "great disappointment" at the delay in his departure for Turkey. "Tired of Liverpool," he wrote, without reference to Hawthorne.

They parted the following day, and again Hawthorne recorded the particulars:

He sailed from Liverpool in a steamer on Tuesday, leaving his trunk behind him at my consulate, and taking only a carpet-bag to hold all his travelling gear. This is the next best thing to going naked; and as he wears his beard and mustache, and so needs no dressing-case—nothing but a tooth-brush—I do not know a more independent personage. He learned his traveling habits by drifting about, all over the South Sea, with no other clothes or equipage than a red flannel shirt and a pair of duck trowsers. Yet we seldom see men of less criticizable manners than he.[34]

The image of Melville's setting sail with "only a carpet-bag" brings to mind the letter Melville wrote Hawthorne about *The House of the Seven Gables*—the resounding letter in which he hails his new friend for saying "NO! in thunder":

> For all men who say *yes,* lie; and all men who say *no,*—why, they are in the happy condition of judicious, unincumbered travellers in Europe; they cross the frontiers into Eternity with nothing but a carpet-bag,—that is to say, the Ego.[35]

This was written in the heady spring of 1851; but by November 1856, even the carpetbag/ego had become an intolerable encumbrance. The friends saw each other briefly once more, when Melville returned to Liverpool to pick up his trunk before sailing back to New York. Melville's journal entry for May 4, 1857 reads simply: "Saw Hawthorne." Hawthorne himself let the encounter pass without comment.

And so the friendship ended as it had begun—with the confluence of the domestic and the mystical. Linen and annihilation, providence and veal pies, ale and immortality enfolded their final encounter just as turkey and thunder had enfolded their first. In six years, Melville had changed from a bold and nimble mountain climber to a listless, weary traveler embarked on a healing journey that failed to restore his health. The real sadness at the heart of this friendship is that only in their final encounter did Hawthorne feel disposed to sympathize with Melville. His Liverpool journal entries show more affection and concern for Melville than anything he had written in Lenox. Hawthorne allowed himself at last to peer within Melville's shadow, to fathom the "very high and noble nature" of this independent personage who preferred to go naked. But Hawthorne's caring came too late. By the time he reached Liverpool, Melville's desire for "infinite fraternity" had "gone out of him" along with his "spirit of adventure." Damp, drizzly November would not relax its grip on his soul. "He seemed depressed and aimless," Julian recollected years later of Melville's final visit. "He said goodbye at last, and wandered away. . . ."[36] "He seemed alone, absolutely alone in the universe," the doddering, kindly lawyer-narrator says of Bartleby. "A bit of wreck in the mid-Atlantic." Such was Herman Melville when he parted from Hawthorne.

The impulse toward annihilation, as Henry A. Murray notes, had preyed on Melville throughout his literary career. "If I fail to reach my golden haven, may my annihilation be complete; all or nothing!" he trumpeted in *Mardi*. "I foresee my annihilation," rumbles Ahab, "but against this verdict of fate I shall hurl my everlasting protest." "I am on the verge of annihilation but can't make up my mind to it," he wrote in *Pierre*, and "I accept my annihilation" in *Billy Budd*.[37] The annihilation Melville spoke of to Hawthorne amid the sand and wind of Southport was not a figure of speech, for when he set sail to Great Britain he was already dead as a writer of fiction, the fire of imagination burned out, his material—the adventures he had lost the relish for—pretty much exhausted. Yet his artistic and spiritual death left the body intact. Melville's life dragged on for another three and a half decades after he returned home from Europe. He went on the lecture circuit for three years, attracting smaller and smaller audiences. He tried again to get a consulship and failed again. In 1863, he and his brother Allan traded houses, Allan taking over Arrowhead and Herman moving his family into 104 East Twenty-sixth Street, a few blocks uptown from where he had spent his briefly prosperous childhood.

Hawthorne, meanwhile, had returned from abroad and moved back to Wayside, the house he had purchased in Concord in 1852. *The Marble Faun* was a great success when it was published in 1860, but in the last four years of his life, Hawthorne's creative powers flagged. He started writing several romances in the fanciful tower he had added to Wayside, but got stuck in each. In Concord, Hawthorne resumed his friendships with Emerson, Thoreau, and other local literati, but there is no record of any attempt to contact Melville. The shadow of despair that Hawthorne perceived in Melville in November of 1856 now descended on him as well. Hawthorne's inability to finish a work of fiction made him extremely anxious about money, and he fretted constantly to Sophia that he would die in the poorhouse. In fact, with no steady income and prices rising during the Civil War, the family was pinched. In the last years of his life, Hawthorne seemed to waste away in mind and body like one of his tormented characters. He died, in May 1864, two months shy of his sixtieth birthday, while traveling in New Hampshire with Franklin Pierce.

Two years after Hawthorne's death, Melville at last secured an official appointment—as deputy inspector of customs at the port of New York—and for nineteen years he remained on the government payroll, earning four dollars a day (he spent much of his time at the docks at the foot of Gansevoort Street, which was named for his mother's illustrious family, as he was painfully aware). Unlike Hawthorne, Melville left no record of his years in the customs service; but he did continue to write while holding his job, something Hawthorne had never been able to do.

Having given up on prose, he turned his hand to poetry. Melville expected no recognition or praise for his verse and sought no contact with the literary world. Supposedly, he owned no copies of his own books. Family tragedies darkened Melville's life in his declining years. Malcolm, the Melvilles' first child, died in 1867 at age eighteen of a bullet fired from his own gun, apparently a suicide. Stanwix, his second son, went to sea, drifted aimlessly to the Far East, England, and Central America, and died of tuberculosis in San Francisco in 1886, two months after his father had retired from the customs service. Melville kept his feelings about these losses to himself. In the final years of his life, Melville returned to prose, completing the short novel *Billy Budd* before his death in 1891.

Melville died in almost total obscurity, but the publication of *Billy Budd* in 1924 sparked the "Melville revival," which burns on unabated today.

All mention of the friendship vanishes from both Melville's and Hawthorne's papers after their encounter in Liverpool. In Melville's case, one might surmise that the memories and associations of the most intense period of his creative life were too painful. Hawthorne, burdened by his own mortality, may simply have put this short chapter of his past behind him. At Hawthorne's funeral in Concord, Emerson, Longfellow, James Russell Lowell, James Fields, and Oliver Wendell Holmes were among the pall-bearers, but Melville was not present—uninvited or unwilling to attend, we do not know.

There is a legend, yet another legend, that Melville commemorated Hawthorne's death in his haunting poem "Monody":

> To have known him, to have loved him,
>   After loneness long;

And then to be estranged in life,
And neither in the wrong;
And now for death to set his seal—
Ease me, a little ease, my song![38]

The poem is lovely, and even more moving if we imagine that it was written for Hawthorne. But was it? The truth about "Monody," like so much else in this brief, radiant, heartbreaking friendship, shrinks from our touch.

Hawthorne and Melville to James and Wharton

FEW MEN of equal genius and of equal eminence can have led on the whole a simpler life. . . . Hawthorne's career had few vicissitudes or variations; it was passed for the most part in a small and homogeneous society, in a provincial, rural community; it had few perceptible points of contact with what is called the world. . . . He produced, in quantity, but little. . . . And yet some account of the man and the writer is well worth giving. Whatever may have been Hawthorne's private lot, he has the importance of being the most beautiful and most eminent representative of a literature. The importance of the literature may be questioned, but at any rate, in the field of letters, Hawthorne is the most valuable example of the American genius. That genius has not, as a whole, been literary; but Hawthorne was on his limited scale a master of expression. He is the writer to whom his countrymen most confidently point when they wish to make a claim to have enriched the mother-tongue, and, judging from present appearances, he will long occupy this honourable position.[1]

Thus the thirty-six-year-old Henry James, a newly minted Londoner, wrestled with the specter of his literary forerunner in the opening pages of *Hawthorne,* the critical biography he wrote in 1878 for the English Men of Letters series. The mixture of esteem, condescension, self-assurance, defensiveness, and apology is utterly characteristic of the slender volume. And so is the urbane English point of view. Throughout the book, James implicitly (and sometimes explicitly) declared his independence from the homogeneous, provincial, rural society that had produced Hawthorne and shaped his imagination. Writing in England and for English readers, he served up Hawthorne as the very model of everything that he himself grandly intended to supersede in his own literary career (he had already published *The American* and *Daisy Miller* but not yet *The Portrait of a Lady*).

The book stands as perhaps the most extraordinary case of literary parricide in American letters. Yet it is by no means a hatchet job. Admiration, affection, and a good deal of brilliant appreciation figure in the smooth narrative. James embraces before he topples. The "anxiety of influence" sharpens his critical faculty even as it skews his motives. James's book remains one of the cornerstones of Hawthorne studies—but what a very queer cornerstone it is. *Hawthorne*, as Harold Bloom points out, "requires to be read between the lines."[2] The subtext that one hears rumbling beneath its pages is James's aggressive justification of his own decision *not* to follow in his subject's footsteps. If Hawthorne was provincial, he would be cosmopolitan. If Hawthorne was rural, he would be urban. If Hawthorne shrank from contact with what is called the world, he would pursue it.

The irony, of course, is that James, even while pledging his allegiance to Flaubert, Balzac, and Turgenev, marched steadily under Hawthorne's banner. No other writer had as deep or as enduring an influence on him. Parricide or no, James never ceased to be his father's son.

In the book's most famous passage, James compiles a long and damning list of the "items of high civilization . . . which are absent from the texture of American life" and the absence of which was, in his view, fatal to Hawthorne's opportunities as a novelist:

> No State, in the European sense of the word, and indeed barely a specific national name. No sovereign, no court, no personal loyalty, no aristocracy, no church, no clergy, no army, no diplomatic service, no country gentlemen, no palaces, no castles, nor manors, nor old country-houses, nor parsonages, nor thatched cottages nor ivied ruins; no cathedrals, nor abbeys, nor little Norman churches; no great Universities nor public schools—no Oxford, nor Eton, nor Harrow; no literature, no novels, no museums, no pictures, no political society, no sporting class—no Epsom nor Ascot![3]

James was well aware that he was echoing a similar list that Hawthorne had put in the preface to *The Marble Faun* to explain why he felt compelled to situate his romance in Italy:

> No author, without a trial, can conceive of the difficulty of writing a romance about a country where there is no shadow, no antiquity, no mystery, no picturesque and gloomy wrong, nor anything but commonplace prosperity, in broad and simple daylight, as is happily the case with my dear native land. . . . Romance and poetry, ivy, lichens, and wallflowers need ruin to make them grow.[4]

It is striking that James's list focuses on art, architecture, and social and political institutions while Hawthorne's focuses on historic and spiritual qualities—shadow, antiquity, mystery, and gloomy wrong. Yet, in fact, though James might have believed he was moving abroad to soak up palaces, ivied ruins, and Ascot, his fictions were steeped in Hawthorne's shadow, antiquity, and mystery. For every little Norman church in James there are ten gloomy wrongs. James, like Hawthorne before him, kept his eye trained on the inner landscape—the heavings and quiverings of the stricken American conscience. When he did draw on the "items of high civilization" from his list—the Carmelite convent in *The American*, Lord Warburton in *The Portrait of a Lady*, Milly Theale's Venetian palazzo in *The Wings of the Dove*, Notre Dame in *The Ambassadors*—he fixed as much on their *moral values* as on their aesthetic atmosphere. James's protagonists, the "conscious centres" through whose senses we take in Europe, are spiritual descendants of Hawthorne—not of Hawthorne's characters, but of Hawthorne himself, "the last pure American," as James once called him. James surrendered to the seductions of European art and culture far more readily than Hawthorne would permit himself to do on his single long sojourn abroad; James instantly felt more at ease with the subtle pleasures of complexity; but he never shook free of Hawthorne's habit of moralizing, of finding the "figure in the carpet" and the symbol in the scenery. Neither of them ever learned to take the shadow and the mystery for granted. They both knew that experience glittered all the more richly and strangely when set beside innocence.

In many ways, James picked up artistically where Hawthorne left off, choosing Rome, the setting of Hawthorne's final

novel, as the scene of his first, *Roderick Hudson* (the earliest novel
he cared to acknowledge in later years). Like Hawthorne, James
used artists, writers, and social reformers as his heroes; like Hawthorne, he wrote brilliantly of strong, intelligent women, though
James's heroines tend to keep their eroticism more under wraps
than Hawthorne's "dark ladies"; like Hawthorne, he was drawn
to outside observers, attenuated gentlemen obsessed with the
plumper lives led by their friends and neighbors. The brooding
hermetic atmosphere of *The Golden Bowl*—in which two couples
enact a private drama sealed off from the demands of "real life"
and in which symbols play so large a part—is strangely reminiscent of Hawthorne's "interior" fictions such as "The Birthmark"
or "Rappaccini's Daughter." Isabel Archer, as Bloom points out,
traces her ancestry back to Hester Prynne. The adultery in *The
Scarlet Letter* gave birth to the adulteries that haunted James's
imagination at the end of his life. The utopian dreamers of *The
Blithedale Romance* foreshadow the bustling reformers of *The
Bostonians*. Ethan Brand is the progenitor of James's Gilbert Osmond, the heartless villain of *The Portrait of a Lady,* and more
distantly of John Marcher in "The Beast in the Jungle" who commits a Jamesian version of the unpardonable sin—the failure to
live his life. The "thin-skinned" Arthur Dimmesdale, as Philip
Rahv writes, "is the ancestor of all those characters in Henry
James who invent excruciatingly subtle reasons for renouncing
their heart's desire once they are on the verge of attaining it."[5]

"It is wise . . . to come back betimes, or never," Hawthorne
wrote at the end of *The Marble Faun* to explain why he is sending
his pair of implausibly happily married American artists back
home to America. James took the latter course, choosing to come
back less and less frequently and finally *never,* even going so far as
to renounce his American citizenship. But in a more fundamental
way, for all his European airs and graces, James never ceased to be
an American. To place James in the "school" of Hawthorne is to
distort and oversimplify both of their work. Yet it is undeniable
that James, patronize Hawthorne though he might, stood squarely
on his predecessor's shoulders. If James did manage to supersede
Hawthorne, to see further and deeper into human nature, as he
clearly set out to do, this boost up may explain why.

In *Notes of a Son and Brother,* the second volume of his
autobiography, James fondly recalls how Hawthorne's *The*

Wonder-Book and *Twice-Told Tales* had "helped to enchant our childhood" and he describes how he had unaccountably put off reading Hawthorne's romances until one summer when, as a young man in Newport, he gulped down "at one straight draught the full sweet sense" of them.[6] Hawthorne was, as far back as James could remember, a familiar name in his household—his books read and discussed, his stature as *the* American literary genius beyond dispute. Of Herman Melville, however, James says not a word in his memoirs—though he does make a passing reference to reading Melville as a youth in some notes he wrote about American literature. This is all the more extraordinary since the James family and the Melville family had ties to intersecting upper-middle-class circles in old New York. James and Melville were both born in lower Manhattan and spent part of their childhoods there, though of course a generation apart. They were, moreover, neighbors for six months in 1875 when James returned from Europe for a spell and rented two rooms at 111 East Twenty-fifth Street—practically back-to-back with the house at 104 East Twenty-sixth where Melville had been living since 1863. James was very busy at the time seeing *Roderick Hudson* through serial publication in *The Atlantic* and writing literary journalism, but he was never averse to mixing in literary society and making the acquaintance of anyone who was anyone. It was a sign of the depths of obscurity to which Melville had sunk by the 1870s that James was utterly unaware that he could practically peer into the back bedrooms of the author of *Moby-Dick*. Indeed, he was utterly unaware of *Moby-Dick* itself.

Edith Wharton, on the other hand, was acquainted with both Melville's social position and his writing. She mentions in her memoirs that Melville was a cousin of the Van Rensselaers, which would make him a relative of her dear friend Walter Van Rensselaer Berry, the distinguished international lawyer who later became a close friend of Marcel Proust (Proust dedicated his *Pastiches et mélanges* to Berry). One's imagination staggers at the idea of a connection, however remote, between Melville and Proust! Born in 1862, the year before Melville moved back to New York, Wharton spent much of her childhood on West Twenty-third Street, just a stone's throw away from where Melville was living—but of course his "deplorable Bohemianism" kept him out of her parents' impeccable parlor.

Wharton mentions in a 1911 letter to her lover Morton

Fullerton that among the stack of books that she had brought with her to the Italian spa at Salsomaggiore is *Moby-Dick:* "Do you share my taste for Melville? I like him almost as well, & in the same way, as Borrow."[7] (George Henry Borrow was an English writer of fictionalized travel adventures.) This was more than a decade before the so-called Melville revival, when Melville's readership had dwindled to a tiny cult based mostly in England. That Wharton should have had a "taste for Melville" at all in 1911 is an indication of how impressively wide ranging her reading was. Like Melville (another adventurous reader), Wharton was largely self-educated: A whale ship had been his Yale and Harvard; hers was her father's well-stocked library.

Wharton, coincidentally, also lived quite near Hawthorne—although, again, more than fifty years later—for her beloved country estate, the Mount, was just a few miles from Hawthorne's red farmhouse on the other side of Lenox. As a novelist, Wharton did not labor in Hawthorne's shadow the way James did, but she certainly knew of his work and she did absorb some of his characteristic chilly atmosphere of guilt and gloom into her short novel *Ethan Frome.* As the critic Cynthia Griffin Wolff points out, Wharton's Ethan Frome harks back to Hawthorne's Ethan Brand and Frome's sour, suspicious wife gets her name from Zenobia in *The Blithedale Romance,* one of Hawthorne's passionate dark ladies. "Wharton was not interested in sin," writes Wolff, "but she was interested in the effect of isolation upon the workings of man's emotional life: thus *Ethan Frome* is related to *Ethan Brand.*"[8]

Nathaniel Hawthorne died two years after Edith Wharton was born. When Herman Melville died in September 1891, Henry James, in London, having completed *The Tragic Muse,* was embarking upon his unhappy (and notably unsuccessful) career as a playwright. That same summer, Edith Wharton, who had just purchased a small house on Park Avenue, published her first short story, "Mrs. Manstey's View," in *Scribner's Magazine.*

PART TWO

Henry James
and
Edith Wharton

FIVE

On the Road

*When Americans went abroad in 1820 there was
something romantic, almost heroic in it, as compared
with the perpetual ferryings of the present hour, the
hour at which photography and other conveniences
have annihilated surprise.*

—HENRY JAMES, The Aspern Papers

*The motor-car has restored the romance of travel. . . .
It has given us back the wonder, the adventure and
the novelty which enlivened the way of our posting
grand-parents.*

—EDITH WHARTON, A Motor-Flight Through France

FROM HENRY JAMES'S LETTERS to friends, one would think that a
car ride with Edith Wharton was an experience akin to the rape of
the Sabine women. Here is the sixty-nine-year-old Master cower-
ing in abject, comic anticipation as Wharton's chariot of fire draws
near:

Lamb House Rye
Reign of Terror
ce vingt juillet, 1912

My dear, dear Howard [Sturgis],
This is a sort of signal of distress thrown out to you *in the last*

confidence, at the approach of the Bird o'freedom—the whirr and wind of whose great pinions is already cold on my fore-doomed brow! She is close at hand, she arrives tomorrow, and the poor old Ryebird, with the majestic Paddingtonia no longer to defend him, feels his barnyard hurry and huddle, emitting desperate and incoherent sounds, while its otherwise serene air begins ominously to darken. *Bref,* the Angel, ("half-angel and half-bird," as Browning so vividly prefigures her,) has a *plan,* of course; which is that, struggling in her talons, as you will say, I am yet to be rapt off . . .[1]

Rapt off, in this case, to nothing more treacherous than tea at Howard Sturgis's house followed by dinner with Lady Ripon at Coombe—but rapt off on other more prodigious occasions on motor trips through most of France, a good deal of the south of England, and the Massachusetts countryside surrounding Wharton's house at Lenox. James's magniloquent, mock-hysterical alarm is the *note* of his relationship with Wharton—the mixed dread and relish of her energy, her high style, the imperious manner, and freedom of movement that her considerable funds made possible. James wrung his hands over the way Wharton interrupted his work, drained his comparatively meager resources, threw his prim, orderly bachelor's existence into a tumult—but secretly, the poor huddling Ryebird was a willing victim of the golden ravening eagle. Clearly, if surprisingly (most of all to himself), James enjoyed these motor trips, delighted in the rapid-fire impressions that driving in the countryside threw up to him, and basked in the blazing light reflected off Wharton's rich armor.

Motoring was not a style of travel that one associates with James's conservative, ponderous, tortoiselike sensibility, nor was the flashy, opulent Wharton his style of friend, but he came to value, even to depend on, both. Motoring was the medium of their finest, most pleasurable communication; her various cars—mostly large, black, glossy, French-made Panhard-Levassors—were the scenes of the best moments of their friendship. Different—in many important ways opposite—as they were in their style of travel, different as were their *reasons* for travel and their manners of receiving and recording the sensations of a journey, they were always to enchant each other as traveling companions.

James and Wharton became acquainted over lunch in London on a somber December afternoon in 1903, although, as Wharton recalls in her memoirs, they had actually crossed paths twice before in the 1880s. The first occasion was a Paris dinner party, possibly in 1887, and Wharton, then in her twenties, freshly married to a man she didn't love, and terribly shy, had thought to impress the already famous writer by wearing her newest Doucet dress; at the second encounter, a party in Venice, she relied on a becoming new hat to catch his penetrating glance—but James "noticed neither the hat nor its wearer—" Wharton wrote nearly fifty years later, "and the second of our meetings fell as flat as the first."[2] It wasn't until Wharton began publishing fiction, starting with a story in *Scribner's Magazine* in 1891, that she summoned up the nerve to *make* James notice her. She sent him her first story collection, *The Greater Inclination*, in 1899 and later *The Valley of Decision,* her historical novel set in eighteenth-century Italy. James, meanwhile, was hearing intriguing accounts of Wharton's literary and social arts from various friends they had in common, particularly the French writer Paul Bourget; he found her work and her reputation impressive enough to initiate a correspondence.

The 1903 London lunch came, like all of the first encounters in this book, at a turning point in both of the writers' lives. Wharton's literary career was about to take off: Her third story collection appeared the following year and *The House of Mirth,* her first major success, followed it in 1905. On the verge of attaining fame and even greater wealth than she already commanded, Wharton was, at forty-one years old, finally emerging from the hard, dull, protective shell of her social class. Her well-bred parents and handsome outdoorsy husband shunned the society of writers and artists ("The Four Hundred would have fled in a body from a poet, a painter, a musician or a clever Frenchman," as her friend Margaret Terry Chanler once said[3]), but Wharton was now determined to make up the lack of good company and good conversation as rapidly as possible. Henry James was a trophy she desperately wanted to carry off.

James, whose distinguished literary career already stretched back over three and a half decades, was just embarked upon his "major phase," the period when he wrote in rapid succession his three final and demanding masterpieces—*The Wings of the Dove* (1902), *The Ambassadors* (1903), and *The Golden Bowl* (1904). To the rising generation of writers in London and New York, James was the Master—the supreme artist of English prose fiction; but journalists attacked and parodied his ornate, convoluted, hyperconscious "late" style, and his readership steadily declined from the high-water mark of *Daisy Miller,* published in 1879. James was bitter over the popular failure of his books and plays. He was also increasingly lonely after his move in 1898 from a London flat to Lamb House, a comfortable russet-brick Georgian house in the mellow little southern coast town of Rye.

James, who had always had a tremendous gift for friendship and a huge roster of eminent companions, relied on his friends as never before in the final decades of his life. But, of course, he did not let his craving for company interfere with his critical faculties. James had learned to be suspicious of "literary ladies" after one of them—Wharton's friend Violet Paget, who wrote under the name Vernon Lee—roasted him, and another—Constance Fenimore Woolson—fell hopelessly in love with him and committed suicide (there may well have been a connection). Though Wharton was a member of this scribbling tribe, James, almost despite himself, seems rather to have enjoyed her from the very start. Their backgrounds and their circles overlapped, and they shared a taste for wicked gossip, French literature, titled dining companions, social intrigue, and travel. Like so many of James's heroines, Wharton was rich and energetic and eager to live all she could, which in her case, as he was soon to find out, amounted to a very great deal indeed. James wrote a mutual friend after the December lunch that he found Wharton "really conversable (rare characteristic, *par le temps qui court!*) and sympathetic in every way." To other friends he sniffed that Mrs. Wharton was *"sèche"* (dry) and "slightly cold," but, clearly, he was intrigued.[4] And once he was intrigued, James could be extremely tenacious.

Like James, Wharton revered the past, the fineness and elegance of good *old* society, and she abhorred the new, particularly the millionaire newcomers of the gilded age—the Vanderbilts, Fricks, and Goulds whose standing on the social ladder she described with Proustian exactness in *The House of Mirth* and *The Custom of the Country.* Yet for all her disdain for the vulgarity and ostentation of the arrivistes, Wharton was always quick to join them in acquiring the newest and finest technology money could buy, be it indoor plumbing and electric lights for the Mount, her country house in the Berkshires, or a sleek steam yacht chartered for a tour of the Greek islands shortly after her marriage. When it came to satisfying her craving for comfort and diversion,

Wharton spared no expense. And so it was with her automobiles. Of course Wharton, as James never tired of bemoaning in his letters, had the *means* to acquire these new machines—which he most emphatically did not.

Their friendship endured James's envy and Wharton's splendor because the two of them could laugh—at each other and at themselves. "Perhaps it was our common sense of fun that first brought about our understanding," Wharton notes in her memoirs, *A Backward Glance*. "The real marriage of true minds is for any two people to possess a sense of humor or irony pitched in exactly the same key, so that their joint glances at any subject cross like interarching search-lights . . . [I]n that sense Henry James was perhaps the most intimate friend I ever had, though in many ways we were so different."[5]

Motor cars had been in existence for some years when the Whartons bought their first Panhard-Levassor in Paris in 1904—an open hoodless, doorless, windshieldless four-seater that broke down as regularly though less disastrously as spacecraft do today. But in these pre-Model T days, cars were still something of a novelty. At the Chicago Exposition of 1893 (the technology fair at which James's friend Henry Adams confronted the dynamo and suffered his revelation about "the whole mechanical consolidation of force" on which America's capitalist system was based), the car was displayed as an oddity, a luxurious, newfangled toy. A decade later only the very rich had cars of their own; the conservative rich, suspicious that the fad for motoring would blow over, kept their horses and carriages.

Wharton, however, fell in love with her Panhard at once, as much, one suspects, for the rarity of owning one as for the freedom it allowed her to travel at her own speed (fast) and to get to places not accessible to run-of-the-mill tourists. The private motor perfectly suited her idea of travel as escape from the commonplace (and escape, perhaps as well, from the emotional deadness of her marriage, just as the trapped lovers Lydia Tillotson and Ralph Gannett in her fine story "Souls Belated" chase through Europe to escape the falsity and emptiness at the core of their illicit passion). In her car, Wharton could, like the mythical creature "half-angel and half-bird" James makes her out to be, soar past the less privileged tourists chugging dutifully to the monuments and vistas imposed on them by their *Baedekers*. The car was her mode of making her own travels distinguished and adventurous at a time when the first great wave of mass tourism was breaking over Europe.

Wharton's Panhard (which James dubbed "Hortense" after the sexually adventurous French writer Hortense Allart, Mme. de Méritens) was put into service to transport only the principal players in her entourage—a choice companion, preferably James or Walter Berry, tucked in beside her in the backseat while her husband, Teddy, rode up front beside their indispensable chauffeur, Charles Cook, a lean and resourceful Yankee whom she pried out of the Berkshire Hills and pressed into her overseas service for many years. (Wharton was as fiercely loyal to worthy servants as she was fearsomely chilly to unwanted acquaintances: She conserved her warmth for those she loved.) The mountain of luggage and servants went separately by van.

With her Panhard, even laden as it was with both husband and Henry James, Edith Wharton could poke and pry. She could take possession. And she could speed—that was the great thing— she could cover vast distances. This, in any case, was what impressed James most about the style of travel of the "Edith Whartons." "The rich, rushing, ravening Whartons," he branded them in a letter to a friend after an early and not altogether successful trip (a "fragmentary merely-motory trip" he called it) with them in England; and to another friend he wrote even more severely (referring to himself in the third person, like Henry Adams in *The Education*) that he "thanked goodness . . . that such fantastic wealth and freedom were not *his* portion—such incoherence, such a nightmare of perpetually renewable choice and decision, such a luxury of bloated alternatives, do they seem to burden life withal."[6] *His* portion was always considerably smaller, his alternatives slimmer—and his style, of life and travel, if not of prose, far less extravagant.

But it wasn't just that James lacked the means to zoom around in the fashion of the "rich, rushing, ravening Whartons"; he positively shunned speed as inimical to gathering the finer, deeper impressions, the impressions he amassed slowly, sedulously, and with due deliberation all his life. In his travel piece on Venice, James mocks the "fatal rashness" of those "shallow inquirers" who come to Venice for a week and hasten away disappointed, even irritated with the city. For James, rather, it is by living there from day to day that you feel the fulness of her charm; that you invite her exquisite influence to sink into your spirit. The creature varies like a nervous woman, whom you know only when you know all the aspects of her beauty. . . . Tenderly fond you become; there is something indefinable in those depths of personal acquaintance that gradually establish themselves. The place seems to personify itself, to become human and sentient and conscious of your affection. You desire to embrace it, to caress it, to possess it; and finally a soft sense of possession grows up and your visit becomes a perpetual love-affair.[7]

James, who never, apparently, made love to a woman (or a man), offers himself here (albeit in the second person) as the practiced seducer of cities, a connoisseur who has refined his powers of appreciation in many and varied love affairs. One fairly sees before one the early middle-aged, not yet rotund and still bearded Henry James (he was thirty-nine when he wrote this) drifting solemnly down the narrow side canals, alighting at obscure, damp, incense-reeking churches, rubbing at old inscriptions until they yield an impression, the more precious because the fainter and slower to emerge.

There is a comic side, as well, to James's loitering, lingering, hesitant style of travel (as of speaking and writing), which Wharton describes with relish in *A Backward Glance*. One of her best set pieces on James is about how a heat wave laid low the urbane but overweight Master during his 1904 sojourn at the Mount. Taking pity on his discomfort (but exasperated by his fussing), she suggested that he might be better off returning to England on a boat that sailed from Boston in two days. "His bodily surface, already broad, seemed to expand to meet [the heat]," she writes, "and his imagination to become part of his body, so that the one dripped words of distress as the other did moisture." She goes on to describe how James, "a mountain of misery" with "a pile of sucked oranges at his elbow," moaned, "Good God, what a woman—what a woman! Her imagination boggles at nothing! She does not even scruple to project me in naked flight across the Atlantic . . ."[8] "He took a great deal of space to turn round in," Wharton wrote of James's literary style shortly after his death; the same could be said of his personal deportment.[9]

For one so inclined, the automobile, particularly the automobile careening from cathedral to château at breakneck speed, would seem the very least suitable mode of transportation, but such was not the case. The extraordinary thing is that when James *did* reconcile himself to the car, he got so much out of it, took so much pleasure in it. Eventually, despite his initial antipathy, he came near to agreeing with Edith Wharton that "the motor-car has restored the romance of travel," though, of course, for him it was always the motor car of a friend, since he never "set up" a motor of his own.

It was the series of motor trips he and Wharton took through western Massachusetts during this 1904 visit that made a convert of him. Seeing cars "from within," as he writes, is "the only way," and from within Wharton's motor car James found the "rural vastness" of the New England countryside "quite unexpectedly and almost uncannily delightful and sympathetic . . . with weather like tinkling crystal and colours like molten jewels."[10] To his brother William he raves about the way a car "deals with a country large enough for it not to *rudoyer,* but to rope in, in big free hauls, a huge netful of impressions at once—this came home to me beautifully. . . . A great transformer of life and of the future!" And he confides to his old friend Jessie Allen that "I have been won over to motoring, for which the region is, in spite of bad roads, delightful—the mountain-and-valley, lake-and-river beauty extends so far, and goes so on and on that even the longest spins do not take one out of it." The beauty of the Massachusetts countryside, which he had never visited in his youth, strikes him as infused with "a really romantic freshness." "The region is lovely," he continues, "and—or rather *but*—everyone is oppressively rich and *cossu* . . . and 'a million a year' seems to be the usual income."[11] In *The American Scene,* he called the Berkshires the "land beyond any other today . . . of leisure on the way to legitimation, of the social idyll, of the workable, the expensively workable, American form of country life."[12]

The oppressions of wealth and leisure had wrought most remarkable changes on the Berkshires in the half century since Hawthorne and Melville walked its hills and fields. Yet James well knew that the "social idyll" did not cover the entire landscape. In their many afternoon drives, Wharton also spun him past the bleak isolated farmhouses that she would fix on, several years later, as the setting for *Ethan Frome,* her most Hawthornesque

novel. "Ah, the thin, empty, lonely, melancholy American 'beauty'
—which I yet find a cold prudish charm in!" James once rhapso-
dized in a letter to her, perfectly capturing the rural austerity that
both Wharton and Hawthorne evoked in their fiction.[13]

James scrutinized not only the Berkshire scenery, but also
his hostess and her house, which he described to Howard Sturgis
as "an exquisite and marvellous place, a delicate French chateau
mirrored in a Massachusetts pond (repeat not this formula), a
monument to the almost too impeccable taste of its so accomplished mistress." The veteran of countless dinner and country
house parties notes that "every comfort prevails, and you needn't
bring supplementary apples or candies in your dressing-bag. The
Whartons are kindness and hospitality incarnate."[14] Later, when
their intimacy was more deeply established, James came to appreciate Wharton as a woman and a companion, not merely as a
gracious hostess (he *never* really appreciated her as a writer); but
at this stage of the friendship, he viewed her above all as a striking
product of "the expensively workable American form of country
life."

On balance the visit, and particularly the motoring, was a
success, and it set the stage for more prolonged and even more
successful motor trips abroad in the coming years.

Wharton and James motored together again in England
two years later, in the spring of 1906, a trip that was cut short by
bad weather and perhaps as well by James's anxiety about the
expense of being part of the Whartons' entourage. For even though
they provided the car and the gas, he was forced, when with them,
to stay at hotels far more luxurious than those he would have
chosen on his own, and to dispense tips to the numerous servants
he came in contact with. Traveling with the Whartons, he wrote a
friend, is "a proof again of the old story that it's one's rich friends
who cost one!"

These anxieties welled up again when he faced the prospect
of another motor journey with them the next year, this time starting from Paris, where the Whartons were subletting George
Vanderbilt's apartment in an old hotel at 58 rue de Varenne.
(Edith had already embarked upon her great siege of the old aristocratic society of the Faubourg St. Germain and her project of
forming her own literary salon. The Faubourg was to be her base
of operations for the next twenty years.) James writes to a Paris

friend, Edward Lee Childe, that in agreeing to the prolonged stay with the Whartons he had done "a rare & rash thing (for *me*) to go to spend some 10 or 12 days with some friends, the Edward Whartons . . . during which time I shall enjoy but imperfect freedom of movement & circulation (always the precious penalty for staying with people in complicated capitals)."

But this time, even after three weeks and a day on the road in their "motor-flight" through France, and a subsequent stay with Wharton in Paris for a good month longer, the two were better friends than ever (it was after this trip that James began addressing his letters to "My dear Edith" instead of "Dear Mrs. Wharton"). Indeed, the success of this joint sojourn in France seems to have put the seal on their relationship: Henceforth they were no longer merely well-acquainted members of the same social and literary circles but true intimates. It was their finest and most memorable time together.

A flight it truly was for in their three weeks on the road, the friends (with Teddy along for the ride) inscribed a huge circle through France, dropping down from Paris to Blois, Poitiers, Bordeaux, south to the Pyrenees, east to the Riviera for a spell, and then back up through Burgundy and home to Paris again. The experience of whirling around luxuriously with the Whartons struck James as "an expensive fairy tale."

In *A Motor-Flight Through France*, Wharton writes that the car gives one a "sense of continuity" and a "general topography" that one can get from no other means of transport. From the window of the Panhard, the landscape around Arras looks like "rich juicy land bathed in blond light" and "the wonderful white road" to Beauvais "fling(s) itself in great coils and arrow-flights." "The motorist sometimes misses details by going too fast," she admits, but then "he sometimes has them stamped onto his memory by an opportune puncture or a recalcitrant 'magneto'; and if, on windy days, he has to rush through nature blindfold, on golden afternoons such as this he can drain every drop of her precious essence."[15] Wharton, in fact, had little cause to apologize for missing "details," for despite her furious pace, she took in an amazing amount. She was a speed reader of landscapes and architecture.

Together, James and Wharton took the French provinces by storm, searching out the fine bits of carving on the ancient church at Poitiers, scorning the "vast sea of vulgarism" they found at Lourdes, deploring the "hairless pink monster" of the Albi

Cathedral, applauding the view at Pau, which Wharton describes as an "astonishing balcony hung above the great amphitheatre of southwestern France. . . ." Coupled in the back of the Panhard, she with her shining array of facts and her fierce desire to be original, he with a vast store of memories and associations rising up from the depths of his mind to meet and enhance new impressions, James and Wharton were a twin engine of supreme consciousness. Together they blazed down the narrow rutted provincial roads at the fastest speed then attainable, in hot pursuit of the precious and the beautiful, the brighter, more suggestive light, the high structures of the past made sacred by the centuries of life and death.

American tourism never again reached the heights to which James and Wharton brought it—the high intelligence, high style, high tone, the ample means, and the boundless will to deploy these means in travel. Travel for both of them was an art, almost a religion, and their journeys through Europe were like pilgrimages to their spiritual home. In fact, Europe had been James's *actual* home for three decades, and it was soon to become Wharton's permanent home as well for, like James, she found the native American air too thin and poor to sustain her, and the native manners too offensive to abide ("What horror it is for a whole nation to be developing without a sense of beauty, and eating bananas for breakfast," she once wrote in disgust, though she fails to mention whether bananas would have been less horrid for lunch or dinner). "One's friends are delightful; but *we* are none of us Americans," she wrote a friend of the culture shock she invariably suffered after returning from Europe to the land of her birth. "We don't think or feel as Americans do, we are the wretched exotics produced in a European glass-house."[16]

Such national renunciation would have been unthinkable to Hawthorne and Melville, engaged as they were in demonstrating that "Shakespeares are this day being born on the banks of the Ohio." Hawthorne does flirt with the idea of expatriation in *The Marble Faun,* when he writes that "when we have once known Rome," even with all her depravity and decay, "we are astonished by the discovery, by and by, that our heartstrings have mysteriously attached themselves to the Eternal City, and are drawing us thitherward again, as if it were more familiar, more intimately our home, than even the spot where we were born."[17] But at the end of the book, Hawthorne's expatriate American artists "resolved to go back to their own land; because the years, after all, have a kind of emptiness, when we spend too many of them on a foreign shore."[18] "Excessively detached Mr. Hawthorne remains, from the first, from Continental life," James wrote at the start of his own literary career, "touching it throughout mistrustfully, shrinkingly, and at the rare points at which he, for the time, unlearned his nationality. . . ."[19]

Melville, by temperament, could never be "excessively detached"—and yet on his tour through the Near East and Europe during 1856 and 1857 he noted in his journal that he was repeatedly "afflicted with the great curse of modern travel—skepticism."[20] Melville sneers in *Pierre* that "among the evils of enlarged foreign travel, that in young and unsolid minds, it dislodges some of the finest feelings of the home-born nature; replacing them with a fastidious superciliousness."[21] Melville eerily prefigures here the attacks that red-blooded American jingo journalists were to launch a half century later on James and Wharton. Melville's own ardor for new places had burned out in his youth. Even if he had had the means to expatriate himself and his large family, he would not have done so. For better or worse, he had taken his stand in America.

In transplanting themselves to Europe, James and Wharton were in a sense American pioneers. Certainly they plowed up the way for future generations of American writers. Robert Lowell said he felt like a "pioneer going into the wilderness," when he moved from New York to England in 1970. "After a while the wilderness changes into the Europe of Henry James and Eliot."[22]

James was enchanted both by Wharton's company and her car while their French motor flight lasted; but the trip drained him both physically and emotionally, and exhausted as well his desire to travel farther, especially with Edith Wharton. Back home in "poor frowsy tea-and-toasty Lamb House," out of the clutches of the golden eagle, free again to move as he pleased and to dwell alone with his own thoughts, he begins to have misgivings about the venture, as he confides in a letter to Mary Cadwalader:

> I've really and absolutely crossed the absurd channel for the last time of my life. It's fantastic, it's grotesque—if you or they will; but nothing can exceed henceforth my aversion to "going abroad." . . . The energy of our friends meanwhile—of Edith's

and Teddy's (though I think in him it *must* wane) fills me with a deep and solemn awe. Such an arrangement of my life would be to me the grimmest of nightmares. But my conception of felicity is more and more to crouch behind a Chinese wall; or at least behind a good old English russet brick one.[23]

In fact, despite these elaborate protestations, he was back for a briefer encounter with "the Social monster" at the Whartons' Paris flat the next spring. But this time it really *was* his final visit. "The Continent," as he later wrote Wharton, "is an utterly & finally closed chapter: that book, sharply & inevitably padlocked, stands now on the highest thinkable shelf, far out of my reach."

James's time on the road was not, despite his complaints, a total loss professionally for he did squeeze one rather wicked story from the trip—and more particularly from the character and circumstances of his traveling companion. "The Velvet Glove" is in a sense the revenge that James's muse exacted for his ten weeks of disloyalty with Wharton—revenge not only for the time she consumed by her seductive possessive generosity, but for her presumption in trespassing on the precincts most sacred to James—the precincts of art. The golden impressions of their trip, when recollected in the tranquillity of Lamb House, assumed a thin, oily sheen of poison.

In the story "poor John Berridge," an expatriate American writer of middling talent and middle age, finds himself suddenly afloat on the "golden stream" of literary success because of a hit play he has written called *The Heart of Gold*. All at once, the *bel monde* falls at his feet, and at a party at the Paris studio of the artist Gloriani (the same setting used so memorably in *The Ambassadors*), a handsome young lord contrives to introduce the writer to a friend of his, a "fellow Olympian," a princess, in fact, who also happens to be the romance writer Amy Evans (a name as plain and flat as Edith Jones, Wharton's maiden name). Berridge, in thrall to the high aristocratic splendor of this stunning woman, practically swoons in bliss when she sweeps him away from the party and into her "chariot of fire" to go motoring around Paris. It is here, "shut intimately in together" in the close, cushioned, expensive confines of her car, that the story comes to its breathless climax. As the motor carries the two of them through the "dim fire-dust" of the Paris night with its "vague consecrated lamp-studded heights [overlooking] . . . the great scroll of all its irresistible story," the princess, ever so charmingly, with ever so seductive a rustle of her pale gold gown and her perfumed presence, reveals to poor John Berridge the reason she has pursued him: She wants him to write a little preface for her latest book to help boost its American sales. Like so many of James's plots, it is the stuff of soap opera—sex for publicity, seduction for career advancement— transmuted by the alchemy of his art.

Berridge is utterly devastated—disillusioned with his Olympian, humiliated by the immense blow to his pride (he had thought, vainly, that she wanted him for himself, or at least for his aura of success). "Her motive," he feels, is "disconcerting, deplorable, dreadful . . . and she was doing it, above all, with the clearest coolness of her general privilege." His revulsion is twofold—first for the personal affront, but even more for the idea that a creature of her noble race should sully herself with the inky, grubby business of writing professionally. "The really 'decadent' perversity," he rails, "recalling that of the most irresponsibly insolent of the old Romans and Byzantines, that could lead a creature so formed for living and breathing her Romance, and so committed, up to the eyes, to the constant fact of her personal immersion in it and genius for it, the dreadful amateurish dance of ungrammatical scribbling it, with editions and advertisements and reviews and royalties and every other futile item."[24]

By *writing* her romance instead of *living* it, the princess is not only stealing Berridge's material, but she is also spoiling it. He prefers his Olympians pure and ignorant of art—the more witless the better. Once they begin to think, to become self-conscious, they shed the rich haze of association that appeals to the true artist's imagination: By trying themselves to create, they die for art. And so, at the end of the story, refusing the princess the favor she has tried to wrest from him, Berridge priggishly lectures her: "You don't need to understand. Don't attempt such base things. Only live. Only be. *We'll* do the rest." Having leaped from her car before it enters the gate of her palace, he pokes his head back inside, where she sits "in her narrow niche, as with the liquefaction of her pearls, the glimmer of her tears," like "some miraculously humanised idol, all sacred, all jewelled, all votively hung about, but made mysterious, in the recess of its shrine, by the very thickness of the accumulated lustre." Whispering "You *are* romance" to this weeping false goddess, he steals a single long kiss and then backs off to let the car disappear into the "great floridly-framed aperture" of her palace gate.

"The Velvet Glove" is not, of course, a direct transcription of James's relationship with Wharton: The princess is younger and far more beautiful than Wharton and Berridge both younger and more starry-eyed about the aristocracy than James was by this point in his career. (Berridge was also a popular success as a writer, which James was not.) But the parallels are too strong to be dismissed: Wharton's current book was called *The Fruit of the Tree* and Amy Evans's volume is *The Top of the Tree;* Leon Edel, in his five-volume biography of James, points out passages in the story in which James parodies the rather awkward rhapsodic style Wharton used in this minor novel; and there was in fact an incident in which a small American journal solicited James for a "puff" on the book, supposedly at Wharton's request (though she denied this).

The story conveys, more richly and evocatively than the letters, James's deep ambivalence about Wharton, her money, and her rank, and her way of putting them into service to further her literary career. The progression of John Berridge's emotional states—from distant worshiper to would-be lover to outraged pawn—parallels the evolution of James's feelings about Wharton—from admiring fellow writer to intimate traveling companion to exhausted victim of her "devastation." In Berridge's panic to escape the cushioned prison of the princess's car, one feels James's revulsion from the long weeks of confinement with Wharton, from being too much under her sway, too tightly wound in the web of her possessiveness, too caught up in her frantic pace and her sharp need to see everything and see it quickly. He took his revenge by sending her up—comically, slyly, fondly, but also, just a touch maliciously.

In "The Velvet Glove," James recoils from Wharton the writer even more than Wharton the hyper traveling companion. Berridge shudders at the idea of "literary friendship" with the princess—by which he means mutual back scratching in print, sharing "material," pulling strings for one another—and there is no question that James shuddered at the prospect of such a relationship with Wharton. In matters of his art, the Master had to stand alone. Homage, not sympathy, was what he exacted from his literary friends, Wharton included.

An act of literary sniping that is rescued from meanness only by its humor, the "motor story," as Wharton called "The Velvet Glove," is a strange and slightly jarring capstone to the friends' career as fellow travelers. And yet, remarkably, Wharton claimed to like the story, calling it "perhaps the most beautiful of his later short stories." Actually, it is just possible that Wharton believed what she wrote. In fact, there is some discrepancy in the record, for though James wrote to Wharton at the time that the story "reeks of you," Wharton in her memoirs, written nearly three decades later, goes to some length to disassociate herself—disingenuously?—from it, insisting that the inspiration for the tale was "a very beautiful young Englishwoman of great position, and unappeased literary ambition."[25]

Possibly, Wharton was too proud to admit that James had wounded her. Or perhaps she was simply too possessive of James to let any story, however nasty, ruffle her. In any case, she got her own revenge in the fondly barbed portrait she drew of him in *A Backward Glance*.

"The Velvet Glove" may finally be James's way of washing his hands of the literary aspect of their relationship—and placing it on the firmer footing, for both of them, of deepening personal regard and intimacy. Having been the prisoner of her hospitality for months, James, as he makes clear in the story, was determined *not* to become the prisoner of her writing. But he was only too happy to become the confidant and consoler of her private passions and sufferings—her love affair, the seeds of which had already been planted, with American journalist and erotic adventurer Morton Fullerton and the painful unraveling of her marriage to Teddy over the next few years.

Though the friends never repeated the "monstrous" length of their 1907 French expedition, James and Wharton kept in close touch, writing more and more often to one another and seeing each other, mostly in England, for short visits. Wharton held fast to James on whatever terms she could get for he was a feather in her cap, the biggest literary prize she had ever bagged, and she was not about to let him get away, no matter how much an unflattering story of his might "reek" of her. James, despite his extravagant dread of her swooping descents, continued to be the willing victim of his "angel of devastation." After all, he could not resist her.

SIX

Sex and Money

*Thank goodness you're a failure—it's why I so dis-
tinguish you! Anything else to-day is too hideous.
Look about you—look at the successes. Would you
be one, on your honour?*

—Maria Gostrey to Lambert Strether,
The Ambassadors

*She was realizing for the first time that a woman's
dignity may cost more to keep up than her carriage;
and that the maintenance of a moral attribute should
be dependent on dollars and cents, made the world
appear a more sordid place than she had conceived it.*

—EDITH WHARTON, The House of Mirth

ONE THINKS of Henry James's novels as revolving in a rarefied
world of infinite delicacy, superfine moral niceties, motives so subtle as to disappear like silken thread when exposed to the light of
day. But in truth, beneath the shimmering surfaces of his fictions
lurk ugly, crude, intractably crass problems of sex and money,
usually intertwined. Kate Croy, Charlotte Stant, Prince Amerigo,
Madame Merle, and a crowd of James's lesser characters—all are
entangled by their impossible desires to have both sex and money,
desires that are usually impossible to satisfy simultaneously. Sex is
never free: It is traded on an exchange according to strict unwrit-
ten rules. Marriage is the ultimate deal, and it entitles both partners to enormously increased purchasing power—for a price, of

course. The link between money and sex is a secret that James's characters, and even more his narrators, work hard to conceal: But it's there, in story after story, novel after novel, waiting to pounce like one more beast in the jungle. "What values are *not* pecuniary?" asks a character in *The Outcry*, James's last finished novel, referring to the value of a painting that an English lord needs to sell in order to raise money to finance a convenient marriage for his daughter, a young woman who is herself described as "a value so great and so charming."[1]

James's friend Edith Wharton knew the secret too, knew it perhaps even better than the Master. She certainly took it more for granted than James. The fact that sex and money can be traded doesn't shock Wharton: It's the way of the world, and anyone who harbors illusions about it will be crushed. Lily Bart in *The House of Mirth* is Wharton's most famous victim of the sex-money nexus; Undine Spragg in *The Custom of the Country* is the most blatant manipulator of the market. Like James, Wharton wrings a sexual meaning from the very vocabulary of finance: *Pay, owe, sacrifice, own, trade, bargain, advantage, interest, collect* are the terms in which sexual relationships are conducted in both their work. Even more than the European theme or the upper-class setting, the knowledge and use of this secret about sex and money linked Henry James and Edith Wharton artistically. They both pick up where the age of innocence leaves off.

It should not be surprising, then, that sex and money played so large a role in their long friendship, but somehow it *is* surprising. Somehow we don't expect quite so much raw scandal to have occupied two such august literary personages, but it did.

It was scandal that opened their hearts to each other in 1908, which was the *annus mirabilis* for Wharton, the year that a series of seismic convulsions rippled through her life. Edith Newbold Jones, as she was christened in 1862, had been born into the very best old New York society. Her ancestors included the solidly upper-middle-class Gallatins, Ledyards, Rhinelanders, and Schermerhorns, and there was money in the family—not the huge piles of filthy lucre that gilded age arrivistes amassed, but nice neat bundles of carefully invested old money. Enough for frequent trips to Europe, houses in New York and Newport, motor cars, new dresses, frequent dinner parties. Edith, after a mysteriously broken engagement to one Harry Stevens, married the handsome, leisured, sporting, but incurably dull Edward Robbins Wharton—Teddy—

the scion of a "good" but no longer very wealthy Boston family. He was thirty-six, she twenty-three (considered rather old for a "girl" on the marriage market), and the only things they had in common, aside from social background, were a devotion to small dogs and European travel. It was not a happy marriage, not a joining of kindred spirits or sympathetic intellects, certainly not a passionate marriage (there is much speculation that it was a sexless union: Leon Edel, terming Edith a "demivirgin," notes that she and Teddy always slept in separate bedrooms: "to sleep in the same room with her husband gave Mrs. Wharton allergies"[2]); but whatever its shortcomings, the marriage more or less worked for quite a long time. Teddy followed rather docilely in Edith's ever-broader wake as she traveled energetically through Europe; he lived quietly in the gorgeous houses she bought or built and decorated; and he allowed her to do her writing—which she did with increasing zest and success and fervor from the turn of the century on.

Her writing, indeed, might have been the germ of the problems between them for it was in prose fiction that Wharton first freed herself psychologically from the tight corset of her class. In such novels as *The House of Mirth, The Age of Innocence, The Reef,* and in such stories as "The Line of Least Resistance," "Souls Belated," and "Autres Temps . . ." she examined with unflinching candor the morals and manners of her class in the New World and the Old and revealed how painfully these conventions trapped people with any spirit or intelligence, especially women. Wharton herself was a woman of spirit and intelligence and also a highly conventional member of her class. Tense, self-conscious, a touch stiff and cold in her bearing, not pretty but rather "handsome" with clear deep brown eyes and a strong mouth and jaw, Wharton as a young woman combined a great hunger for experience with a painful sense that so much appetite was somehow gauche. The feminist critic Cynthia Griffin Wolff notes that Wharton's family ridiculed her for wanting to read and write and for being less attractive than her two brothers, and she blames this for the insecurity and "almost morbid shyness" that paralyzed Wharton for so many years.[3]

The conflict between Wharton's emotional and intellectual impulses and the dictates of her upbringing fissured her character. She could be imperious and deferential, regal and timid, decisive and abject, exuberant and prostrate, robust and chronically ill.

Wharton suffered from "such conflict and confusion," writes Wolff, "that during her years of apprenticeship there were long periods when she was too depressed to write."[4] Nausea accompanied by extreme fatigue, headaches, and weight loss plagued her for much of her thirties. Her fiction did not really begin to flow until she was nearly forty. Later, in her maturity, Wharton became something of a grande dame, and she mastered the grande dame's art of harmonizing the seemingly irreconcilable under the sleek mantle of her style. The more she saw through the follies of society, the stricter and more scrupulous she became about keeping up appearances. She adhered to all the conventions, but for her own reasons. With maturity, she gained self-confidence and a sense of freedom that she steadfastly refused to abuse. She abhorred the license of bohemians as much as the blindness of bores. She lived more and more at her own brisk pace, and let others run panting behind her.

In 1908, that pace quickened considerably when Wharton began an adulterous affair with an American journalist living in Paris named William Morton Fullerton. This liaison precipitated one of the most celebrated sexual awakenings in modern letters. But, of course, such passion in such a world came at a steep price, as Wharton and James knew all too well. Wharton, like Anna Leath in *The Reef* (which R.W.B. Lewis calls "possibly the most autobiographical work of fiction she ever wrote"[5]), had to pay for her discovery of passion with her pride, her happiness, her peace of mind. But at least Wharton did not have to suffer her payment alone. In the autumn of 1908, she allowed herself the comfort of unburdening herself to James.[6] James assumed the role not only of her confidant, but also of a sort of eager observer and even participant in the intrigue. The affair turned out to be one of the most revealing chapters of their friendship.

James was a highly interested party in the Wharton–Fullerton affair for it was he who had helped bring the lovers together, paving the way for Fullerton to visit Wharton at the Mount in the autumn of 1907, a few months after the motor flight through France. James had known Fullerton since the early 1890s, when the twenty-five-year-old Harvard-educated journalist had come from Connecticut to take up a position with *The Times* of London. James's biographer Leon Edel describes Fullerton as "a dashing well-tailored man with large Victorian moustaches and languid eyes, a bright flower in his button-hole and the style of a 'masher.' "[7] In his photographs he appears both sleek and sensual, with a melting, soulful gaze, slicked-back hair, broad shoulders, and long white fingers. Fullerton ingratiated himself with James and an affectionate correspondence ensued.

James, nearing fifty at the time, was just assuming his role as the Master—*cher maître,* as Wharton customarily addressed him. He had certainly earned this honorific. By 1892, James had lived a life that was extraordinarily full by some measures and unutterably empty by others. He had made himself, really with little help aside from a few connections and a small legacy of inherited money, into one of the literary lions of England—the consummate man of letters who had known Turgenev, Flaubert, and Zola in Paris in the 1870s; who had traveled widely and deeply in France, Italy, Germany, and Switzerland, always in the best international society; who had already written such master-pieces as *Daisy Miller,* "The Aspern Papers," and *The Portrait of a Lady* and would soon publish *The Turn of the Screw* and *What Maisie Knew.* By 1892, James had been living permanently in England for a decade and a half, during which time he had met *everybody,* from Thackeray to Browning to Matthew Arnold to Trollope to Lord Rosebery to Leslie Stephen (Virginia Woolf's father). His boast that he dined out 140 times during the London winter "season" of 1878–79 is legendary.[8] Yet for all his connec-tions, his celebrity, his status, James knew that there was a great void at the center of his life. Single, celibate, and more alone than he cared to be, he peered deeper and deeper down a well of des-olation.

Though he had deliberately distanced himself from the dis-tractions of London when he moved to Rye in 1898, James found that solitude weighed heavier as he aged. He joked in letters about being an old bachelor and an intractable, unspoilable celibate, but the consequences of celibacy became a matter of much somber rumination and often a cause of depression. As he wrote to Ful-lerton, beautifully, touchingly, in 1900, when he was fifty-seven:

> The grey years gather; the arid spaces lengthen, damn them—or at any rate don't shorten; what doesn't come doesn't, and what goes *does.* . . . The port from which I set out was, I think, that of the *essential loneliness of my life*—and it seems to be the port also, in sooth to which my course again finally directs itself! This loneliness, (since I mention it!)—

what is it still but the deepest thing about one? Deeper about *me*, at any rate, than anything else: deeper than my 'genius,' deeper than my 'discipline,' deeper than my pride, deeper, above all, than the deep countermining of art.[9]

James's lament about the "essential loneliness" of his existence rings true for most writers—and certainly for the writers in this book. Melville and Hawthorne cemented their friendship during the long solitude of a Berkshires winter, and Melville fantasized about breaching his isolation by having an endless spool of paper connect him to Hawthorne. Elizabeth Bishop supposedly told Robert Lowell that she was "the loneliest person who ever lived." Eudora Welty complained to Katherine Anne Porter of how isolated and numb she felt at home, and loneliness preyed on Porter too despite her numerous marriages and love affairs. The loneliness of writing makes friendship, especially friendship with another sympathetic writer, precious—and even more precious as "the grey years gather and the arid spaces lengthen." James writes of art as "countermining" loneliness; for him, as for the others, there was also considerable solace in the deep countermining of friendship.

The aging James's penchant for friendships with handsome young men has roused inevitable speculation about his sexuality. Was he a repressed—or an active—homosexual? Did he die a virgin? Was he impotent? For year James was thought of as essentially sexless—a hyper-refined, stuttering, obscurely "wounded" aesthete who would have been revolted by the grossness of the sex act had the opportunity to perform it ever come his way. But more recently a different view of Henry James has come to light—an affectionate, warmhearted, fondly avuncular old soul, much given to bear hugs, embraces, and fond pats, both verbal and physical, especially with his circle of handsome young men. Whether these led to greater intimacy is something we'll never know, though it seems highly unlikely. The prevailing opinion these days is that James was predominantly homosexual in his inclination, but that he never acted on it. Edel, in his introduction to the final volume of James's letters, explores all the rumors, gossip, and innuendos surrounding James's sexuality, including the story (recounted by Somerset Maugham) that the writer Hugh Walpole "once offered himself to the Master" but "James recoiled with 'I can't, I can't, I *can't.*' "[10]

James, for whatever reason, probably *couldn't,* but that didn't stop him from enjoying and relying on the company of attractive young men, and even loving some of them—Walpole, Hendrik Andersen, Jocelyn Persse—in whatever way he could. His affection for these men made him both more accepting of and more curious about the physical side of love. As Edel notes, James's late fiction reflects his increasing, though always oblique and voyeuristic, obsession with sex—his "intense wish to know what goes on in adult bedrooms."[11] The passage in *The Wings of the Dove* in which Merton Densher luxuriates in the afterglow of having Kate Croy "come, that once, to stay, as people called it" in his rooms is unthinkable in early James: "What had come to pass within his walls lingered there as an obsession importunate to all his senses . . . it made everything else irrelevant and tasteless."[12] And what, after all, is the whole movement of *The Ambassadors* but the slow, wonderful dawning of the *fact* of sex on the super-refined consciousness of Lambert Strether?

Morton Fullerton was one of the "dear, dear boys" who gathered around the Master at this time of his life. James was extremely fond of him and worried over him a good deal. "Down there, alone at Rye, I used to lie & think of Morton, & *ache* over him," he once told Wharton,[13] and it may well be that James preferred the company of the charming, smooth Fullerton to the driven, demanding Firebird. Fullerton, evidently, was "dear" to a wide circle composed of both sexes for he was an active bisexual of "considerable sexual versatility," as Edel puts it. Among his more socially prominent partners were the aging but still lovely Margaret Brooke, the ranee of Sarawak, and Lord Ronald Gower, an aristocratic English sculptor, a well-known homosexual and a member of Oscar Wilde's circle. At the time he met Wharton, Fullerton was freshly divorced from a French singer named Camille Chabert, entangled in an affair with an older and very possessive Frenchwoman, who might have been his landlady, and engaged to marry his cousin Katharine, a passionate young woman fourteen years his junior, who had been raised believing that she was his sister.[14] Highly creative lying must have been essential to float so complicated a life. Despite his suave deceptions and Frenchified dandyism, Fullerton was not a cad. He was, however, monumentally unreliable. Edel claims that Fullerton was the model for Merton Densher in *The Wings of the Dove*—the rather weak but appealing journalist who loves Kate Croy and allows her to manipulate him into a plot against the affections (and wealth) of Milly Theale.

Fullerton was an unfortunate choice to inspire in Wharton the passion of a lifetime. Wharton, at forty-six, was just three years Fullerton's senior, but she was a mere infant compared to him in the affairs of the heart. Over the twenty-three barren years of her marriage to Teddy, Edith had reconciled herself to a life without passion and steeled herself against disappointment. As R.W.B. Lewis wrote, "She had rigidly guarded herself against . . . emotional buffeting; she had created a personality severely immune to the enticing dangers of life. . . ."[15] When Fullerton opened the floodgates of her heart, Wharton, to her own intense surprise, found herself drowning in her love for him. "I am a little humbled, a little ashamed to find how poor a thing I am, how the personality I had moulded into such firm lines has crumbled to a pinch of ashes in this flame!" she wrote in the journal that she began just after meeting Fullerton and that she addressed to him, like a secret love letter, really almost a confession. "Oh, my free, proud, secure soul, where are you?"[16]

"She never lost the sense that what was to her the central crisis of experience must be a mere episode in a life so predestined as his to romantic incidents," Wharton noted dryly of the pair of lovers in "The Letters," a short story written in 1910.[17] She might have been describing her affair with Fullerton. Her awareness of the number and variety of romantic incidents in Fullerton's life kept her pinned in a painfully inferior position, especially when his ardor cooled and his attentions wandered. In her journal and in the letters she posted to Fullerton, she continually prostrates herself before "the lover I worshipped."[18] "I am so afraid—*so* afraid—of seeming to expect more than you can give, & of thus making my love for you less helpful to you, less what I wish it to be," she wrote at the beginning of the affair.[19] And in another letter: "You can't come into the room without my feeling all over me a ripple of flame . . . whenever you touch me . . . all the words in me seem to have become throbbing pulses, & all my thoughts are a great golden blur—."[20]

In an extraordinarily revealing letter written in the early days of their romance, Wharton confesses her fear that "the treasures" she wants to lay at Fullerton's feet will strike him as "familiar" trash: "I'm so afraid of this, that often & often I stuff my shining treasures back into their box, lest I should see you smiling at them!"[21] Wharton is terrified of appearing ridiculous in Fullerton's eyes, but even more in her own. And her terror leads her to cede all power to Fullerton: With a smile he can turn her treasures to trash. The stiff little girl whose mother and brothers laughed at her passion for making up stories now burns with shame over the awakening of her sexual passion. *"I'm so afraid . . ."*

All her life, Wharton had harbored a secret conviction that other women lived and loved "more richly and recklessly" than she, that she was doomed never to have "any warm personal life, like other, luckier people."[22] Hawthorne was also haunted by this shameful sense of being *different,* but perhaps because he was a man and managed to find an adoring wife, he was able to channel it without undue conflict into his art. For Wharton the anxiety that she was born with some sort of curse—the curse of being a woman "to whom *nothing had ever happened*"[23]—made her abase herself to Fullerton for redeeming her. Fullerton at a stroke reduced her life, and her work, to nothing. From a feminist perspective, their relationship was appalling.

One must, however, keep in mind that Wharton, despite the power and acuity with which she portrayed trapped and suffering women, was no feminist, and thus might have felt her humiliation less than we feel it for her. "She had no interest or belief in institutional reform," writes Lewis, "and rather shied away from literary women who did."[24] In simultaneously rejecting the ideology of feminism and dramatizing its origins, Wharton stands as a spiritual ancestor to Katherine Anne Porter, Eudora Welty, even Elizabeth Bishop—all of whom spoke out against feminism (or ignored it) while at the same time creating powerful feminist fictions: Porter most notably in "The Old Order" stories about a strong-willed grandmother who feels contempt for her menfolk; Welty in the matriarchal society of *Delta Wedding* and in her admiration for fiercely independent female teachers such as Miss Eckhart in "June Recital" and Julia Mortimer in *Losing Battles;* and Bishop in the savage poem "Pink Dog," which recounts, comically but heartbreakingly, the struggle of a mangy bitch to survive the violence and disease of Rio.

Lewis recounts the story of the Wharton–Fullerton affair in considerable detail, following the partners back and forth across the Atlantic, describing their clandestine meetings in Paris during the spring of 1908, and pinpointing the week in May when they consummated their love. James, by sheer coincidence, was on the scene for this crucial chapter of the story, having come to Paris from Lamb House to be Wharton's guest for two weeks in late April. Wharton, in the midst of her usual social maelstrom, took both James and Fullerton off in her automobile on May 2 to visit the old town of Beauvais. She confided afterward to the journal addressed to Fullerton: "Alone with you I am often shy and awkward, tormented by the fear that I may not please you—but with our dear H.J. I felt at my ease, and full of the 'motor-nonsense' that always seizes me after one of these long flights through the air."[25]

One can only speculate how much James surmised about the relationship unfolding literally before his eyes. It was *the* Jamesian situation—Chad and Madame de Vionnet, Prince Amerigo and Charlotte, Gilbert Osmond and Madame Merle—a hidden affair with unfathomable consequences. Did James *know* about Wharton and Fullerton, as Strether, Maggie Verver, and Isabel Archer gradually, excruciatingly come to *know* of the adulterous liaisons being conducted under their noses? If he did, he was, as one might expect, impeccably discreet about it. In any case, James did not have to endure his "rage of wonderment" very long, for that autumn, when Wharton was back at the Mount, she confided in him the increasing difficulty she was having with Teddy and also, possibly, the affair with Fullerton. Teddy, around the time of the Fullerton affair (and no doubt in part because of it), started going steadily off the deep end—his behavior became more and more erratic, vacillating wildly between euphoria and depression, and he became abusive toward his wife. Neurasthenia was the contemporary diagnosis. "Borderline psychosis" or "manic-depression" would probably be the term employed today. Edith was only too glad to pack her husband off on extended journeys and prolonged "cures" at various spas and watering holes. Curiously, she seems never to have recognized the possibility of a connection between Teddy's condition and her adultery, and she expressed little guilt about breaking her marriage vows. Perhaps after two decades of marital torpor, she felt a love affair was her due.

Deeply touched at being taken into Wharton's confidence and terribly upset at her situation, James despatched a fascinating letter advising her how best to weather the emotional storm:

Only sit tight yourself & *go through the movements of life.* That keeps up our connection with life—I mean of the immediate & apparent life; behind which, all the while, the deeper & darker and the unapparent, in which things *really* happen to us, learns, under that hygiene, to stay in its place. . . . Live it all through, every inch of it—out of it something valuable will come—but live it ever so quietly; &—*je maintiens mon dire*—waitingly![26]

The advice he gives here is central to his own code of both life and art: to keep "the deeper & darker" *down,* not by ignoring it, but by living "through" it in privacy. James here joins hands with Hawthorne and looks ahead to Bishop and Welty: All of them preferred to veil their inner darkness behind the "immediate & apparent life;" all of them believed in what Bishop called the "indirect approach" of masks, tropes, allegory, or myth when dealing with emotionally charged subjects.

James, for all his gnashing of teeth and racking of brain, was not above a bit of double-dealing in this affair. On the same day he wrote Wharton to "live it all through," he confided to their mutual friend Gaillard Lapsley, "Her arrangement of life is to me one of the prodigies of the time. I don't 'keep pace.' "[27] James would continue to vacillate between sympathy and skepticism as Wharton whirled from crisis to crisis.

As James penetrated deeper and deeper into the secrets of Wharton's heart over the next few months, a kind of voyeuristic relish crept into his tone: "Oh how I want your news, the real, the *intime*—" he begs her with comic exaggeration, "how I want it, how I want it! . . . The things, things, the things—i.e. the details—I yearn for—!"[28] This, of course, is meant to be funny, but one could make a serious case that voyeurism was James's primary form of sexual gratification. The snooping narrator of *The Sacred Fount* all but salivates over the sexual complications of his fellow guests ("I could cry over the ruins of such a talent," Wharton lamented when she read the book[29]); and the narrator of *The Aspern Papers* is also a rather creepy voyeur, albeit a literary one, a "publishing scoundrel" desperate to lay his hands on a packet of love letters. Lambert Strether is also something of a voyeur, though a much nobler and less willing one, since he spies at the behest of the stern (and wealthy) woman he loves.

James's peeping narrators and heroes are spiritual descendants of Hawthorne's Miles Coverdale—and in a sense of Hawthorne himself, for whom the role of Paul Pry had immense appeal. But James, in both his life and his work, takes hidden observation to a far higher pitch than Hawthorne: He and his characters peep not simply out of curiosity about the sexual practices of others, but as a *substitute* for sex.

James was to approach very near to "the real, the intime" that summer when Fullerton and Wharton met and traveled together in England. James traveled with them through the English countryside and he dined with them at the Charing Cross Hotel on June 4, 1909. When the meal ended, James went off to his club, and the lovers took a room together at the seedy railway hotel. Wharton commemorated their night of passion in her poem "Terminus":

> Wonderful was the long secret night you gave me, my
>   Lover,
> Palm to palm, breast to breast in the gloom.[30]

And so on for fifty more rolling Whitmanesque lines in which she juxtaposes the misery that numberless weary travelers have known in this "soot-sodden" room with the ecstasy that she and Fullerton experienced on "the low wide bed, as rutted and worn as a highroad." She later wrote to Fullerton of this summer, "during that month I have been completely happy. I have had everything in life that I ever longed for, & more than I ever imagined!"[31]

Fullerton left for a brief trip to the States after the night at the Charing Cross Hotel, but he was back in England in July, and the lovers were again with James, staying as his guests at Lamb House and motoring him off to Folkestone and Canterbury. Fullerton put a damper on this trip when he revealed to his friends the dire straits he was in due to complications in his love life. One of his former mistresses (her name and identity remain shrouded in obscurity) had somehow gotten hold of letters that implicated Fullerton in affairs with both Margaret Brooke and Ronald Gower, and she was using her discovery to blackmail him. Fullerton believed he could buy her off, but he lacked the means to do so. (Marion Mainwaring supplies the intriguing detail that this was no simple blackmail, since Fullerton might have borrowed the money his mistress was trying to get out of him. He later welshed on some debts to Wharton as well.[32])

Whatever the exact circumstances of the case, it was clear that some woman was making things extremely hot for Fullerton, and Wharton and James were commiserating and wringing their hands over his plight. James could wring his hands—eloquently, of course—forever, but Wharton characteristically took action. The bailout scheme she finally fixed on was as delicate and convoluted as the plot of a James novel. Wharton had been approached by the London publisher Frederick Macmillan to write a book about Paris, but pleading that she was too busy, she urged Macmillan to give the assignment—and the £100 advance—to Fullerton. Then she enlisted James as a kind of bagman to float Fullerton an additional £100 out of her own pocket: She would mail James a check for that amount and James in turn would send the money on to Macmillan and tell him to pay it out to Fullerton under the guise of increasing his fee for so important and commercially promising a project. In the event, Wharton did not have to draw on her own account for Macmillan offered to double Fullerton's advance on his own, provided that James stood as guarantor.

Lewis is absolutely convinced that Fullerton "had been privy to the plot from the outset" but this surely would have made the whole business a farce.[33] Also, if Fullerton knew about it, why would James write Wharton in high mock solemnity, "Of course I shall breathe, nor write, no shadow of a word of what I have been hearing from you to him" and why would he write Macmillan that he (James) wished to "remain wholly unmentioned in the affair"?[34] On the other hand, if Fullerton was *really* in the dark, how explain this passage in a letter from James to Wharton: "That he will *let* you do it will seem . . . almost as beautiful as that you should do it . . ."[35] There are abysses of darkness and mystery that we may never penetrate.

Whether or not Fullerton really knew that he owed the additional hundred pounds to the intervention of James and Wharton, and whether or not he cared, the plan succeeded. Fullerton took the money, he bought his letters back from his mistress, and recovered his peace of mind. He failed, however, to deliver the book he had promised to Macmillan; but luckily Macmillan did not try to recoup his loss. It would have been extremely awkward for James if he had.

●

Ultimately, the Fullerton rescue scheme proved to be more important for Wharton's friendship with James than for her relationship with Fullerton. Much as she adored Fullerton, Wharton eventually grew sick of the "aching uncertainty" of the relationship ("You write to me like a lover," she accused him near the end, "you treat me like a casual acquaintance! Which are you—what am I?"[36]), and by the summer of 1910 she had ceased to be his lover. Wharton chose to keep Fullerton as a friend, and to help him when she could with literary connections. They continued to correspond occasionally throughout her life.

After their collaboration in the Fullerton business, Wharton made a place for James in the small circle of truly intimate friends in whom she confided and on whom she relied. The friendship had passed beyond "motor-nonsense" to the "deeper & darker" level "in which things *really* happen." Wharton now knew how much weight their friendship was capable of bearing. Having trusted James with her darkest secret, she need keep nothing back.

Wharton's life grew more complicated, and more painful, over the next few years. In November 1909, she learned that Teddy, who was a trustee of her estate, had embezzled approximately fifty thousand dollars (a fortune by today's standards) of her money to buy an apartment in Boston for his mistresses and to speculate in unsound investments. It's unclear whether this was revenge for the Fullerton affair or an expression of his psychological derangement. Whatever the motive, it was devastating to Wharton. The situation of a husband's *pocketing* a wife's money at the same time that she was secretly trying to *give* some of it to her lover has all the cruel, punishing irony of a Wharton tale. Only now the author herself was the victim. And there was more: Teddy returned to her in a state of physical and psychological collapse, and Wharton, the betrayed and betraying wife, was forced to take on the role of nursemaid. Once again, sex and money had spilled from her books into her life.

Money, at last, was all that held husband and wife together ("my presence still seems associated in his mind solely with the idea of money," Edith wrote Teddy's brother[37]), and when she severed this connection by forcing Teddy to resign as co-trustee of her estate, the marriage collapsed. James, fortuitously, was present to witness one of the critical "scenes" that preceded the long drawn-out rupture. Ailing himself, he had accompanied his gravely ill brother William to America in August of 1910, and he remained in America for nearly a year after William died on August 26, 1910. In July 1911, during a spell of blistering weather, he paid a visit to Wharton at the Mount (the occasion of the sucked oranges, discussed above, when he quailed at her suggestion that he book an earlier boat to England to escape the heat). The friends had a few relatively idyllic days before Teddy arrived from one of his numerous cures.

His physical health was much improved, but mentally he was more off the rails than ever. Despite the presence of house guests (or perhaps because of them), Teddy began hurling violent accusations over the issue of his wife's estate. When he wasn't berating Edith, he was pathetically begging her forgiveness. She was frantic, but held firm to her position: Teddy must surrender his trusteeship and in exchange she would deposit five hundred dollars a month in his Boston bank account so that he could "maintain" himself and manage the Mount. "The violent and scenic Teddy is negotiable," James wrote to a mutual friend, "but the pleading, suffering, clinging, helpless Teddy is a very awful and irreducible quantity indeed." The disaster of this marriage left James "howl[ing] with an almost equal pity for both of them."[38]

The operatic domestic situation sent the Whartons' house guests flying, and James, who took shelter in Nahant, promptly wrote her that "you must *trancher* [make a break] at all costs."[39] He also advised her to sell the Mount, which in his opinion had become an "absolutely unworkable burden & complication." Wharton reluctantly agreed to the sale of her beloved country home by the end of the year, but the divorce from Teddy turned out to be a far more difficult and protracted business. The marriage limped along for nearly two more years, with uneasy reconciliations, a great deal of travel both together and apart (often on different continents), more violent scenes, and further revelations of Teddy's scandalous behavior with mistresses in France. Finally, as 1912 drew to a close, Wharton initiated the necessary legal steps and the divorce decree was issued on April 16, 1913, a day after James turned seventy.

James was unflagging in his devotion and his *interest* throughout this difficult time. "What types, what cases, what *hideurs* [hideousnesses], such situations throw up!" he wrote Wharton when her cousin arrived in France to begin assembling the evidence of Teddy's adulteries. "Planez, planez [soar, soar]—to find how one *can* is a magnificent resource."[40] He took, for once, the same line in letters *to* Wharton and *about* her—that divorce was "the only thing." James congratulated her on her "definite liberation" when he received word that she had succeeded at last and he promptly dispatched word to their mutual friends. "Teddy is now howling in space," he wrote jubilantly to Percy Lubbock.[41]

Edith's tone was far more restrained. Though she could jest about divorce in her fiction—"there was a divorce and a case of appendicitis in every family one knows," says the stately, rich, and blandly open-minded Judy Trenor in *The House of Mirth*[42]—the entire business was painfully humiliating when it happened to her. Divorce *was* certainly more tolerated, and more common, among society people in 1913 than it had been just a generation back. But Wharton, who had come of age at a time when the word *divorce* was not even *spoken* in proper drawing rooms, wondered anxiously whether the new laxness in morals would extend to her—and whether it *should*. "I wonder if she did not a bit hate herself" for going ahead with the divorce, writes Louis Auchincloss, a member of her social world. "To a woman of her intense conscience the price of freedom must have been terrible."[43]

In "Autres Temps . . . ," written on the eve of her divorce, she tells the sad story of Mrs. Lidcote, a divorced society lady who returns from her exile in Europe to stand by her daughter after *her* divorce, only to find that her daughter is perfectly "all right"—happily and richly remarried, visited by the best families—while she herself remains an outcast. The change of manners is not retroactive: "My case had been passed on and classified," wails Mrs. Lidcote. "I'm the woman who has been cut for nearly twenty years. The older people have half-forgotten why, and the younger ones have never really known: it's simply become a tradition to cut me. And traditions that have lost their meaning are the hardest of all to destroy."[44]

In the country as a whole, the numbers of divorced women age fifteen and over had crept up from 3.0 per thousand in 1890 to 4.7 per thousand in 1910—and a decade later would jump to 8.0 per thousand (as compared with 20.7 per thousand in 1988).[45] Though at the turn of the century divorce was more common among the lower classes (servants, actresses, circus performers),[46] it was more feasible for upper-class women like Wharton for the simple reason that they could *afford* to divorce. It wasn't until women acquired the education and job skills to support themselves and their children that divorce became a practical alternative for the less privileged. In Wharton's fictional world, divorce is a symptom of the retreat of the old guard of New York society before the onslaught of the crass, uncouth, valueless, and immensely wealthy nouveau riche—the "big money-makers from the West" who arrived in the 1880s and were soon reinforced by "the lords of Pittsburgh" as Wharton writes in her memoirs.[47] Undine Spragg in *The Custom of the Country,* the arriviste par excellence, acquires and discards husbands as casually as she does fur coats and jewels. Carry Fisher in *The House of Mirth* is another memorably divorced Wharton character—shallow, weak, and reduced to scheming to hang on to whatever respectable toehold (and living) society would grant her. Wharton abhorred being associated with such creatures (and their models in real life), and she abhorred the humiliation of public exposure. But her life with Teddy had become more abhorrent than any social embarrassment. By the end, she felt she had no choice.

Meanwhile, as Wharton's marriage dragged intolerably to its end, a serious disagreement roiled the smooth surface of her friendship with James. Before it blew over, the storm came close to severing their bond. Once again, money was the root of the trouble. James and Wharton's rivalry over money (and, by extension, over the commercial success of their work) was complicated by the fact that they were products of the same comfortably privileged old New York society (or, as Louis Auchincloss precisely fixes their social standing, "two intersecting circles of the same small *haute bourgeoisie*"—the intellectual James circle embracing "the arts and sciences" and the "more fashionable" Wharton circle that cared more for clothing, food, and sports[48]). Several generations back, their families had been distantly connected through business—Ebenezer Stevens, Wharton's great grandfather and a Revolutionary War hero, was the business partner of a relative by marriage of William James, Sr., Henry's grandfather. William James, the founder of the James family in America, was one of those titans who rose to the challenge of the virgin American republic. In 1789, at the age of eighteen, he migrated from Ireland to Albany with a few coins in his pocket; and over the next four decades, by dint of heroic industry and unfailing business acumen, he amassed a fortune that was commonly reckoned to be second only to that of John Jacob Astor.[49]

The James family fortune dissipated almost as quickly as it had been accumulated. Henry's father, also named Henry, supposedly breathed "leisured for life" when he came into his inheritance, and the eleven siblings, half siblings, niece, and nephew with whom he shared the fortune evidently had much the same attitude for none of them worked to increase their inherited wealth. "What had become of the spirit of the pioneers and the revolutionaries?" Wharton wonders in her memoirs as she contemplates the idle mild-mannered generation of her parents and James's father and uncles. "Perhaps the very violence of their effort had caused it to exhaust itself in the next generation. . . . Even the acquiring of wealth had ceased to interest the little society into which I was born."[50]

As they approached maturity, Henry Junior and his three brothers and sisters often wondered together what had become of their grandfather's "admirable three millions." Precious little of it came down to their generation. Henry did receive a monthly income from rents from Syracuse real estate (about $250 per month, which he shared with his brother William),[51] but this was by no means sufficient to make him "leisured for life." Unlike his father and his uncles, Henry James, Jr., had to work for a living.

James shared with Melville and Katherine Anne Porter (and to a lesser extent Elizabeth Bishop and Robert Lowell) the peculiar perspective of the heir of a family in decline. Though he never knew actual poverty, as Melville and Porter did, James certainly did know the embarrassment of having less money than he wanted, less than he had grown up with, and far less than many of his grand friends and "connexions" had. As an adult, James lived comfortably but modestly. By the time he met Edith Wharton, he had grown accustomed, but by no means reconciled, to seeing his earnings shrink. Like Melville, James had achieved his biggest financial success early in his career: *Daisy Miller* and *The Portrait of a Lady,* both written when he was in his thirties, were far more popular than *The Golden Bowl* or *The Ambassadors,* just as Melville's first novel, *Typee,* brought him far more recognition and cash than *Moby-Dick.* The black depression that seized James in the late winter of 1910 arose, at least in part, from his bitter disappointment over the sales of the so-called New York edition of his life's work on which he had staked such high hopes (from 1909 to 1911, the twenty-four books in the series earned only two thousand dollars).[52] Given this family background and personal history, it is little wonder, as Lewis notes, that "money, for evil or good, in actuality and in metaphor, so gripped the Jamesian imagination."[53]

One of James's last stories, "The Jolly Corner," is one of the most fascinating examples of just how violently money gripped his imagination. In the tale, an aging expatriate American named Spencer Brydon returns to New York to look after the houses he has inherited. He makes a lot of money by converting one house to a high-rise apartment building, but he cannot part with the other house, the "jolly corner" of the title, because it was the home in which he grew up. Night after night, Brydon returns alone to the untenanted house, obsessed with the "confronting presence" that he senses lurking there. On an all-night vigil he finally encounters this presence, which is a ghostly embodiment of what he himself *might have been* had he remained in New York to pile up money rather than moved to Europe to idle it away. At the climax of the story, Brydon retreats in horror before the apparition of his "other self"—an "evil, odious, blatant, vulgar" gentleman with stumps where two fingers had been shot away. Sick with the realization that this "stranger" possessed "a life larger than his own, a rage of personality before which his own collapsed," Brydon faints away. The idea that he might have had a "million a year" and a life of passion and action nearly destroys him. In the end, he recovers thanks to the ministrations of the devoted spinster Alice Staverton, a fellow survivor of old New York, and James breaks off with the two in each other's arms. The happy ending, however, cannot gloss over the tormenting question at the heart of the story: Has Brydon really wasted his life and his talents? Has he—has James himself—done anything to compensate for the loss of a "million a year"? Compared with the "admirable three millions" that his grandfather made, what is his own life worth? James wrote "The Jolly Corner" after his 1904 trip to America. The return to the scenes of his childhood inevitably raised the specter of the past—a specter that haunted him and *was* haunted with the vastness of a fortune won and lost.[54]

Edith Wharton's financial situation diverged sharply from Henry James's after their childhoods. Her father, like his, led a life of inherited leisure, with a house on Gramercy Park and another in Newport, Rhode Island. To economize when the post-Civil War depreciation of American currency considerably reduced his income, George Frederic Jones rented out the houses and took his young family to Europe, just as Henry James, Sr., had done for rather different reasons at frequent intervals during the 1840s and 1850s. Jones's economy measure worked for he, like most of his close relatives, managed to keep his wealth intact. When he died in 1882, he left his daughter, who was twenty years old, $20,000 outright and a one-third share in his estate, which spun off income of about $8,000 or $9,000 a year (multiply by about ten for the approximate current equivalent).[55] Teddy Wharton, whom she married in 1885, also came from a wealthy, leisured family, and though he had inherited no money, he could count on an allowance of $2,000 a year from his devoted parents. In 1888, Edith and Teddy were "leisured for life" when a remote eccentric and miserly relative of hers died and left her more than $120,000 in real estate and shares in Chemical Bank. Even before she published a word, Edith had enough money to buy two small adjoining town houses in Manhattan and a house on the ocean in Newport, and to travel wherever and whenever she wanted.

But the income from her inherited wealth paled beside the income she earned from her books. Wharton, almost from the very first, was a far more popular writer than James; and unlike James, she kept her audience as she matured. Not all of her books were best-sellers, but enough of them were to give her a queenly income nearly all her life. From 1905 to 1908, she earned about $22,000 a year from advances, serial rights, and royalties—James's writing, by comparison, brought him about $7,400 in 1909.[56] (In terms of *total* annual income, Edel says that Wharton was pulling in about five times what James earned in the early 1900s: $50,000 versus $10,000.[57])

Wharton's lavish style of living—the summer palace in the Berkshires, the chauffeur-driven cars, the apartment in Paris, the trips—would not have been possible without her writing. James knew this, and it was a constant source of vexation and jealousy. Odd as it may seem now, James was desperately hopeful to the end of his days that he would write another best-selling novel or a hit play. Each successive best-seller that Wharton produced rubbed salt in the wound of his comparative failure. James, for the most part, kept his jealousy in check or made light of it; but it may explain the faint breath of contempt in some of his letters to friends describing Wharton's extravagant exploits. As he wrote of her scornfully to Lapsley, "I can't help regretting . . . that an *intellectuelle*—and an Angel—should require such a big pecuniary basis. How much more consistently intellectual and angelic are *we* in our unmoneyed state."[58]

James and Wharton's near breach takes on more vivid colors when viewed against this financial/emotional background. Wharton, like many people accustomed to considerable wealth, had a rather myopic view of the fiscal situations of her friends, and with James her myopia approached blindness. This was not totally her fault. According to Edel, James enjoyed playing humble country squire to her great aristocratic lady, constantly (and ironically) comparing his lowly poverty with her exalted fathomless wealth. Who was to blame if she took this game more seriously than it was intended?

When James became seriously ill and suicidally depressed in early 1910, Wharton got it into her head that he was in dire straits financially and she rushed in to offer her assistance. "He has incessant preoccupations about money," she confided to Fullerton after seeing James in England. "He talked of it constantly. . . . I hope to induce him to let me arrange that matter for him."[59] James promptly, proudly, and emphatically refused to let her "arrange that matter": "really I am not—absolutely & positively not—in need," he insisted on February 2. Wharton evidently took offense at this brush-off for in his next letter James stammered out a tentative apology for "vulgarly speaking a little 'wounded,' or [having] a bit unduly disconcerted you by my poor (as yet) embarrassed & clumsy form of response to all your goodness. . . ."[60] Wharton had to content herself for the moment with making him a gift of heaps of grapes, but she had by no means abandoned her scheme of enriching James.

In 1911, she tried to secure the Nobel Prize (and its hefty cash honorarium) for him, but the judges ruled in favor of Maurice Maeterlinck. Wharton's concern for James's financial security turned to outright alarm after her brief descent on Lamb House during the summer of 1912. This time, she took direct action. She wrote her American publisher, Charles Scribner, instructing him to draw eight thousand dollars against her royalty account and pay this sum out to James in two installments as the advance for "an important American novel" that he was to undertake. It was the exact same ruse she and James had used a few years back with Fullerton, only this time the stakes were higher and the secrecy stricter. Though Scribner complained to her that this "fell purpose" made him feel "rather mean and caddish," he never breathed a word of it to James, who pocketed "with lively appreciation" the $3,600 he was entitled to on signing the contract ($400 went to his agent), the largest advance he had ever received.[61] He struggled intermittently in the final years of his life to write *The Ivory Tower,* but died before the book was completed. James went to the grave unaware that he had been the "victim" of Wharton's aggressive benevolence.

Wharton, however, did not let matters rest there. The year 1913 marked James's seventieth birthday, and Wharton organized a kind of subscription among his American friends to raise money for a hefty cash gift ("not less than $5000" she stipulated in the note she circulated to "a restricted number of his personal friends and admirers"[62]) to be presented on April 15. James's English friends had embarked on a similar subscription, though they discreetly limited the contributions to £5 a head; the English funds were used to purchase a golden bowl (a silver-gilt porringer) and to commission a portrait of James by John Singer Sargent (as Sargent refused to accept any fee, another commission was issued to the young English sculptor Derwent Wood). Wharton hoped that the far more lavish American birthday fund would be sufficient to allow James to buy a fine piece of old furniture or to "set up a motor" of his own. But it all came to grief.

James's nephews Harry and Billy (William's sons) learned of the scheme and informed their uncle indignantly, and James exploded in embarrassed humiliation. He cabled immediately to Billy "please express to individuals approached my horror money absolutely returned" and then wrote him more expansively: "A more reckless and indiscreet undertaking, with no ghost of preliminary leave asked, no hint of a sounding taken, I cannot possibly conceive." James also wrote a shattering rebuke to Wharton, who was traveling in Italy to recover from her divorce; though the letter has not survived, one can judge his severity by the impact it had on her. She wrote to Lapsley from La Spezia that her journey has been "poisoned" by James's reaction to the gift. "There was nothing on earth I valued as much as his affection—I can never get over this. . . . The idea that he pictures me as a meddling philanthropist is too intolerable."[63] Wharton had to return the money to the American donors with a stiff, shamefaced note about the "unfriendly misinterpretation of the nature and intention of the Birthday Gift."[64] For a while a serious rift seemed likely, but eventually both friends tacitly agreed to let the whole "unhappy Birthday enterprise," as Wharton called it, drop.

Wharton supplied an odd gloss on this episode—really on all her financial conflicts with James—two decades later when she published her memoirs. The portrait she draws of James in the book is for the most part affectionate, nostalgic, and fondly teasing; but when she got to the subject of James's attitudes toward money, she indulged herself in a rather wicked bit of cattiness. "At Lamb House," she writes, "an anxious frugality was combined with the wish that the usually solitary guest . . . should not suffer too greatly from the contrast between his or her supposed habits of luxury, and the privations imposed by the host's conviction that he was on the brink of ruin." She admits that James was generous to friends in need, but he stinted when it came to himself, for he was "haunted by the spectre of impoverishment." Her evocation of the same "dreary pudding or pie" served day after day "with its ravages unrepaired" is especially damning, though rather funny.[65]

Yet, in the light of Wharton's actions during James's lifetime, this portrait of the miser of Lamb House appears quite fantastic. If James, as she heavily implies, harbored neurotic delusions about his financial situation, if he was merely and absurdly miserly rather than in any real fiscal peril, then why did she take such pains to fill his coffers with her own gold? Edel notes that Wharton alone, of all James's guests, grumbled about the quality of his hospitality, an attitude he attributes to "failures in perception" on her part.[66] Wharton's immense wealth blinded her to the secure if a trifle threadbare comfort James enjoyed at Lamb House; arrogance deafened her to the mocking tone that James adopted whenever he had to entertain her there.

The truth is that James *did* fuss unnecessarily about money, especially to Wharton and *about* Wharton (she "consumes the world as you and I . . . consume apples," he complained to a friend after one of her visitations to Lamb House. "She uses up everything and every one"[67]) and that Wharton, perhaps a bit defensive about her comparative opulence, took his fussing seriously and moved grandly to eliminate its cause. James's fussing itself might well have had a sour competitive edge to it—as indeed what writer of moderate means and dwindling royalties could avoid feeling sour in the company of so rich and so successful a colleague as

Edith Wharton? Wharton's blunder was to misinterpret James's irony, and she paid dearly for it.

Wharton's prime motive in coming to the rescue of Fullerton and James was generosity, but there was a taint of selfishness too, a desire to glorify herself—and to control the men. She liked the idea of incurring obligations, even unknown obligations. And she liked the boldness and the flashy originality of the gesture. It was just a touch risqué for the world of fashion (proper matrons might support the *arts* but not by writing checks to artists). Fullerton might have squirmed a bit, though in the end he pocketed the cash, but with James her calculations were seriously off. Above all, she failed to reckon with the large sum of his pride. Wharton had trespassed on some inviolable inner chamber of the self, the chamber where he kept the secrets of money and power and sex. James exposed the secrets in his art, as Wharton did herself. But he would not tolerate having the glaring light trained on his own life. In James's story "The Bench of Desolation," the shabby bookseller Herbert Dodd knows to the last shilling the price that has been fixed to his dignity, and he pays it out until he is literally bled dry. James himself commanded far vaster resources. He alone would hold the keys to his inner chamber. No one must enter. No one must know. To accept a large sum of cash raised by Edith Wharton would be to surrender a share of his privacy. He would sooner die.

The incident of the seventieth birthday gift points up the limits of the James and Wharton friendship—perhaps one of the limits of friendship itself. Gift giving, as the critic Ronald A. Sharp has explored, is one of the essential forms of friendship; yet a true gift is not a form of charity or relief, but a tribute to shared feelings and common sensibilities. Melville's dedication of *Moby-Dick* to Hawthorne; the little French trinkets that Eudora Welty picked up for Katherine Anne Porter in New Orleans when France fell to the Germans during the Second World War; the *ex-voto* carved head that Bishop sent to Lowell when he was recovering from a mental breakdown—these are among the true gifts of friendship. Their value derives not from their cost but from their affirmation of what the friends hold in common. Wharton's seventieth birthday present to James was not a gift in this spirit for a gift of cash, no matter how well intended, can never have any meaning beyond the size of the sum. Wharton knew all too well how money changes everything in sexual relationships. She had learned this lesson, bitterly, painfully, in her life and she expounded it beautifully in her fiction. But James taught her that the lesson applied as much to friendship as to love. In the three years that remained to them, Wharton refrained from further bequests.

"The great thing is that we always tumble together—more & more never apart," James wrote Wharton to smooth over his refusal of the first sum she offered him, back in the winter of 1910 when he was so ill; "& that for that happy exercise & sweet coincidence of agility we may trust ourselves & each other to the end of time."[68] After the embarrassment of the birthday gift, *that* was the note that sustained and deepened their friendship in its final years.

SEVEN

Literary Rough and Tumbles

Art is long & everything else is accidental & unimportant.

—HENRY JAMES *to Edith Wharton,*
January 7, 1908

I had never doubted Henry James was great, though how great I could not guess till I came to know the man as well as I did his books.

—EDITH WHARTON, A Backward Glance

OVER THE THIRTEEN YEARS of their relationship, James and Wharton came to cherish each other as friends, but strangely enough, they never fully understood or appreciated each other as writers. If anything, their friendship endured and flourished *despite* their work. Melville and Hawthorne, Welty and Porter, Bishop and Lowell all at times resented each other's successes and disparaged aspects of each other's works—but for all of them, the work was essential to the life of friendship, was indeed its *raison d'être*. This was definitely not the case for James and Wharton. Though their fellowship in the craft of fiction brought them together in the first place, it became over the years a recurrent source of unease, embarrassment, and rivalry between them, and both of them intensely disliked seeing their names paired as kindred artists. Theirs was a rich literary friendship in that they loved talking about and sharing books, but only when the books were written by someone else.

Wharton was positively obtuse in her readings of James, especially once he adopted the dense, convoluted, intricately associative manner of his later style. "He . . . talks, thank heaven, more lucidly than he writes" was her relieved comment to William Crary Brownell (her Scribner's editor) after her first real meeting with James over lunch on a dark London December afternoon in 1903;[1] and she later confessed frankly, even proudly, to Brownell that she couldn't read anything James wrote after 1894. (She knew she was on safe ground here, for Brownell, despite the fact that he was also James's editor, disliked the later style as much as she and published an article in the *Atlantic* in 1905 attacking it.) Many other readers, including James's older brother William, shared their frustration with his ever-lengthening, parenthesis-ridden sentences. "Say it *out* for God's sake and have done with it," William once thundered in irritation at Henry after struggling through some of his denser passages.[2] In her memoirs, written seventeen years after James's death, Wharton is still railing against James's last novels. She couches her attack in the form of a snide anecdote about James's "morbidly delicate sensibility":

> His latest novels, for all their profound moral beauty, seemed to me more and more lacking in atmosphere, more and more severed from that thick nourishing human air in which we all live and move. . . . Preoccupied by this, I one day said to him: "What was your idea in suspending the four principal characters in 'The Golden Bowl' in the void? What sort of life did they lead when they were not watching each other, and fencing with each other? Why have you stripped them of all the *human fringes* we necessarily trail after us through life?"
>
> He looked at me in surprise, and I saw at once that the surprise was painful, and wished I had not spoken. . . . But after a pause of reflection he answered in a disturbed voice: "My dear—I didn't know I had!" and I saw that my question, instead of starting one of our absorbing literary discussions, had only turned his startled attention on a peculiarity of which he had been completely unconscious.[3]

Wharton goes on to insist graciously that James's "sensitiveness to criticism" arose from his bitter disappointment over the failure of his mature work to sell as well as *Daisy Miller* and *The Portrait of a Lady* had. "[T]he sense of protracted failure made him miserably alive to the least hint of criticism," she writes, "even from those who most completely understood, and sympathized with, his later experiments in technique and style."[4]

Though Wharton tries to imply that she belonged to this latter group of distinguished savants, she in fact was one of the vulgar pack of readers who had failed to progress beyond *Daisy Miller*—a pack that numbered most of the daily newspaper reviewers of the day. Brownell sneered in his critical essay about James, "He has never, at any rate, yielded to the temptation to give the public what it wanted."[5] But posterity has, of course, given James the last laugh.

Since Wharton disliked James's later style, it's hardly surprising that she resented having her own work compared with his. The charge of being "the heir of Henry James" or the "pupil of James" or "James and water" haunted her throughout her literary career, especially at its debut. As Millicent Bell shows in her study of the writers' friendship, nearly all the reviewers of Wharton's first short story collection (*The Greater Inclination*, published in 1899) found her guilty of copying James—a rather serious offense at a time when critical opinion, particularly in America, had turned sharply against James. "If imitation is indeed the sincerest form of flattery," the reviewer in the *Philadelphia Telegraph* wrote, "Mr. Henry James must regard himself complimented in the highest degree in the appearance of this book." Perhaps the only reviewer she could forgive was the one who called her "a masculine Henry James."[6]

The fact that the charge of imitating James was largely without grounds made it all the more galling. Yes, Wharton's characters move in roughly the same social sphere as James's—just as she herself did. And yes, she followed James's example in working the "international theme," just as she followed his example in moving abroad. But in their work these are really only superficial resemblances. In style, and above all in vision, Wharton and James were utterly distinct. Wharton in her memoirs described James as "essentially a novelist of manners" but the tag fit her own work far better.[7] At least as early as *The Portrait of a Lady*, James had worked a far deeper psychological vein than Wharton ever reached.

Think of *The House of Mirth* next to *The Portrait of a Lady:* Both concern the plight of attractive, spirited, well-born young women of limited means and both unfold against the backdrop of great houses, magnificent gardens, wealth, and leisure. Sex and money and power set the plots of both books in motion. Yet *Mirth* is at heart a novel about how the social monster, as James called it, must inevitably crush an individual—a woman—who fails to abide by its rules. By the novel's end, we have learned far more about the anatomy of the monster—the clothing and architecture and diction and codes of behavior that separate class from class, the migration and breeding patterns of rich New Yorkers, the financial and erotic privileges that "ladies" acquire when they marry, the penalties inflicted on unmarried "girls" when they attempt to slip out of the "great gilt cage"—than we have about the mind or motives of Lily Bart. We know practically everything we will ever know (or need to know) about Lily from the first scene in which she appears in Grand Central Station looking "radiant" but not "new" and proceeds to flout convention by visiting Lawrence Selden in his rooms.

Portrait, on the other hand, is fundamentally not about how people in society behave but what they *know*. Isabel's fate hangs on the relationships between knowledge and corruption, knowledge and power, knowledge and pain. The more she knows, the more she suffers—yet knowing is the only way to live fully, deeply *into* her life. We glimpse, in the course of *Portrait,* the country house society of English aristocracy and the expatriate communities of Paris, Florence, and Rome. But what we *know* best, by the novel's end, is the mind and the character and the passions of its heroine.

By the late phase—in such masterpieces as *The Ambassadors, The Wings of the Dove, The Golden Bowl*—James was really writing about consciousness in a social setting. The manners and customs of "the little vanishing group of people" whom Wharton claimed he chose as his subjects were only a springboard into his dark voyage to the interior. Wharton for the most part remained very brilliantly content to stop at the threshold. She learned something about moral shadings and the choice of rich and yielding "situations" from James and on several occasions she adopted his narrative technique employing a "center of consciousness"; but deep down they belonged to different breeds. In her gift for satire and social observation, Wharton is kin to Dreiser, Sinclair Lewis, and Fitzgerald. In her depiction of the passionate individual trapped and sexually thwarted by deadly social codes, she anticipates E. M. Forster and, more faintly, Katherine Anne Porter. We read Wharton's books to find out what happens, to see how it all hangs together, to revel in the charming oddness of the past; and part of their pleasure is that the follies and the sufferings of the rich are, for some reason, more engrossing than those of the middle and lower classes. We read James not for the plot, nor even principally for the style, highly polished though it often is, but because he opens for us, magnificently wide, a window on the workings of the mind.

Despite her irritation at seeing herself described in reviews as an imitator of James's style, Wharton was eager to make her work known to James himself. Even before they became acquainted, Wharton sent James her first volume of stories when it appeared in 1899, and the following year she sent him a story, "The Line of Least Resistance," that she had just published in *Lippincott's Magazine*. The first surviving item in their correspondence is the letter James wrote her in October 1900 to thank her for her "brilliant little tale" about a rich Newport husband who agrees out of cowardice and stupidity to become reconciled with his unfaithful wife. James, in his characteristic fashion, begins by carefully praising the story's "admirable sharpness & neatness & infinite wit & point" and then proceeds to shoot a few poisoned arrows of criticism: "[T]he *Lippincott* tale is a little *hard,* a little purely derisive. . . . It *is* a needle-point!"[8]
Wharton was so upset by this criticism that she instructed Brownell to remove the story from her forthcoming collection. In her memoirs she gives further evidence of how acutely sensitive she was to James's "irresistible tendency to speak the truth" about her literary efforts. Though she tries hard to sound a note of fond amusement over James's "tiptoe malices," she clearly did not relish being their victim. Once, during one of his visits to the Mount, Teddy asked James whether he had seen Edith's new story in *Scribner's Magazine*. James replied:

> "Oh, yes, my dear Edward, I've read the little work—of course I've read it." A gentle pause, which I knew boded no good; then he softly continued: "Admirable, admirable; a masterly little achievement." He turned to me, full of a terrifying be-

nevolence. "Of course so accomplished a mistress of the art would not, without deliberate intention, have given the tale so curiously conventional a treatment. Though indeed, in the given case, no treatment *but* the conventional was possible; which might conceivably, my dear lady, on further consideration, have led you to reject your subject as—er—in itself a totally unsuitable one."[9]

Another time when James was staying at Wharton's Paris apartment, someone asked him in her presence about a short story she had written in French. "I do congratulate you, my dear," James said, his eyes twinkling wickedly, "on the way in which you've picked up every old worn-out literary phrase that's been lying about the streets of Paris for the last twenty years, and managed to pack them all into those few pages."[10]

Wharton goes on to insist that she really enjoyed these "literary rough-and-tumbles" with James, but surely this is a touch disingenuous, for if she hadn't been stung by James's remarks, she certainly would not have remembered them in such detail for all those years.

James dished out another serving of "the whole truth" in his second letter to Wharton, written in response to her first full-length novel, *The Valley of Decision,* a long and rather cumbersome historical novel set in eighteenth-century Italy. Again he praises the book first, calling it "a serious & achieved work of art," and though "there is a thing or two I should like to say" in criticism, he will reserve them for a face-to-face encounter. (Considering that he wrote Sarah Orne Jewett about her *The Tory Lover* that "the 'historic' novel is, for me, condemned, even in cases of labour as delicate as yours, to a fatal *cheapness,*"[11] James has let Wharton off very gently.) Instead of dismembering *The Valley of Decision,* James offers Wharton some very blunt advice about her literary future, admonishing her to forgo Europe "in favour of the *American Subject.*"

> There it is round you. Don't pass it by—the immediate, the real, the ours, the yours, the novelist's that it waits for. Take hold of it & keep hold, & let it pull you where it will. . . . What I would say in a word is: Profit, be warned, by my awful example of exile & ignorance. . . . DO NEW YORK! The 1st-hand account is precious.[12]

A few days later, he wrote even more colorfully in the same vein to Mary Cadwalader Jones, a connection he and Wharton had in common (Mrs. Jones had been married to Wharton's brother, Frederic, and the two women remained devoted to each other even after the marriage ended; James and "Minnie" Jones had become friends years before in New York). Jones had sent James two of Wharton's early literary efforts, *Crucial Instances*, her second collection of stories, and *The Touchstone,* a short novel published in 1900. After thanking her for the "valued missives," James directed his attention to their author:

> I take to her very kindly as regards her diabolical little cleverness, the quantity of intention and intelligence in her style, and her sharp eye for an interesting *kind* of subject. . . . [These two books have] made me, again, as I hinted to you other things had, want to get hold of the little lady and pump the pure essence of my wisdom and experience into her. She *must* be tethered in native pastures, even if it reduce her to backyard in New York. If a work of imagination, of fiction, interests me at all (and very few, alas, do!) I always want to write it over in my own way, handle the subject from my own sense of it. . . . But I can't speak more highly for any book, or at least for my interest in any. I take liberties with the greatest.[13]

The diabolical "little lady" was, as James would soon enough discover for himself, hardly the type to submit to being tethered or having essences pumped into her, even such pure essence as flowed from the mind of Henry James. Nor would she ever prove receptive to his impulse to write her stories over "in my own way." Indeed, this impulse, Wharton felt, seriously impaired James's literary judgment, blinding him to the merits of works unlike his own. James, in time and with deepening personal regard, would descend a few steps from the Olympian heights in his literary dealings with Wharton. And Wharton would learn to take his lofty pronouncements and tiptoe malices with a grain of salt. But rough and tumble remained to the end the "note" of their literary relationship. Ironically, though Wharton was a most unwilling "pupil," she proved at least some of the Master's advice to be quite sound. She did, in fact, perform most brilliantly when she "did" New York—in *The House of Mirth* (written in 1905, just a couple of years after James proposed tethering her in native pastures), in the early sections of *The Custom of the Country* (1913), and later, after his death, in *The Age of Innocence* (1920). And *Ethan Frome* (1911) was tethered quite literally in native pastures.

Through the years of their friendship, James continued to read Wharton's novels and stories with "the highest sympathy, highest criticism, highest consideration & generally most intimate participation" as he put it,[14] and he continued to judge them according to how closely they adhered to his own tastes and principles. Thus he found fault with *The House of Mirth,* despite the fact it does New York "with a high, strong hand & an admirable touch," for being "better written than composed"—that is, for lacking the "architecture" that he found so essential in a work of fiction. It rambled where, in his view, it should have circled; it chronicled where it should have shaped. In short, it wasn't sufficiently Jamesian. *The Custom of the Country* was even less so.

Wharton recounts in her memoirs how James, after generously praising this book, abruptly and "irrepressibly" launched into an attack of her total failure to perceive that the true subject of the work should have been the encounter between her "crude young" American heroine, the gold-digging social-climbing Undine Spragg, and "the mysterious labyrinth of family life in the old French aristocracy." Wharton argued back that her idea in *The Custom* was to chronicle "the career of a particular young woman," but James did not buy it. Since in the novel he "cared only for the elaborate working out on all sides of a central situation," as Wharton puts it, he simply could not see *The Custom* as a true novel.[15] Again, James failed to perceive or appreciate that Wharton's strengths were distinctly different from his own.

He was far more enthusiastic about *The Reef* (1912), predictably enough, since this was Wharton's most Jamesian effort (and, also predictably, one of the least popular in her day). It's worth quoting his response to the novel at length because it is so revealing of the way his mind played over a work of art, reading his own concerns into it, turning it over and over imaginatively until he has made it *his,* until, indeed, he practically feels that he has written it himself.

> The whole of the finest part is, I think, quite the finest thing you have done; both *more* done than even the best of your other doing, and more worth it through intrinsic value, interest and beauty. . . .

Each of these two figures [Anna Leath and George Darrow] is admirable for truth and justesse; the woman an exquisite thing and with her characteristic finest, scarce differentiated notes (that is some of them) sounded with a wonder of delicacy. I'm not sure her oscillations are not beyond our notation; yet they are all so held in your hand, so felt and known and shown, and everything seems so to come of itself. . . . Anna is really of Racine and one presently begins to feel her throughout as an Eriphyle [sic] or a Berenice: which, by the way, helps to account a little for something que me chiffonne [that rankles me] throughout; which is why the whole thing, unrelated and unreferred save in the most superficial way to its milieu and background, and to any determining or qualifying *entourage,* takes place comme cela, and in a specified, localised way, in France—these non-French people "electing," as it were, to have their story out there. . . . [After comparing her favorably with "the good George Eliot," he notes that] your only drawback is not having the homeliness and the inevitability and the happy limitation and the affluent poverty, of a Country of your Own (comme moi pour example!). It makes you, this does, as you exquisitely say of somebody or something at some moment, elegiac . . . but leaves you more in the desert (for everything else) that surrounds Apex City [the Kansas town that Undine Spragg hails from].[16]

This is the most marvelous mixture of penetrating insight and myopic misreading. James's description of the book as "Racinian" is brilliant. He gets at the heart of the matter when he questions why the story had to be set in France. And he is superb when he points out that Wharton's "only drawback is not having the homeliness and the inevitability and the happy limitation and the affluent poverty, of a Country of your Own"—a remark that inadvertently sheds light on the shortcomings of some of his own works, particularly those set in England and populated by English characters, such as *The Awkward Age, The Sacred Fount,* and *The Outcry,* all of which lack the moral complexity and depth of his stories about Americans at home and abroad.

James is also right in noting that "the situation" between Anna Leath and George Darrow is "more gone into . . . than anything you have done"—yet far from being a strength, it is precisely this "going into" that drags the novel down. *The Reef* opens promisingly enough with the brief, chance, half-hearted Parisian fling between George Darrow, an early middle-aged American diplomat who believes himself to have been unceremoniously rejected by his fiancée (Anna Leath), and Sophy Viner, a young, blooming, worldly American girl of limited means and strong desires who finds herself "between situations." After unfolding this affair from Darrow's point of view, Wharton shifts the center of consciousness to Anna, just as James had done in "The Prince" and "The Princess" sections of *The Golden Bowl*. She moves the action from the tawdry damp hotel in Paris to château Givré, and it is here that *The Reef* stalls out.

Wharton, following James's example deliberately or not, belabors in exquisite detail what he calls Anna's "oscillations"—her widening and deepening knowledge about the true relationship between Darrow (who comes to stay at Givré after a reconciliation) and her daughter's governess (who turns out to be none other than Sophy Viner) and her attendant scruples about whether or not she can live with such knowledge. James was able to take a similar situation—most notably in *The Golden Bowl*—and infuse it with a high interior drama, an all-encompassing significance that transcends the sordidness of the plot (which is, after all, the rankest soap opera about a daughter and her father ignorantly marrying a pair of lovers and then unwittingly encouraging them to resume their affair). But in Wharton's hands, the situation slowly dies of starvation. Nothing about Anna's crisis with Darrow and Sophy Viner is as compelling as Wharton's deft introductory sketch of her background and character—her painful girlhood awareness of being different from the bland old New York society she was born into, where "the unusual was regarded as either immoral or ill-bred"; her sense of being shut out of "some vital secret" that made "normal" girls far more confident than she; and her passionless marriage to Fraser Leath, a kind of declawed Gilbert Osmond who occupies himself collecting antique snuff boxes and "formulating the conventions of the unconventional," but who has, at least, the decency to die young.[17]

R. W. B. Lewis writes that "in the presentation of Anna Leath, Edith Wharton almost literally began to write her autobiography."[18] Lewis also finds parallels between Darrow's Paris fling with Sophy Viner and Wharton's night of passion with Morton Fullerton at London's Charing Cross Hotel in June 1909. Though Lewis fails to mention it, there is also a striking resemblance between Darrow and Fullerton: Both feature a certain moral and sexual slipperiness, conveniently short memories of their emotional entanglements, a facility at deception, great personal charm, and "promise" that they are doomed never to fulfill.

By the end of the novel, Anna has "explored the intricacies and darknesses of her own heart . . . [and] she knew now—knew weaknesses and strengths she had not dreamed of, and the deep discord and still deeper complicities between what thought in her and what blindly wanted . . ."[19] But Anna fails to progress beyond the discord and the complicities. The real problem with *The Reef* is that by the final scene, the reader has ceased to care. Ultimately, *The Reef* is a Jamesian novel that suffers from not being Jamesian enough: Wharton fails to delve sufficiently deep into what James called "the soil of consequence." Wharton's real talents lay elsewhere—in what she called the chronicle novel, in satire, plotting, in exposing the social and sexual imprisonment of women. Wharton herself had extremely mixed feelings about *The Reef,* confessing to Bernard Berenson that she was "sick" about it and insisting that "it's not *me,* though I thought it was when I was writing it."[20] In her oeuvre, the novel stands as an interesting experiment that she wisely never repeated.

It no doubt struck Wharton, who always had a keen interest in the sales and marketing of her books, that the one novel of hers that James singled out for elaborate praise sold just about as poorly as the Master's own books did at the time. Appleton, her new publisher, paid her an advance of $15,000 for the book, three times more than Scribner's had ever laid out for one of her novels, but sales barely went over 7,000 copies.[21] With her next novel, however, *The Custom of the Country,* Wharton recaptured her audience, selling 60,000 copies within a few months of publication (*The House of Mirth,* by comparison, sold 140,000 copies in its first three months). James, casting a greedy eye on Wharton's heaping royalties, was not so mean-spirited as to criticize her *because* she outsold him. But envy might well have been a factor in his skewed readings of her work. He simply couldn't see—or didn't want to—that what made her popular was also what made her good.

James and Wharton, with their difficulties over each other's work, rarely wrote about each other for publication. Wharton did have a "finger," as she put it, in the composition of Morton Fullerton's laudatory article about the massive reissue and—in some cases—rewriting of James's finest work, known as the New York Edition, and she pushed hard to get *Scribner's Magazine* to run it. "I want very much to have a ringing word said for H.J. just now," she wrote to Edward L. Burlingame, the editor of *Scribner's Magazine*, in February 1908, and a month later: "I *long* so to have someone speak intelligently and resolutely for James."[22] Her desire to enrich James by boosting his sales proved stronger than her personal distaste for the later style. She might have known, however, that Scribner's would refuse the Fullerton piece, given how low James's stock had sunk there. The essay eventually ran in the April 1910 issue of the English publication *Quarterly Review*. After reading the Fullerton–Wharton hosannas of praise in manuscript, James told Wharton he felt "embarrassed . . . fairly to anguish,"[23] though that didn't stop him from "rejoicing" when the piece was Americanized and reprinted in Boston's *Living Age* in June.

Around the same time that Wharton was midwifing Fullerton's essay, James was considering writing a laudatory essay about her to mark the publication of her new novel, *The Fruit of the Tree*. The incident, which supplied the "germ" for the story "The Velvet Glove" (see above), is curious in the extreme. The American publisher of an obscure Socialist journal had written to James claiming that Wharton had expressed a wish that he write something about her. James, dubious about the undertaking, asked Wharton for verification, whereupon she flatly denied any involvement. Rather than let the whole thing slide, James told Wharton he wanted to proceed with the essay, but only, of course, with due caution. "As the matter stands," he wrote her, "the seed having been dropped, by however crooked a *geste*, into my mind, I am conscious of a lively & spontaneous disposition to really dedicate a few lucid remarks to the mystery of your genius. . . ."[24] (Wharton nervously joked to a friend that it looked "as if he meant to make mince-meat of me."[25])

In the event, however, James chose not to nurture the dropped seed to germination. "I don't feel that I can 'enthuse' over you in a hole-&-corner publication," he wrote her a few weeks later. "It doesn't seem to me the proper place of either of us. . . ." Perhaps more to the point, as he goes on to say, is that he has finally sat down and read her new novel, *The Fruit of the Tree*, straight through "with acute appreciation" (one can practically feel Wharton's jaw tense up) and he feels compelled to inform her that he deems it "a thing" of "a great deal of (though not perhaps of a completely) superior art."[26] James acknowledges that he bores her by harping on the "terrible question" of composition, but for him it was always *the* question about a work of art, and Wharton's not completely superior art was no exception. Clearly, his polite protests notwithstanding, James refrained from "enthusing" over Wharton in print because he could not enthuse enough.

James did dedicate himself to the mystery of Wharton's genius once—and only once—in an essay called "The New Novel" published in the London *Times Literary Supplement* in 1914. After glancing critically (and rather obtusely, for him) at the "looseness" and lack of "method" in the works of a number of contemporary novelists, including Arnold Bennett, Joseph Conrad, D. H. Lawrence, and H. G. Wells, he singled out Wharton for special praise, citing the superiority of her *The Custom of the Country* to other "slice of life" novels:

> "The Custom of the Country" is . . . consistently, almost scientifically satiric, as indeed the satiric light was doubtless the only one in which the elements engaged could at all be focussed together. But this happens directly to the profit of something that, as we read, becomes more and more one with the principle of authority at work; the light that gathers is a dry light, of great intensity, and the effect, if not rather the very essence of its dryness is a particular fine asperity. The usual "creative" conditions and associations, as we have elsewhere languished among them, are thanks to this ever so sensibly altered; the general authoritative relation attested becomes clear—we move in an air purged at a stroke of the old sentimental and romantic values, the perversions with the maximum waste of perversions, and we shall not here attempt to state what this makes for in the way of esthetic refreshment and relief . . .

James ends by justifying Wharton's "shade of asperity" as an essential aspect of her "rare identity." This he characterizes aptly as "the hard intellectual touch in the soft, or call it perhaps the humid temperamental air; in other words of the masculine conclusion tending so to crown the feminine observation."[27]

Though Millicent Bell feels that James's piece has "just a

little flavor of being a complimentary gesture" written to bolster Wharton in the year of her divorce,[28] it contains nonetheless some shrewd commentary not only on the tone and color of *The Custom of the Country* but also on the distinctive style of its author. Dry—or the French *seche,* which sounds so much more withered—is a word that James used on several occasions to describe Wharton. "A dry light of great intensity" was exactly the kind of illumination that Edith Wharton shed, especially in the presence of the vague dim gleams and golden shafts that emanated from James. As the years passed—and in 1914, when he wrote this essay, only two years remained to him—James came to appreciate and value Wharton's dryness and intensity more and more. If her art, in his view, was not completely superior, she more than made up for it by the superiority of her life. Wharton felt exactly the same way. For both of them, the life ultimately took precedence over the work. They valued each other that much.

EIGHT

Little Old New York

*New York ... never changed without changing for
the worse ...*

—EDITH WHARTON, *The Age of Innocence*

"THE TRUTH IS that he belonged irrevocably to the old America
out of which I also came," Wharton wrote of James in her memoirs.[1] What she really meant, of course, was the old New York,
where less than a mile separated the homes of their birth (James on
April 15, 1843, at 21 Washington Place; Wharton on January 24,
1862, on West Twenty-third Street near Fifth Avenue). Although,
as Leon Edel accurately notes, they "belonged to two different
periods of Manhattan's history,"[2] nonetheless, their childhoods in
"Little Old New York," as James persisted in calling it, gave them
a considerable expanse of common ground, both in their friendship and, in a special way, in their work. Their circles and their
memories overlapped, and so did their attitudes toward the city—a

funny mix of satirical contempt, outright disgust, and nostalgia. Like their common sense of humor, New York was something they understood implicitly, instinctively about each other. The New York background was a bass note that echoed back and forth between their fictions—one of the few notes they sounded repeatedly together.

It was a note first and foremost of antipathy. "He hated the place," Wharton insisted in her memoirs of James and New York; "its aimless ugliness, its noisy irrelevance, wore on his nerves."[3] Wharton was referring here to the New York of 1904, the "terrible town" that James described with such wonder and revulsion in *The American Scene,* the record of his return to the land of his birth after an absence of nearly a quarter century. James devoted the better part of four chapters of *The American Scene* to explaining how and why he hated what New York had become since he had seen it last. He despised first "that concert of the expensively provisional into which your supreme sense of New York resolves itself";[4] he was alarmed at the "bigness and bravery and insolence, especially, of everything that rushed and shrieked"; he despaired of the glossy Fifth Avenue mansions of the robber barons (a "record, in the last analysis, of individual loneliness"); and he cringed at hearing the Lower East Side immigrants mangle his native tongue.[5] But what pained him most deeply and most personally was the way this roaring, soaring, mechanized megalopolis had "so violently overpainted" the New York of his "extremest youth."

In *A Small Boy and Others,* the first volume of his autobiography written six years after *The American Scene,* James repaints with fond condescending memory "the small warm dusky homogenous New York world of the mid-century" that he had known as a boy. Manhattan, back in those days, was urbanized only as far north as Twentieth Street: Above this there were farms, country houses, and woods (Harlem was frequented by hunters for its abundant woodcock, snipe, and rabbit). At its uptown fringes the "city began to assume a theoretic air," as James wrote of midcentury Manhattan in *Washington Square,* "where poplars grew beside the pavement (when there was one) . . . and where pigs and chickens disported themselves in the gutter."[6] In James's rose-colored recollections, this long narrow island city was a scruffy, comfortable, unpretentious outpost at the edge of a varnished, golden-hazed "wilderness" landscape done in the style of the Hudson River School.

James recalls walking as a lad past a large brown house that stood on Eighteenth Street surrounded by "grounds" in which there roamed "two or three elegant little cows of refined form and colour, two or three nibbling fawns and a large company, above all, of peacocks and guineafowl." He lovingly describes the consumption of fruit, in particular "peaches big and peaches small, peaches white and peaches yellow" as one of the chief social occupations of this innocent society: "What did the stacked boxes and baskets of our youth represent but the boundless fruitage of that more bucolic age of the American world, and what was after all of so strong an assault as the rankness of such a harvest?"[7] (It's fascinating that Melville in *Pierre* described almost exactly the same section of Manhattan at almost exactly the same time period as a dismal, dirty, dangerous, Dickensian urban hell peopled by drunks, whores, cheating cabdrivers, foppish gentlemen, money-hungry editors, and shabby little artists.)

The cityscape, customs, and traditions of this "familiarly fruit-eating time" all but vanished in the course of the next half century. In fact, James's life coincided almost exactly with one of the greatest explosions of urban growth in the history of civilization. By the 1860s, when Wharton was a child, the city had climbed up to Fiftieth Street; the population jumped from 312,710 in 1840 to 814,000 in 1860 (and later to 1,441,216 in 1890 and 3,437,202 in 1900—this last figure reflects the consolidation of the five boroughs into greater New York in 1898). Half of the residents of the newly consolidated metropolis were foreign born. The first modern apartment house—Stuyvesant Apartments—opened at 142 East Eighteenth Street in 1869, and the Metropolitan Museum was incorporated the following year. The proliferation of safe passenger elevators in the 1870s allowed apartment houses to expand vertically, and by the following decade apartment dwelling had lost most of its social stigma among the middle class, although society considered a town house the only proper abode until well into the twentieth century.[8] (James was dismayed to learn in 1902 that a new apartment building had been named for *him;* he wrote William Dean Howells that it was no doubt doomed to failure and would have to reopen as "the Mary Johnston or the K[ate] Wiggin or the James Lane Allen [popular novelists of the day]. Best of all as the Edith Wharton!"[9]) In 1888, the first steel skeleton buildings began to rise in Manhattan; sixteen years later, when James sailed into New York Harbor, he compared Manhattan's skyscraper-

Anthony Trollope called Hawthorne "the handsomest Yankee that ever walked the planet," and this oil portrait by Cephas Giovanni Thompson shows him still quite striking at the age of forty-six. It was painted in 1850, the year Hawthorne met Melville.

Melville was forty-two years old and approaching the end of his thirteen-year residence in the Berkshires when Rodney Dewey took this photograph in 1861. Melville had seen Hawthorne for the last time four years earlier in Liverpool, England.

The craggy summit of Monument Mountain, where Hawthorne and Melville met during a literary picnic on August 5, 1850. The heavens opened when the party gained the summit, but Melville, "the boldest of all," according to his New York editor Evert Duyckinck, braved the storm "astride a projecting bowsprit of rock."

Melville's Arrowhead, near Pittsfield, Massachusetts, circa 1862. Melville added the famous "piazza" with its view of Mount Greylock after acquiring the house in 1850. When Hawthorne came to visit, Melville bundled him off to the barn (*far right*) and up to his study (second-floor left window of the farmhouse) for brandy drinking and cigar smoking.

PHOTO BY THE AUTHOR

Melville's wife, the former Elizabeth Shaw, around the time of their marriage in 1847. The daughter of the wealthy and socially prominent chief justice of the Massachusetts Supreme Court, Lizzie Melville was ill prepared for the cramped, fraught, and often impoverished life she led as Mrs. Herman Melville.

TWO PHOTOS:
BERKSHIRE ATHENAEUM,
HERMAN MELVILLE
MEMORIAL ROOM

Henry James in New York City, 1905. James stayed with the Whartons at their Park Avenue town house for a few weeks during his year-long visit to the States, which he wrote about in *The American Scene*. "I vibrated much there," he later wrote Wharton of the experience of being her guest in Manhattan.

James in the Lamb House garden room, where he dictated the great novels and stories of the "major phase." This photograph was taken sometime between 1905 and 1910, when his friendship with Wharton was in full bloom.

PHOTOGRAPH BY ALICE BOUGHTON.
BY PERMISSION OF THE HOUGHTON LIBRARY, HARVARD UNIVERSITY

BY PERMISSION OF
THE HOUGHTON LIBRARY,
HARVARD UNIVERSITY

Edith Wharton and dogs in Newport around 1889–1890, about
the time that she published her
first poems and story in *Scribner's
Magazine*.

Edward ("Teddy") Wharton in
1898 with three of the dogs he and
Edith loved so dearly—Jules,
Miza, and Mimi. "Ce cher grand
Jules—I'm sure he passed away in
the grand style," James commiserated with Edith Wharton when the
dog died in 1907.

A publicity photo of Edith Wharton in 1905, the year *The House of Mirth* was published. "You look thoroughly in possession of your genius, fame & fortune," James wrote her.

The veiled Edith Wharton and smartly capped Henry James poised for a motor flight with goggled chauffeur, Charles Cook, at the wheel. Teddy, with dogs and pipe, stands typically off to one side.

The Mount and surrounding gardens, the country estate that Edith Wharton built outside Lenox, Massachusetts, as it appeared in 1911. James, who was her guest here in 1904 and again in 1911, described the place as "a delicate French château mirrored in a Massachusetts pond . . . a monument to the almost too impeccable taste of its so accomplished mistress." YALE COLLECTION OF AMERICAN LITERATURE, BEINECKE RARE BOOK & MANUSCRIPT LIBRARY, YALE UNIVERSITY

ABOVE AND OPPOSITE: MCKELDIN LIBRARY, UNIVERSITY OF MARYLAND AT COLLEGE PARK

Opposite top, Katherine Anne Porter at Yaddo, the artists' colony in Saratoga Springs, New York, in 1941. Porter arranged an invitation for Eudora Welty that summer, but Welty didn't like the place and never returned. Porter, however, was a fixture at Yaddo for years.

Opposite bottom, Welty expected Porter to attend a publication party for *A Curtain of Green and Other Stories,* held in November 1941 at New York's Murray Hill Hotel, but she was disappointed. John Woodburn, Welty's editor at Doubleday, is seated next to her at the far left; her agent Diarmuid Russell is standing at the far right.

Below, South Hill, the Colonial farmhouse outside of Saratoga Springs that Porter bought in the winter of 1940. Porter's preoccupation with the costly and prolonged renovation of the house was one of the many interruptions that kept her from writing the introduction to Welty's book during the summer of 1941. Porter hoped this would be her permanent home, but she lived there only thirteen months.

Albert Erskine, age twenty-eight, Baton Rouge, Louisiana, 1939. Porter's fourth and final husband, Erskine was more than twenty years her junior. The marriage lasted less than two years. Decades later, Erskine served as Welty's editor at Random House.

Porter, eighty-two years old, presented Welty with the Gold Medal for Fiction of the National Institute of Arts and Letters in New York City in May 1972. "This is . . . the closing of the circle," Welty wrote her.

TWO PHOTOS: BY PERMISSION OF
THE HOUGHTON LIBRARY, HARVARD UNIVERSITY

Opposite top, Robert Lowell around the time he met Elizabeth Bishop in 1947. Bishop said years later that the young Lowell was as handsome as James Dean, and it amused her tremendously that a Hollywood producer wanted to give him a screen test after seeing his picture in *Life* magazine.

Opposite bottom, the forty-year-old Lowell in 1957 with his daughter, Harriet. Bishop made a brief and tumultuous visit to Lowell in Castine, Maine, later that year, and Lowell's breakthrough on the "Life Studies" poem came a few weeks after her abrupt departure.

Below, Elizabeth Bishop in Brazil, probably in the mid-1950s

Above, Bishop and Lowell on Copacabana Beach ("that famous carte postale beach" Bishop called it) in Rio, August 1962. "There were never better moments," Lowell later recalled of this day, but Bishop noted in her diary at the time that Lowell was becoming "more hysterical every day." He suffered a serious psychotic episode the following month.

Opposite, Bishop wrote to a friend about this photograph, taken in Rio the same day, that she and Lowell were "giving an *abraço,* supposedly, but 2 New Englanders get awfully gingerly & shy."

Bishop receiving an honorary doctor of letters degree from Princeton University in June 1979. "The whitening hair grew thick above a face each year somehow rounder and softer," Bishop's friend James Merrill wrote of her. She died four months later at the age of sixty-eight.

studded skyline to "extravagant pins in a cushion already over-planted, and stuck in as in the dark, anywhere and anyhow."[10] He bemoaned the dwarfing of the city's church spires by the profit-generating towers of commerce (as J. Lincoln Steffens put it, "the enterprise of business has surpassed the aspiration of religion"[11]).

During the decades of James's absence from the city, New York consolidated its position as the financial, transportation, shopping, entertainment, and communications center of the nation. Thirty steamship lines ran boats between New York and Europe at the end of the nineteenth century, and other shipping lines connected New York to the major cities of the Americas, both North and South. New York also served as the port of entry for the largest human migration in the history of the world, with more than twelve million immigrants arriving in the city between 1892 and 1954. The peak years of immigration were from 1900 to 1915, and when James visited Ellis Island in 1904, a "million or so of immigrants [were] annually knocking at our official door," as he put it.[12] In 1907, the high-water mark of immigration, the figure reached nearly 1.3 million. James reported that after his visit to Ellis Island he felt shaken "to the depths of his being" by the spectacle of "ingurgitation" and haunted for days afterward by a "sense of dispossession." "Other impressions might come and go," he wrote, "but this affirmed claim of the alien, however immeasurably alien, to share in one's supreme relation [i.e., to one's country] was everywhere the fixed element, the reminder not to be dodged."[13]

The bucolic age of peaches and Manhattan houses in "grounds" had begun to pass away, as Melville well knew, even during James's boyhood. In 1848, when James was five, his family moved from the "world of quiet harmonies" of Washington Square "so decent in its dignity" up to a new house on Fourteenth Street. "The age of 'brown stone' had just been ushered in," writes James, "and that material, in deplorable, in monstrous form, over all the vacant spaces and eligible sites then numerous between the Fifth and Sixth Avenues, more and more affronted the day."[14] In Wharton's earliest memories, the affront had become an assault. In the portrait of old New York she paints in *A Backward Glance*, brownstone has spread a universal blight over the city. She describes New York as an intolerably ugly city of "untended streets," "narrow houses," and "smug and suffocating upholstery." And yet much as she loathed "this cramped horizontal gridiron" and its "deadly uniformity of mean ugliness," she was still shocked that in fifty years it would vanish like Atlantis, its "social organization . . . swept to oblivion."[15]

As she grew older, Wharton, like James, forgave the city of her birth some of its ugliness and absurdities simply because they had vanished. Again to quote her memoirs: "Not until the successive upheavals which culminated in the catastrophe of 1914 had 'cut all likeness from the name' of my old New York, did I begin to see its pathetic picturesqueness."[16] Or, crudely put, the horrors she had known in her New York childhood smelled positively sweet compared with what came after.

Louis Auchincloss, himself a product of what remained of New York society after the Great War, acutely sums up Wharton's ambivalent feelings toward New York in his introduction to her memoirs: "On one hand she loved it for the very completeness of her understanding of it and for the richness of the material with which it supplied her. It was, after all, her cradle and family. On the other hand she resented the smallness of its imagination, the dryness of its appreciations and its ever turned back (or at the most its condescending smile) towards everything that made life worth while to her."[17] Auchincloss goes on to say that as she grew older, Wharton came to reflect that "in a rootless world the roots of that lost brownstone city were better than none."

Even more than the physical ugliness, it was the spiritual and moral and intellectual ugliness of New York's "genteel monotony" that repelled Wharton—and that she devoted so many of her finest novels and stories to excoriating, including *The House of Mirth, The Custom of the Country, The Age of Innocence,* and *The Mother's Recompense.*

The Age of Innocence, as Lewis and other critics point out, is Wharton's fullest portrait of the New York she had known as a girl (the novel opens with the words "On a January evening of the early seventies," which is just the period when Wharton returned to the city at age ten after nearly six years abroad) and also her most serious treatment of the place New York held in her life. Newland Archer, the novel's hero, is the quintessential New York gentleman—born, like Wharton herself, near the top of the "slippery pyramid" of New York society, and related to the aristocratic families who held the apex. "A contemplative and a dilettante," Archer is polished, educated, sensitive, and gifted with exquisite good taste in books, music, and pictures as well as with sufficient intelligence and self-awareness to take a faintly ironic view of the "inscrutable totem terrors" that ruled New York society. All of this is perfectly conventional, perfectly good form, and "the thing." But Archer parts from the ranks of his fellows in the club box at the new opera house in his susceptibility to both conscience and passion. His engagement to the strictly conventional May Welland forces him, almost despite himself, to reflect on the awful hypocrisy of a society in which the eligible bachelor is permitted his dalliances while the marriageable maiden is expected to be a "miracle of fire and ice"—"the young girl who knew nothing and expected everything."[18] Archer, during the required round of prenuptial visits, muses on the artificiality of his bride-to-be, "that terrifying product of the social system he belonged to and believed in":

> He felt himself oppressed by this creation of factitious purity, so cunningly manufactured by a conspiracy of mothers and aunts and grandmothers and long-dead ancestresses, because it was supposed to be what he wanted, what he had a right to, in order that he might exercise his lordly pleasure in smashing it like an image made of snow.[19]

These dangerously unconventional thoughts might be written off as premarital jitters; but Archer moves even further outside the pale when he becomes involved with his fiancée's cousin Ellen Olenska, a sensual, worldly, mysterious, slightly older woman who has suddenly returned to New York in disgrace after the scandalous failure of her marriage to a blackguardly Polish count. Though he disapproves of Ellen at first, Archer defends her out of loyalty to his wife—"Women ought to be free—as free as we are" he announces to the foppish Sillerton Jackson—and then finds himself falling hopelessly in love with her. To Archer, Ellen represents everything his staid married life in New York would deprive him of: adventure, freedom of thought, culture, daring, beauty, honesty. She breathes the spirit of Europe into his drab brownstone world.

The Age of Innocence is in a sense Archer's sentimental education. His adoration of Ellen opens his eyes wider and wider to the cruelty and falsehood of New York society; yet he cannot quite bring himself to act on his love and run off with her—and Ellen herself won't allow it. Despite himself, Archer remains irreproachably inside the system, "the narrow groove of money-making, sport and society": He marries May and remains faithful to the "dull duty" of marriage, fathering a family, putting in his hours at the law firm, and working quietly and without pay for municipal reform, etc. In a touching coda at the end of the novel, Archer, now a fifty-seven-year-old widower, finds himself an anachronism in the rushing, shrieking, valueless barbarity of post-war New York. He realizes that despite his utter disillusionment with society he has lived the life of a "good citizen," an exemplary upholder of the old values that trapped and nearly destroyed him.

Archer and his grown son, Dallas, travel together to Paris, where Ellen Olenska has lived quietly for years. Dallas, a product of the casual new social order, breezily informs his father that he has known for years that Ellen was "the woman you'd have chucked everything for: only you didn't"—knows because his mother told him on her deathbed—and that he has arranged for the two of them to visit her. Archer, reeling under these shocking revelations, accompanies his son to the apartment building where Ellen lives, but in the end he sends Dallas up without him. "Say I'm old-fashioned," he instructs his son to tell the woman he loved, and he sits alone on a bench in the thickening dusk, holding vigil for the memory of the one shining moment of his life. Though he has long since ceased to believe in the customs and practices of old New York, he continues to honor them because he knows that he belongs to them irrevocably, just as James and Wharton did. "After all," Archer reflects in mournful resignation, "there was good in the old ways."[20]

As Cynthia Griffin Wolff writes in her penetrating discussion of *The Age of Innocence,* "Wharton, a self-conscious product of the old New York she re-creates, had finally come to realize that the children of that time and place must forever bear its mark, cherish its values, and suffer in some degree its inadequacies. . . ." Wolff also believes that "the central meaning grows out of the complex way in which the novel beckons to Wharton's dearest friend, Henry James."[21]

The Age of Innocence (the first novel written by a woman to win the Pulitzer Prize) was one of a series of postwar novels in which Wharton revisits the world of old New York. One striking feature of these fictions is the new candor with which Wharton writes about sex and the anger with which she connects sexual repression and social repression. Wharton herself, like May Welland, was a "terrifying product of the social system . . . the young girl who knew nothing and expected everything." She never forgave her mother (whom she distinguished as the best-dressed woman in New York) for refusing to tell her what would "happen" after she married Teddy. She wrote in an unpublished memoir that a few days before her marriage she "begged" her mother to tell her "what being married was like": "Her handsome face at once took on the look of icy disapproval I most dreaded. 'I never heard such a ridiculous question!' she said impatiently!"[22]

Wharton blamed this horribly damaging reticence on the "totem terrors" of old New York. "It was the old New York way, of taking life 'without effusion of blood,' " she writes in *The Age of Innocence;* "the way of people who dreaded scandal more than disease, who placed decency above courage. . . ."[23] It was not "the thing" to talk about sex, even, or perhaps especially, on the night before a maiden's wedding, and emotion and money were similarly excluded from polite conversation. Wharton's fiction overflows with unhappy marriages, and she drew a direct link between the sexual ignorance of young girls and the wretchedness of young wives. Here in "The Old Maid," one of the novellas in the *Old New York* tetralogy written in the 1920s, Wharton writes of the transformation of dewy virgin into stoic matron:

> Afterward: why, of course, there was the startled puzzled surrender to the incomprehensible exigencies of the young man to whom one had at most yielded a rosy cheek in return for an engagement ring; there was the large double-bed; the terror of seeing him shaving calmly the next morning, in his shirt-sleeves, through the dressing-room door; the evasions, insinuations, resigned smiles and Bible texts of one's Mamma; the reminder of the phrase "to obey" in the glittering blur of the Marriage Service; a week or a month of flushed distress, confusion, embarrassed pleasure; then the growth of habit, the insidious lulling of the matter-of-course, the dreamless double slumbers in the big white bed, the early morning discussions and consultations through that dressing-room door which had once seemed to open into a fiery pit scorching the brow of innocence.[24]

Such transformations were not limited to New York—but in Wharton's imagination New York is particularly culpable because she herself had been a victim of its punishing taboos. The blackest sin of New York's social organization in Wharton's eyes was this conspiracy to corral girls "who knew nothing and expected everything" into marriage and then to bind and gag them into staying married through "the insidious lulling" of habit and the pressure of obligation. This may well explain why Wharton did not share James's nostalgia for "the boundless fruitage of that more bucolic age." There was nothing bucolic about growing up female in old New York.

Wharton, of course, was hardly an advocate of "free love" or unbridled sexual expression either inside New York or abroad. She herself lived a life of careful, reproachless propriety, even in her affair with Fullerton, which she conducted according to the rules of the day—in secret and without compromising her marriage. Wolff argues that Wharton "embraced old New York's customs of repression because they helped to support her resistance against the clamoring of unsuitable internal emotions."[25] But such resistance led to anguish and depression.

In Wharton's fiction, the social edifice rises over a measureless chasm of despair—despair most of all over the impossibility of living with passion. Passion succumbs to the dullness of habit even in marriages made for love; and passion outside marriage is dangerous, poisoned by illusion, and ultimately futile. As Wharton once confided to a friend: "Ah, the poverty, the miserable poverty, of any love that lies outside of marriage, of any love that is not a living together, a sharing of all!" She felt with increasing stringency that there was no escaping the social stage, that, as Lewis puts it, "society, crushing as it might be, was all there was."[26] When people throw over convention and run off, they simply substitute another, shabbier, uglier, more meaningless set of conventions for those they have fled. As Kate Clephane realizes in *The Mother's Recompense,* "the prison of her marriage had been liberty compared with what she had exchanged it for."[27] Far more acutely than James, Wharton saw the terms and consequences of this social entrapment—sexual, social, economic. Far more sympathetically and richly, she depicted its victims.

It's astonishing given the privileges and wealth she had known since birth that Wharton should have been so keenly attuned to the plight of social victims—that she should have depicted over and over again the suffering of the downtrodden, excluded, fallen, rejected. She never forgot that women traded their bodies and their consciences for the spoils of respectability, and that a single slip could plunge them into disgrace and deprivation.

Intolerably ugly as the old brownstone New York was, inexcusably vulgar as nouveau riche Fifth Avenue was, the poverty that lay outside the gilded cage was far more hideous. In letting her imagination dwell on this poverty, in associating economic poverty with social and sexual alienation, in enacting over and over again the drama of dispossession, in placing her stories in an industrialized New York, Wharton strikes a distinctly modern note. Kate Clephane sits in her elegantly appointed bedroom in her daughter's Fifth Avenue town house and realizes that she is a mere transient, that the luxurious respectability of her surroundings is an illusion: "It was as if this house which people called her own were itself no more than the waiting-room of a railway station where she was listening for the coming of another train that was to carry her—whither?"[28] Wharton's New York stories are heavy with the props of the old order—the canvas-back ducks, the landaus and brown coupes, the Worth gowns and thick engraved dinner invitations, the ballrooms and opera boxes—but for Wharton's alienated heroines, these props represent not stability and tradition but the terms of their bondage. The instant they lose faith in the "system," their mansions turn to railway waiting rooms.

In a strange way, Wharton's vision of urban alienation and desperation picks up where Melville leaves off in *Pierre*: Wharton's Lily Bart and the hero of Melville's novel are both dislodged from a cushioned aristocratic Eden and plunged into the hell of New York's mean streets. Both *Pierre* and *The House of Mirth* are novels of dispossession in which being poor in New York represents the lowest depth—really the threshold to death. Melville and Wharton anticipate the bleak New York stories of Katherine Anne Porter (in "Theft" and "A Day's Work") and Eudora Welty (in "Flowers for Marjorie"), as well as Elizabeth Bishop's grim rendering of lower Manhattan in "Varick Street" as a dark industrialized underworld where even love becomes mechanized and commercialized ("*And I shall sell you sell you/sell you of course, my dear, and you'll sell me*"). New York is "the loneliest place in the world if you have no family," Bishop once told a friend. Only Robert Lowell celebrated New York as a modern Rome—a world capital, the center of American intellectual life, at once grand, numbing, violent, and thrillingly corrupt. "It has a sheer feeling of utter freedom," Lowell told an interviewer. "And then when one thinks back a little bit, it seems all confused and naked."[29]

James, too, saw twentieth-century New York as the locale of a new and terrifying kind of urban alienation. In *The American Scene* he records his sensory impressions of the burgeoning metropolis in 1904; but in the short stories he wrote after his return to England, he distills his intimate recognitions and regrets. "Distills" may be too delicate a word for the emotion in these final tales for as Leon Edel puts it, James expresses himself "crudely and at moments savagely":

> [T]he four American tales which he wrote on his return to England reflect a sense of shock. Indeed all his last tales have in them a barely concealed "sacred rage." The Olympian—the acknowledged "Master" of the new generation—sets aside his urbanity and good humor and howls, like Lear: he sees the suffering and waste of human life, the loss of friendship and of personal identity, the loneliness of modern cities; he has the oppressive sense that all is "too late." . . . These are tales of individuals lost in the crowd; and of individuals without identity or self-awareness. They are also angry tales.[30]

Spencer Brydon in "The Jolly Corner" (1908) returns to New York after an absence of thirty-three years (James has added a decade to his own exile) to find "monstrosities" everywhere, the most monstrous of all being the "rank money passion" that has supplanted the gentler civilities of his youth: "the dreadful multiplied numberings . . . seemed to him to reduce the whole place to some vast ledger-page, overgrown, fantastic, of ruled and crisscrossed lines and figures. . . ."[31] (One recalls Ellen Olenska in *The Age of Innocence* rejecting Archer's offer to lead her through the winding ways of New York's social codes: "Is New York such a labyrinth? I thought it so straight up and down—like Fifth Avenue. And with all the cross streets numbered!"[32])

As discussed above, Brydon, in the course of the story, has a near-fatal encounter with the ghost of his "other self"—the figure of what he would have been had he remained in the city to make money instead of moving abroad to spend it. The ghost haunts Brydon's childhood house near Washington Square, but Brydon in turn haunts the ghost, returning night after night to stalk him from room to empty room. James plays with this same notion of the reversal of haunter and haunted in a letter of fond reminiscence to Mary Cadwalader (Minnie) Jones: "My New York of those dear East Eleventh Street 'first-floor-back' hours lives again for me as I write. . . . It's astonishing, it's prodigious, how I find my spirit gratefully haunting them always—or rather how insidiously turning the tables they, the mystic locality itself, haunt and revisit my own departed identity."[33]

A figure very like Minnie Jones appears as the title character of another late New York story, "Crapy Cornelia" (1909). In this decidedly minor tale the wishy-washy hero, White-Mason, contemplates with increasing repugnance the prospect of marrying the thoroughly modern and luxuriously wealthy New York matron Mrs. Worthingham, a "polished and prosperous little person" of gleaming charm and expensive superficiality. (Edel finds a "very strong" resemblance between Mrs. Worthingham and Mrs. Wharton, but others don't.[34] The two women do share wealth, a taste for modern conveniences, and "the most unconscious and instinctive and luxurious assumption," but James would never have befriended Wharton if he thought her as foolish and vulgar and dense as he makes Mrs. Worthingham out to be—"as ignorant as a fish," he calls her at one point; and the name alone would have been a horrible insult.) Mrs. Worthingham fills White-Mason with dread of what lies ahead in modern urban society:

> This was clearly going to be the music of the future—that if people were but rich enough and furnished enough and fed enough, exercised and sanitated and manicured, and generally advised and advertised and made "knowing" enough, *avertis* enough, as the term appeared to be nowadays in Paris, all they had to do for civility was to take the amused ironic view of those who might be less initiated.[35]

White-Mason flees in terror from such a future and takes refuge with Cornelia Rasch, a dowdy, aging, shabbily genteel holdover from the "New York of his already almost legendary past." Though he makes it clear that he can't, that he won't marry Cornelia, White-Mason informs her at the story's end that he *can* live with her "just this way," by which he means by settling into her worn old armchair day after day for long dull afternoons of tea and reminiscence.

In "A Round of Visits" (1910), James's final story, Mark Monteith returns to New York after a lengthy exile abroad because a dear and trusted friend has swindled him out of his inheritance. Monteith, a kind of parody of Jamesian prissy fastidiousness, discovers that no one in the cold harsh city can summon up a speck of interest in his plight. Isolated and overwhelmed by the roaring modern city, he scarcely dares to emerge from his hotel "to face the void and the chill." Monteith feels stripped and violated, both emotionally and financially, and James explicitly draws an analogy between the loss of money and loss of memory—"all the broken bits of the past, the loose ends of old relationships, that he supposed he might pick up again."

In a bizarre twist, Monteith does at last find a sympathetic listener—Newton Winch, an old acquaintance from years before—but Winch turns out to be just such a swindler as the man who ran off with Monteith's money. Winch knows his crime has been discovered and is about to shoot himself at the moment when Monteith, who has no knowledge of the situation, drops in for an unannounced visit. Monteith is so full of his own sense of injury that he fails to perceive that Winch is in far more desperate straits than he and for related reasons. The two men are in a sense reverse sides of the same copper coin, yet Monteith can't draw the connection. In the final moments of the story, Monteith sees the pistol glinting under Winch's armchair and, with the enormity of the situation dawning on him, he makes Winch promise not to use it. The police arrive and Monteith goes to let them in, only to hear the crack of gunshot from the next room. Winch has broken yet another promise—and Monteith is left with nothing at all except a sense of guilt.

Brydon, White-Mason, and Mark Monteith all confront a modern, money-mad, skyscraper-ridden Manhattan which no longer has any place or use for them. "Progress" has made them marginal figures in a city that once was "theirs"; time has isolated them; change has swallowed up the houses, customs, values, and families they once knew and left them only their memories. Monteith literally has nothing; but Brydon and White-Mason at least have fellow refugees—Cornelia for White-Mason and Alice Staverton for Brydon—to console them for their losses, to share their memories, and perhaps, for Brydon, to love and/or marry him for "The Jolly Corner" ends with the couple's embrace.

Despite his own long and bitter acquaintance with loneliness—"the deepest thing about one"—James shrinks in these stories from casting his heroes out *utterly* naked and alone into the urban jungle. Unlike Wharton, who lets Lily Bart commit suicide, alone and broke in a New York boarding house, who leaves Newland Archer alone on a Paris bench, and who consigns Kate Clephane to permanent shabby exile in France, James feels compelled to rescue his twentieth-century New York characters from the lowest depths. In some fundamental way, James had a more hopeful, more nostalgic, more generous nature than Wharton did. Or perhaps he was more afraid of the dark. He approached the edge of the abyss, but drew back. He cherished the rosy glow shed by illusion. He believed that consciousness was a redemptive moral force—was above all a *force* to marshal against the powers of darkness that drag down Wharton's heroines and Melville's heroes.

Everyone quotes the passage in *The Ambassadors* in which Lambert Strether importunes Little Bilham to "live all you can," but the passage that follows it is even more crucial to James's vision of life and consciousness: ". . . now I'm old," Strether continues his great speech in Gloriani's garden, "too old at any rate for what I see."

> Oh, I *do* see, at least; and more than you'd believe or I can express. It's too late. And it's as if the train had fairly waited at the station for me without my having had the gumption to know it was there. Now I hear its faint receding whistle miles and miles down the line. What one loses one loses; make no mistake about that. The affair—I mean the affair of life— couldn't, no doubt, have been different for me; for it's at the best a tin mould, either fluted and embossed, with ornamental excrescences, or else smooth and dreadfully plain, into which, a helpless jelly, one's consciousness is poured—so that one "takes" the form, as the great cook says, and is more or less compactly held by it; one lives in fine as one can. Still, one has the illusion of freedom; therefore don't be, like me, without the memory of that illusion.[36]

The illusion of freedom—of moral freedom—was one that James could never part with, and the memory of that illusion became more and more important to him as he approached the end of his life. An illusion is by definition deceptive, and yet as Strether strives so eagerly to demonstrate, it can also be illuminating—it can irradiate the very essence of life. It may be that the illusion of freedom, acknowledged and grasped and clung to *as* illusion, was what kept James sweet and generous and magnanimous, let him live out his life to the end with hope and forgiveness. The illusion, or the memory of the illusion, let him believe that there could still be some refuge for him, and for his characters, from the hideous darkness that he saw closing over his world.

Wharton did without the illusion; she stopped at the determinism of the "tin mould." Unlike James, she doesn't let her characters escape; she doesn't let them off the hook—and she didn't let herself off, either. I think Millicent Bell is right in pointing to a "thin and wintry quality" in Wharton's work. The bleakness of her vision may strike closer to our own outlook (our "downlook" as Lowell has it—Lowell who oddly enough harks back to Wharton in his merciless exposures of upper-class marriage and adultery); but James saw through and around and beyond the bleakness.

James's is, finally, a more fully rounded vision of life. Where Wharton penetrates, James circles until he has taken in a subject from all sides. Both of them sound the distinctively American note of shock at moral imperfection: Like Melville and Hawthorne, they never ceased to be amazed and outraged at the corruption of innocence, though they described different flanks of the sacred cow. Where Wharton wonders in novel after novel how human society can be at once so stupid and so cruel, James wonders how love can possibly survive the existence of sex. Renunciation—a theme that the friends shared—is death in Wharton, the slow, desiccating, wasting away of the spirit; but in James, renunciation is portal to the higher life, a rising above, an amassing of greater and greater riches in a smaller and smaller space. To quote Bell once more, "James, the true solitary with few unguarded, intimate relationships, really adored life. He could never cease his passionate absorption in it, his wonder at new human revelations. . . . Edith Wharton almost always had closed the case of her characters before her story was under way."[37]

As fundamentally different as they were in artistic temperament and technique, James and Wharton both heard the "music of the future," heard it playing most stridently in New York, and both feared that the monstrous sound would soon spread—even as far as the sacred capitals of Europe. But they could not have known, as they met in England during the golden late summer of 1914, that the true orchestra of the future was just tuning up. The demise of civility in New York that James bewailed in "Crapy Cornelia" was as nothing compared to the crash of European civilization that they beheld together during the Great War.

NINE

"This Crash of Our Civilization"

Life goes on after a fashion, but I find it a nightmare from which there is no waking save by sleep.

—HENRY JAMES *letter to Edith Wharton, August 19, 1914*

Once within the military zone every moment is interesting.

—EDITH WHARTON *letter to Henry James, March 11, 1915*

"I FEEL all but unbearably overdarkened by this crash of our civilization," James wrote Wharton on August 6, 1914, two days after Great Britain had entered what was to become known as the Great War. "The only gleam in the blackness, to me, is the action of the absolute unanimity of this country."[1] James's prescience was extraordinary for when he wrote this, most believed that England, France, and Russia would easily defeat the Central Powers and that the war would be over by Christmas. He *saw*, as few others did at the time, the scope and the meaning of the impending conflict. "You and I, the ornaments of our generation, should have been spared this wreck of our belief that through the long years we had seen civilisation grow and the worst become impossible," he wrote an English friend a few days later.[2] In the end, the crash was more devastating than even James could have imagined. Nine and a half million dead—including nearly one million Britons, the better part of a generation.

To stand witness to this horror sickened and crushed James. He was himself surprised that it failed to kill him. "I am learning to take for granted that I shall probably on the whole *not* die of simple sick horror—than which nothing seems to me at the same time more amazing," he wrote Wharton a year into the war in 1915. "One aches to anguish & rages to suffocation, one is still there to do it again, & the occasion still there to see that one does."[3] James, who had been known to agonize over what Wharton called the "almost insuperable difficulties" of choosing a hat or meeting a friend's train, threw himself decisively into relief work, heading up committees, raising and distributing money, visiting wounded soldiers in London hospitals. He vented his anguish and his rage in whatever action was open to him. As Wharton wrote so movingly and so vividly after his death: "Those who were with him during the autumn days of 1914 will never forget the transfiguration of the whole man. It was as if he who, as long ago as in his thirties, had definitely classified himself as an observer, now suddenly leapt into participation; as if at last the one void in him had been fulfilled."[4] Yet despite this transfiguration, the war weighed more and more heavily on him as it dragged terribly on. Though James in fact died of natural causes in 1916, "what really gave him his death-blow was the war," as Wharton put it in her memoirs. "He struggled through two years of it, then veiled his eyes from the endless perspectives of destruction. It was the gesture of Agamemnon, covering his face with his cloak before the unbearable."[5]

Wharton, though slower than James to recognize the enormity of the war, utterly shared his outrage at its accumulating horrors and his passionate commitment to relief work. Indeed the war revealed, as no other event had done, the common instincts and sympathies that deeply united the friends. One is struck, in reading the correspondence from 1914, how they dropped, overnight, all their accustomed subjects—literary gossip, travel plans, humorous quips and snippets about friends, complaints over ailments and foul moods—and devoted themselves single-mindedly to public events. James ushered in this new stage of their relationship when he wrote Wharton that "the irrelevance of all remark, the utter extinction of everything, in face of these immensities, leaves me as 'all silent & all damned' as you express it leaves *you.* ... Life goes on after a fashion, but I find it a nightmare from which there is no waking save by sleep."[6] The nightmare drew the friends closer together. War consumed the shadow of disdain that had long clouded James's feelings toward Wharton, and it introduced a new and reciprocal emotion into their friendship: reverence.

The outbreak of war caught Wharton at an especially awkward time. In the year and half between her divorce from Teddy and the declaration of hostilities, Wharton had been restless and intermittently ill. She had traveled a good deal (including a motor flight through Germany with Bernard Berenson in August 1913, a visit to the States in December, and a trip to Algeria and Tunisia with the young English writer Percy Lubbock in 1914), and in the breaks between her trips she had cast about for another country house. James trembled when he learned that the Firebird had fixed her sights on England. His letters from 1913 and early 1914 anxiously chart the ups and downs of her negotiations to purchase a country estate called Coopersale just north of London and, when she decided against it for tax reasons, to rent Stocks, the Buckinghamshire estate belonging to the novelist Mrs. Humphry Ward, a friend of James's, and her husband.

Though James bubbled to Wharton of his delight at the prospect of having her so near at hand, he worried behind her back that residence in the same country would leave him excessively vulnerable to her swooping descents. In the event, war broke out before Wharton even took possession of Stocks. She and her dear old friend Walter Berry had been motoring in Spain during July, and they rushed north to Paris as the international situation worsened at the end of the month. Wharton finally established herself at Stocks at the end of September, but she found English country life (without a telephone!) intolerable at such a tense moment in history, and after a couple of weeks, the Wards proposed exchanging Stocks for their town house at 25 Grosvenor Square. James and Wharton spent a few days together in London before Wharton, electrified by the Battle of the Marne and feeling "like a deserter," as she wrote a friend, for having abandoned her adopted country in time of crisis, crossed back to France on September 24. The war had cut down her "life-long dream of a summer in England" to less than a month.

Back in Paris, Wharton marshaled her considerable energy and resources to launch a major campaign of relief work. Even before she had gone to England in August she had opened up an *ouvroir*—a workroom—providing jobs, meals, coal, and medical care for seamstresses who had no relatives at the front and thus did not qualify for government assistance. As Belgian refugees began to stream into Paris during the Battle of Ypres that autumn, Wharton set up a relief outfit, eventually known as the American Hostels for Refugees, which provided shelter, food, free medical care, clothing, coal, and employment for thousands of homeless people (9,330 in its first year alone). "The range of Edith Wharton's activity in 1915 staggers the mind," writes R.W.B. Lewis. "She had to keep busy every minute, Edith declared; otherwise, her awareness of the horror would be too much for her."[7]

James, in recognition of her burgeoning administrative duties, addressed her as "great *generalissima,*" a rare touch of humor in this grim time. Belgian refugees were also arriving in England, and James did what he could for them, donating the old chapel-studio at the corner of his Lamb House property for their use as a common room, giving what money he could spare, and doling out additional funds sent by Wharton. (James reported to her in a series of letters how he was attempting to "distil" and "deal out" her initial £10 bequest bit by bit rather than "pass it on *en bloc*"; though Wharton's responses have not survived, one gathers that she eventually became annoyed at all this fuss and bother over such a meager sum—another sign, to her mind, of James's neurosis about money.)

James agreed to serve as chairman of the American Volunteer Motor-Ambulance Corps that Richard Norton, the son of Harvard's Charles Eliot Norton, organized. But charity and committee work were not enough for him: James also urgently wanted to make contact with individual soldiers and refugees. Edel paints a touching portrait of his "moving from bedside to bedside" comforting the wounded soldiers in London: "Friends of the Master wondered how the soldiers reacted to his subtle leisurely talk—but he seemed quite capable of entertaining and comforting them. He likened himself to Walt Whitman during the Civil War."[8] "Don't you think the martial truculent Henry is by far the best we've seen yet?" Wharton marveled in a letter to a mutual friend.[9]

James railed in letters to Wharton over his frustration at being too old and too sick to participate more actively in the war

effort: I "feel like the chilled vieillards in the old epics, infirm &
helpless at home with the women while the plains are ringing with
battle."[10]

Wharton also chafed at being homebound—but, typically,
she took matters into her own hands. Six months into the war, she
wrote James that she was possessed of "a yearning to get away for
a few days, & also a great desire to find out what was really
wanted in some of the hospitals near the front." So in February
1915, she packed her motor with clothes and medical supplies and
set out, together with Walter Berry, to witness the Battle of Verdun
for herself. Wharton's war letters—the only letters of hers that
James preserved from their fifteen-year correspondence—are vivid
on-the-spot accounts of the shock, and the thrill, of her encounters
with trench warfare.

Writing with a grim terseness worthy of Hemingway, she
describes for James how extraordinary it felt to climb into her car
in Paris and drive (or rather be driven by her trusty chauffeur,
Cook) into the war zone in a mere four hours. She stops at a
hospital where there were nine hundred cases of typhoid and "*everything* was lacking." She lunches at Clermont-en-Argonne, "one
of the most utterly ravaged places in this region" ("It looks exactly
like Pompeii," comments the connoisseur of exquisite places; "I
felt as if I must be going to lunch at the Hotel Diomede!"[11]).
Lunch is interrupted by a roar of cannon, and the party tears
across the street to observe the battle in progress five miles away:
"white puffs & scarlet flashes kept springing up all over the dark
hillside" as the Germans fire down from the top of a hill at the
French trenches below. "And so we saw the reason there are to be
so many wounded at Clermont tonight," she concludes the battle
scene, adding in a postscript, "9 P.M., & and the cannon still
booming."[12]

James was supremely enthralled. "How can I welcome &
applaud enough your splendid thrilling letter," he gushed in return. "I unutterably envy you these sights & suffered assaults of
the *maxima*—condemned as I am by doddering age & 'mean'
infirmity to the poor mesquins [shabby] *minima* . . ."[13] James
ended his letter "shamelessly howling" for more, like Oliver Twist,
and Wharton obliged him a week later with an account of her
second excursion into the war zone.

This time numbness has considerably dimmed her excitement. She paints for him a blighted "Winter War" landscape: "a

snow-covered rolling country sweeping up to the white sky, with no one in sight but now & then a cavalry patrol with a blown cloak struggling along against the wind." She shudders before a church that has been converted to a "human stable": "The poor devils sleep on straw, in queer little compartments made of plaited straw screens, in each of which compartments a dozen or so are crammed . . ."[14] By the end of the letter, after describing a hellish night spent wandering around Châlons trying to find a place to sleep and encountering tight-lipped officers who were her dinner guests in peacetime, she confesses that "it was no use trying to keep up the pretense of reality any longer!"

Much as he appreciated these dispatches from the front, James could not conceal from Wharton how empty and futile they made him feel about his own remoteness from action. He confessed sadly in a letter written in May 1915, "I myself have no adventure of any sort equal to just hearing from you of yours—apart I mean from the unspeakable adventure of being alive in these days."[15] This letter is James's wartime masterpiece—a *cri de coeur* that starts with his own personal despair and opens out to embrace a devastated society: "*Every one* is killed who belongs to any one here, & one looks straight and dry-eyed, hard & arid, at those to whom they belonged." He closes with a resounding salute to Wharton: "Je vous embrace [sic], je vous venere!"—I embrace you, I venerate you!

As we know, James and Wharton had been wary of each other's work in peacetime, but during the war they joined literary forces in assembling *The Book of the Homeless,* a collection of pieces by well-known British, European, and American authors, painters, and composers, which was sold to raise money for the American Hostels for Refugees and the Children of Flanders Rescue Committee. Wharton originated the scheme, and James helped by enlisting English contributors and by donating an essay of his own—"The Long Wards"—about impressions gathered while comforting wounded soldiers in London's St. Bartholomew's Hospital. Wharton was keen on getting a piece from Joseph Conrad, a recent "discovery" of hers, but James was not optimistic about this since Conrad "produces by the sweat of his brow and tosses off, in considerable anguish, at the rate of about a word a month." In the event, James did succeed in wringing a piece out of Conrad, as well as Thomas Hardy and John Singer Sargent, but "the grim

Rudyard," as he styled Kipling, refused. The book, published in October 1915, with an introduction by Theodore Roosevelt, also included pieces by Rupert Brooke, Jean Cocteau, George Santayana, W. B. Yeats, a pastel by Claude Monet, and a score by Igor Stravinsky. Wharton herself translated all but one of the French poems. *The Book of the Homeless* eventually brought in eight thousand dollars, and an additional seven thousand dollars was raised when the manuscripts and some of the artwork were auctioned.[16]

One thinks of Katherine Anne Porter as inhabiting a different epoch from James and Wharton; but in fact, she was born in 1890, just twenty-eight years after Wharton. When the United States entered the First World War in 1917, Porter was twenty-seven and just embarking on her literary career. Like James and Wharton, Porter became active in volunteer work, serving as the Red Cross Corps publicity chairman in Fort Worth, Texas, and writing enthusiastic bits for the local newspaper. But when she turned back to the war period years later in her short novel *Pale Horse, Pale Rider,* Porter was far cooler.

Miranda, Porter's alter ego, resents being pressured to put part of her meager reporter's salary into Liberty Bonds and feels increasingly alienated from the country's rabid patriotism and German bashing. "Oh, the war," Miranda murmurs wearily whenever the subject arises. Porter's political vision hardened during the Second World War, and in her novel *Ship of Fools,* set at the brink of the Nazi rise to power but written mostly during the 1950s and early 1960s, she indulged in the same anti-German caricatures that she satirized in *Pale Horse, Pale Rider.*

It's interesting that none of the other literary friends in this book became as involved in war relief and propaganda work as James and Wharton. Melville visited a cousin at the front during the Civil War and wrote a volume of poems dedicated to "the memory of the THREE HUNDRED THOUSAND" Union dead, but he never ministered to the wounded, as Whitman (his exact contemporary) did and James did fifty years later. Hawthorne held himself even more aloof from the conflict. Always skeptical about the benefits of freeing the slaves (an attitude that shocked his Abolitionist friends in Concord) and doubtful whether the Union was worth preserving, Hawthorne became a rather reluctant convert to the cause. Like Melville (with whom he had lost contact), he traveled south into the war zone, and his political connections gained him an interview with Lincoln. His piece in *The Atlantic* about his impressions of the war ("Chiefly About War Matters," July 1862) raised eyebrows in the North for its less than flattering remarks about Lincoln. Hawthorne blamed the "general heart-quake of the country" for interrupting his literary labors.

James, Wharton, Porter, and Eudora Welty also found it almost impossible to concentrate on their fiction during the wars that they lived through. For a few months during the Second World War, Welty reviewed books about the war for *The New York Times Book Review* under the pseudonym Michael Ravenna; but when word got out that a nonmilitary nonmale was doing this job, she was taken off it. Both of Welty's brothers fought in the war, and she wrote many anguished letters to the front, collected books for soldiers, and listened each night with her mother to news reports on the radio.

Elizabeth Bishop holed up in Key West for much of the war; from her published work, one would never know that a world war was fought during her lifetime. Robert Lowell was, characteristically, far more *engagé*. After trying to enlist in the navy and the army early in the war, Lowell refused to report when he was drafted in 1943. As he explained in a long letter to President Roosevelt, the Allies had already "rolled back" their enemies and were now waging "a war without quarter or principles, to the permanent destruction of Germany and Japan."[17] The government declined to grant him status as a conscientious objector, and Lowell was sentenced to a year and a day in federal prison—an experience he wrote about in some of his most memorable poems, including "Colloquy in Black Rock," "In the Cage," and "Memories of West Street and Lepke." And, of course Lowell was strongly and publicly opposed to the war in Vietnam later.

Perhaps James and Wharton's fervent involvement in volunteer work during the First World War reflects their patrician sense of responsibility (something that Lowell invoked in his letter of refusal to President Roosevelt); or perhaps, living abroad, they were simply *closer* to the action than any of the other literary friends.

James and Wharton's comradeship during the war was seriously strained when James made his most radical wartime gesture: his declaration of British citizenship on July 28, 1915. As Edel notes, James's motives for this controversial step were a mixture of the practical and the propagandistic. James was annoyed that despite his forty-year residence in England he was still officially an alien and as such required to secure police permission to travel down to Rye, which was classified a forbidden zone during the war. Becoming an English subject would allow him to come and go freely in "his" own country. In a letter to Prime Minister Herbert Asquith, requesting him to stand as one of the four character witnesses necessary for naturalization, James also spoke of his desire "to testify at this crisis to the force of my attachment and devotion to England and to the cause for which she is fighting. . . . I can only testify by laying at her feet my explicit, my material and spiritual allegiance, and throwing into the scale of her fortune my all but imponderable moral weight."[18] Even at this solemn public moment, James could not resist the rich ambiguity of that "all but imponderable." In any case, he clearly meant the step as an expression of his "fiendish" fervency for the war and as a slap in the face of American isolationism. The application was rushed through, and *The Times* of London trumpeted the event with the headline: MR. HENRY JAMES. ADOPTION OF BRITISH NATIONALITY. "All lovers of literature in this country will welcome the decision of this writer of genius," the accompanying story proclaimed.[19]

American lovers of literature, however, were anything but welcoming. James had long been criticized in his native country for preferring Europe to America, and his renunciation of American citizenship during this international crisis confirmed in many narrow minds the suspicion that he was anti-American—a label that stuck to James for many, many years. Wharton joined with James's own family in deploring his action. Though she never reproached James directly, she attacked him to friends, writing to Alfred Austin: "You don't really expect me, as an American, to think Mr. James has done well to leave us? It has made me very sad. . . . We don't care much for defections."[20] In time, however, she was to accept his move and even to sympathize with it. "I did not share" his point of view "when he took his decision," she wrote shortly after James's death, "but . . . the subsequent course of things at home has shed a corroborative glare [on it]. It is indeed hard for some of us to 'accept America as it seems to be today,' & his change of citizenship was the revolt of a sensitive conscience bred in the old ideals, & outraged by the divergence between act & utterance which has come to be a matter of course for the new American."[21] In her memoirs she offers a more personal reason for her change of heart: "At the time I considered it a mistake; it seemed to me rather puerile, and altogether unlike him. Not knowing what to say I refrained from writing to him; and I regret it now, for I think the act comforted him, and it deeply touched his old friends in England."[22]

James was already seriously ailing—in body as well as in mind—at the time he changed his citizenship. A notorious hypochondriac, James had for years wailed in his letters to Wharton over an array of infirmities including jaundice, heart trouble ("pectoral passages," as he called them), "food loathing," "digestive & stomachic deviltry," a bad case of shingles in 1912, and extensive dental work ending with the extraction of most of his teeth in 1914. "James's incessant preoccupation with his health gradually led to periods of nervous depression," Wharton noted rather tartly in her memoirs.[23]

In early 1910, he suffered a serious mental and physical collapse—taking to his bed with a "deep inanition & depression & disqualification (for everything—but the tomb)," as he wrote Wharton. Having crossed the Channel to minister to him at his bedside, Wharton reported in alarm to Fullerton that James was unspeakably lonely and despairing and seemed to be on the verge of suicide: " 'Not to wake—not to wake—' that was his refrain."[24] It was during this seizure, probably brought on by the poor sales of the New York Edition, that James burned nearly all the letters that had been written to him, including Wharton's.

James eventually pulled through this black period, and his doctor pronounced him clear of organic disease, but in his final years he complained more and more of palpitations and shortness of breath—signs of weakening of the heart and arteriosclerosis. In September 1913 he pictured himself pathetically to Wharton as "a poor old person pulled up by the roadside, supported against the nearest object & ruefully panting, not to say woefully groaning, while he faces the next 'rising ground.' "[25] By the autumn of 1915, his angina had become acute and he was taking almost no food. Perhaps sensing that the end was near, in October he went down to Rye from his lodgings in Chelsea to burn the remainder of his papers. Wharton, despite the danger of crossing the Channel, came from Paris to visit him that month, but her week in London proved to be frustrating and depressing.

The few glimpses she had of James convinced her that he was in very bad shape. "*Our* Henry was gone when I was in

London in October," she wrote their common friend Gaillard Lapsley in January 1916, regretting bitterly that she had "not even . . . had a real goodbye from him before leaving England."[26] It was after this visit that Wharton asked James's secretary, Theodora Bosanquet, to send her regular (and confidential) bulletins on the Master's state of health (she had done the same thing several times already during previous bouts of illness). Wharton wanted to be able to rush to England at a moment's notice, although, as it turned out, the moment never arose: Wharton feared that her sudden appearance at his bedside would agitate James, and so she had to content herself with fretting in France.

The news from Bosanquet was less and less encouraging. James suffered a stroke at the beginning of December, which seriously impaired his mental and physical powers. Bosanquet wrote on December 11 that he was "quite delirious" and the paralysis was so severe at times that he was unable to move his eyes. The next day she reported to Wharton that despite the serious damage to his brain, James insisted on dictating to her a book about Napoleon: "There is the extraordinary fact that his mind *does* retain the power to frame perfectly characteristic sentences—even whole pages of pure 'Henry James' prose composition. . . . And the fragments he dictates do, in the queerest way, hang together. . . ."[27]

During one of his more lucid intervals, the Master was told that he had won the Order of Merit—the highest civilian honor awarded in England. "Turn off the light so as to spare my blushes," he told his maid.[28] At another moment of clarity he asked Bosanquet to thank Wharton for her concern, promising that when "these strange and difficult conditions" abated he would "get into a closer relation with her."[29] The idea of going mad, of losing his grip on reality, appalled James and he spoke of nights "of horror and terror." Bosanquet's last few dispatches are heartbreaking. James failed to recognize his London lodgings, believing himself at various times to be in a third-rate Irish hotel, on board a ship, or in Rome. One day he insisted on being moved constantly from one chair to another until his household staff collapsed in exhaustion.

By the end of December, the great light of James's mind had all but gone out. It came as a huge relief to his friends and family when death finally ended his suffering on the afternoon of February 28, 1916. "I was so glad to know the end was quiet & unconscious," Wharton wrote to Bosanquet when she heard the news. "We who knew him well know how great he would have been if he had never written a line."[30] Years later, when she wrote her memoirs, Wharton gave this vivid picture of James's final days:

> His dying was slow and harrowing. The final stroke had been preceded by one or two premonitory ones, each causing a diminution just marked enough for the still conscious intelligence to register it, and the sense of disintegration must have been tragically intensified to a man like James, who had so often and deeply pondered on it, so intently watched for its first symptoms. He is said to have told his old friend Lady Prothero, when she saw him after the first stroke, that in the very act of falling (he was dressing at the time) he heard in the room a voice which was distinctly, it seemed, not his own, saying: "So here it is at last, the distinguished thing!" The phrase is too beautifully characteristic not to be recorded. He saw the distinguished thing coming, faced it, and received it with words worthy of all his dealings with life.[31]

"All my 'blue distances' will be shut out forever when he goes," Wharton wrote Gaillard Lapsley as James dwindled away in London. "His friendship has been the pride & honour of my life. Plus ne m'est rien [nothing means anything to me anymore] after such a gift as that—except the memory of it."[32] "We had a Henry that *no one* else knew," she wrote later, "and it was *the* Henry we had!"[33] Wharton exerted herself after James's death to retain possession of "her" Henry—*the* Henry—to keep her memories of him alive and to transmit him intact to posterity. With her characteristic desire for control, she entered into a protracted wrangle with the James family over the choice of editor for his collected letters, refusing to turn over her own letters from James if "the family persist in their idea," as she put it, "of editing the letters themselves." The negotiations were immensely complicated by the fact that the leader of the James family delegation, William James's widow, detested Wharton, having been scandalized by the adultery in *The Reef* and having fixed on her as the sole culprit in the debacle over the Master's seventieth birthday present. Eventually, Percy Lubbock—Wharton's candidate—was awarded the job, and a rather prim, tidied-up slice of James's Everest of correspondence appeared a few years after his death.

Wharton was aware that "her" Henry appeared only fleetingly in Lubbock's volume; and so she took pains to remedy the situation by publishing a long and lively review of the book. She uses rich, warm colors in her portrait of the Master, fondly recalling his "elaborate politeness" and his "simplicity of heart," his twinkling sense of humor (his "memory for a joke was prodigious"), and his "deep central loneliness." Wharton is most affecting when she writes of James's final burst of impassioned involvement in the war. She recalls that he once said of himself, "It would be hard to imagine a life with less chiaroscuro in it than mine." "In reality," she writes, he had "depths under depths of shadowy unexplored feeling; and it may never be known by what accident it remained in bondage to his art till the great breaking-up of the foundations of the world."[34]

The piece is a grand tribute not only to the Master, but also to the depth of Wharton's feeling for him and the strength of her desire to have their friendship remembered. Though she outlived James by twenty-one years—like him, she suffered a number of strokes, and she died on August 11, 1937, at age seventy-five, at her home in St. Brice-sous-Fôret outside of Paris—Wharton never ceased to regard his friendship as "the pride and honour" of her life.

It rather jars our sense of literary history to realize that Wharton lived into and through the jazz age, meeting the young F. Scott Fitzgerald at St. Brice (the encounter did not come off well—he was tipsy and she was haughty), befriending Aldous Huxley and art historian Kenneth Clark, suffering serious financial setbacks during the Depression, and continuing to write prolifically until very near the end (*The Age of Innocence* in 1920, *The Glimpses of the Moon* in 1922, *The Mother's Recompense* in 1925, *The Children* in 1928, *Hudson River Bracketed* in 1929, and her memoirs, *A Backward Glance,* in 1934). It's jarring because in our minds, Wharton, as she wrote of James, belongs "irrevocably to the old America"—the premodern, prewar, pre-Freudian America that they both evoked so memorably in their fiction.

Wharton herself felt like a refugee amid the "turmoil and mediocrity" of the shattered postwar world; like Newland Archer in *The Age of Innocence,* she despised the old New York society that had formed her, but she despised what followed it even more. Nowadays, the phrase "The age of James and Wharton" conjures up images of ladies in long tight-bodiced dresses engaged in secret love affairs, endless gleaming summers in Newport, and expensive, morally fraught sojourns abroad: Certainly it does *not* conjure up images of corpses rotting in trenches, country churches converted into military hospitals, flappers swilling gin, and bread lines snaking through the canyons of Manhattan, and yet Wharton's life spanned all of this history.

The James–Wharton friendship, as it turns out, supplies some of the most memorable images of "their" age: motor flights in Wharton's splendid "chariot of fire" through the slumbering Berkshire Hills and the villages of central France; hushed glimmering evenings of incomparable conversation on the great terrace of the Mount; the crumbling towers of old English ruins at Bodiam that inspired James's remark about the phrase "Summer afternoon";[35] the intrigue they hatched to rescue Fullerton from a blackmailing mistress; the marvelous Edwardian garden parties they attended together at Cliveden and Stanway. Through all of these scenes rang the sound of their shared laughter—"our common sense of fun," as Wharton puts it. Laughter gave their friendship its long life, its richness and sparkle, and even, oddly enough, its depth.

But the deepest abysses came only after the laughter died and the friends stood witness together to "the great breaking-up of the foundations of the world." James knew at the first resounding gunshots that this *was* the end, abruptly and for all time; he knew that the war instantly and forever changed the "meaning" of his world—that it made a mockery of everything high and noble and fine that had been thought and accomplished in "his" time. Three months into the conflict he wrote to Wharton of the impossibility of working on any fiction "locate[d] in our time": "Our time has been *this* time for the last 50 years, & if it was ignorantly & fatuously so the only light in which to show it is now the light of that tragic delusion. And that's too awful a subject."[36] "It seems to me to *undo* everything," he wrote another friend, "everything that was ours, in the most horrible retroactive way."[37]

In the light of this terrible *éclaircissement*, their friendship shone on as a tremendous consolation. For all the little tempests of envy, competition, financial misunderstanding, and literary spite that had blown up between them over the years, their friendship was at last an unutterable blessing to both of them. Wharton never showed herself a truer friend than in her willingness to forgo this blessing. "I should have liked to have [Henry James] standing beside me the day the victorious armies rode by," she wrote of the war's end in her memoirs: "but when I think of the years intervening between his death and that brief burst of radiance I have not the heart to wish that he had seen it. The waiting would have been too bitter."[38]

James and Wharton to Porter and Welty

"I WAS FOR YEARS upon years compared with Katherine Mansfield," Katherine Anne Porter complained to Flannery O'Connor in a letter. "Then it was Hemingway and even Faulkner, now and then. And now I have graduated into the society of Flaubert, Melville, Stendhal, Henry James, and even Tolstoy. Fast company, I call it, and it does me no earthly good, and it is the device of lazy-minded third-rate reviewers who can't read."[1] Porter is, of course, tooting her own horn under the guise of critic bashing for how could she not have enjoyed such flattering comparisons? Of all the "fast company" reviewers threw her in with, Henry James was the most congenial.

Porter learned far better than Edith Wharton did the crucial lessons of the Master: when to appear and when to disappear in her narratives; how to use historically evocative settings, objects, and family memories to summon up the shades of the past; how to reveal the moral perils of the adult world through the wide eyes of children; how to transcribe the contents of a character's mind without resorting to arty stream-of-consciousness techniques; how to turn a central situation from side to side to side until a perfect ring of ambiguity revolves around it; how to infuse her fiction with the pressure of inevitability.

"My devotion to [James] grows as I study his life," Porter wrote her nephew, "the most admirable life I know, lived as it was in the mind, the imagination, the heart, and the most unwavering fidelity to his own knowledge and convictions. . . . With no support, almost no encouragement or understanding from anybody, he just went on being an artist from his cradle to his grave. . . ."[2]

To just go on being an artist from cradle to grave was the first tenet in Porter's credo. As she responded to a magazine questionnaire: "I choose Henry James, holding as I do with the conscious, disciplined artist, the serious expert, against the expansive, indiscriminating, 'cosmic' sort."[3] Porter did have an indirect personal link with James through Ford Madox Ford, who was a friend of hers at the end of his life and who, as a young man, had known James well in literary London.

It may be stretching things a bit to say that James stood in the same relation to Porter as Hawthorne stood to James—but there was certainly a close and conscious connection in both cases. To seal her devotion to the life and art of Henry James, Porter wrote a long biographical essay about him, based largely on his autobiography, in 1943. Like James's critical biography of Hawthorne, Porter's piece, called "The Days Before," reveals almost as much about her as about her subject. She dwells on James's ancestry, his peculiar childhood and haphazard education (acquired, as she points out with approval, in the streets, theaters, galleries, parties, boats, and hotels of Europe, New York, and Newport— not at a university), his sense of time and place, his "destiny as artist," his fascination with Europe, and his agitating financial situation—all subjects that preoccupied her in her own fiction and nonfictional reminiscences (which are sometimes indistinguishable).

"If people are superior to begin with, as they were," Porter writes of the James family, "the freedom of money is an added freedom of grace and the power of choice in many desirable ways."[4] Porter sounds as if she is speaking from personal experience about such financial freedoms, as indeed she sometimes pretended was the case: But in fact, she grew up dirt poor and was plagued by insufficient funds nearly all her life until *Ship of Fools* became a best-seller when she was in her seventies. The idea of being born into a wealthy superior family—even one whose fortune had "misted away somewhat," as she wrote of the Jameses— appealed to Porter so much that she incorporated it into her own personal myth. And, as friends note, she always lived as if she were rich anyway, parting company here with the anxiously frugal Master.

Edith Wharton appealed to Porter for much the same reasons. The composer David Diamond, a friend of Porter's, recalls one day at Yaddo when Porter found Delmore Schwartz reading an Edith Wharton novel: " 'Now there's a woman I wish I had been!' she told me. 'Not as a writer—but the woman who had all that money, all that admiration.' Of course we didn't know about Fullerton then. I had the feeling that Katherine Anne was modeling herself on Wharton. The desire to live in Paris, to have money, to have the admiration of men—these were mirrored in Katherine Anne's life."[5] According to Diamond, Porter preferred Wharton's post–World War I novels *The Children* (1928) and *Hudson River Bracketed* (1929) to *Ethan Frome* (1911), and she adored her wonderfully creepy short story "The Eyes" about a detached epicene Jamesian gentleman who is haunted each time he contemplates making an emotional commitment by a pair of piercing, hideously depraved eyes.

Wharton's literary influence on Porter, though fainter than James's, is detectable in Porter's penchant for satire (in *Ship of Fools* and "Hacienda") and in her keen eye for the details of dress, manner, and speech that reveal a character's social standing. Porter's mix of veneration and contempt for the "old order" in the South parallels Wharton's ambivalent feelings toward old New York. Both women were convinced that the old orders, for all of their provincial fatuity and binding codes, were being replaced by something far more vicious and ugly. It's also worth noting that Porter's married women are as trapped and miserable as Wharton's, or even *more* trapped for most of them have far less money.

Katherine Anne Porter lived in Paris for several years during the 1930s when Edith Wharton was spending the final summers of her life at her villa in the Paris suburb of St. Brice (she wintered at another home on the Riviera). Porter would undoubtedly have loved to come out to St. Brice to pay homage to Wharton, as F. Scott Fitzgerald had done in the 1920s, but there is no record of any contact between the two women. In Wharton's eyes, Porter, like Melville, might have been too unspeakably bohemian. Or she simply might never have heard of the younger writer, whose reputation had not yet penetrated beyond a small American literary circle.

Porter's inclusion of Melville in her list of fast literary company is not as far-fetched as it seems on first blush. Porter's masterpiece "Noon Wine" has a number of strong echoes to Melville's *Billy Budd,* which was first published posthumously in 1924, just twelve years before Porter composed her short novel in a week.

Both works explore the clash between abstract justice and the mysteries of the human heart. Both delve deeply into what Melville, harking back to the Bible, calls "the mystery of iniquity." Porter's slimy, slick-talking villain Homer T. Hatch is another John Claggart, the sneaking, jealous master-at-arms aboard the *Bellipotent* who engineers Billy's downfall. Porter's industrious, harmonica-playing Swedish farmhand Olaf Helton is another Billy Budd: Both are holy innocents whose violent impulses get the better of them. In both works, the slaying of the villain introduces unanswerable questions about the nature of right and wrong, good and evil, human nature and society.

Billy Budd, as R.W.B. Lewis points out in his study *The American Adam,* is "the type of scapegoat hero" whose fall from innocence parallels Adam's fall and whose sacrifice parallels Christ's.[6] Though Lewis does not mention Porter, she clearly writes out of the "American Adam" tradition he identifies, even naming the doomed soldier-hero of her *Pale Horse, Pale Rider* Adam and explicitly calling him "the sacrificial lamb."

The influence of Hawthorne also turns up in Porter's brief but richly varied opus. The allegory of *Ship of Fools* resonates to Hawthorne, the only real master of allegory in American fiction, and Porter's characters, like Hawthorne's, are tormented by their guilty consciences: Think of the unnamed woman in "Theft," Rosaleen in "The Cracked Looking-Glass," and, of course, Mr. Thompson in "Noon Wine," whose sense of guilt compels him to justify himself over and over to all his neighbors, even though the court declared him innocent. These stern, judgmental Texas farmers in "Noon Wine" are the direct descendants of the black-browed Boston Puritans of *The Scarlet Letter*. Porter's "The Jilting of Granny Weatherall" in which an old woman looks back on her life from the brink of death is a situation right out of Hawthorne. And her Laura in "Flowering Judas" protects herself from life by "denying everything" just as Hawthorne's Ethan Brand denies the warm promptings of the heart and so commits the unpardonable sin.

Porter planted herself squarely in the great American tradition, the tradition of Melville and James, Hawthorne and Wharton. Actually, "planted" conveys the wrong impression for her art (with the exception of the belabored *Ship of Fools*) has the feeling of spontaneity and freedom, as if the stories just "came to her." But of course they didn't. A conscious consummate artist, like her beloved Master, Henry James, Porter always worked very hard to cover her tracks.

Eudora Welty offers fewer clues than Porter does about her connections to the great tradition. The celebrant of "place in fiction," Welty has closer affinities with fellow southerners like William Faulkner, Peter Taylor, and Porter than with her predecessors from New York and New England. Artistically, she has more in common with Virginia Woolf than with Edith Wharton. Stylistically, she learned more from Chekhov than from James. Still, there is something of Melville's swagger and dark whimsy in some of Welty's early stories (doesn't "Why I Live at the P.O." make a crazy nod at "Bartleby"?), and a muted strain of Melville's rhapsodic music echoes through some of her lyrical passages. Welty inherited something of Melville's restlessness too—all those hopped-up lonely boys and frustrated young women eager to bust out of their prisonlike homes to hit the road and to see "the world," even if the world is nothing more exotic than San Francisco or Chicago.

Yet Welty's nearest kin in American fiction may be Hawthorne. We see both of them peering out, unseen, from upstairs windows at the petty, complicated, funny, and horrible lives of their neighbors. We see both of them flitting through the garden at dusk, painfully aware that those same neighbors are now peering at them through "the curtain of green." America's dark, dangerous, heathen forest hems in their sparse, gossipy little towns, and whether the forest is northern hemlock or southern live oak, the devil stalks through it. In Welty the devil is more likely to rape you than thrust you into the ring of fire—but he's the same old devil that tempted Young Goodman Brown. In her memoirs Welty writes of her fascination with processions and parades: The appalling, torch-lit midnight procession at the climax of "My Kinsman, Major Molineux" marches directly into her work, most memorably in "The Wide Net," which is also a story of surprising discoveries.

When Eudora Welty was born on April 13, 1909, Edith Wharton, in Paris, was in the throes of her love affair with Morton Fullerton, and Henry James was on the verge of the suicidal depression brought on by the failure of his New York Edition. "Hideous & horrible has been my long silence, but there have been inevitabilities in *its* depths of inevitability," the ailing James wrote to Wharton from Lamb House on the day after Welty's birth. Katherine Anne Porter, then nineteen years old, was three years into what she later called her "preposterous first marriage," which endured for another six years before ending in divorce. Although they were both daughters of the South, it is hard to imagine two women writers who had less in common than Katherine Anne Porter and Eudora Welty when they met nearly three decades later in Baton Rouge.

PART THREE

Katherine Anne Porter and Eudora Welty

Wanda Landowska once said, about an argument with some English friends over the ascription of some old music . . . "Friendship is more important than truth." I would not go so far: but I know friendship when I see it, and none of us, not one man or woman in the whole world, since we got up on our hind legs and started looking for the Truth, has ever been sure he has found it.

—KATHERINE ANNE PORTER,
The Collected Essays and
Occasional Writings of
Katherine Anne Porter

In New York you may have the greatest and most congenial friends, but it's extraordinary if you ever know anything about them except that little wedge of their life that you meet with the little wedge of your life. You don't get the sense of a continuous narrative line. You never see the full circle. But in the South, where people don't move about as much, even now, and where they once hardly ever moved away at all, the pattern of life was always right there.

—EUDORA WELTY,
Conversations with Eudora Welty

TEN

The Most Unburdensome Friendship

> *I will make my own mistakes, not yours.*
> —Katherine Anne Porter, *"Old Mortality"*

> *She began writing spontaneously when she was a child, being a born writer; she continued without any plan for a profession, without any particular encouragement, and, as it proved, not needing any.*
> —Katherine Anne Porter *on Eudora Welty in her introduction to Welty's*
> A Curtain of Green and Other Stories

Writers, if they're lucky and if they're good, cross the threshold between anonymity and recognition while still young. Some, like Byron or Melville, awake one bright morning to find themselves famous; others get towed into fame by an older, or at least more established, writer friend. Hemingway had Fitzgerald and Gertrude Stein, both of whom helped him with contacts and connections in Paris and New York when he was an unknown newspaper reporter trying his hand at fiction. Willa Cather, on the eve of her literary breakthrough in *O Pioneers!*, profited from the sisterly benevolence of Sarah Orne Jewett, who advised her to stop wasting her talent on magazine work and to turn to the subjects closest to her heart—her childhood memories of Virginia and Nebraska. Edith Wharton, as we have seen, had Henry James, who, though stingy with praise and hospitality, gave freely of criticism and companionship.

Eudora Welty, at the beginning of her career as a published writer, had Katherine Anne Porter. Welty was lucky and much more than good when Porter took her up "out of the blue" and helped find her a place in the golden circle of renown. The friendship came, for Welty, at the perfect time—the pivotal moment between obscurity and first success; it rose on the secure foundation of instant instinctive understanding and esteem for each other's work and it flourished, at least initially, in the warmth of generosity. But in every other way theirs was one of the odder pairings in American letters. Porter and Welty, when they met, were nearly polar opposites in character, habits, appearance, experience and personal style, in the way they lived their lives and did their work. Their friendship did not make them any more alike. Nonetheless, both of them cherished the relationship, although they didn't always cherish each other.

Porter, indeed, thought little enough of her new friend to delay publication of her first book while she dallied over writing the thirty-three-hundred-word introduction that she boasted would increase Welty's income from its sales by ten thousand dollars. Welty, though reverent in print about Porter, has been known to mock her privately for her appalling taste and her ceaseless self-centered chatter. Still, the friendship endured for some forty years. A strange friendship, certainly, but also strangely revealing of the attitudes and passions of both women.

They met in Baton Rouge, Louisiana, in July 1939. "It was hot midsummer," Porter writes in her introduction to Welty's first book, *A Curtain of Green and Other Stories,* and they "spent a pleasant evening together talking in the cool old house with all the windows open. Miss Welty sat listening, as she must have done a great deal of listening on many such occasions. She was and is a quiet, tranquil-looking, modest girl. . . ." There was, without a doubt, an elaborate meal and a free flow of wine for Porter was a passionate cook and canny hostess. One sees her fluttering like a moth in the soft Louisiana darkness, her silver-white hair and pale smooth skin gathering in the last light, her slight, graceful figure perched on the edge of a chair or silhouetted against an open window, her hands ever busy carrying a glass or a cigarette to her lips, her throaty voice filling the room with stories, gossip, political ruminations as her cigarette filled it with smoke.

Porter, then forty-nine, was still a beauty—indeed, she would be beautiful at seventy—and here, briefly, in Louisiana, and surrounded by southern friends and, briefly, a southern husband, she could give full rein to her southern belle persona. A "lady," never a woman, and an "artist," never an author, Porter was as famous for her persona—her conversation, her looks, her style—as for her writing. She was, as Welty was to recall years and years later, "the first person I met or knew who very consciously was aware she was an artist and that she was practicing an art and who respected it above all things that anyone could do."[1] At parties and literary gatherings she was always at the center of a group of men, always smoking and talking, almost always about herself. She surely put on quite a show for the "quiet, tranquil-looking, modest girl" from Mississippi.

Welty, then thirty, had driven down for the day from Jackson, Mississippi, where she was living in a fine, lofty, red-brick, 1920s-vintage Tudor house with her widowed mother. "Tranquil-looking" was about the kindest thing Porter could say about her appearance for Welty has never been pretty. "I don't think she had a redeeming feature—except maybe her eyes," remarked a painter who did her portrait, "but that didn't seem to matter at all." Her frame is too lean and angular to be elegant, her back too curved, her face too large and too soft, with teeth and nose too prominent and chin not prominent enough. Having been born and raised in the Deep South, Welty knew the whole southern belle routine by heart, so Porter's performance would not have struck her as especially novel. Now and then she would emit a little gasp of astonishment or a great whoop of laughter for laughter has always come easily to Welty, surprisingly easy for someone as shy as she is. She said very little except to thank her hostess profusely. Southerners have such excellent manners, and Welty has the additional excellences of sweetness and modesty.

Porter refers to Welty as a "girl," which is odd considering that she was thirty at the time of their meeting, but others who knew her well have used the same word to describe Welty. "She was a very sweet, wholesome, charming girl with a lot of talent who was delighted to find people liked her stories," the critic Cleanth Brooks recalls of his first impression of her in 1939. "She is one of the most modest writers I've ever known. There was not a bit of ego in her."[2] Of course, Brooks and Porter might have called her a girl simply because she was unmarried, but it may be something more than that. There was a quality of freshness and seeming innocence, of being untried and unspoiled, of shying away from the viciousness of desire and the shabbiness of remorse that made Welty seem girlish. Though (like Melville, James, and Lowell) she knew violence, madness, grief, anger, and desperate, furious loneliness to the bone—as all the world could see by reading her stories—she refused to know lust or bitterness. And in this she was and remained a girl.

Shy and modest and cautious and very unassuming at first meeting, Welty could shine when she relaxed. The blistering humor of stories like "Why I Live at the P.O." and "Petrified Man" enters her conversation, too, and she laughs as quickly and naturally as she gets others to laugh. "She could just go off into peals of laughter over something that other people would not have found funny," said an acquaintance from the 1940s. "This was her most engaging feature." She talks, as she writes, with a rare sense of timing, and with perfect pitch for the droll, incongruous, absurd. Her accent is deeply and purely southern, her voice as soft and sweet as her manner, except when someone crosses her. Then she can turn hard as brick. A very plain, always very private, sweet southern woman of thirty with a towering gift for fiction and an adamantine core: such was the unknown writer who came to visit the celebrated Katherine Anne Porter that hot July evening in Baton Rouge.

Unmarried, and never to be married, Welty nonetheless had a rather hectic social life with a lot of the "nice" people in Jackson. She is so much "underfoot locally," as Porter reports her saying in the introduction to her first collection of stories, that "the only comment her friends make when a new story appears is, 'Why, Eudora, when did you write that?' Not how, or even why, just when. They see her about so much, what time has she for writing."[3]

Though certainly not wealthy, the Welty family was comfortable, especially by the standards of Mississippi, the nation's poorest state, at the end of the Great Depression. Several years before he died in 1931, Welty's father, who had attained the position of president of the Lamar Life Insurance Company, built the family a rather grand house on a wooded plot of land at the edge of Jackson. The house and garden that her mother laid out reflected the prosperity and optimism of the mid-1920s. It was built for the ages "in a style very much of its day," as Welty writes in her memoirs, "of stucco and brick and beams."[4] The style was Tudor, the domestic architectural style that broadcast new and increasing wealth in the twenties, just as postmodernist arches and lattices and columns do today. The house was more than ample enough for Christian and Chestina Welty and their three children (Eudora had two younger brothers); its size and solidity must have seemed cruelly mocking to Eudora and her mother after Christian Welty died in 1931 and the boys went off to war a decade later.

Though neither of her parents came from Jackson originally (her father, in fact, was a Yankee, the son of Ohio farmers of Swiss extraction, and her mother hailed from an old Virginia family that had moved to West Virginia around the time of the Civil War), their oldest child and only daughter was rooted deeply and unshakably in the town of her birth. She went away to university (two years at Madison, Wisconsin, to complete her B.A. at the University of Wisconsin and a year in New York studying advertising at the Columbia University School of Business); she plunged into New York for six months in 1944 to work as an editor for *The New York Times Book Review* and later she stayed for two long stretches in San Francisco in 1946 and 1947. But Welty never really *lived,* never settled, away from her parents' Tudor house on Pinehurst Street and never would. The nice southern girl living at home with her mother: It was a fact of her life that she brooded over a good deal.

In 1943, after their friendship was firmly cemented, Welty wrote Porter wistfully that she felt "lulled" by the quietness of life at home and she wondered if she would ever make the "tremendous leap" and break away. But as soon as she expresses the possibility of leaving home, she dismisses it as a fond dream.[5]

The "tremendous leap" never came and the fond dream faded, especially after her mother became an invalid. Even to travel away from home—as she has done often and with great relish all over America and Europe whenever she could get away—"tore all of us up inside," Welty confesses in her memoirs, "for they seemed, each journey away from home . . . something that had better be momentous, to justify such a leap into the dark. The torment and guilt—the torment of having the loved one go, the guilt of being the loved one gone—comes into my fiction as it did and does into my life."[6]

When her mother died in 1966, Eudora continued in the family home alone, and now, in her eighties, she lives there still. "As you have seen," she concludes *One Writer's Beginnings,* "I am a writer who came of a sheltered life. A sheltered life can be a daring life as well. For all serious daring starts from within."[7]

Welty's parents, for better or worse, gave her a sheltered life, but they could not shelter her from the torment and guilt of their separations or from the ordeal of losing them. Her father died suddenly of leukemia when he was fifty-two. It was 1931, the start of the Great Depression, and Welty's younger brothers were still in high school and college. The sudden loss of her father when she was twenty-two and the stark visions of toil and endurance that she witnessed and photographed when she traveled around Mississippi as a publicist for the WPA from 1933 to 1936 were the shocks that launched her on the "serious daring" of her early work. Years later in an interview, she said that her work for the WPA (Works Progress Administration) was "the real germ of my wanting to become a real writer, a true writer. It caused me to seriously attempt it. It made me see, for the first time, what life was really like in this state."[8]

Without much encouragement from friends or family— "Why, Eudora, when did you write that?"—Welty retreated whenever she could to the "semi-privacy," as she termed it in a letter to Porter, of her long, airy, many-windowed bedroom to write the stories of madness, betrayal, murder, rape, deformity, shame, suicide, alienation, and man's bafflement before the lush, cruel mysteries of nature that were later to be published together in *A Curtain of Green and Other Stories,* perhaps her strongest collection. Welty's first published story, "Death of a Traveling Salesman," ran in the spring of 1936 in a literary magazine called *Manuscript* published out of Akron, Ohio. She received no money for the story—"I didn't care a hoot that they couldn't, they didn't pay me anything," she said later. "If they had paid me a million dollars it wouldn't have made any difference"[9]—but she did get the unreserved admiration of John Rood, the editor of *Manuscript.* It was a start.

Welty kept sending work out and more stories began appearing in other literary magazines. "I believe I've always been lucky—my work has always landed safely and among friends," she told an interviewer years later.[10] One great stroke of luck came when her work "landed safely" among Robert Penn Warren,

Cleanth Brooks, and Albert Erskine, who were then in charge of the influential *Southern Review* published out of Louisiana State University at Baton Rouge. Thirty-five years later, when asked whether it helped her that Warren, Brooks, and Erskine took an interest in her work, Welty gasped in reply: "*Helped* me? Why, it just gave me, you know, my life to get my stories in print at that time."[11] *Southern Review* ran "A Piece of News" in the summer issue of 1937, "A Memory" followed in the autumn, then "Old Mr. Grenada" (later retitled "Old Mr. Marblehall") in the spring of 1938, and "A Curtain of Green" that autumn. Of the editors who were giving this young woman her life, Warren and Brooks are well known as charter members of the group of southern writers and critics who called themselves the Agrarians, as practitioners of New Criticism, instigators and celebrants of the southern renaissance, and, in Warren's case, poet and novelist. Erskine, who has failed to win fame, was a twenty-seven-year-old graduate student who was getting his Ph.D. in English literature at LSU and working as business manager on the *Review*. He also happened to be blond, hazel-eyed, tawny-skinned, classically handsome, and married (at least for the time being) to Katherine Anne Porter. Porter says in her introduction to Welty's stories that Erskine regarded Welty as "his personal discovery" and became her enduring partisan. (More enduring than Porter knew at the time, for years later he was to become her editor again, when she moved from Harcourt Brace to Random House.) So in a sense, the friendship between the two women began as a kind of family concern.

Porter read the stories that her husband and their friends were enthusiastically publishing, and liked what she read. On October 25, 1938, she wrote "out of the blue," as Welty puts it, to express "admiration for your very fine work," to suggest to her that she contact Ford Madox Ford about publishing her work, and to propose naming her as a candidate for a Guggenheim Fellowship. The tone of Porter's initial letter is both grand and gracious—and Porter relished being both. Welty was indeed a "find" and Porter was proud to be among the very first to find her and set her on her way. They also had some common ground for several of Porter's finest stories, including "Old Mortality" and "Pale Horse, Pale Rider," were appearing in *Southern Review* at the same time. Baton Rouge and Jackson were only a few hours' drive apart, even in those days before interstates, so it was natural that such keen and shared admiration should lead to a meeting.

Welty, characteristically, was both delighted at the recognition—most delighted that the praise came from a "*writer . . . the writer of short stories I revered,*"[12]—and terrified at the prospect of meeting Miss Porter. "It took me, I suppose, six months or a year to fully get up my nerve," she recalled. "Twice I got as far as Natchez and turned around and came back. But I finally did get there, and Katherine Anne couldn't have been more welcoming."[13] Long afterward, a friend of Welty's remarked that "Porter's accepting her as a fellow writer was one of the things that made her feel that she *was* a writer." Two fine short story writers recognizing and appreciating each other's gifts: that is how their friendship started in July 1939.

Welty describes Porter as being "out in the world," a phrase that in her fiction, particularly in *The Golden Apples,* signifies the very opposite of the sheltered confines of home, family, and small town. To be out in the world is to expose oneself to the hazards of adventure, poverty, passion, maybe even art—and all this Katherine Anne Porter had done by the time she befriended Eudora Welty in 1939. Her life, nearly from infancy, had been as restless, rootless, and unpredictable as Eudora Welty's life was fixed, sedentary, and apparently monotonous.

Starting at age sixteen, Porter had acquired and discarded a string of husbands and lovers (she once claimed to have enjoyed thirty-seven of the latter before she was forty),[14] moved ceaselessly and compulsively from Texas to Denver to New York to Mexico to Bermuda to Berlin to Paris to Basel, changing direction and locale nearly as often as she changed sexual partners. In the spring of 1938 she had come to roost in Baton Rouge with Erskine, her fourth and final husband, a man more than twenty years her junior whom she had married after a whirlwind courtship and under somewhat false pretenses (he didn't learn her age—forty-seven—until the wedding ceremony in New Orleans in April 1938). The marriage, she said later, ended on the day it began,[15] and by the autumn of that year, Porter was trying to disentangle herself from Erskine. She finally succeeded in the spring of 1940, when she left Baton Rouge for Yaddo, the writers' colony in Saratoga Springs, New York.

Porter's life, depending on how you look at it, appears chaotic, shabby, painful, and wasteful—or passionate, protean, committed, and thrilling. Perhaps all. Perhaps the passion and excitement were masks for the pain—or the delicate, exposed nerve ends that transmit pain to an overwrought mind given to "fabulous ups and downs." She needed to live at the center of a small storm, a perpetual, ever-changing crisis of her own making. The storm might brew material for her stories; more often it made work difficult or impossible. When the storm raged too severely, her health, always delicate after she contracted tuberculosis in 1916 and a near-fatal influenza infection during the pandemic of 1918, gave out, and she withdrew. She "led a maximum life," her lifelong friend Glenway Wescott wrote of her, "concomitantly with her perfect, even perfectionist story writing."[16]

She was never one to plod dutifully through a piece of work, pounding away at the typewriter every day until she rolled the piece out from beginning to end. "She had to be in the mood and be in the right place, and then she would dash it off," said the painter Marcella Comès Winslow,[17] at whose Georgetown house Porter lived while working at the Library of Congress in the mid-1940s. She worked in the lulls of her personal storm or in the teeth of a storm. Sometimes a lull coincided blessedly with a burst of incandescent creativity—a period of "trancelike absorption" as she called it[18] that left her outwardly serene (and temporarily moored fast) while she seethed inwardly to transcribe all the perfect sentences that welled up one after another with that pure, sharp, ringing clarity that is a hallmark of her style.

Such a calm came over her in 1936 when she holed up at the Water Wheel Tavern in Bucks County, Pennsylvania, to race through in a matter of weeks two of her three finest short novels. About a week each for her masterpiece "Noon Wine" and "Old Mortality," with "Pale Horse, Pale Rider" completed in New Orleans a few months later. It was the most sustained successful creative period of her literary life, and the last one to descend on her for a long, long time. Her final burst came in 1961 when she pushed *Ship of Fools* into port at a small hotel on Cape Ann, Massachusetts, but by most accounts the completion of the novel was not a period of "trancelike absorption" but a sweaty, agonizing wrestling match with the demon that had been clutching at her throat for decades.

The creative burst that produced her three finest short novels ended the decade—the 1930s—in which she had found her truest, clearest voice in fiction. By the end of the 1930s, Porter had won a very grand place for herself in American letters based on a rather slim, but impressive body of work. "Her fame," said Glenway Wescott, "has been out of proportion to the amount of her work, however highly one might think of it."[19] Her story "Flowering Judas" about a dazed and numb American girl's unwitting participation in Mexico's bloody revolutionary politics was received with rapture by critics when it was published in *Hound and Horn* in the spring of 1930. Robert Penn Warren later called it "one of the most famous [stories] of our time."[20] When *Pale Horse, Pale Rider,* the volume containing the short novel by that name as well as "Old Mortality" and "Noon Wine," appeared in 1939, reviewers compared Porter to Hawthorne, Flaubert, Milton, and Henry James.[21] *Ship of Fools,* already embarked on in an early version called "Promised Land," threw the literary world into an agony of protracted anticipation that gave new meaning to the phrase "long-awaited."

Porter's sterling reputation was not based solely on her considerable gifts as a writer of short fiction. She was one of those writers around whom shimmered the silvery aura of celebrity: Like Byron (the godfather of all literary personalities), Dickens, the young Melville, Oscar Wilde, Edith Wharton, Ernest Hemingway, Norman Mailer, Robert Lowell, she satisfied (or pandered to) our need for literary "stars," figures whose lives and loves seem larger, deeper, more significant than our own, people whose behavior in bars, wars, bedrooms, public stages, or simply in conversation with their friends seems far more wonderful and romantic than anything their characters do on the printed page.

The elements of Porter's fame were already firmly in place by the time she and Welty met. The prime element, after her literary talent, was her beauty—an attribute that remained undimmed well into her middle and even old age. Cleanth Brooks, a neighbor of hers in Baton Rouge and a friend from then on, recalled that her face had that wonderful bone structure that ages well. "Katherine Anne knew how beautiful she was," Brooks said, "and she loved being beautiful. I'm sure she thanked God on her knees every night for making her beautiful."[22] Glenway Wescott described her this way in the early 1960s: "She has in fact a lovely face, of the utmost distinction in the Southern way; moonflower-pale, never sunburned, perhaps not burnable. She is a small woman, with a fine figure still; sometimes very slender, sometimes not. Her eyes are large, dark, and lustrous. . . . Her voice is sweet, a little velvety or husky."[23] The composer David Diamond, who knew her well at this time, had a dissenting opinion: "Hers was not a soft, feminine body. She was bony and hard. There was no succulence to her. There was a hardness of body and character."[24] As a young woman, Porter, bony or not, had been pretty enough to work in the movies, and approaching fifty, she looked at least a decade younger, with the sleek poised demeanor of a mature woman of the world. After a three-year residence in Paris from 1933 to 1936, she had become the epitome of literary chic.

She was also incredibly charming when she wanted to be. Porter's gifts as a conversationalist were as legendary as her beauty. The southern writer Caroline Gordon, who knew Porter very well, described her as "an actress who happens to have a talent for setting down her emotions in felicitous prose."[25] Whenever she attended a party or literary gathering, a circle of mostly male rapt listeners would gather around her to hear her spin tales, reminisce, and drop names. Dressed expensively and luxuriously, chain-smoking, using her expressive fiery deep-blue eyes to fix and tease her listeners, Porter would upstage any other woman in the room, even women accustomed to taking center stage.[26] In a tête-à-tête, Porter's talk flowed just as freely and entertainingly but after a while oppressively. Marcella Winslow said that when Katherine Anne was around, "you had to let her take over because that was what she wanted to do. It was not a back and forth conversation—it was more or less on Katherine Anne."[27] It could become exhausting.

By the late 1930s, Porter had been on the literary "scene" for the better part of two decades. She had made swarms of literary friends (Josephine Herbst, Allen Tate, Robert Penn Warren, Ford Madox Ford, the southern writer Andrew Lytle, Robert McAlmon, an American expatriate writer) and nearly as many enemies (among them were Elinor Wylie and Hart Crane, both then dead). She was indeed a "Great Personage," as Tate called her, and someone to be reckoned with.

Porter's personal beauty and charm were all the more alluring because they belonged to a writer not only gifted, but tormented. Although she just failed to die (of tuberculosis and influenza) in the first flush of brilliant youth like Keats or Shelley, or drink herself into middle-age heart failure like Fitzgerald or James Agee, Porter belonged, like these colleagues, to the school of suffering Romantic writers. Her art was like a high-strung Thoroughbred horse—expensive to keep, hard to mount, impossible to stay on for very long. The dark background of her glamour was the enormous difficulty she had in getting her work—her fiction—done. Welty wrote that one of the most enduring lessons she learned as a writer from Porter was to value "the role of difficulty in writing . . . Katherine Anne was helping me to recognize living with difficulty as a form of passion."[28]

But the difficulty, and her perfectionism, kept Porter's output down to a trickle—a problem that Elizabeth Bishop also suffered from. Porter was almost as famous for what she didn't write, what she promised to write and couldn't or wouldn't finish, as for what she did. Elizabeth Hardwick says she was as vain about her writing as about her beauty[29]: The endless delays ensured that the world would see only an unblemished image. Her inability to "buckle down" to work, her infinite distractibility, the torment and guilt of missing deadlines, spending her advances before she'd set a word to paper, taking on new work to bail herself out of hopelessly stalled old work—this ceaseless, punishing, often fruitless pursuit of her Muse was to color Porter's friendship with Welty as it did all her close relationships.

When she took up Welty and helped get her writing career aloft, Porter had awakened from the brief "trancelike absorption" of "Noon Wine" and was entering the worst and longest stretch of procrastination of her career, the twenty-year agony of writing *Ship of Fools*. The fact that the friendship began when Porter was having a long dry spell creatively was surely a coincidence. Welty no more caused Porter's creative drought than Hawthorne caused Melville's. Perhaps the events are unrelated. But it's possible that Porter's willingness to "adopt" Welty, a writer twenty years her junior just starting out on her literary career, reveals an internal shift in focus or attitude, a settling into the role of grande dame or mentor, a passing of the mantle. In any case, it's certainly true that Porter had an easier time writing letters, nominating her friend for fellowships, and reading and commenting on Welty's stories than working on her own.

Why did Porter adopt this particular writer? First, of course, there was the work. Porter, whatever else she was in the way of southern belle and sexual adventuress, was above all else an artist, and she immediately recognized the artist in Welty as well. "You are as good as there is in your time," she wrote Welty on the event of the publication of her first book, "and you have a long way to go and to grow. I can't see the end of it, thank God. . . ."[30]

In her introduction to *A Curtain of Green,* Porter insists approvingly that "there is in none of these stories any trace of autobiography" (a perverse kind of praise since she claimed proudly that "everything I ever wrote in the way of fiction is based very securely on something in real life"); but she recognizes that in "A Memory" "there might be something of early personal history." Indeed, yes. Porter describes it as "the story of the child on the beach, alienated from the world of adult knowledge by her state of childhood, who hoped to learn the secrets of life by looking at everything, squaring her hands before her eyes to bring the observed thing into a frame."[31]

What the girl in the story observes is a grotesquely real redneck family—a slovenly woman with lumpy breasts and arms on which the "fat hung . . . like an arrested earthslide," her flabby husband, and their weedy, noisy, sulking children. In their solid, immutable, vulgar fleshiness, these "common" people blot out a silken fantasy the girl has been spinning about a blond, handsome boy she loves from a distance at school. "It did not matter to me what I looked at," the girl confesses. "I was obsessed with notions about concealment, and from the smallest gesture of a stranger I would wrest what was to me a communication or a presentiment."[32] If we didn't know this was Eudora Welty, we might identify it as Nathaniel Hawthorne. From the large, sloppy, grossly erotic gestures of the "common" family Welty's girl wrests terrified disgust; from the boy she wrests her first "hopelessly unexpressed" passion—but they are equally strangers and her relationship with them is the same: that of the hidden observer.

The girl in the story who tells her "memory" is as obsessed with remaining concealed herself as she is with the concealment of others. And so was (and is) Eudora Welty. "I wished to be, not effaced, but invisible—actually a powerful position," she writes in her memoirs.[33] When she does come out of hiding—as all writers must who do not burn their pages—it is only on her own terms, with her art mediating. The young girl who peers at the world through squared hands now, as an elderly woman and celebrated artist, lets the world peer back at her, but only through a frame of her own choosing. Even the copious interviews and the television appearances are carefully managed to keep the image of pervading sweetness, kindness, gentility, and a kind of aw-shucks innocence intact.

Welty has written that her acute sense of privacy makes her dread the nosiness of biographers and critics: ". . . I have become over-sensitive to it."[34] She has also instructed her friends not to talk with reporters or biographers about her private life. "Like Willa Cather, like T. S. Eliot's widow, she wishes to keep meddling hands off the life," writes Carolyn G. Heilbrun of Welty's extreme privacy. "To her, this is the only proper behavior for the Mississippi lady she so proudly is." Welty's life is her own and she has chosen to keep a tight grip on its intimacies. But of course one must wonder why she hides and what she is hiding.

If Porter's interest in Welty was aroused by her work, it was sustained and warmed into friendship at least in part by Welty's girlishness—by the quietness and tranquillity, the shyness and modesty, the readiness to efface herself and oblige another, by her silent retreat from romance. In the public arenas of parties and conferences where Porter needed to radiate at the center of attention, Welty would drop into the shadows in her dual role of "observer and dreamer." And there would be no men to stir up serious trouble between them. All of this suited Porter fine.

This is not to say that the friendship was based mainly on negatives—an absence of sexual rivalry, a blatant disparity in appearance, connections, experience, reputations. Welty was a type Porter approved of—from a "nice" southern (or at least semi-southern) background; literary in her bent and her gift without having any "literary life" (that is, no fancy powerful friends in New York, not yet, anyway); totally unpretentious; a young writer who was (or seemed) a pure, innocent product of the old order so dear to Porter's heart and to her sometimes-fabricated memories. They also shared some of the same prejudices and exclusions, sneering together at Jews (there is an appalling reference to "horns" and "Jew-phobia" in one of Welty's letters to Porter), lesbians (although both of them had many close gay male friends), and "women's libbers."

Like Elizabeth Bishop, Porter and Welty pretty much denied that their gender had any bearing on their own careers or reputations as writers. "All that talk of women's lib doesn't apply *at all* to women writers," Welty told an interviewer in 1972. "We've always been able to do what we've wished."[35] Porter was even more derisive: "I don't care about my rights," she told an interviewer. "Rights never did me any good. I want my privileges. . . . While I was going through [Betty Friedan's book], I thought, 'Oh, Betty, why don't you go and mix a good cocktail for your husband and yourself and forget about this business.' "[36] Both agreed that the real flaw in feminism is that it is beside the point: Women hold the true power, the power of land and family and memory—and then, as Welty writes in *Delta Wedding,* "so as to be all gracious and noble, they had let it out of their hands— with a play of the reins—to the men."

All of this common ground made Welty not only an artistic "find" for Katherine Anne, but also a personal find as well. For her part, Welty felt quite breathless with excitement at the interest that Porter took in her and in her work. Welty benefited not only from Porter's support but also from her example. Here was a refined southern woman working—and succeeding—as an independent artist. In the critic Norman McMillan's view, Porter's "most significant" gift to Welty was "her contribution to a distinct heritage for women writers."[37]

Nonetheless, despite their deeply shared admiration and their common literary heritage, the enormous abyss of differences that separated Porter and Welty—in looks, in style, in upbringing, in position—must have been immediately, maybe even shockingly apparent to both of them when they met in Baton Rouge. The abyss narrowed as Welty grew up and grew into a literary life, but it never closed. It continued to be a strange pairing, but the very strangeness offered a kind of protection. It made them, for each other, special cases.

ELEVEN

Fellow Colonists

> *Run-down rose gardens, rotting cantaloupes, fountains, a bust of Dante with a hole in the head. . . . It doesn't drug me but I get fantastic and uncivilized.*
>
> —ROBERT LOWELL *letter*
> *to Elizabeth Bishop on Yaddo*

PORTER BEGAN HELPING WELTY professionally even before their acquaintance had blossomed into friendship. She offered to name Welty as a candidate for a 1940 Guggenheim Fellowship and later on she was among those who recommended Welty for a place at the writer's conference at Bread Loaf. Welty's Guggenheim did not come through until 1942, but Bread Loaf accepted her as a fellow, the most prestigious of the student slots, and she set off for the green northern fastness of Middlebury, Vermont, late in the summer of 1940. It was not a good experience. It might have been that Bread Loaf—a high-powered two-week summer conference for promising writers, established in 1926 and administered through Middlebury College under the watchful eye of Robert Frost—was just too arty, too New England, too self-consciously, preciously "literary" for Eudora's tastes. Perhaps Welty, who has written that both she and Porter taught themselves to write and worked with fierce independence in their "own patch of garden,"[1] objected to the invasions of her privacy at workshops and tutorials. Certainly a writers' workshop can be a lacerating experience, particularly for someone as sensitive and reserved as Welty.

In any case, we know Welty was unhappy at Bread Loaf because she asked Porter to delete a reference to her "quiet horror" of the place in the introduction to *A Curtain of Green*. She admitted to Porter that she did in fact have a horror (not always quiet) about the things Bread Loaf "professes to do," but she worried that she'd offend people and appear ungrateful if Porter broadcast this horror.[2] And so with many apologies for the trouble she was putting Porter to, Welty pleaded that "the quiet horror" be erased from the record. This episode is utterly characteristic of the young Welty: the distaste for her fellow writers in groups; the embarrassment at having the distaste made known; the acute concern with good manners (she mentions that, as a fellow, she stayed at Bread Loaf for free and hated the idea of looking like an ungrateful guest); the eagerness to suppress anything mean-spirited, nasty, or sharply critical that she might have said or thought. Nice southern girls do not voice horror, even quiet horror, about their hosts in public.

Also characteristic is the abjection of Welty's gratitude for Porter's help and the profusion of her apology for asking for it. "Please remember that my recommendation of your work costs me nothing," Porter wrote her around the time of sponsoring her for Bread Loaf. "It is no doubt one of the marks of your seriousness of character and intention that you take obligation for any little help offered or received; in this case, let me assure you, a purely imaginary, self-assumed sense of obligation. . . . I would much prefer your friendship, in the most unburdensome meaning of that word."[3] This is the note on which their friendship commenced: Welty's scrupulous, overnice, painful sense of obligation; Porter's high-handed generosity and haughty aristocratic disdain for reckoning the cost of favors. Something of the same tension over debts and obligations cropped up in the relationship between James and Wharton, though for them the medium of exchange was not so much literary as social and, more awkwardly, financial.

Much as it flatters one's vanity to be able to lavish favors on a new friend in the form of praise, parties, trips, or prefaces, ultimately it bars the way to true intimacy. The giver feels used if there is no return; the beneficiary feels demeaned if he or she lacks means of repayment or opportunities to repay. The "most unburdensome" friendship that Porter writes of is either that in which favors play no part or in which the balance can be somehow made to come out even. Welty and Porter never really got their friendship on that equal footing. Porter was even more exacting of attention, deference, admiration than she was generous. Welty, an increasingly uneasy protégée, never found a way that suited her to repay the favors. Though the connection was long and "cherished," in Welty's words, it was never truly intimate.

Whatever her horror of Bread Loaf, Welty evidently convinced herself that she would not feel the same at Yaddo for she allowed Porter to secure her an invitation for the summer of 1941, and arrived there in early June "as one in a dream."[4] Yaddo is the Harvard of artists' colonies: old, revered, comfortably endowed early in the century by its blueblood founders Katrina Nichols Trask and her philanthropist husband, George Foster Peabody; situated on five hundred acres of woods, landscaped grounds, and formal gardens near the upper-crust resort and horse-racing town of Saratoga Springs, New York. Like a private and very exclusive club, Yaddo protects itself carefully from incursions by the "wrong sort." Invitations are issued to worthy applicants only with the support of prominent colleagues. (Elizabeth Bishop and Robert Lowell were also invited to Yaddo, and Lowell turned the place on its head in 1949 when he accused the colony's director, Elizabeth Ames, of harboring Communists—see below.) Welty, in her reminiscence of how her friendship with Porter began, paints a clear picture of the place: "Yaddo was in the old, rural, comfortably settled part of New York State west of Albany. . . . The estate was private and well guarded. . . . The Mansion faced you head-on as you approached it through forest trees; it was huge, elaborately constructed: it looked made by impulse for eternity, out of the rock on which it stood."[5] In addition to the mansion, there were smaller studios and houses hidden away on the estate, including North Farm, where Welty and Porter lived across the hall from each other.

Porter had been in residence at this enchanted cost-free fairyland for artists (visual artists and composers as well as writers) for a year already, having taken refuge here in June 1940 after the breakup of her marriage to Albert Erskine. She had been received like royalty in exile and was initially put up in the mansion's huge tower room, which had seventeen windows opening on views of trees, hills, and gardens.[6] The aristocratic aura of the place suited Porter, and its proximity to the horse-racing scene at Saratoga added even more cachet for she loved to recall the stories her aunt Annie Gay told of trips here with strings of race horses; she had incorporated some of these cherished memories into "Old Mortality."

When she joined Katherine Anne at Yaddo in June 1941, Eudora Welty was in a very different frame of mind than she had been in the previous summer at Bread Loaf. She stood at that brink of breathless, glorious expectation known to all young writers: the eve of publication of her first book. Welty had acquired (or rather had been acquired by) the literary agent Diarmuid Russell in 1940, and Russell, though new at the profession (Welty thought she might have been his first client), managed to accomplish what Porter, Ford Madox Ford, and Welty herself had failed to do since the late 1930s: find a publisher who would bring out a collection of her short stories (the story of Welty's perseverance through many setbacks and rejections, told in detail by the critic Michael Kreyling in *Author and Agent,* is a tale to inspire all struggling writers).

Russell (the son of the Irish poet and mystic George Russell, a close friend of Yeats, who published under the name AE) and Welty were a match made in literary heaven, and she has always spoken of him with warm appreciation (she dedicated her first book to him). After placing "A Worn Path," "Why I Live at the P.O.," and "Powerhouse" in the *Atlantic Monthly,* Russell had amassed the ammunition to launch his attack on the New York publishing houses. John Woodburn of Doubleday, Doran had already expressed interest in Welty's work (it was he who had given her name to Russell), and now he was at last able to offer her a contract and an advance of $250 for *A Curtain of Green.* "To cap this," Welty writes in her *Georgia Review* essay about the friendship with Porter, Woodburn "had invited and persuaded Katherine Anne Porter to write an Introduction to it."[7] "It has seemed like a magical year," Welty wrote Russell in thanks for all he had done for her.[8]

As she set off for Yaddo, all the pieces of her literary debut were falling neatly into place. The one loose board that was left to nail down was the actual writing of the introduction. Herein lay the germ of a small, tense drama that was to be played out against the rich green backdrop of Yaddo all that summer.

Welty, in her memoir about the friendship, ironically casts the Yaddo experience as a grand opera: The stage was the rock-built mansion with its murmuring interior fountain, its great windowed dining room, and beyond it, on the other side of a stone balustrade, the silent, fragrant garden presided over by statues of the Graces. The chorus was the resident artists, many of them refugees from the political storm that was engulfing Europe. And the star, the great diva, was Porter herself, who "rose to the occasion—her clear voice [entering] as if on cue with cries of *'Au contraire!'* " Welty, typically self-effacing, places herself well off in the shadowy wings—following the elegant Katherine Anne "with her spring-heeled step," as they marched single file through the woods from North Farm to the mansion each evening; silently watching and listening to her brilliant friend at dinner; letting her attention drift from the glittering action within to the soft, pale flowers—summer stock and nicotiana—blooming in the moonlit darkness. "They made me think of home," she writes, homesick for her mother, the great gardener of Pinehurst Street. "That first night, I knew for certain only what the *garden* was doing."[9]

Breaking in on the high Romantic aura of the Yaddo opera were the crude, comic, almost daily dispatches from John Woodburn, who was becoming more and more anxious about the introduction that Porter promised to write in February but had still failed to produce in June. "Kid, you keep after her!" Woodburn pleads with Welty. "She promised to write it *now*! Remind her we've got a deadline." "Get it out of her, baby." Welty modestly terms Woodburn "my champion, who had staked so much in bringing out this first book by an unknown, young, Southern, female, short-story writer." But in the *Georgia Review* piece she makes him out, comically, of course, to be her torturer. The more urgently Woodburn begs Welty to strap Porter to her writing table and squeeze the introduction out of her, the more miserably Welty retreats into anxiety and guilt. "I knew it was to be a wonderfully happy and carefree summer for me—if only I didn't have Katherine Anne's awful deadline hanging over my head: the unmentionable."[10]

All summer long, the tension of the awful deadline builds. As Welty describes it, she and Katherine Anne did almost everything *but* write. Rather than listen like a hopeful, guilty eavesdropper for the sounds of Porter's Olivetti clicking out her introduction, Welty strolls into Saratoga Springs to move "with a wonderful crowd of perambulators here for the waters, the races, the sights and parades." Porter, always a proud and inspired cook (Peter Taylor described her as a "great artist as a cook and party-giver"[11]), devotes her days to making onion soup, playing operas on her phonograph, and hosting picnics. And there are frequent trips to the house.

Porter, in the winter of her fifty-first year, satisfied at last her perennial urge to own a house. In an essay entitled "A House of My Own" (enlarging considerably on Virginia Woolf, who was willing to settle for a room), Porter describes how she happened upon the modest "modified Georgian" dwelling set in a valley near Saratoga Lake and how she knew at once, at first sight, that it was *her* house. She neglects to make clear in the charming little essay that buying the property, which she named South Hill, and restoring the lovely but totally unlivable house seriously interrupted her writing and stretched her finances past the breaking point. South Hill also took its toll on Welty's time and energy that summer.

Porter owned a brand-new Studebaker that she couldn't *quite* drive yet (in true southern belle fashion, she was never too steady at the wheel), so she pressed Welty into service as chauffeur for excursions to the house. "It became a part of nearly every day to jump into the Studebaker and drive out to South Hill," Welty reports. There they would "supervise" the ever-changing ranks of unreliable workmen by stretching out in the meadow grass to smoke cigarettes, listen to the bird song, and chat and laugh about books and people. On days off from house renovation, the friends would drive up to Albany to shop for "treasures" for the house—French antique chairs, ruby-red carpeting. Welty, privately, has mocked Porter's awful taste for French brothel interior decor[12]—lots of red velvet and gilt—but in the *Georgia Review* reminiscence she is respectful, even reverent, about South Hill, its furnishings, and its owner.

Meanwhile, the introduction to *A Curtain of Green* was

conspicuously *not* getting written, and the pleas from Woodburn were getting ever more shrill ("Get it out of her *now,* kid! Do you want our book *postponed?*"). Welty herself seemed to have pretty much written off the summer at Yaddo as far as work was concerned. In an interview years later, she laughed about how the sign on her door—SILENCE. WRITER AT WORK WITHIN—made her so self-conscious that she could not write at all[13] (though in letters to her agent she mentions revising the short story "First Love"[14]). And of course there was the constant enticement of ditching work to gad about with Porter—or do her shopping. "At Yaddo there is every temptation in the world to get swept away and not do your own work," remarked a friend of Welty's who spent some time at the colony a few years later.[15] Porter, however, though she neglected the promised introduction and consumed a good deal of Welty's time, was not idle that summer. Welty describes with a sense of hushed momentousness the day Katherine Anne "tapped at my door and came in holding out to me a whole sheaf of typewritten pages"—the first seventy-five pages of the novel that was to be published, twenty years later, as *Ship of Fools.* "You may read this," Katherine Anne said to Eudora with Olympian condescension, "if you would like."

Welty's comment on the incident is wonderfully strange, under the circumstances: "In allowing me to read it, and at its beginning, she had made me a gift of her clear confidence in me. As far as I was concerned, the Introduction she was going to write for me had been conveyed to me by way of a blessing. If its significance was to relate to her literary trust in me, I had already received it."[16] Blessing or not, the introduction would not be written until August (seven months after Porter had promised to write it), and publication of *A Curtain of Green* was postponed by several months. Welty was, understandably, frantic, and by some accounts furious,[17] as what first-time author wouldn't be, but she fails to mention this in her memoir of the friendship. Nor does she say what she thought of the opening of *Ship of Fools,* aside from the honor of living across the hall from its author and witnessing "something of the terror . . . of its pages coming into being one by one . . . the living words coming through her fingers and out of her skin."[18] Here, once again, Welty holds the frame of art in front of her face to compose her features into a sweet, wistful smile and delete all sign of the grimace of anger, hurt, and disappointment.

Welty not only exonerates Porter of the guilt of holding up

publication of her book, but she also goes so far as to take the blame for the whole business of the introduction onto her own shoulders. (Porter herself was well aware of the dangerous psychological alchemy that makes victim and villain trade places. She depicts such a reversal in her story "Theft," in which the nameless heroine, a female writer past her first youth and extremely down and out in New York, has her lovely gold cloth purse stolen by a demonic female janitor. In confronting the janitor and demanding the purse back, the writer is made to feel that she herself is the thief. At the story's end she is left alone with the golden purse and the bitter thought: "I was right not to be afraid of any thief but myself, who will end by leaving me nothing.") Welty, in her reminiscence, makes herself out to be the thief who robbed Porter of her peace of mind. Who but Eudora Welty would think to apologize, fifty years after the event, because it had never even occurred to her to depart Yaddo early so as to cease putting Katherine Anne "on the spot" with the daily nuisance of her presence? Though Welty reports that Porter could spend an entire day making onion soup for her friends ("and as we all agreed, it was worth every minute of it") and though Porter was "scrupulously attentive" to her house in progress, taking it on as a "self-assignment . . . an autobiographical deadline," Welty nonetheless blames herself and the "awful deadline" of that introduction for halting the progress of *Ship of Fools*.

Isn't this extraordinary—and more than a touch disingenuous? After all, despite her outward self-abasement and awe of her friend's chic bohemian ways, Welty supplies the careful reader of this little essay plenty of rope with which to hang Porter. Mightn't Katherine Anne have turned the soup making over to Eudora for a day while she banged out the introduction? (Porter's sometime friend Caroline Gordon "wickedly believed" that a good part of Porter's "domestic passions" were "just to get out of work."[19]) But then, of course, one wonders why Welty didn't gently mention to her friend that she'd waited four years to see these stories come out as a book and why the *hell* did she have to wait several months longer while Katherine Anne made soup and picnics and small talk? No, of course not. Welty could never have said anything of the sort, given *her* nature and the nature of her wonderful, preposterous friend. Is it possible that after this summer, Welty had come to despise Porter just a little, and perhaps even more to despise herself for the person she became in Porter's presence, just as James despised *himself* a little for succumbing to Wharton's golden rush? Porter made Welty more of a girl than she wanted to be, imposed on her good nature, kept her down even as she seemed to be singing her praises. In the end, Welty found her friend easier to stand from afar.

Welty concludes of Porter, with a sigh, "She was constitutionally a besieged woman. . . . Her whole writing life was one of interruptions, and interruptions of the interruptions. I was to learn that writers do generally live that way, and not without their own collusion. No help ever comes, unless in the form of still another interruption."[20]

Caroline Gordon, less kind than Welty, finds Porter constitutionally unreliable. "She would walk miles to get you a bouquet of flowers," Gordon writes to her friend Jean Stafford, Robert Lowell's first wife, "or a jug of wine and present the gift gracefully but you cannot *depend* on her for anything. The very thought of anyone depending on her makes her wild. This is partly because she is always in a crisis herself and partly because of her histrionic gifts. . . ."[21]

There were other, deeper and darker, truths that Welty learned from and about Porter that summer, but she only alludes to them in this essay. "Certainly I was slower in learning to know Katherine Anne than I believed I was in the summer at Yaddo," she writes near the end of the *Georgia Review* piece. "Our friendship had shown me day after day the enchanting brightness she could shed around her, but it was later, through letters she wrote when we were no longer in the same place, laughing, that I became to any degree aware of the dark, its other side, which she lived with on its own terms in equally close commune. . . . She was combatting unhappiness, even desolation, I now think, through that whole summer and for times longer than that, and bravely."[22] Since Welty won't discuss her friendship with Porter and has kept most of Porter's letters to herself, we are left to wonder about the nature of the ghosts that haunted her.

Welty twitches the curtain before Porter's desolation only to let it fall heavily into place again. But as for her own darker feelings, she refuses even to admit they exist. She says nothing of her resentment at being pressed into service as Porter's chauffeur. She suppresses the pain of being neglected by her friend the moment they entered on the great stage of Yaddo's dining room, the stage on which Porter performed as star and on which Welty shrank into the shadows to commune with the garden. She breathes not a word about the interruptions Porter inflicted on *her* work in the midst of what we can now see was her most fertile period. (In the course of the 1940s, she wrote her second collection of stories; her short novel *The Robber Bridegroom,* which she dedicated to Porter; her first full-length novel, *Delta Wedding;* and the related stories of *The Golden Apples,* the book she considers her masterpiece. Porter, by contrast, finished a single long story, "The Leaning Tower," and a single short story, "The Source," in 1941, and after that surrendered to her interruptions for the rest of the decade, and the next decade as well.) And most of all, Welty conceals whatever furious disappointment she must have felt at having the publication of her book postponed.

"It's hot here and I feel depressed and ready to go," Welty wrote to Diarmuid Russell at the end of July. The crowds gathered for the races strike her as "one long procession" of grotesques, and far from wanting to study it, she confessed to Russell that she only wants to run away. "For somebody who undertakes to write I feel far too easily battered & bruised. . . . Maybe it's my dreamlike life in Mississippi where things are long ago or far ahead but never now."[23] At summer's end, when she returned to her mother in Jackson, Welty had little enough to show for her weeks at Yaddo: no substantial new work done, no prospect of seeing her book appear until her friend saw fit to write the introduction, the breathless excitement of June deflated by the dry gusts of August.

Porter finally reports to Welty on August 27 that she "batted out" the introduction "in two evenings' very pleasant work," but then she managed to miss the book's publication party in November at New York's Murray Hill Hotel, even though she had promised to attend. Afterwards, Welty wrote Porter that she was disappointed at her absence from the party and she confessed that she probably wouldn't have made the trip herself had she known Porter would not be there.[24] "Anyone can sympathise with the sufferings of a friend," wrote Oscar Wilde, an authority, if ever there was one, on the perils of literary friendship, "but it requires a very fine nature—it requires, in fact, the nature of a true Individualist to sympathise with a friend's success."[25]

It is, perhaps, possible that Welty was as sweet, selfless, and forgiving as she makes herself out to be in her reminiscence of her friendship with Porter, but one frankly doubts it. In letters from this period she can be as venomous as a startled snake. She concocts her deadliest venom of all for an acquaintance from Bread Loaf—a young female writer from the South who also happened to be at Yaddo that summer: Carson McCullers. The sad, strange, farcical drama played out by McCullers and Porter, with Welty as attendant chorus, is another piece of ugliness that Welty omits from her memories of that summer.

TWELVE

Too Much Life
and Too Little

> I find it sometimes a question how to keep my time
> and energy defended from certain kinds of people
> who try to attach their empty and unattractive lives
> to mine in one way or another—people I am sur-
> prised to find on the same planet with me, much less
> in the same house.
>
> —KATHERINE ANNE PORTER letter to Glenway Wescott

> It took me a long time to manage the independence,
> for I loved those who protected me—and I wanted
> inevitably to protect them back. I have never man-
> aged to handle the guilt.
>
> —EUDORA WELTY, One Writer's Beginnings

LIKE KATHERINE ANNE PORTER and Eudora Welty, Carson Mc-
Cullers was from the South—she was born and raised in Colum-
bus, Georgia—and, like Porter, she had left the South at a tender
age to seek literary fame and fortune out in the world. But there
the common ground comes sharply to an end. Porter and Welty
knew at once and for all time that McCullers was not *their* kind of
southerner. Nor was she their kind of woman or their kind of
writer. McCullers was not, in their opinion or really in just about
anybody's opinion, a nice girl—in fact, just the opposite. Welty
called her a nasty little girl who wrote nasty stories,[1] and even
friends described her as a "street brat" very much in the mold of
Mick Kelly, the tomboy heroine of *The Heart Is a Lonely Hunter*.

But McCullers, whatever her shortcomings, was an original, and by 1940 she was already notorious in literary circles for the extreme oddness of her personality and her talent. The publication that year of *The Heart Is a Lonely Hunter,* her first novel, made her an overnight sensation. Her picture—Edwin Peacock's famous publicity shot of the puppy-dog brown eyes, the bangs, the pug nose, the man-tailored shirt, the grin of a wicked schoolboy—was all over New York. She was the new enfant terrible. At twenty-three, McCullers had been married for three years to Reeves McCullers, a perpetually struggling writer whom she would shortly divorce and then remarry, and she had a well-advanced drinking problem (she considered her drinking a solution for she said she needed a steady stream of sherry to make her writing flow). She was a fragile, clinging, demonstrative, demanding, tortured, childlike person, forever falling madly in love at first sight and suffering extravagantly when her love was not reciprocated. "She oozed love," recalls a friend. "She lived in a constant state of agony."[2] She was also bisexual with a yearning for chic, worldly, and famous women (Garbo was one of the objects of her unrequited affection). Even those who liked Carson and admired her work (Truman Capote for a time, Tennessee Williams, Edith Sitwell) frequently found her impossible. Welty and Porter, who emphatically neither liked nor admired her, found her unbearable.

Welty was a natural target for comparison with McCullers because they made their literary debut just a year apart, and they appeared, at least on the surface, to be sorority sisters in the school of the southern grotesque. Dwarfs and cripples, deaf-mutes and psychopaths, love-warped ladies and history-crazed gentlemen, rapists and killers turn up in the stories and novels of both Welty and McCullers, as they do in the work of Flannery O'Connor and, to a lesser extent, of Katherine Anne Porter.

But Welty and McCullers were attracted to the grotesque for very different reasons, and they use grotesque characters to very different purpose in their work. The grotesque emanates a thick, stifling, erotic perfume in McCullers's work that is largely absent from Welty's work and entirely absent from her life. Welty's grotesques—the clubfooted black man in "Keela, the Outcast Indian Maiden," the mad old maid in "Clytie," the deaf-mute couple in "The Key," the crazed, doomed sisters Miss Myra and Miss Theo in "The Burning"—are cut off by their deformities from contact with a larger world, from the satisfaction of speech or from the pleasure of love. Their grotesqueness is but an extreme outward sign of the alienation that afflicts nearly all of her characters. As she herself once told an interviewer who asked her about the grotesque in her early work, "It is easier to show somebody as lonely if you make him deaf and dumb than if you go feeling your way into his mind."[3]

In McCullers's fiction, grotesqueness is also a token of alienation—but it goes way beyond this. It is not just that her angry tomboys and cripples, sadomasochist soldiers and Amazonian wives, mutes and hunchbacks don't fit into the suffocating small town life around them. McCullers populated her books with unlovable characters because she believed that love is essentially perverse. The characteristic situation of her stories is the bisexual love triangle—Captain Penderton lusting after his wife's many lovers in *Reflections in a Golden Eye*; the hunchback Cousin Lymon shifting his attention from Miss Amelia to her no-count ex-con husband Marvin Macy in "The Ballad of the Sad Café." The prevailing theme of her work—that love's equation can never be balanced, that "there are the lover and the beloved, but these two come from different countries . . . [because] the beloved fears and hates the lover"[4]—gains power and eerie clarity from being enacted by freaks. McCullers, with her strange fits of passion, her thermos of sherry, her monologues and moping, her habit of hurling herself physically and emotionally at people who aroused her, was just such a freak herself in the eyes of Porter and Welty. Welty, understandably, recoiled from the idea that reviewers and readers might lump the two of them together. Porter recoiled from her in every way.

McCullers arrived at Yaddo around the same time as Welty, early in the summer of 1941, with her life in a characteristic shambles. Her consuming flare-up of love for Annemarie Clarac-Schwarzenbach, a very beautiful and aristocratic Swiss émigrée and a member of Thomas Mann's circle, had come to naught. She had separated from Reeves, but the two of them remained joined after a fashion by their shared obsession with the composer David Diamond. Diamond was a pivotal figure not only between Carson and Reeves but also between Carson and Katherine Anne as well. Diamond had met Porter in Paris a few years earlier and became "smitten with her—as smitten as I was to become with Carson."[5] Porter was fond of Diamond—like most of her male friends, he was charming, cultivated, and homosexual—but she was not fond

enough to tolerate McCullers for his sake. It was a very complicated situation.

Diamond was in residence at Yaddo only a short time before Elizabeth Ames, the director, asked him to leave. Diamond
says she made him the scapegoat for the trouble that was brewing
between Porter and McCullers. He stayed on for a time in Saratoga Springs and later in the summer returned to his parents'
home in Rochester, where Reeves joined him, without telling Carson. When Carson discovered not only this betrayal (Diamond
had, after all, proposed marriage to *her*), but also the fact that
Reeves had been forging checks in her name, she started divorce
proceedings.[6] Somehow, in the thick of her personal mess, Mc-
Cullers managed to forge ahead with "The Ballad of the Sad Café,"
considered by many to be her finest work.

Although Welty was one of the few people whom McCullers knew when she arrived at Yaddo (the two of them had been
together at Bread Loaf the previous summer), McCullers had small
interest in deepening that acquaintance. Rather, she found the
chic, celebrated Porter in every way more desirable. Fifty-one at
the time, recently separated from Erskine, drowning in debt after
the purchase of South Hill, Porter was vulnerable, "exposed" as
one friend put it.[7] She had reached the age, as she later wrote of
Mary Treadwell in *Ship of Fools,* when women "attract every
species of parasite, and Lesbians lurk in the offing." Even had
Porter been rich and radiantly in love, the attentions of Carson
McCullers would not have been welcome; but because she was
poor and bereft, she found McCullers and everything she represented—bisexuality, youth, a slovenly bohemianism, a famished
craving after love and attention, a seemingly effortless outpouring
of fresh work, instant critical and popular success—particularly
threatening. It was infuriating that such a creature should claim to
love her.

The story of Carson McCullers's infatuation with Katherine Anne Porter at Yaddo has become a set piece of literary gossip—a tale of intimate embarrassment like the unconsummated
marriage of John Ruskin and Effie Gray or the occasion when
F. Scott Fitzgerald dropped his trousers in a Paris café so Hemingway could pass judgment on the size of his penis. Who can
resist the sexual folly of the famous? In the standard version,
which Virginia Spencer Carr records in her biography of McCullers, Carson fell in love with Katherine Anne at first sight at Yaddo

and began following her around the place, "mooning" over her, and declaring her love. Carr even provides the dialogue, recollected by Porter thirty years afterward. "I love you, Katherine Anne," Carson told her. "You're the *only* famous writer I have ever known." "No, I'm not famous, Carson," Porter supposedly snapped back. "I've just had the good luck to have critics who like what I write."[8] Porter had a tendency to flare up when annoyed, and she no doubt gave McCullers a thorough dressing down, but she could not ward her off. Every time she turned around, there was McCullers, dying for attention, approval, recognition.

The climax came one evening just before dinner, a rather formal occasion at which Yaddo residents were expected to appear well dressed and on time. Porter was dressing for dinner inside her tower room in the main house (she had not yet moved to North Farm). McCullers stood outside her room, pounding on the door and wailing, "Please, Katherine Anne, let me come in and talk with you—I do love you so very much." Incensed at being hounded down in her room, Porter commanded McCullers to go away at once and she believed she had prevailed upon her. However, when she emerged to go to dinner, Porter found McCullers stretched out full length along her threshold. (In one version, surely apocryphal, McCullers was lying there nude.) "I had had enough," Porter told Carr. "I merely stepped over her and continued on my way to dinner. And that was the last time she ever bothered me."[9]

Porter never yielded an inch in her loathing of McCullers. David Diamond remembers imploring Katherine Anne on one occasion to put her arms around Carson: " 'It wouldn't kill you,' I told her. 'Carson is such a child.' Katherine Anne replied, 'I would vomit.' " Years later, Diamond mentioned to Porter the terrible end that Carson and Reeves had come to (Reeves, an alcoholic, committed suicide in Paris, Carson died at age fifty after suffering a series of strokes). "They deserved it," Porter told Diamond. "They were evil."[10] "She [Porter] could be real *nasty* about people, there was no doubt about that," recalls Marcella Winslow.[11]

Whether McCullers was really making a sexual play for Porter or merely expressing her literary admiration (and ambition) in a particularly cloying way remains in doubt. Diamond feels that Carson's "oozing love" was not sexual but rather an expression of her irrepressible need for affection—her "constant state of agony." Whatever McCullers's intentions, Porter regarded her behavior in the worst possible light. Porter's biographer Joan Givner believes that Porter was excessively sensitive to lesbians, perhaps because of a hidden lesbian undercurrent in her own nature, and that this fear kept her from forming close relationships with other women.[12] Welty was an acceptable, though never a truly intimate, female friend because she was, as Porter put it, "150 per cent female." When a woman's female percentage was too low, as McCullers's certainly was, Porter considered her degenerate. (Porter seems to have made an exception of Elizabeth Bishop, another Yaddo lesbian, for the two women were friendly acquaintances; but Bishop, unlike McCullers, believed in "closets, closets, and more closets," as she once told a friend, so perhaps Porter never knew.)

Porter had rather different feelings toward male homosexuals. Though she rails in letters to straight men (among them Robert Lowell, who railed back) about "pansies" and "queers" and "café cowboys,"[13] some of her closest and most enduring relationships were with homosexuals, including the writers Glenway Wescott and Monroe Wheeler. "It was so nice to relax with that kind of man," she told an interviewer, "to enjoy his delightfully malicious wit and intelligence, without having to worry about bruising his male ego, his machismo, and having to deal with all that ritualized wrestling around at the end of an otherwise cheerful evening."[14] "Far from being threatened by homosexual men," says Diamond, "she felt most comfortable with them. She trusted them."[15]

But then male companionship and admiration in just about any form was acceptable, indeed indispensable, to Porter, and a number of her friends have spoken of how she liked to have men around her as much as possible.[16] "She was partial to men," one woman friend noted. "She didn't like to go out unless a man was taking her."[17] The idea of a party, a lunch, or trip to the theater or a museum without a male escort was utterly unappealing to her: Where was the fun if one couldn't flirt?

In her ever-hopeful pursuit of romance Porter was strangely like Carson McCullers. Both of them were scarcely ever *not* in love and rarely happy in it. And both had a way of falling in love at first sight and demanding far more in love than they received. The critic Ruth Vande Kieft lumps them together as "two big infantile egos," who suffered alike from a narcissistic craving for attention.[18] Porter, like McCullers, loved unwisely and improbably, choosing men who would abandon or humiliate or bore her and, as she got older, choosing men who were far, far younger than she. "She had unfortunate romantic relations," said the poet William Jay Smith, a friend of both Porter and Welty. "She had a way of choosing the wrong man. For a woman that strong, it was not easy to find the right man. Her romances seemed always doomed to failure."[19] Givner believes that Porter, for all her romantic entanglements, was always uneasy with her own sexuality and that she gravitated toward men who would demand little or nothing of her sexually. In Givner's view, Porter preferred the trappings of romance—the moonlight and roses—to the "ritualized wrestling around" of sex. Adam, the dashing, golden hero of "Pale Horse, Pale Rider," was in a sense Porter's fondest sexual fantasy: a man of godlike beauty and natural gallantry who dies before he can tarnish his love with more than a tender, chaste embrace.

But there was also another, more cynical side to Porter's view of love and sex and marriage. Porter jokingly told an interviewer, "The only time men get a little tiresome is in love—oh, they're OK at first, but they do tend, don't they, to get a little bossy and theological about the whole business?"[20] Her stories and novels contain some of the most memorably awful marriages in modern fiction: the unnamed bickering couple in "Rope," Gabriel and Miss Honey in "Old Mortality," the Hallorans in "A Day's Work," and the Baumgartners in *Ship of Fools* spring immediately to mind. In each instance, the man is vain, idle, arrogant, drunken, pathetically weak or oppressively foolish, and the woman is put-upon, long-suffering, and bitterly enraged about what life has handed her. When their rage gets the better of them, Porter's women explode with sadistic violence. Mrs. Halloran's assault on her drunken husband's face with a wet, stiffly knotted bath towel and Mary Treadwell's attack on William Denny's face with the metal-capped high heel of her sandal are rendered in excruciating, bloody slow motion: Porter packs the full power of her art in every blow to the faces of these worthless men.

"To be an artist—no marriage was worth giving up what I had," she once remarked.[21] And no romantic affair, either. In her art, Porter evened the score as much as she could between herself and the men who had disappointed her, oppressed her, drained her of her time and energy. "It is a disaster to have a man fall in love with me," she told an interviewer near the end of her life. "They aren't content to take what I can give; they want everything from me."[22] The flirtatious southern belle and the hard-bitten modern artist never ceased to claw at each other in Porter's heart.

•

While Carson McCullers was mooning around after Porter at Yaddo, Welty seems to have stayed pretty much on the sidelines, but she was by no means an indifferent observer. Carr claims McCullers and Welty might have become friends but for Porter's "vigilant eye," yet the letters the friends exchanged tell a different story. Welty, in writing Porter, never missed an opportunity to blacken McCullers's name. One can imagine how the two of them raked her over in private conversation. Diamond recalls that when Porter and Welty were together at Yaddo "they had a way of ripping people up. Katherine Anne would do the talking and Eudora would just listen, giggle, and agree."[23] Carson was their prime target, and Carson bashing remained a bond between them for a good long time. Even before Yaddo, Welty was writing to Porter with horror about how "that little wretch Carson" is being hailed by book reviewers as "the climax of *Southern* writing."[24] In a letter written after the summer, she seethes over "the little Curson" and "her scenes" and she predicts that "one day she will simply poison herself." Welty works herself up to such a frenzy of disgust that she mixes her metaphors, but then she claims that she's done this deliberately as a kind of verbal potion.[25]

Welty, characteristically, offers a far sunnier picture of her feelings for public consumption. When Carr went to Jackson to interview Welty for the McCullers biography in 1971, Welty told her that she was sorry she had never gotten to know Carson better: "I wish Carson's and my own paths had crossed more.... We were never to know each other very well, though I do know we always liked, right along, each other's work."[26] This last part about liking Carson's work flatly contradicts what she wrote privately to Porter, and when their paths *did* cross at a New York theater in 1950, Welty ducked down in her seat so that McCullers wouldn't spot her, or so she wrote to Porter.[27]

At least part of Welty's loathing for McCullers was loyalty to Porter. The letters she wrote to Porter after leaving Yaddo are full of a fluttering kind of solicitude for Katherine Anne's health, the state of her nerves, and the halting progress on her house and novel—and Eudora lumps Carson together with such nuisances as lazy workmen, frigid winter temperatures, and inept postal service. Her nastiness about "Curson" may well have been a way of ingratiating herself to Porter.

Yet Welty had her own reasons for disliking McCullers that

had nothing to do with loyalty to Porter. She cannot have enjoyed seeing the great splash McCullers, eight years her junior, made with *The Heart Is a Lonely Hunter* in 1940, while her own first book raised a comparative ripple. Compared with the raves several critics gave McCullers—"The book goes on living in an astonishing way in the mind," wrote May Sarton in the *Boston Transcript*. "Something has been added to our life"[28]; McCullers "writes with a sweep and certainty that are overwhelming," wrote Rose Feld in *The New York Times*[29]—the notices for *A Curtain of Green and Other Stories* were respectful but rather tepid. Welty must also have been chagrined to see *The Heart Is a Lonely Hunter* climb the best-seller list while sales of *A Curtain of Green* remained decidedly sluggish (her advance for the book was $250, and a total of 6,700 copies were sold over the next thirty years).

Quite aside from her jealousy, Welty might have felt repelled by McCullers's blatant bisexuality in life and art, though we have no direct record of this. Welty's own sexuality remains something of a mystery. Male acquaintances from the 1940s noted that she lacked a sexual presence and was not known to date. The writer Michael Seide, who knew her well at Yaddo and kept in touch with her afterward, says that he found her "closed up" sexually: "She was not good-looking, and her manner was quiet, shy, and sensitive, though she had a tough side too. Katherine Anne was more exposed, but Eudora did not have much to expose. And she did not know much about romance, judging from her books."[30] Diamond recalls that she "had a lovely voice that would hold your attention, but she had no degree of temperament except for her sweetness. She was always on an even keel, and this annoyed people."[31] A friend who has known Welty well from middle age on remembers hearing her say with comic emphasis "I *love* men!" and remarks that Eudora becomes more animated, even flirtatious in the presence of handsome young men.

In the correspondence with Porter there are frequent references to John Fraiser Robinson, who came from Mississippi's delta region and served in the air force during the war. Robinson and Welty were an acknowledged couple, both in Jackson and outside it, during the 1940s; they went to dinner parties and picnics together and Welty spent time with him in Florida during one of his leaves from the military. Welty drew on Robinson's family stories for *Delta Wedding* and dedicated the book to him; later she visited him for several months in San Francisco and in Italy, and they collaborated on the dramatization of *The Robber Bridegroom*. In *Author and Agent* the critic Michael Kreyling, who had access to Welty's letters to her agent, describes the relationship with Robinson as "serious," but he discreetly avoids raising the questions of *how* serious and why it never progressed to marriage.[32] Robinson, like Welty, was struggling to succeed as a writer after the war, and it's possible that they found it too stressful to be nurturing both their careers at the same time. Some acquaintances speculate that the heaviness of heart that weighs on stories such as "No Place for You, My Love" and "The Bride of the Innisfallen" arose from Welty's disappointment over Robinson. After Robinson, there seem to have been no other serious romantic involvements.

Welty's work reveals far more about her sexuality and her sexual imagination than anything she has said in interviews or written in publicly available letters. "A Memory," "Lily Daw and the Three Ladies," "Petrified Man," and "Clytie" all reveal horror at sex and the bizarre behavior sex provokes. Rape figures directly or indirectly in a number of Welty's stories, including "The Petrified Man," "At the Landing," "Sir Rabbit," *The Robber Bridegroom,* and in her very strange Civil War story, "The Burning." And in *Delta Wedding* and "The Whole World Knows" potent, if disturbed, male characters pick up girls for passing sexual encounters that result in suicide or fatal accidents. In Welty's work "rape appears to be a natural, if sometimes inconvenient, sexual encounter from which women, like slightly annoyed hens, pick themselves up, shake their feathers, and go on about their business," writes the critic Louise Westling.[33] Male sexual energy in characters such as George Fairchild or Troy Flavin in *Delta Wedding,* Jamie Lockhart in *The Robber Bridegroom,* King MacLain in *The Golden Apples,* or Billy Floyd in "At the Landing" is both compelling and frightening. These males are almost godlike in their potency, but they are also violent, unreliable, emotionally stunted, and in some cases just plain foolish. Sex with such men, we are left to imagine, is hasty, forced, exciting, but ultimately unsatisfying: Like sudden thunderstorms, they make a lot of noise and quickly dissipate.

The female counterparts to these potent, violating males are Welty's cheap, spoiled, floozy blondes—characters such as Bonnie Dee Peacock in the *Ponder Heart,* Jinny Love Stark in *The Golden Apples,* Robbie Reid in *Delta Wedding,* and most vividly Wanda Fay Chisom in *The Optimist's Daughter,* who use their sticky airhead feminine charms and wiles to ensnare men into marriage.

Robbie is the only one of the lot who seems to take any pleasure in sex for its own sake. Jinny marries and then carries on an extramarital affair out of boredom; Bonnie Dee and Fay marry older or infirm men for money, hoping for the greatest security with the fewest sexual demands.

In her stronger, fuller, more serious female characters, Welty probes a more complex female sexuality. In her memoir, *One Writer's Beginnings,* Welty singles out two characters in *The Golden Apples*—Miss Eckhart and Virgie Rainey—as reflecting most intensely herself and the concerns of her art. Of Miss Eckhart, the town of Morgana's old maid music teacher, Welty writes, "As I looked longer and longer for the origins of this passionate and strange character, at last I realized that Miss Eckhart came from me.... She derived from what I already knew for myself, even felt I had always known. What I have put into her is my passion for my own life work, my own art. Exposing yourself to risk is a truth Miss Eckhart and I had in common. What animates and possesses me is what drives Miss Eckhart, the love of her art and the love of giving it, the desire to give it until there is no more left." Of Virgie, Morgana's sexually uninhibited free spirit, Welty writes, "Passionate, recalcitrant, stubbornly undefeated by failure or hurt or disgrace or bereavement, all the while heedlessly wasting of her gifts, she knows to the last that there is a world that remains out there, a world living and mysterious, and that she is of it." And she concludes this passage: "Inasmuch as Miss Eckhart might have been said to come from me, the author, Virgie, at her moments, might have always been my subject."[34]

Welty calls attention to the opposition between Virgie and Miss Eckhart; she plants more deeply in "June Recital" clues to the traits they have in common. Miss Eckhart, with her mysterious foreign origin and old maidish eccentricities, and Virgie, with her wildness, her talents, and precocity, are linked in being both outsiders to the tight core of the Morgana community. And they are linked as well in being essentially solitary. Virgie, for all her gypsylike sexual freedom, is a loner and a wanderer who feels most alive not in the throes of erotic ecstasy but swimming naked and alone in the moonlit river or sitting with an old black woman on a stile, under a tree, near the graveyard where her mother has been buried. Virgie's swim in the Big Black River before her mother's funeral in "The Wanderers" is one of the most erotic passages in Welty's fiction: "She saw her waist disappear into reflectionless water; it was like walking into sky, some impurity of skies. . . . Her breasts around which she felt the water curving were as sensitive at that moment as the tips of wings must feel to birds, or antenna to insects. . . . She moved but like a cloud in skies, aware but only of the nebulous edges of her feeling and the vanishing opacity of her will . . . the water . . . like any other arms, took the body under too, running without visibility into the mouth."[35]

Welty, like Elizabeth Bishop, like Henry Miller, loves the image of flowing water, and she chooses rivers or bayous again and again as the scene of erotic surrender. Rosamond in *The Robber Bridegroom* is raped on a bluff over the Mississippi, with the water flowing "slow as sand" beneath her; Jenny Lockhart is raped on a houseboat in the Mississippi in "At the Landing"; in "The Wide Net," William Wallace fears that his wife, Hazel, has drowned herself in the Pearl River, and when he plunges into the water's depth he experiences a revelation of how Hazel "had been filled to the brim with . . . elation. . . ." But in none of these stories does the river's water flow as voluptuously, as seductively as the Big Black River in which Virgie loses herself, alone and "suspended in felicity."

The critic Harold Bloom asserts that both Welty and Hemingway "emerge from *Huckleberry Finn*. . . . Their obsessive American concern is Huck's: the freedom of a solitary joy, intimately allied to a superstitious fear of solitude." Welty's characters, Bloom continues, like Hemingway's and like the "self-representations of our major poets" including Whitman, Stevens, Crane, and Elizabeth Bishop "all secretly believe themselves to be no part of the creation and all feel free only when they are quite alone. . . . The truth of Welty's fictive cosmos, for all her preternatural gentleness, is that love always does come first, and always does yield to an irreparable separateness."[36] After sexual passion subsides, solitude endures: It is the condition that fosters and protects memory, vision, even love.

Welty's stance finally is not that of the wise, merry spinster or that of the bitter, stifled old maid: It is the sharp-eyed solitary woman gathering strength for herself in love's absence but not in its defeat. Like Virgie at the end of "The Wanderers" and emphatically unlike Porter, Welty is "all to herself."

Given the fundamental differences, really the almost total opposition of their sexual natures and the way they lived their lives, one wonders what Porter and Welty made of each other as sexual creatures. The available letters they exchanged are gossipy and playful, but Porter notably refrains from confiding in Welty the details of her erotic adventures, as she does with Glenway Wescott, Josephine Herbst, her nephew Paul Porter, and others close to her, and Welty characteristically keeps quiet about her private life.

Like Wharton and James, like Lowell and Bishop, Porter and Welty remained good friends despite the abyss that divided them in matters pertaining to sex. But it's likely that each felt a touch of disdain for the other. Acquaintances have speculated that Welty disapproved of the way Porter used her southern belle aura to command attention and manipulate men. Paul Porter tells a story that sheds some light on this. He recalls attending a party for Martha Graham with Porter, Welty, and lots of other famous people:

> Aunt Katherine made her way through the mob to a sofa and sat down, and in merely minutes she was surrounded by an audience, some literally at her feet. Surrounded, she sat there talking for the rest of the evening. In the cab afterwards, which we shared with Eudora Welty, Aunt Katherine chattered in a gay, excited way about the praise and attention she had received. Suddenly Eudora patted her on the knee and said gently, "Now Katherine Anne, don't be so girlish." My heart stopped. I waited for an explosion, but it never came. Aunt Katherine just laughed, took Eudora's hand in hers, and said, "You're right, my darling; but it WAS a good party, wasn't it!" I wonder if anybody else in the world could have said what Eudora Welty said to Aunt Katherine and have had such an affectionate response. Perhaps, but I don't know who."[37]

It may be that Welty was simply peeved at Porter's vanity. Porter was a consummate actress in social settings, a prima donna, and a ham who *expected* adulation. Welty might well have grown tired of being upstaged by her friend's routine. But it's also possible that she was disgusted by the way Porter lit up whenever there were men around to flirt with. It was embarrassing to see a woman well advanced in years feeding so avidly, so girlishly on male attention.

Joan Givner, Porter's biographer, believes that Welty was far more deeply threatened by some of the consequences of Porter's "girlish" behavior. Givner recalls that when she interviewed

Welty for the Porter biography, she seemed avid to hear the intimate details of her friend's personal life, but that her curiosity turned abruptly to fury when Givner mentioned that Porter might have had a stillborn baby out of wedlock. The anger was directed at Givner for gossip mongering—Welty evidently threw Givner out of her house and did her best to blacken her name in literary circles as a "bone-picker."[38] But Givner wonders whether Welty found the idea that Porter might have conceived a child out of wedlock too upsetting to deal with. Implacably genteel, a lifetime member of the Junior League, a fixture of Jackson society, Welty might have been horrified by such a lapse from propriety.

Porter and Welty's shared loathing for Carson McCullers takes on a new aspect when viewed in the light of their own differences in sexual attitudes and experiences. In loathing McCullers they staked out what small patch of common ground that they could find. In belittling McCullers for her nasty effusions, they could shake hands as fellow "normal" females and then promptly turn their backs on the fact that "normal" signified something quite distinct for each of them. Miss Porter with her four divorces and numerous lovers was hardly Junior League material. Miss Welty certainly never felt at home in bohemia, with its casual and frequent couplings and uncouplings. But at least they were both 150 percent female and proud of it. Nothing more on the subject need—or could—be said by either one of them.

THIRTEEN

House and Garden

> Ah, the family ... the whole hideous institution
> should be wiped from the face of the earth. It is the
> root of all human wrongs.
>
> —Cousin Eva in
> Katherine Anne Porter's "Old Mortality"

> The home tie is the blood tie.
>
> —EUDORA WELTY, "Place in Fiction"

AFTER YADDO, the friendship proceeded more erratically, with a series of missed connections, hoped-for reunions that never came to pass, book parties not attended, travels that failed to intersect. The friends exchanged gifts and letters, books, and gossip; they admired and criticized each other's new stories—but from afar. The war, which the United States entered in December 1941 after the Japanese bombed Pearl Harbor, preyed on both their minds, interrupted their work, and threw a pall of absurdity over mundane occupations. As Welty puts it in a letter to Porter, the momentus events overseas were making it difficult for her to focus her thoughts in a "small straight line."[1]

For Welty, with her two brothers serving on minesweep-

ers in the Pacific and her dear friend John Robinson posted to
Africa and Italy in military intelligence, the war was a personal
invasion, a "bastard child," as she calls it in a letter to Porter,
that she, along with everyone else, has to endure. Her instinctive
way of enduring the horror was to "keep down" her personal
anxieties and go through the motions of her daily routine. The
mental strain blocked the flow of her writing, but she could always garden, in fact she felt compelled to keep the garden up as
the rest of the world seemed to disintegrate. In a letter to Porter
she blesses her garden for the pleasure it continues to bring her
in this dark time.

As on her first lonely nights at Yaddo, Welty turns to the
garden for solace, for distraction from worry, for the numbing
pleasure of drudgery, for the inspiring mystery of growing things.
"The true lover of flowers is born . . . to a certain amount of the
purest joy that earth can give her children," writes Celia Thaxter
in her charming volume *An Island Garden*, "joy that is tranquil,
innocent, uplifting, unfailing."[2] Along with writing, music, and
cooking, gardening was a passion that Welty and Porter shared,
and perhaps the one that brought them most pleasurably together.
Gardening may strike the nonenthusiast as a nice, harmless, but
rather trivial hobby. But the devotee knows that gardening can
take on a symbolic, almost mystical significance that far outweighs
its decorative "lady's club" aura. In their exchanges on gardening,
Porter and Welty reveal a good deal about themselves as women,
as daughters, as artists; and they reveal as well something very
deep in their friendship—a spiritual kinship they held despite all
their differences.

Welty evokes both the practical and the mystical aspects
of gardening in letters she wrote to her agent, Diarmuid Russell,
after her return from Yaddo in August 1941. She tells him that
the first thing she did when she arrived home at night was to
take a flashlight and inspect the garden: "lo the big pink insects
were cutting away at my little camellias, and the closer I held the
light and the more I said 'ouch' the better they worked, just like
surgeons. It was time I came back to them."[3] This is rather sweet
and funny—but there is a little stab of guilt in the last line. A
few days later she tries to describe to Russell a moment of spiritual transcendence that she experienced when watering the garden in the evening:

Every evening when the sun is going down and it is cool enough to water the garden, and it is all quiet except for the locusts in great waves of sound, and I stand still in one place for a long time putting water on the plants, I feel something new—that is all I can say—as if my will went out of me, as if I had a stubbornness and it was melting. . . . I feel without ceasing every change in the garden itself, the changes of light as the atmosphere grows darker, and the springing up of a wind, and the rhythm of the locusts, and the colors of certain flowers that become very moving—they all seem to be a part of some happiness or unhappiness, an unhappiness that something is lost or left unknown or undone perhaps—and no longer simple in their own beautiful but *outward* way. And the identity of the garden itself is lost.[4]

The image of Welty's standing still in the twilight garden and feeling her inner being merge with the outward beauty of the wind, the locusts, the flowers is strangely reminiscent of Melville's youthful sailor dreaming at the top of the masthead in *Moby-Dick*:

. . . lulled into such an opium-like listlessness of vacant, un-conscious reverie is this absent-minded youth by the blend-ing cadence of waves with thoughts, that at last he loses his identity; takes the mystic ocean at his feet for the visible im-age of that deep, blue, bottomless soul, pervading mankind and nature; and every strange, half-seen, gliding, beautiful thing that eludes him; every dimly-discovered, uprising fin of some undiscernible form, seems to him the embodiment of those elusive thoughts that only people the soul by contin-ually flitting through it. In this enchanted mood, thy spirit ebbs away to whence it came; becomes diffused through time and space . . . forming at last a part of every shore the round globe over.[5]

Both Melville and Welty sing out in the full-throated strain of the American sublime. Yet how telling that such a moment should come to Melville's dreamer on a whaling ship and to Welty in her mother's backyard. And that the merging of the "bottomless soul" into nature takes Welty not to the brink of oblivion, as in Melville, but to a mournful sense that "something is lost or left unknown or undone."

"In deep and mysterious ways Mississippi was home, and the garden an intensification of home," writes Michael Kreyling.[6] The garden was also an intensification of her deep, troubling, guilt-ridden devotion to her mother, "a great gardener," as Welty calls her, "and really a horticulturalist by inclination and study."[7]

Whenever she was away from home, there always came a moment when "it was time I came back to them"—to the plants and to the widowed mother who had been left to tend them alone. To make the garden grow well (Welty's success at growing flowers is one of the very few personal details Porter mentions in the introduction to *A Curtain of Green*) was to enter most fully, most reassuringly into her mother's world. Behind the curtain of green there was serenity, fecundity, safety, even transcendence, but also strangeness, isolation, and restriction. Entering her mother's garden meant withdrawing from the world "out there."

Welty explores the mysterious connections between gardening, grieving, penetrating, and withdrawing in her story "A Curtain of Green." After the sudden, senseless death of her husband (a Chinaberry tree fell on his car and killed him instantly), Mrs. Larkin buries herself in an ever more luxuriant garden. So entangled does Mrs. Larkin become in her backyard jungle that "quite possibly by now she was unable to conceive of any other place."[8] Her gardening is not a pursuit of order or beauty, but rather a kind of deliberate plunging of the self into the dark, wet, irrational otherness of the natural world: "She seemed not to seek for order, but to allow an overflowering, as if she consciously ventured forever a little farther, a little deeper into her life in the garden."[9] Mrs. Larkin's appearance becomes more and more disreputable. The neighbors begin to talk. At the climax of the story, she stands in a silent rage behind her young black helper, holding a hoe over his innocent head and seriously contemplating killing him: "Such a head she could strike off, intentionally, so deeply did she know, from the effect of a man's danger and death, its cause in oblivion: and so helpless was she, too helpless to defy the workings of accident, of life and death, of unaccountability."[10] In the end, the daily rain comes and releases Mrs. Larkin from her existential agony. Fainting, she sinks down into the garden, surrendering to her exhaustion.

"Welty's fiction is full of flowers and the women who nurture them," notes Ruth Vande Kieft,[11] and surely Mrs. Larkin is the most disturbing, most fiercely imagined of Welty's many women gardeners. "A Curtain of Green" is not strictly autobiographical, but is does reflect the situation Chestina Welty and her daughter were in after Christian Welty died. "The events of a story may have much or little to do with the writer's own life;" Welty once wrote, "but the story *pattern* is the nearest thing to a mirror image of his mind and heart."[12] The story pattern in "A Curtain of Green"—withdrawal and rage, delving deeper and recoiling in horror, violence and surrender, nurturing and suffocating—braids together the plight of widowed mother and fatherless daughter. Unlike Mrs. Larkin, Mrs. Welty was lucky enough to have a daughter to help her in the garden and to hide with her there, but it was not so lucky to be the daughter. In gardening beside her mother Eudora had the satisfaction of bringing beautiful, pleasuring, fragrant things into the world. But there was also the betrayal that she could bring forth nothing else aside from flowers, nothing of her own flesh: For the dutiful daughter there would be no fruitful marriage. Gardening came to symbolize both the love and the loss of living at home. Eudora found transcendence in her mother's garden, but she lost her freedom.

Welty blessed her garden in a letter to Porter in 1942, but on other occasions, she came close to cursing it. She rails against gardening as slave work. She writes of placing individual hoods over each camellia to protect them from cold and spending dull, utterly nontranscendent hours soaking them during droughts. When her mother is away visiting relatives, Welty complains to Porter about feeding the plants and neglecting herself until she is as wilted as the plants. The endless rounds of domestic chores lull her into a kind of stupor from which she yearns to escape—to New York, to California—to *someplace* where she can have total privacy and independence. She confides to Porter, in a letter already mentioned, that she feels she "*should* leave," but meanwhile she tends her garden, performs the drudgery that she dares not ask the maid to do, writes letters to John Robinson in Africa, and listens to music.[13]

More and far heavier responsibilities fell on Eudora once

her mother and her brother Walter became invalids in the mid-1950s. During the painful decade of these illnesses—Walter died in 1959 at age forty-three of complications from a rare form of arthritis; Chestina Welty died after a series of strokes in 1966—house and garden were to be Welty's virtual prison, with even the escape into writing shut off. She was truly "immured," to use a word Porter loved.

How poignant, how sweet and touching Welty's blessings and laments over the garden must have seemed to Porter. The desire to have a garden, to see the same flowers return to bloom each spring and summer and the trees and shrubs spread from year to year, played no small part in Porter's yearning for a house of her own. "Oh Eudora, how I do love growing things, and helping them grow," she wrote to Welty from Washington in 1966. "It is a joy to stay long enough in one place to see something I planted actually in bloom."[14] She knew Welty would understand. Like Edith Wharton, Porter conceived of house and garden as complementary spaces forming a harmonious continuum from indoor to outdoor "rooms." Both women took interior design and gardening very seriously as forms of self-expression, akin to creating works of art.

South Hill, the run-down old farm near Saratoga Springs that Porter purchased and restored while at Yaddo, was to be both her dream house and dream garden. In the depths of the winter of 1942, months before taking possession, Porter described to a friend the fantastic pleasure garden she intended to lay out at South Hill:

> I am going to plant about four dozen peonies, all colors. . . . I am putting in an asparagus bed—one year old roots, 150 of them. I am going to plant white lilacs and mock orange all over the place, and a hedge of primitive roses, rosa rugosa. I am going to plant sweet smelling things near enough to the house that when they bloom the perfumes will come into the house at night and keep me awake for joy. . . . When I was a child I used to get up at night and sit in an old swing under an oak branch just to smell honeysuckle and roses and cape jessamine. . . . It is really an act of faith, and I know that faith makes the difference between life and death.[15]

This lush fantasy, like that of a mother dreaming of her unborn child, recalls the beautiful evocation of the "summer country of my childhood" that Porter wrote in her essay "Noon Wine: The Sources": "that soft blackland farming country, full of fruits and flowers and birds, with good hunting and good fishing; with plenty of water, many little and big rivers."[16] In Porter's imagination, to garden, to live in one place long enough to plant the roots and watch them come up and smell the perfume of their flowers, is to regain the lost Eden of her childhood. South Hill was her bravest, fiercest attempt, and also her saddest failure. When she sank all her money and her heart into the place, she didn't reckon with the bitter winters of the north or her loneliness and delicate health. "South Hill, like some earlier dreams, but a dream complete this time, had to be put behind her," Welty writes in her reminiscence of Porter.[17] When Porter reprinted her wry little essay "A House of My Own," written at the time she bought South Hill and figured on staying forever, she appended a terse note without apology or explanation: "Note. July, 1952: I lived there just thirteen months."[18]

That "summer country of my childhood" was also a short-lived paradise—a paradise that Porter had lost when her childhood had scarcely begun and that she would regain and re-create only in her fiction. Porter was descended from landowners, farmers, and traders from Kentucky, Tennessee, and Georgia—"a good old family of solid wealth and property," as Porter herself put it.[19] A few years before the Civil War, Porter's paternal grandfather sold his farm in Kentucky and moved with his new wife to Hays County, Texas, where he bought 368 acres of fertile virgin blackland. It was a promising spot to farm in, but the war put an abrupt end to whatever prosperity the Texas Porters hoped for.

By the time Callie Russell (the future Katherine Anne's given name) was born in 1890, the family was "running down," as Porter wrote in her story "The Grave." Porter's mother died when she was not yet two, and her father, like Welty's mother, never recovered from the death of his spouse. The mother's death was the great divide in the family's fortunes. Never a very forceful or steady character, Harrison Porter lapsed into a permanent attitude of mournful defeat. Callie Russell and her brother and two sisters endured a childhood of desperate poverty, dirt, crowding, raggedness, and the embarrassment of social decline—circumstances she shared with Melville and, to a lesser extent, with Hawthorne. The sole force staying their downward spiral was the grandmother, the former Catherine Anne Skaggs—Aunt Cat, as she was known all over that part of Texas—who took over the upbringing of her son's four children.

Unlike her son, Aunt Cat was a very formidable person indeed. She appears in Porter's stories as Miss Sophia Jane Rhea—a stiff-backed, iron-willed, vain, rigid, opinionated woman possessed of a "tremendous rightness" in matters pertaining to dress, deportment, education, child rearing, religion, and morality. She was "altogether just, humane, proud, and simple," Porter wrote of her in a story called "The Journey," with a "feeling of superiority in judgment and sensibility to almost everyone around her."[20] "In a Southern sense, the Grandmother embodied the Old Order," says Welty of the position Aunt Cat held in Porter's life. "That was the real genuine Old Order that was in the old lady. Everything that came after her, that depended on her . . . wasn't the *true* Old Order."[21] The style, the traditions, the values, the fastidious codes of conduct of the ancien régime: Aunt Cat, with her ferocious arrogance, had the last word on all these matters.

Of course, there is some question about how "true" even the "real genuine Old Order" was. As Joan Givner has shown exhaustively in her biography, Porter devoted considerable energy to fabricating her personal history, magnifying her family's wealth and aristocratic social standing, and laying false claim to distinguished forebears, including Daniel Boone, William Sydney Porter, who wrote as O. Henry, Revolutionary War Colonel Andrew Porter, and the Duke of Suffolk.[22] "She suppresses her age, baptismal name, lowly origin as the daughter of a poor dirt-farmer, childhood religion, and at least one of her husbands," writes Givner, who threw herself into the enormous task of setting the record straight on these and many other matters.[23]

It's worth mentioning that just about everyone who knew Porter despises the Givner biography and insists that in her zeal for pinning down certifiable facts and "digging up the dirt" Givner failed to portray the complicated woman and the superb artist. "It's possible that the facts are correct," says Cleanth Brooks, "but the woman that I knew does not appear in the book, nor is there any sign of the great artist. Givner turns her family into rednecks, and you wonder how could this waif have learned to read and write, how was it that she could turn out as she did? She didn't fake her reading or rely on editors to rewrite her stories. Her spelling was correct, her grammar was impeccable, her prose was beautiful—she had the real touch."[24] Welty takes the most extreme position, savaging Givner as a mudslinger who made Porter a "victim" of her "biographical speculation."[25] Welty vehemently denies that Porter lied about her personal history: "No conversation I ever had with Katherine Anne had any deceit in it whatsoever or any wish to deceive. It would have bored the devil out of her to try to fabricate some sort of fancy [background]. She had more to think about than that."[26] This is the voice of friendship speaking.

To the extent that Porter did fabricate or embroider or glorify her past history—however one chooses to describe it—the impulse arose, at least in part, from her relationship with her grandmother. In "embodying the Old Order," as Welty puts it, Aunt Cat embodied everything that Porter most cherished in her family life—and everything she found most impossible to live with. In her story "The Old Order," Porter writes of her grandmother as a "tyrant ... a tireless, just and efficient slave driver of every creature" on her country property.[27] "The Grandmother's role was authority ... it was her duty to portion out activities, to urge or restrain where necessary, to teach morals, manners, and religion, to punish and reward her own household according to a fixed code."[28] Authority was something Porter never could abide. In the Miranda stories, we feel the child straining against the grandmother's control, her narrow-mindedness, her implacable conviction that she "knew best about everything and children knew nothing."[29] And as Miranda grows up, her rebellion extends to everything and everyone that tries to hold her. "She was not going to stay in any place, with anyone, that threatened to forbid her making her own discoveries, that said 'No' to her."[30] To the child Callie Russell, Aunt Cat was a heroine and a tyrant both, and the adult Porter never really resolved her conflicting feelings. "She loved her family best when they were about twenty-five hundred miles away," comments her nephew Paul,[31] and she maintained more or less that distance for most of her adult life. "She had to get away," says Welty.[32] She did get away—first in a hasty marriage to John Henry Koontz, the son of an east Texas rancher, when she was sixteen; then to a new life, a new career, a new identity as a reporter in Denver, a film actress in Chicago, a fiction writer and editor in New York, a bohemian adventurer in Mexico, Paris, Germany, Switzerland, Baton Rouge . . .

The same ambivalence Porter felt toward her grand-mother—heroine and tyrant—colored her feelings about owning a house and growing a garden of her own. "I don't mind being homeless, really, I have always been and can probably not do-mesticate very easily," she wrote her friend Josephine Herbst in 1937. "I want a *place,* and I love the south, but my feeling of security is somewhere in my own self, and not in any given spot of land or under any given roof."[33] (She was a true spiritual descendant of the wandering, rootless Nathaniel Hawthorne, who told Longfellow that "I feel quite homeless and astray, and as if I belonged nowhere.") And yet she wrote to Welty after one of their rare meetings in the early 1960s, "You looked so fresh and well, sometimes I think there is no beauty cure better than just staying at home, no matter how much one has to do there, or how much one misses the world and one's friends and amuse-ments: I get fresh life if I can just stay in my own house and back yard. . . . I remember now three truly happy times in my life, and all three I was in a house by myself in the country some-where, minding my own business."[34]

"She kept trying to establish herself bases," says Welty of Porter's lifelong oscillation between home and homeless-ness. "She kept buying houses and fixing them up as somewhere to be the center of where she wanted to be, but it never worked."[35] Elizabeth Bishop was another torn nomadic descen-dant of Nathaniel Hawthorne: Like Porter, she craved a perma-nent house and garden but always ended up losing them—or fleeing them.

Porter was "the real romantic," as Cleanth Brooks puts it, "always looking for that bluebird of happiness right around the corner. She searched all her life for the perfect lover and hus-band, the perfect place to live, the perfect set of friends."[36] She searched, in a sense, for her dream of the old order. The roman-tic quest doomed her in many ways to a life of folly and wretch-edness, but it furnished one of the most powerful themes of her fiction.

It is one of Porter's great strengths as a writer that she saw through the illusions that she cherished: In the story sequence

"The Old Order" and even more in "Old Mortality," she conjures up the noble and thrilling beauty of the past only to expose it as a sham and a lie. Miranda grows up in a world of "living memory" in which "the floating ends of narrative" hang in the air like dust. Nothing that happens to Miranda in the present can possibly measure up to the stories of the golden past for "there was always a voice recalling other and greater occasions."[37]

As Porter shows in the course of "Old Mortality," narrative itself traps and cripples the grandmother, the father, Uncle Gabriel, Aunt Eva, and it reaches out to clutch Miranda. Every time a story about the incomparable belle Amy is hauled out, the bonds of deception tighten. In the end, Miranda comes to hate her family because they "could not tell her the truth, not in the smallest thing,"[38] and to hate love itself because of the falsity she has seen and heard piled on the word. She flees this childhood world of narrative, vowing to forget the stories, to forget the very people who told the stories, and to find "something new of her own." " 'At least I can know the truth about what happens to me,' she assured herself silently, making a promise to herself, in her hopefulness, her ignorance."[39] In the story's famous last sentence, Porter gives Miranda a swift ironic shove into the world "out there." For all her brave new thoughts, Miranda still inhabits a dream not of her own making. She has not yet learned that she too is doomed to find not *the* truth, but "*a* truth," as Robert Penn Warren puts it, and "it, too, will be a myth."[40]

Welty notes acutely in "Katherine Anne Porter: The Eye of the Story," her essay about Porter's work, that "throughout the stories we watch the romantic and the anti-romantic pulling each other to pieces. . . . That battle is in itself a romance."[41] That battle also raged at the center of Porter's life, and she herself was pulled to pieces by it. It is utterly characteristic of Porter that she should fail to profit in her life from the wisdom she distilled in her art. Just as she sneered in her fiction at women's dependence on men but went on desperately needing them, so she exposed the myth of the past but continued to revere it, to pursue it, to claim it as the truth about herself, maybe even to believe her claim. "She created her private myth, only to find it wanting," said one critic.[42] But the more she found it wanting, the more elaborately she created and re-created it.

Of all Porter's doomed Romantic pursuits, gardening was the most innocent, the sweetest, in a sense the most childlike. "Oh Eudora, how I do love growing things, and helping them grow. . . ." In gardening she could join hands untroubled with her grandmother; she could take up the struggles of her dirt farmer ancestors and turn them into something beautiful. In gardening, Porter could cast a spell of exquisite order; she could re-create and repossess the paradise that she never really had. "It is lovely to know you grow Helen Traubel and Dainty Bess too," she wrote to Welty about the roses they grew in common. "I have besides the ones I named, Red American beauty, Soeur Therese, The Doctor, Queen Elizabeth, Kordes Perfecta, King's Ransom, Polynesian Sunset, and fifteen fine old roses that were here when I came, all shades of pink, red, and several pure white, whose names I do not know and can't find them in the catalogues, but whose faces I love dearly."[43]

For both Porter and Welty, gardening was an act of reverence to their female ancestors, a carrying on of old lore amassed by generations of ladies. But of course the two friends approached their female heritage from opposite directions—Welty the daughter who never left her mother; Porter the daughter who never really had a mother. Once her mother became an invalid, and especially after her mother died in 1966, Welty took over the house and garden, though she insisted modestly that she could never rival her mother as a gardener. "You wouldn't know it," she told an interviewer in 1972, "but this garden was once beautiful. My mother really kept after it."[44] The roses suffered terribly from an infestation of nematodes in the mid-1960s, the years when Mrs. Welty was bedridden with her final illness. Among the casualties were Gloire de Dijon, Fortune's Yellow Climbers, and Mermaid— Porter would have loved the names and mourned the loss.[45] Eudora spared her mother the knowledge of the true devastation by planting a crab apple tree at the head of the rosebeds. ("Sparing was our family trait," she wrote in "Kin," her most flower-bedecked story.[46]) It was a beautiful deception only a gardener could appreciate, a deception only the most dutiful daughter could have dreamed up and executed. Now old and increasingly infirm herself, Welty feels ashamed and depressed that she can no longer keep up her mother's garden.[47]

Porter abandoned every garden she ever planted or

bought—South Hill; Roxbury, Connecticut; Georgetown—living out her final years in a high-rise double apartment in the Washington suburb of College Park with lots of potted plants. The urge to grow things never left either one of them. The garden as dream, the garden as prison: These were motifs in both their lives. It was something that the two proud, lonely, childless women understood deeply and silently about each other.

Cooking was another traditionally female art that linked Porter and Welty with each other and with their female ancestors. Though less mystical than gardening, cooking represented to both of them a way to carry on the pleasurable womanly wisdom of the past. Both of them were fine cooks, and Porter was famous among her friends for her dinner parties and her yearly Twelfth Night parties, as lavish in their way as those she recollected her grandmother hosting. Eating and drinking together is also, of course, a medium of friendship—and so, as Welty tells us, is cooking. "I often think to make a friend's recipe is to celebrate her once more," she writes in her introduction to *The Jackson Cookbook*, "and in that cheeriest, most aromatic of places to celebrate in, the home kitchen."[48] Especially as they grew older, Porter and Welty devoted considerable space in their correspondence to describing and thanking each other for memorable meals. In Welty's *Georgia Review* reminiscence of Porter written a decade after her death, she lists the subjects of their "long life of correspondence," as "reading, recipes, anxieties and aspirations, garden seeds and gossip"—with no distinctions made among them.[49]

In letters, and no doubt in conversation, their exchanges about gardening sounded rather frivolous and banal, as all chat about gardening sounds at one level. But it's not what they said, but what they felt—the emotional essence that they inhaled with the perfume of flowers—that gave gardening an importance in their lives. "One famous grower of Old Roses . . . advises one to bury a big beef bone, cooked or raw, deep under the new plant," wrote Porter in her essay "The Flower of Flowers," "so that its growing roots may in time descend, embrace and feed slowly upon this decayed animal stuff in the private darkness. Above, meanwhile, it brings to light its young pure buds, opening shyly as the breasts of virgins . . . out of this tranced absorption with the rot and heat and moisture of the earth, there is distilled the perfume of perfumes from this flower of flowers."[50] To garden, if only in one's thoughts, was to plunge one's hands deep into the rot and heat and moisture of Mother Earth, to submit to this tranced absorption. In sharing, however casually, a passion for gardening, the friends—each of whom worked her private garden with fierce independence, as Welty wrote both literally and figuratively of herself and Porter[51]—found their easiest and most affecting way of being daughters together.

FOURTEEN

Drifting Apart

> I am harder to amuse than Queen Victoria, though
> for very different reasons, and for society I love only
> the company of a good familiar friend or two at a
> time, and talk; this grows rarer and harder to come
> by, everybody complains of it, but still we must all
> run like sheep from one mob-occasion to another,
> and there is no time left for keeping friendships
> warm.
>
> —KATHERINE ANNE PORTER
> letter to Eudora Welty,
> November 8, 1951

"I THINK I'VE ONLY SPENT about ten percent of my energies on writing," Porter once told her friend Barbara Thompson in an interview. "The other ninety percent went to keeping my head above water."[1] For Welty, during her most productive stretch in the 1940s, the percentages were pretty much the reverse. She published five books in the course of the decade, and entered the next decade with a renewal of her Guggenheim Fellowship, on the strength of which she traveled to France, Italy, England, and Ireland. While in Ireland she summoned up the pluck to contact Elizabeth Bowen, who had written an admiring review of Welty's *Delta Wedding*, and she stayed as a guest at Bowen's Court, Bowen's country estate in County Cork. The two women became

251

fast friends and remained in close touch until Bowen's death in 1973. On subsequent trips to Europe, Welty lectured at Cambridge University and made the acquaintance of E. M. Forster. V. S. Pritchett was also to become a dear friend. The "girl" whom Porter had launched back in 1941 was doing just fine under her own steam.

Katherine Anne was, in some ways, proud of Eudora's success. After all, hadn't she been the one to "discover" her and hadn't she been writing for years to her nephew Paul, himself a struggling writer, that he could find no better model for how to write a modern story than Eudora's work? But Porter's pride was not so consuming as to scour away her jealously. It was galling to Porter to see Welty's novel *Delta Wedding* published—and even appear briefly on the best-seller list—when she was still hopelessly bogged down in *Ship of Fools*. Diarmuid Russell wrote his client that Porter was "a little miffed" that "her protégé . . . had the impudence to bring out a novel first, almost going behind her back. I don't know where she got the idea she has, probably her own subtle way of slighting the work."[2] Kreyling says that Porter felt "blind-sided" by the publication of *Delta Wedding,* and that a coolness set into the relationship after this.[3]

Porter was even more miffed two years later when she read Welty's essay "The Reading and Writing of Short Stories," in the February and March 1949 issues of *The Atlantic*. The piece, which was adapted from a lecture Welty gave on the West Coast in 1947, reads like Welty's own personal road map to the landmarks of the modernist short story, a celebration of the writers who made her think the hardest about her craft—Stephen Crane, Ernest Hemingway, Chekhov, William Faulkner, D. H. Lawrence, with briefer asides on E. M. Forster and Virginia Woolf. There is, however, not a single word about the work of her dear friend and sponsor, Katherine Anne Porter. Porter did not take this kindly. Her nephew Paul recalls hearing a "mild grumble" from his Aunt Katherine that "Eudora had managed to write an entire article on the subject of the short story without mentioning her once!"[4] Givner says Porter was "astonished and furious," and she notes that it was soon after reading the essay that Porter snapped off a letter to Paul attacking *The Golden Apples* as "technical virtuosity gone into a dizzy spin absolutely drunk on language, a personal showing off as shameless as a slackwire dancer with pinwheels. It is a great pity . . ."[5]

Considering that *The Golden Apples* is the work that Welty

said "is closest to my heart of all my books"[6] and that many judge her best, that is a serious attack indeed. (Paul Porter reports that his aunt changed her opinion about *The Golden Apples*. He recalls that "she later read 'Moon Lake' [one of the volume's strongest stories] to me from beginning to end, interrupting herself with laughter and interjecting little comments. . . . 'Isn't that delicious!' and 'Oh God! that is wonderful!' and so on." Paul once challenged his aunt Katherine about her contradictions and she responded, with Whitmanesque expansiveness, that "when she talked or wrote letters, it was off the top of her head, but when she was WORKING she had to answer to God."[7])

Other literary friendships have smashed up on far slighter grievances than the ones Porter and Welty had created in their criticism and neglect of each other. And Porter herself had a reputation for blowing up at friends, picking fights, and dropping people from her life, sometimes for no apparent reason. She and Hart Crane parted on bad terms in Mexico back in the late 1920s, shortly before his suicide in 1932. She and Caroline Gordon had a terrific row in Washington in 1944. She fell out with her old and once very close friend Josephine Herbst after Herbst publicly criticized her scathing attack on Gertrude Stein. (Several years before this Porter had told an FBI agent that Herbst was a Communist organizer and that she had acted as a secret courier for Moscow during the 1930s—a charge that Porter fabricated for no known reason aside from malice.[8]) Especially as she got older, Porter became extremely prickly and hypersensitive, lashing out at friends, even old friends, over the slightest insult.

Porter never quite forgave Welty for leaving her out of that essay (she was still grumbling about it to her agent a decade later.)[9] And Welty had been working on a grudge of her own ever since Porter had pressed her into service as her personal chauffeur at Yaddo. In 1946–1947, when she was in San Francisco for five months with John Robinson, Welty conspicuously failed to travel to Los Angeles to visit Porter, who was putting in a short stint writing for the movies. Their letters tapered off considerably during the late 1940s and the 1950s, and in the letters they did write there was little of the liveliness and freshness of their early exchanges. But however great a strain the friendship sustained, the bond did not snap. Porter forgave her "protégée" for being so much more prolific than she herself had ever been. Whatever resentment Welty harbored over Porter's condescension or competitiveness, she kept it quiet. Like Wharton and James, like Bishop and Lowell, Porter and Welty valued each other enough as literary allies to overlook their personal differences. It also helped that they saw each other so infrequently—which also held true for Wharton, James, Bishop, and Lowell.

One of their rare prolonged encounters came in March 1952, more than a decade after their summer as housemates at Yaddo, when Porter came to Jackson to lecture at Millsaps College. The friends exchanged a flurry of excited letters beforehand, planning the visit and discussing clothes and weather. ("I never had the right clothes for ANY occasion in my life," Porter confesses, "and it's too late to start worrying now."[10]) It was decided that after Porter's professional duties were over the two of them would take a little jaunt down to the Gulf Coast in Welty's car. Katherine Anne announced in advance that she expected to get no work done and hoped that Eudora would shelve her writing as well. "I am the highly distractible sort," she wrote Eudora, who certainly didn't need to be told, "and it is no good for me to start out thinking I should be able to write anything amid such changing scenes. I'd just ruin my fun. . . . The mainest thing is to see each other, catch up on our gossip, tie up floating ends into little bow knots, and just enjoy our visit."[11] Despite some friction, they seem to have succeeded on all counts.

A story, perhaps distorted in the retelling, has come out of this visit that suggests how cool and skeptical their feelings for each other had become by this time. Though Katherine Anne stayed at a hotel in Jackson rather than with the Weltys ("since they are giving me it for free, shame to waste it!"), Eudora naturally wanted to have her to the house for dinner. But it wasn't as simple as issuing an invitation: First, she had to obtain her mother's approval. Porter, or so the story goes, was amazed by this. Eudora at forty-two years old could not invite a friend to dinner without clearance from her mother! It was outrageous! How could any woman live this way?[12]

Of the Gulf Coast trip itself we know little. Welty, as usual, drove, and on the way down they stopped at the coastal resort town of Pass Christian to visit with the novelist Elizabeth Spencer, a fellow Mississippian who was working there. Pass Christian was a favorite resort of prosperous Deep South planters before the Civil War and prosperous Yankee tourists after it, but Hurricane Camille pretty much destroyed it, along with much of the Gulf

Coast, in 1969. Porter and Welty stayed at the Hotel Miramar, a rather grand old place on the water that was a favorite of Welty's.[13]

From Pass Christian they drove on through southwest Mississippi into Louisiana. "Katherine Anne loves that part of the world," Eudora remarked years later. "We were getting near—you know she is from Texas near Louisiana—so . . . we were nearing her bailiwick and I think she felt that. . . . All of that country meant something to her, which Jackson didn't."[14] Porter, writing to thank her afterward, recalled their "fine escapade to the Gulf Coast" as "a shimmer of greenery and warmth."[15] On the open road together, they could shake off the constraints they must have felt in Jackson. They didn't have to worry about interrupting each other's work. Like James and Wharton motoring through France, the friends abandoned themselves to the pure pleasure of driving through a dense green landscape and hauling in fresh impressions. Welty has always loved to travel, and like James, she is accustomed to traveling alone or passing alone from one set of friends to the next. With Porter, she had a voluble companion who loved nothing better than to bask in distraction and hoist a glass of bourbon each evening. The trip sounds like a wonderful, though brief, lark.

The other event of note that occurred during the friends' Mississippi reunion was Welty's delivery of a radio address about Porter and her work. In the speech, Welty included what she called "a little potted biography" in which she both glamorizes Porter (she quotes Porter's oft-quoted remark about how she was "precocious, nervous, rebellious, unteachable," like a high-strung racehorse) and also reveres her as a "pioneer by heritage," who taught herself how to write, alone and unassisted, in the howling Texas wilderness. Welty told the Jackson radio audience that some of Porter's most popular stories came right out of Texas "and the family life of tradition, story, and memory"—a remark that is certainly true and that just as truly describes her own work.[16] She praises Porter for helping "the young and promising," and she mentions in a personal aside that Porter encouraged her own early stories.[17]

The speech is thin on literary criticism. Welty cites her favorite stories and summarizes their subjects and themes (she ranks "Noon Wine" highest, describing it aptly as "pure and strong in its form as anything Greek").[18] She does, however, throw out one idea of some substance: that Porter conjures up reality in her work not so much through concrete images and sense impressions but by evoking psychological states and moral conceptions— "the seasonless, placeless, dateless conflicts of the soul." She also emphasizes the centrality of good and evil in Porter's work: "There may not be a smell of jasmine, but there is very likely to be a smell of the Devil."[19] Welty was to elaborate this point as the central thesis of her essay "Katherine Anne Porter: The Eye of the Story," which she published in the *Yale Review* in 1965 and which became one of the cornerstones of Porter critical studies.

On the whole, the speech is rather pious and reverential, but Welty was troubled by it. In speaking publicly about a friend, she worried she was betraying some kind of sacred trust: She was posing as an impartial critic of someone whom she could not possibly judge impartially.

Porter, characteristically, took Welty's speech as no more than her due. "Maybe we are wrong to be uneasy about writing about the friends whose work we like," she gently chided Eudora. "I love to praise what I love, and I don't for a minute believe that love is blind—indeed, it gives clearness without sharpness, and surely that is the best light in which to look at anything."[20] And so, with an elegant shrug, she dismisses the matter.

Welty's reluctance to get involved in literary back scratching was akin to her reluctance to put people she knows and loves in her stories. In both cases she is constrained by her fierce sense of privacy, her fear of exposing herself and her intimates to public scrutiny. All her instincts as a writer forbade her from mixing the facts of her life into her stories or her personal affections into her criticism.

Welty's Jackson radio speech about Porter, marginal as it is as literary criticism or biography, marks a change in their friendship. It inaugurated their honorific phase. As the friends drifted apart, by circumstance and also by choice, their contact became more formal and more public—more purely literary. There were to be no more jaunts like their fine escapade to the Gulf Coast, but instead essays, book reviews, written and spoken tributes, the bestowing of awards—and the rare lunch or dinner together. As Welty wrote Porter, their encounters came mostly during "occasions."[21]

With the radio speech and later, in 1965, with her essay "Katherine Anne Porter: The Eye of the Story," Welty more than repaid Porter for the introduction to *A Curtain of Green* and made ample amends for leaving her out of the 1949 *Atlantic* piece on the short story. Unlike the radio speech, "The Eye of the Story" is pure literary criticism, a smooth, well-wrought, penetrating hymn of praise in which Welty treats with grave respect all that is finest in Porter's work. She expands considerably on the idea tossed out in the speech that Porter is not primarily a "visual" writer—that unlike most story writers (including Welty herself), Porter refuses "to cast her stories in scenes" and eschews "sensory imagery." "Most good stories are about the interior of our lives," she writes, "but Katherine Anne Porter's stories take place there; they show surface only at her choosing." (Welty admits that "Noon Wine" is a stunning exception to this rule: It established "forever that when she wants a story to be visible, it is."[22])

Her other major point is that Porter is essentially a moralist whose "deep sense of fairness and justice" has been outraged by betrayal: "All the stories she has written are moral stories about love and the hate that is love's twin, love's impostor and enemy and death. Rejection, betrayal, desertion, theft roam the pages of her stories as they roam the world."[23] Just as Porter notes in her introduction to *A Curtain of Green* that Welty uses her "just cruelty" to expose vulgarity and evil, so Welty praises Porter here for using her outrage as a "cool instrument" by which she shows "with precision . . . what monstrosities of feeling come about not from the lack of the existence of love but from love's repudiation, betrayal."[24] Welty concludes the essay with a crescendo of acclaim, celebrating Porter for inventing "a style as invisible as the rhythm of a voice," for refusing to repeat herself in her stories, for filling her readers "with a rising joy," for being above all things an artist of radiance and grace and natural gaiety whose name "shines in the mind."[25] With choruses of hallelujah, Eudora summons a flaming chariot to bear Katherine Anne straight up to literary heaven. The essay stands in the celebratory tradition of Melville's "Hawthorne and His Mosses" and Robert Lowell's sequence of poems for Elizabeth Bishop in *History*.

Strangely, Welty omitted any reference to *Ship of Fools*, though of course the publication of this book three years earlier really did elevate Porter into the heaven of wealth and celebrity. It may be that the novel didn't fit with the themes of her essay, but acquaintances have speculated that she couldn't abide the book's dark view of human nature. Ever considerate, Welty probably decided that it was better to leave it out altogether than to risk offending Porter by slighting it.

The essay about Porter cannot have been an easy one to write for the late 1950s and most of the 1960s—"the bad 60s" as she called the decade in an interview[26]—was a terrible time for Welty. Her mother had her first operation for cataracts in 1955, and from then until her death in January 1966, Chestina Welty was almost continually ill, enduring a protracted convalescence after the operation and suffering recurrent infections and strokes as well as debilitating arteriosclerosis. Over the course of a decade, Eudora watched this strong-willed mountain woman lose her eyesight, her mobility, and eventually her lucidity. Most of Eudora's own energies went to nursing her mother and looking after the house and garden. In the late 1950s, Welty's burdens became even heavier when her brother Walter was stricken with a rare form of arthritis. Eudora spent a good deal of time caring for her nieces while Walter and his wife consulted doctors in New Orleans. Walter died in 1959. Chestina Welty was in and out of a convalescent home during the 1960s, but visiting her entailed fifty miles of driving each way. Then in late 1965, her brother Edward fell sick as well. Welty wrote Porter on January 4, 1966, that she would love to take the train to Washington to attend the annual Twelfth Night party, but that since Thanksgiving she had spent every day shuttling back and forth between her mother and her brother, in two hospitals forty miles apart.[27] Three weeks after this letter, both Chestina Welty and her son Edward were dead. As the critic Louise Westling noted, Chestina Welty died like Becky McKelva, the character in *The Optimist's Daughter* loosely based on her—blind, raving, and reciting passages from a McGuffey's Reader.[28]

The prolonged illnesses had drained Welty both emotionally and financially. They had also made it almost impossible for her to work. Fifteen years elapsed between the publication of *The Bride of the Innisfallen and Other Stories* and her next book, *Losing Battles,* which finally appeared in 1970.

These were also the years when the fires of the civil rights movement ("the troubles" Welty called it) blazed across the South, burning most fiercely in Mississippi. With civil rights workers being gunned down or lynched, churches burned, protesters taking to the streets, federal troops marching on schools, and reporters and TV crews swarming all over the state, it was not an easy time to be black *or* white in Mississippi. The old bond between the races, however grounded in fear and ignorance and inequality, was torn asunder. As but one small example of the new social climate, Welty, in an interview, recalls how she could photograph blacks back in the 1930s without self-consciousness or suspicion[29]—something that was no longer possible after the troubles.

As a white southern writer, Welty suddenly found herself under attack by Yankee intellectuals such as Diana Trilling and Isaac Rosenfeld for failing to address social and racial issues head on in her fiction. She has spoken often in interviews of being awakened at midnight by phone calls from angry liberals, especially from Boston (which she found "rather laughable" later when racial violence erupted in that city in the 1970s). "All right, Eudora Welty, what are you going to do about it? Sit down there with your mouth shut?"[30] she reports one of these callers demanding. Such accusations were particularly painful to Welty because of her lifelong fascination with African Americans—indeed, her veneration for certain aspects of black culture.

The critic Ruth Vande Kieft, who knew Welty well, spoke of her "instinctive liking for blacks" and her admiration for their imaginativeness and courage, and she points to such stories as "Powerhouse," "Livvie," and "A Worn Path" and nonfiction pieces such as "Ida M'Toy" as evidence of Welty's deep sympathy with African Americans.[31] Her sympathy is also apparent in the photographs she took of blacks while traveling around Mississippi for the WPA: She captures the gracefulness and dignity of her black subjects without sentimentality and without hiding the poverty and sadness of their lives. Elizabeth Bishop, though she met Welty only once, sensed her attunement to blacks after reading her first collection of stories in the summer of 1948. Bishop wrote to Robert Lowell that " 'The Worn Path' is really marvellous. It's too bad her novel [*Delta Wedding*] was so awful—I should think she could write a long, long, really good Negro novel if anyone could, if she wanted to."[32]

Welty's background might have had something to do with her liberal attitude toward African Americans for neither of her parents came from the Deep South and neither had had much contact with blacks until they moved to Jackson (few blacks lived in the mountains of West Virginia where Chestina Welty grew up; fewer still in the Ohio farming country where her father was raised). The kindly, paternalistic racism of "good" Jackson families was not part of Welty's heritage.

This benevolent racism was, on the other hand, very much part of Porter's heritage—and it shows up in the way she portrays blacks in her stories. Nannie and Uncle Jimbilly, the former slaves and loyal family retainers of the Rhea family in "The Old Order," are as proud, starched, and head-strong as Miranda's grandmother, Miss Sophia Jane, and they are drawn, like her, with a full round measure of humanity. Sophia Jane loves Nannie as much as she loves anyone, even shocks the white community when she suckles Nannie's black baby at her breast when Nannie falls ill after childbirth. But the friendship between mistress and servant only works because the servant knows and keeps her place. Ultimately, Nannie and Uncle Jimbilly are valued most of all not as individuals but as trappings of the Rhea family status in the old order, like the "wonderful old slaves" that Porter told a *Time* magazine reporter had been "companions" in her own family.[33] Their purpose in the stories is to show how noble and humane the grandmother is and how *different* from her bigoted neighbors. Though Porter works hard to make her black characters sharp-tongued and tough-minded, Nannie and Jimbilly are really clichés of uppity, indulged black servants. They fairly glow with nostalgia for the good old days when a little girl received a pony and a servant as presents, and kept the servant as a "beloved friend" all her life.

One recalls Melville writing in "Benito Cereno" that "there is something in the negro which, in a peculiar way, fits him for avocations about one's person. . . . There is, too, a smooth tact about them in this employment, with a marvelous, noiseless, gliding briskness, not ungraceful in its way. . . . Captain Delano took to negroes, not philanthropically, but genially, just as other men to Newfoundland dogs."[34] But of course, the seemingly docile congenial blacks that inspire these heavily ironic reflections have actually murdered their Spanish master in a gruesome mutiny and hung his skeleton at the prow of the slave ship. Porter, writing nearly a century later, chose to disregard the terrible irony of Melville's story.

Welty's written response to the multiple ruptures that "the troubles" opened up in her world was two stories—"Where Is the Voice Coming From?" (written in a single night after the killing of NAACP field director Medgar Evers and published in July 1963) and "The Demonstrators" (published in November 1966)—and the essay "Must the Novelist Crusade?" (published in October

1965) in which she firmly and passionately denies that she (or any writer) has a moral responsibility to "do something about it" in her art. The novelist, she argues, is responsible only to the integrity of his material and to the demands of the imagination; to "crusade" for a political or social cause is to stifle the imagination, to cheapen feelings, and finally to turn fiction into ranting. She has always resisted the pressure to crusade in her own work, she told an interviewer, because "I didn't want to be swerved into preaching disguised as a work of fiction."[35] "Fiction has, and must keep, a private address," she writes in what has become the most famous passage of "Must the Novelist Crusade?" "For life is *lived* in a private place; where it means anything is inside the mind and heart."[36]

This might almost be taken as her creed in art and life alike. For Eudora Welty, privacy is a requirement of the imagination and the foundation of decency. The "agonizing of our times" as she calls it in "Must the Novelist Crusade?" lay in the continued persecution of blacks, the murder of civil rights workers, "the atmosphere of hate" in which white and black southerners had come to live. The agony for her personally lay in the assault on her privacy. She didn't give in, but there is no question that she suffered. Hounded by sickness and death in her family, by the racial violence that was burning holes in the social fabric of her town, by irate midnight callers and hostile northern critics, Welty suffered terribly during the 1960s. When she could work, she hauled out the immense fragmentary manuscript of *Losing Battles,* her longest novel, in which she was bogged down for most of the decade (Michael Kreyling reports that the idea for the book had been "running in her head" since 1955).[37] The fact that she managed to produce the essay about Porter's work is a real tribute to her loyalty to the friendship.

Porter's fortunes took a very different turn during the 1960s for when *Ship of Fools* was finally published on April 1, 1962, it became an instant and huge best-seller, and later a successful movie. Welty, nursing her mother in Jackson, missed the publication party at New York's "21"—by now missing book parties was a tradition between them—but she telegraphed her regrets. After seven decades of living pretty much hand to mouth, Katherine Anne awoke to find herself both rich and famous—not just literary famous, as she had been since the 1930s, but really a star (Givner reports that John

Kennedy brushed aside the crisis in Cuba to chat about the book at a White House dinner party).[38] Having lived all her life as if she had money, Porter really *did* have money now, and the first thing she did was to buy herself the huge emerald ring she had always craved. ("I did it all for this!" she told a friend as she flashed the twenty-thousand-dollar ring at him[39]). Then in the summer, she went to Italy on holiday and returned to Europe again in the fall for a year's stay, mostly in Rome.

Fame and fortune did not make Porter happy. Like many celebrities before and after her, she complained of the burdens it brought and looked back nostalgically, at least when speaking to reporters, to the relative simplicity of her prestar days. She felt crushed by the avalanche of requests for interviews, public appearances, book endorsements that arrived daily. She was bitter that so much of her newfound wealth instantly vanished into the jaws of the IRS. And most of all she was stung by the bad press she and her novel began receiving. The first flush of reviews for *Ship of Fools* were glowing tributes: Mark Schorer, for example, wrote on the front page of *The New York Times Book Review:* "This novel has been famous for years. It has been awaited through an entire literary generation. . . . Now it is suddenly, superbly here. . . . It is our good fortune that it comes at last still in our time. It will endure, one hardly risks anything in saying, far beyond it, for many literary generations."[40] But increasingly vehement attacks started to appear once the initial hoopla died down. Porter was accused of anti-Semitism, anti-Teutonism, and a blinding misanthropy that reduced her immense cast of characters to cartoon figures.

The most withering—and influential—attack was an essay by Theodore Solotaroff published as the cover story in *Commentary* six months after the book appeared. Solotaroff described Porter as an "unreconstructed short-story writer" who failed to build any momentum into her story or her characters. He dismissed her characters as predictable and shallow and savaged her as "morally vicious" for her hideous portrayal of Julius Lowenthal, the one Jew in the book. "The trifling attitude that lies behind the treatment of Lowenthal," writes Solotaroff, "is only one example of Miss Porter's compulsive tendency to simplify and close her characters and issues, to look down upon life from the perspective of a towering arrogance, contempt, and disgust."[41]

Robert Lowell, who had known and liked Porter since the

famous gathering at the Tates' Tennessee house in 1937, joined the fray on Porter's side in a letter to the editor of *Commentary:* "A little sense on Katherine Anne Porter's *Ship of Fools!* . . . *Ship of Fools* should not be read after or placed beside the masterpieces of the ages, but rather with such a book as Edith Wharton's *Age of Innocence.* In such a context, its virtues, to me at least, are obvious: it is one of the very few American novels . . . that deserves to be long; the writing is always alert, modest, and honest. . . . For what it is worth, *Ship of Fools* is in the American Liberal Tradition, a tradition that most of us follow in our non-fiction, but one that is hardly attempted any more in imaginative work. For the Liberal, 1931, just as now, is a time to look blue!"[42]

Porter, inexplicably, resented the comparison with Wharton, insisting it was the "one truly frightful thing said about my work." But Lowell was onto something, even if Porter couldn't recognize it. Both Porter and Wharton expose the fatuity and viciousness of social conventions, especially as they victimize women. Jenny Brown, the ambitious but insecure American artist in *Ship of Fools,* is a distant bohemian cousin of Wharton's Lily Bart; the doomed romance between Dr. Schumann and the drug-addicted Condesa recalls the unrequited love between Wharton's Newland Archer and Ellen Olenska; Mary Treadwell, Porter's embittered middle-aged divorcée, is a desperate and déclassée descendant of Wharton's Anna Leath, the widowed heroine of *The Reef* who is betrayed by the man who awakens her sexually. Porter, however, digs far deeper than Wharton into the dark and ugly recesses of the human heart.

Like Melville and Hawthorne, she believes in "Evil with a capital *E,*" as Robert Penn Warren said[43]—both the evil "out there" in the brute indifference of fate and circumstance and the evil "inside" in man's own indifference to his fellow man. "There may not be a smell of jasmine," to quote once more Welty's remark about Porter's fictional world, "but there is very likely to be a smell of the Devil"—*Ship of Fools* fairly reeks of him. In Wharton, collusion in the lies of society leads to suffering, wasted passion, even death; in Porter it leads to the Nazi Holocaust. The parallels between *The Age of Innocence* and *Ship of Fools* are mostly on the surface; in its vision of evil, its epic scope, and its shipboard setting, Porter's novel has more in common with Melville's *Moby-Dick* and Lowell's "The Quaker Graveyard in Nantucket" than with Wharton's *The Age of Innocence.* But

Lowell is right in saying that *Ship of Fools* falls short of a masterpiece: Ultimately there is something rather mechanical and repetitive about the claustrophobic world of the *Vera*. Porter's darkness is too unrelieved, her people too easily corrupted, her devil too triumphant.

The controversy over *Ship of Fools* and the book's failure to win either the Pulitzer Prize or the National Book Award angered Porter but did not surprise her. As her publisher, Seymour Lawrence, said, "Porter always predicted that people would come out of the woodwork if she had a great success. As long as she wrote short stories and earned $2000 a year everyone would love her. But when she produced a bestseller and earned a million dollars all those so-called fans and devotees would turn on her, out of malice or envy or whatever. She predicted all this long before *Ship of Fools* was published. And after it was published she said, 'Nothing quite fails like success.' "[44]

FIFTEEN

Battles Lost and Won

Now there are only three degrees of age—young, mature and remarkable.

—KATHERINE ANNE PORTER, *1960 panel discussion*

The fantasies of dying could be no stranger than the fantasies of living. Surviving is perhaps the strangest fantasy of them all.

—EUDORA WELTY, *The Optimist's Daughter*

WELTY, CONSUMED by the problems at home, remained rather remote from Porter during the launching of *Ship of Fools*. Even after her mother died and she was free to travel again, Welty kept her distance. When she was in Washington, D.C., where Porter had settled in the early 1960s, Welty stayed with other friends and saw Porter only briefly for a meal or a drink. After one of these Washington visits, Porter complained of being left out: "I had a little impression of you being pulled in all directions, gently of course, lovingly of course, by friends who are going to see you if they have to pull you in pieces and hand you around—I just never could join the pack, angel. . . . I don't doubt you loved seeing them all, but one more is too many."[1] Welty, for her part, complained that Porter's rapid-fire self-centered chatter gave her a headache. Porter used her as a sounding board, she felt, and gave her little in return. A very occasional lunch was *more* than enough of Katherine Anne. What Welty called the "good old gaiety" of their first encounters was more and more supplanted by exasperated, peevish affection—but again, the bond remained too important to both of them to break. As the 1960s passed, the connection continued in the rather formal manner of old friendships that run on a fund of memories.

Welty emerged from her personal trials of the "bad sixties" in glory for at the start of the new decade she finally published *Losing Battles,* her biggest commercial success thus far. Her advances for the book, including paperback and book club rights, came to about $100,000, and it appeared for a time on best-seller lists[2] (its success, however, was modest compared with *Ship of Fools,* which reportedly earned more than $1 million for Porter's publisher). *One Time, One Place,* a collection of Welty's photographs from the 1930s, appeared in 1971, thirty-five years after she had unsuccessfully peddled them in New York from publisher to publisher. *The Optimist's Daughter* came out in book form the following year (Welty had sold a slightly different version of the short novel to *The New Yorker* back in 1967; the magazine held on to it for nearly two years, before devoting almost the entire March 15, 1969, issue to it).[3] A shower of prizes, awards, and medals ensued. In 1971, Welty was elected to the American Academy of Arts and Letters and in 1972, she received the Gold Medal for Fiction of the National Institute of Arts and Letters. Porter, now eighty-two years old, presented her with the award at the official ceremony in New York City in May: This occasion marked "the closing of the circle," Welty wrote her.[4] (Another circle had neatly closed when Welty moved with *Losing Battles* from Harcourt Brace to Random House and editor Albert Erskine, who had been married to Porter and had "discovered" Welty for the *Southern Review* in the 1930s.) As the final effusion of grace, *The Optimist's Daughter* won the Pulitzer Prize in 1973. It is from this period that one can date Welty's assumption of the role of the "Eleanor Roosevelt of American letters" as some irreverent younger writer has dubbed her (Solotaroff had earlier awarded Porter the same title in his scathing attack on *Ship of Fools*). Welty, however, was never one to be blinded by her own celebrity. She told an interviewer in 1972, "I know a literary reputation is a fragile thing. Somebody told me once, watch out when a woman writer passes fifty; they all turn on you. Sometimes I think they decide, 'Oh, we're so damned tired of saying she writes well.' "[5]

Though *Losing Battles* was the product of the long years Welty spent caring for her mother, the book reflects almost nothing of the grim confinement of her actual life. With its huge cast of characters, its multiplicity of voices and stories, its frequently cartoonlike incidents, and its essentially comic vision, *Losing Battles* was a sort of escape hatch for Welty—a way of keeping herself sane. She has spoken of being glared at by her mother's nurses for laughing out loud during its composition. *The Optimist's Daughter,* written in a six-week-long creative burst shortly after the deaths of her mother and brother, cuts far deeper and closer to the bone. The book is a breakthrough both emotionally and artistically for Welty not only draws for the first time on autobiographical material ("the mother is based on my mother," she told an interviewer, the "boys are her brothers") but she also writes with a cold, austere fury that is new for her. Stylistically, *The Optimist's Daughter* is Welty's sparest, most straightforward book, its narrative voice swept clean of metaphor, color, brooding lyricism, and aggressive mythological allusion. It is the style of bitter knowledge that Yeats describes in "The Circus Animals' Desertion" when he writes of lying down "where all the ladders start,/In the foul rag-and-bone shop of the heart."

If *One Writer's Beginnings* depicts family life as a shower of gold, *The Optimist's Daughter* depicts it as a frayed, painfully binding cord. "Rejection, betrayal, desertion, theft roam the pages" of this novel just as surely as they roam the pages of Porter's stories. Wounds, inflicted by chance, by sickness, by moral and spiritual blindness, and by death, go unhealed and undisclosed. Or disclosed only to open fresh wounds. Laurel's mother, Becky McKelva, the character patterned on Chestina Welty, dies raving against her family, *blaming* her husband and her daughter for her own suffering. Laurel's father, the "optimist" of the title, dies through the cruel whim of his horrible new wife, the blond, mean-spirited, emptyheaded Wanda Fay Chisom in whom Welty compresses everything she hates most about the new South, the new order, the modern world.

The Optimist's Daughter, like Welty's early work, contains a dream of escape from the confines of a home—but Welty now contemplates the dream from a new perspective for Laurel, who is in a sense an artist (she works in Chicago as a freelance fabric designer), *had* escaped from the house and garden of her mother. She had married, though her marriage ended swiftly when her architect husband, Phil Hand (a character who has much in common with Welty's father), died in the Second World War. She had defied convention by refusing to return home once she became a widow, and refusing once more when her father became a widower. But now that she has come back to Mississippi to see her father through his final illness, she is forced to confront the terms and the consequences of her departure.

In Laurel's night vigil at the climax of the novel—a great sustained scene of *recognition* reminiscent of Isabel Archer's night vigil in *The Portrait of a Lady*—she faces the "betrayal on betrayal" that ruined her parents' marriage and that ended her own before it had really begun. She faces the resentment that inevitably springs from the love between parent and child: "Parents and children take turns back and forth," she thinks, "changing places, protecting and protesting each other."[6] Swept by "love's deep anger," Laurel finally weeps for how much life has taken from her, and she embraces what she has left: memory.

At first presented with maddening passivity, silence, remoteness, Laurel gathers force as Welty draws us deeper into her pain and isolation. By the end Laurel comes very close to exploding in fury as she looms before Fay, holding aloft the bread board that her husband made and her mother used. With the board in her hands she grasps "the whole story . . . the whole solid past" as she tells the uncomprehending Fay—and Welty achieves an almost Proustian resonance with the phrase. The image of Laurel brandishing the board at Fay recalls Mrs. Larkin in "A Curtain of Green" standing behind the black boy with her hoe, ready to strike at his head. But Laurel, like Mrs. Larkin, drops her weapon. She hands the sacred bread board over to Fay and returns to her life in Chicago, secure in her possession of her memories and her dreams. "Memory lived not in initial possession but in the freed hands," Welty writes at the end of the novel, "pardoned and freed, and in the heart that can empty but fill again, in the patterns restored by dreams."[7]

With Laurel, Welty imagines for herself the other life that she might have had—the happy marriage, however brief, the flight away from the shelter of her mother's house and garden, the unencumbered existence in a strange city. She takes possession of this life, she feels her way through it, and she forgives herself for never having it. Laurel, by the end, has truly won her independence— won it the hard way by losing almost everything else in her life and by staring down into the depths of these losses. The final image of the novel is the "twinkling of ... hands, the many small and unknown hands" of the local schoolchildren waving good-bye. The love of a child is one more thing she will never have, and that she knows she does not really need. She is the last of her line. In the end, Laurel, like Virgie Rainey, like Miss Eckhart, like Eudora Welty herself, holds tightly to the fulfillment of solitude.

Porter responded deeply to the intimate revelations of *The Optimist's Daughter*. She read through the book in one sitting and with the story still glowing in her mind she wrote in the pages of her copy:

> This book, a self-portrait by Eudora, at last, sacredly, inviolably human, winning her long glorious battle by losing it—with the courage of angels and the faith of her own heart—How happy I am in having our love and friendship all these bitter and terrible years. But one great thing we knew together and it does not fail—life is to be lived, endured, fulfilled and loved.[8]

The Optimist's Daughter was indeed a triumph—but it was also a tremendously draining effort. Welty herself has spoken of how hard it was for her to write the book: "It was very painful," she told an interviewer, "but also, it helped me to understand ... my own feelings."[9] A daughter no longer, Welty at sixty-three was also no longer young when she published *The Optimist's Daughter*. The 1960s had stripped her of her prime and her family both. Porter, who had known Welty at the dawn of her literary career, fathomed to the lowest depth what it cost her friend to produce at last this "sacredly, inviolably human" self-portrait. It might, indeed, have cost her everything for *The Optimist's Daughter* is the last sustained piece of fiction Welty has written, the last she is likely to write.

SIXTEEN

The Legend of the Past

> *Memory is the corrector of a life.*
>
> —EUDORA WELTY, *interview in the film documentary*
> Katherine Anne Porter: The Eye of Memory

> *What is the truth, she asked herself as intently as if
> the question had never been asked, the truth, even
> about the smallest, the least important of all the
> things I must find out? and where shall I begin to
> look for it?*
>
> —KATHERINE ANNE PORTER, *"Old Mortality"*

IN THE FINAL DECADE of their friendship, Porter and Welty looked back together, often in astonishment, at a literary relation that had endured all the "bitter and terrible years" since 1938. "My dear Eudora, 'dear' is a very little word to say what you mean to me, and have, nearly uncountable years," Porter opens one of her letters; "they feel like a century at least to me—and I have missed you heavily since those times when one way or another we did manage to see each other now and again."[1] Porter and Welty had in a sense become part of each other's pasts, and in the letters they exchanged during the 1970s they touch on the friendship with reverence and delicacy—the fond, forgiving tone we reserve for ancient difficult relatives or impossible houses we have lived in too long to sell. It had become a friendship more on paper than in fact. Yes, there were dinners now and then in College Park, Maryland, with Porter still talking a mile a minute, and a flurry of notes about Porter's plans to come down to Jackson to join the celebration for Eudora Welty Day, which Mississippi Governor William L. Waller declared as May 2, 1973. (Porter begged off on account of ill health at the last minute.) But the long shadow of the past lay over the present.

Porter's nephew Paul tells a revealing story of the special tenderness that his aunt felt toward Welty near the end of her life. During one of Paul's visits to College Park in the late 1970s, Porter, who had suffered a series of crippling strokes in 1977, asked him to read aloud Welty's essay "The Eye of the Story": "I gave a good loud rather hammy reading, emphasizing the praise," Paul recalls. "When I finished, she said, 'Oh, darling . . .' and stopped, seemed to be looking for words, perhaps even speech itself, staring at and stroking the blanket over her lap. Then she raised her head and said, perfectly and clearly and in a strong voice, 'Something like that makes it all worthwhile, all of it. Do you understand?' 'Yes, I think so,' I said. Another long silence, and then, in a low voice, she said, 'She's been a dear friend for many years, you know.' 'I know,' I said. Again a silence. 'Well . . .' she sighed, and rested her head back on the pillow without saying anything more."[2]

As the real friendship faded, a kind of mythical idealized friendship grew in its place. Memory restored, refurbished, and reinvented the past. Porter, as we know, had long been a great mythologizer of her own life. In the years since Porter's death at age ninety in 1980, Welty has taken up the reins of myth making herself; she dutifully tends the altar on which the legend of the past, as Porter calls it in "Old Mortality," has been laid out. In looking back over her long life, Welty tends to remember the good and the pleasing, and to recolor or suppress the rest. "It may be that so deeply does she want things to be nice and agreeable that she is forgetting the disagreeable," said one friend who prefers to remain anonymous. "But at least the rose-colored glasses of nostalgia are better than dark glasses."

Porter has been one of the prime beneficiaries of Welty's rosy recollections. In her recent writings and spoken comments about Porter, Welty makes no mention of her resentment over being Porter's chauffeur, her flunky, the victim of her procrastination. Gone is her disapproval of Porter's girlishness, her vanity, her misanthropy and cynicism, her bad taste, her head-splitting monologues. In the Calvin Skaggs documentary film about Porter, Welty speaks lovingly of the long dresses Katherine Anne wore at Yaddo and her "spring-heeled walk" as she went from the farmhouse to dinner each night, "anticipating no telling what." She imitates fondly Porter's quavering voice, crooning "Bury me beneath the willar, bo-neath the weeping willar tree . . ." "I remember . . . most," Welty says smiling into the camera, "the pleasure she took in life. She could show her pleasure, as I used to hear said as a compliment: 'She knows how to show her pleasure.' And she did—and her displeasure."[3]

Skaggs believes that Welty has come to cherish Porter's "lovely, lilting way of dealing with the world, how she cooked, making catfish fingers in Georgetown, buying emeralds with the money from *Ship of Fools*." She cherishes these things all the more highly now that Porter is dead. Porter has come to represent what Welty loves and misses most about the old order. At a deeper level, she has always represented to Welty the "serious daring" of being an artist. Skaggs says that Welty knows, perhaps better than anyone, how Porter threw away her talent as she indulged her "lovely, lilting" way of life. But her admiration of Porter as a person, as an artist, and as a "wonderful presence," as Skaggs puts it, has grown stronger than ever. "I am an artist and that's what I'm going to be" was Porter's lifelong motto, and Welty as a southern woman writer knew what a tremendous thing this was to do—how original it was and what a *stand* Porter took by doing it.[4] Never mind that at age seventy Porter acted like a silly, fluttering southern belle. Her memory is sacred now.

"Memory is the corrector of a life," Welty says in the Skaggs film, referring to Porter's stories about her alter ego Miranda. "In the stories [set] in Texas, memory is often used in an ironic sense because the things that people remember and tell of the old stories Miranda comes to see were not really the truth but were the romantic compulsions that had to see things in a certain way and that they were not to be trusted and that she would have none of it. From then on she would live her own life as she said in 'her hopes and ignorance.' " Memory, like the narratives it engenders, is subjective, creative, distorting—it corrects a life by calling up the version of the past that we each need to believe most. But for all its unreliability, memory is all we have to give our lives meaning.

Welty's *The Optimist's Daughter,* like Porter's "Old Mortality," is about a woman's need to redeem her memories. Before they can truly claim their independence from their families, Laurel Hand and Miranda Gay both must face down their family stories—the homebred compulsions, romantic and otherwise—and find their own stories, the myths that they can live by. (Miranda calls it "the truth about what happens to me"; Laurel, being older and wiser and more willing to accept her connection to previous generations, calls it "the whole solid past"—but it amounts to much the same thing.) Welty in her memoirs of becoming a writer and in her recollections of her friendship with Porter seems to be engaged in the same process. She is using memory to make and to keep what she loves best.

All of us do this, especially as we grow older and our memories accumulate. But writers save the corrections of memory by writing them down; and when the corrections are important enough, they continue to refine and correct them until they have taken on a form of their own. The finer the mind, the greater the life, the more nearly perfect the corrections of memory become. Recollections of friendships are special because they are portraits of adult life: Unlike family memoirs, which describe the trials of becoming, tributes to friends are usually drawn from the flush of maturity or from the final flowering before death. They are often as much self-portraits as portraits. Think of Welty's *Georgia Review* piece about Porter. Think of Wharton's recollections of James in her memoirs. And Bishop's elegy for Lowell. And Melville's "Monody" (if it was in fact written for Hawthorne). Each is a record of artistic exchange—of demands made and gifts given, of initiation into new standards, of the difficult fellowship of art. Each is a highly refined, painstakingly corrected version of the past. The writers and the subjects of these tributes knew well that the finest versions, the versions that hold us most in thrall, the versions we finally *believe* are truth. As Porter wrote of the art of Henry James, "Once the circle is truly drawn around its contents, it too becomes truth."[5]

Porter and Welty
to Bishop and Lowell

DURING THE FIERY summer of 1937, a number of high-voltage literary power lines converged on the home of poet Allen Tate and his wife, novelist Caroline Gordon, in Clarksville, Tennessee. The Tates, southern literary gentry whom Robert Lowell described as "stately yet bohemian, leisurely yet dedicated," had known Katherine Anne Porter for some time. Both husband and wife admired her work, and Allen Tate and Porter had slept together a few times, which was practically inevitable given how promiscuous both of them were. That summer, Porter and the Tates were together at a writers' conference at Olivet College in Michigan, and afterward, they all drove to Benfolly, the Tates' plantation house (a material manifestation of their Agrarian literary ideology).

The threesome was soon joined by the sixty-four-year-old Ford Madox Ford and his young wife, a Polish Jewish American artist named Janice Biala. The critic Cleanth Brooks (one of Eudora Welty's editors at the *Southern Review*) and his wife, Tinkum, came up from Baton Rouge. Albert Erskine, the young business manager of the *Southern Review* and a graduate student at Louisiana State University, also stopped by the house. Erskine and Porter talked late into the night, enchanted with each other for very different reasons, and they later married. "In every room in the house there's a typewriter and at every typewriter there sits a genius," Biala wrote a friend of hers. "Each genius is wilted and says that he or she can do no more but the typewritten sheets keep on mounting."[1] Actually, Porter alone among the geniuses was not typing anything for, as she wrote her friend Josephine Herbst, "I cannot settle and work in any one else's house, no matter how pleasant or how promising the situation."[2] She spent most of her time cooking and talking.

And then at some point in the proceedings, the twenty-year-old wild-eyed would-be poet Robert Lowell descended. Lowell had already visited the Tates once before that spring, heralding his arrival at Benfolly by crushing their mailbox with the bumper of his car (his disastrous driving would seriously injure and disfigure his first wife, Jean Stafford, several years later) and emptying his bladder on their gatepost. Twenty-two years later, Lowell remembered the legendary summer at the Tates' house like this:

> The household groaned with the fatigued valor of Southern hospitality. Ida, the colored day-help, had grown squint-eyed, balky, and aboriginal from the confusion of labors, the clash of cultures. Instantly, and with keen, idealistic, adolescent heedlessness, I offered myself as a guest. The Tates' way of refusing was to say there was no room for me unless I pitched a tent on the lawn. A few days later, I returned from Nashville with an olive Sears, Roebuck umbrella tent. I stayed three months. Every other day, I turned out grimly unromantic poems—organized, hard, and classical as a cabinet. . . . Indoors, life was Olympian and somehow crackling. . . . Like a torn cat, I was taken in when I needed help, and in a sense I have never left.[3]

Porter remembered Lowell that summer as "this solitary, strange, gifted child . . . among us."[4]

Lowell did, of course, eventually leave, physically if not spiritually—but the summer visit altered the course of his life. At Tate's bidding, Lowell transferred from Harvard to Kenyon College so he could study with the distinguished southern poet John Crowe Ransom. At Kenyon, Lowell's closest friends were southerners—the fiction writer Peter Taylor and poet and critic Randall Jarrell. And he continued to move in southern literary circles for years, studying for a time with Cleanth Brooks and Robert Penn Warren at LSU in Baton Rouge and holing up in Monteagle, Tennessee, with the Tates and Jean Stafford to write during the winter of 1942–43. Lowell forever after spoke with a soft, faint southern drawl, which deepened after he married Kentucky-born novelist and critic Elizabeth Hardwick. The scion of one of Boston's most distinguished literary families, the inheritor of the stiff black mantle of Hawthorne and Melville, Lowell attempted single-handedly to twist together the literary traditions of North and South. He was that ambitious.

Years after the summer at Benfolly, Porter boasted, "I was the first person Robert Lowell ever brought his poems to" and she took credit for steering him toward Allen Tate. "I think your poetry is wonderful," she remembered telling Lowell, "and you are going to be a poet, so why not go to Allen Tate?"[5] This is not strictly accurate for Lowell was showing his poems to anyone he could collar and he had already met the Tates on his own. But, in any case, Porter and Lowell made favorable impressions on each other that summer and they struck up a casual friendship that lasted all his life. They crossed paths now and then in New York and exchanged a few friendly letters over the years. The relationship even survived their fierce opposition during the witch-hunt that Lowell instigated against the director of Yaddo in 1949 (see p. 318).

In 1952 both of them attended the Congress for Cultural Freedom in Paris; fellow Catholic converts, they lit a candle together at the church of St. Germain-des-Pres. (The Congress for Cultural Freedom—which was funded by the CIA—also sponsored Lowell's trip to South America in 1962, during which he visited Elizabeth Bishop in Rio and suffered a serious manic episode.) In 1961 they were together in Washington at the Kennedy inauguration. Lowell ranked Porter as one of the finest short story writers in America ("You have been *the* short story writer of our country for so long," he wrote her in 1960),[6] and he rose gallantly to defend Porter in a letter to the editor of *Commentary* when critics began to savage *Ship of Fools* in the 1960s. Privately, Lowell wrote her that the book was "the most ambitious and sustained novel that any American has published in the twenty years" that it took her to write it. And he compared the chaotic final party to the end of *Moby-Dick*.[7] Porter, for some reason, did not take kindly to his comparison of *Ship of Fools* and *The Age of Innocence:* "What possessed poor Robert Lowell to say I was a sort of Mrs. Wharton?" she demanded in a letter to Robert Penn Warren. "Suppose I should call him a sort of W. B. Yeats? It would be a damn sight more flattering, but no nearer the facts in the case!"[8]

Elizabeth Bishop was also connected with Porter, though more remotely than Lowell. Bishop, with the help of Lowell's considerable influence, was appointed Consultant in Poetry to the Library of Congress in 1949 and thus became embroiled in the controversy that erupted when the Fellows of the Library of Congress in American Letters awarded Ezra Pound the first Bollingen Prize for poetry. Porter was one of the fellows who had voted for Pound, and she defended her action in a long open letter to the *Saturday Review of Literature.* When Porter then received what she called "a flood of abusive letters from strangers accusing me of assorted crimes," including anti-Semitism and Fascism, she wrote to Bishop that she wished to resign from the Society of Fellows. Bishop sympathized with Porter's disgust over the whole business for she loathed her official functions at the Library of Congress and was miserable in Washington, but she wondered what good Porter's resignation would do. In the event, Porter decided to withdraw her resignation, more, it seems, out of inertia than ideology. Bishop saved her own views about Pound for her poem "Visits to St. Elizabeths" (which, like Porter's letter to *Saturday Review,* incited a good deal of anger, despite its profound, indeed its central, ambivalence).

Over the years, Bishop and Porter exchanged a few letters, and Porter came to admire Bishop's poetry (influenced, no doubt, by Lowell, who raved about Bishop's work to everyone he knew). They were also both ardent fans and correspondents of Flannery O'Connor, as was Lowell, who had befriended her at Yaddo. In the 1970s, Porter wrote Bishop of her wish to have a framed photograph of her, "to be with my company of artists whose work I love and whose faces I wish to see in the room where I have collected their books."[9] Bishop, who hated all photographs of herself, evidently did not comply for there is no photograph of her in the Porter archives.

Bishop did not rank Porter's fiction as highly as Lowell did. She wrote Lowell in the spring of 1962 that she was eager to read *Ship of Fools* because years before she had read the opening chapter set in Vera Cruz and thought it was "the best thing I'd ever read about Mexico." But after finishing the novel late that summer, she wasn't quite so enthusiastic: She confessed to Lowell that she was "a little baffled by some of it" and questioned Porter's use of allegory.[10] In another letter to Lowell, Bishop proffered some shrewd insight into Porter's social pretensions as a writer. She described her theory of "the 'our beautiful old silver' school of female writing which is really boasting about how 'nice' *we* were. V. Woolfe [sic], K.A.P., [Elizabeth] Bowen, R[ebecca] West, etc.—they are all full of it. They have to make quite sure that the reader is not going to misplace them socially, first—and that nervousness interferes constantly with what they think they'd like to say. . . ."[11] Porter would have been furious had she ever gotten wind of this, but it rings extremely true. Bishop puts her finger on Porter's characteristic stance in the Miranda stories—really, she exposes the "airs" Porter put on whenever she wrote of her fabulous old South past. Bishop, of course, could not know that Porter's "niceness" was something of a fraud since her family had lost its "beautiful old silver" and had precious little social status left to boast about—but this only made Porter *more* nervous as an artist.

Bishop, as middle age approached, once joked waspishly in a letter to Lowell that she felt "as old as Katherine Anne Porter." Porter was in a sense the grand old lady of their crowd, an honorific she would have despised. In any case, Porter had the last laugh for though she was twenty-one years older than Bishop and twenty-seven years older than Lowell, she outlived them both.

Though Lowell, like Henry James, knew just about everyone on the literary circuit, Eudora Welty seems to have eluded him, despite her strong ties to Lowell's southern circle, including Cleanth Brooks, Robert Penn Warren, Porter, of course, and Peter Taylor. Welty and Bishop, however, did have some contact with each other (including one lunch in New York) and they admired each other's writing, which is fitting since they had a good deal in common temperamentally. Born two years apart, both women were extremely shy, modest about their work, protective of their privacy, and quite funny, even scathing, around those who knew them well. Both published most of their new work in *The New Yorker*. It's tempting to think that they might have become good friends had they really gotten to know one another—but perhaps they were too much alike to have felt comfortable with each other. And Bishop's lesbianism would have been a serious strike against her in Welty's book.

Bishop wrote Welty in the summer of 1948 to praise her portrayal of an old lady (possibly Phoenix Jackson in "The Worn Path," a story that she mentioned approvingly in a letter to Lowell the month before) and Welty wrote back to say she would look forward to making the acquaintance of one of Bishop's old ladies—very likely Faustina, the subject (and title) of a poem that *The New Yorker* ran in February 1947. Both works are attempts by youngish white women to get inside the heads of life-battered old black women. Bishop's poem is more skeptical and less sentimental; Welty's story more lyrical and life affirming. Welty certainly did *not* belong in the "our beautiful old silver" school of female writing. Both Welty and Bishop were also drawn to African American music—jazz in their day—and both projected themselves imaginatively into the souls of black musicians: Welty in her story "Powerhouse" (about Fats Waller) and Bishop in "Songs for a Colored Singer" (written for Billie Holiday, whom Bishop knew). This was a "power of blackness" that Harry Levin failed to mention in his book on the topic.

A fascinating essay could be written comparing the use of houses in Welty's and Bishop's work. Welty and Bishop both picture themselves as thrilled children eavesdropping on the adult conversations going on in the dim mysterious rooms of their childhood houses—Welty most memorably in her memoirs; Bishop in her great story "In the Village" and her late poem "The Moose." Both of them probe the tension between the safe (sometimes suffocatingly safe) house and the wild allure of the river—Welty in "At the Landing," "The Wide Net," and *The Robber Bridegroom*; Bishop in "The Riverman," "Song for the Rainy Season" (where the river is a waterfall), and "Santarém." Melville's land and sea dreams remained potent in both their imaginations.

Indeed, the house is a rich subject of conjecture in the lives and work of all of the eight friends, particularly the women. "No one fully knows our Edith who hasn't seen her in the act of creating a habitation for herself," James once said of Wharton—and the same could also have been said of Porter and Bishop, both in fact and fiction. While Welty stayed put in the Tudor house her father built for the family in Jackson, the other three women pursued passionate lifelong quests for the perfect house. But only Wharton, by virtue of her wealth and tenacity, succeeded in realizing her dreams, not once, but half a dozen times, most notably at Land's End in Newport, Rhode Island, the Mount in the Berkshires, and the Pavillon Colombe outside Paris.

When they were in their fifties, both Porter and Bishop sank their money and their hearts into renovating lovely historically evocative dream houses—Porter's South Hill farmhouse outside Saratoga, dating from the North American colonial period, Bishop's Casa Mariana in Ouro Prêto, Brazil, dating from the even earlier South American colonial period. In the end, both houses proved ruinous, and the women were forced to sell them before they were properly settled in. Both Porter and Bishop ended their days in apartments—the gardens they, like Welty and Wharton, loved so passionately reduced to potted plants set before sunny windows.

Wharton, Porter, Welty, and Bishop were all famous among their friends for the high style of hospitality they offered. "All observers agree that Edith carried her household duties into the realm of art," writes Louis Auchincloss. "There was something almost relentless in her perfectionism."[12] Porter, Welty, and Bishop were far more relaxed as hostesses, though no less attentive to the details of good living. They were also more adventurous than Wharton in the food they served—Bishop's Boston apartment was a little temple of Brazilian cuisine and folk culture; Porter drew on her long years in Mexico, Louisiana, and France in her cooking, and her repertoire of breads was renowned; Welty dishes up the "flavor of Jackson" to jaded guests from New York. Of course, Porter, Welty, and Bishop did the cooking themselves, which was unthinkable to Wharton with her squadron of devoted servants.

The servants—and the wealth that made them possible—were no doubt part of the reason why Wharton's output was so much greater than Porter's or Bishop's. (Welty had her mother to protect and minister to her in the first decades of her career, when she was most productive; once her mother fell seriously ill, her writing all but ceased.) Like Lowell, Wharton wrote in bed: She lay in state in her pink wrapper each morning, writing longhand and tossing the pages onto the floor for her secretary to collect and transcribe later. By the time her houseguests were ready to embark on the day's motoring, a chapter of the next novel or a section of another story would be finished. The servants, meanwhile, were doing the marketing, cooking, and cleaning.

Bishop once complained to Lowell that she had "no talent for protecting myself or my working time the way I should," and the same lament runs bitterly through Porter's letters and interviews. Both felt they would have written a good deal more had they been born male. How many, many working hours the women sacrificed to the baking of breads, roasting of meats, arrangement of flowers, and selection of whiskeys and wines, which they both loved to drink far too much, especially Bishop (Wharton hated the taste of wine ever since her older brother tricked her into consuming a glass of claret as a child, which actually might have been to her benefit as a productive writer). The choice of lovely evenings with friends *or* hard days of work tormented both Porter and Bishop. Why couldn't they have both, as Wharton did, and as Hawthorne, Melville, James, and Lowell assumed was their due? Why must a woman be a millionaire to keep the house, the life, and the book going all at once?

The houses that Hawthorne, Melville, James, and Lowell conjured up in their imaginative works were often dark and dangerous places haunted by the ghosts of slain ancestors, stained with ancient sins, torn by marital discord, illicit sex, or diseased fantasies. In "real life" however, Hawthorne and Melville filled their houses with children, and Lowell fathered a daughter with his second wife and a son with his third. James alone among the men was childless, as were all of the women: Of the four, not one of them brought a child of her own into the beautiful sheltering houses she built or inherited. But as Virginia Woolf has taught us, this is no coincidence. In our culture, childlessness has been practically the sine qua non for women writers.

PART FOUR

Elizabeth Bishop
and
Robert Lowell

Sometimes, I think I would die, if it weren't for a few
platonic relations with women. . . .

—ROBERT LOWELL letter to Elizabeth Bishop,
February 25, 1966

You have no idea, Cal, how really grateful to you I
am and how fortunate I feel myself in knowing you,
having you for a friend—when I think how the world
and my life would look to me if you weren't in either
of them at all—they'd look very empty, I think. . . .
I don't seem to need or enjoy a lot of intellectual
society—but I certainly need you. . . .

—ELIZABETH BISHOP letter to Robert Lowell,
January 22, 1962

SEVENTEEN

Castine, Maine, August 1957: Ten Years Later

> . . . I myself am hell;
> nobody's here—
>
> —ROBERT LOWELL, "Skunk Hour"

> All the untidy activity continues,
> awful but cheerful.
>
> —ELIZABETH BISHOP, "The Bight"

AT THE END of August 1957 the dam burst for Robert Lowell. It had been six years since his last book of verse was published, and the few poems he had finished in the interim were crabbed, diffi-cult, and, with one exception, slight. "It was . . . a slack of eter-nity," Lowell told an interviewer. "Five messy poems in five years."[1] Then in a few blue, incandescent weeks at summer's end, the poems that form the core of *Life Studies* came pouring out of him. He had been writing "furiously . . . at poems," Lowell wrote to Elizabeth Bishop from his summer house in Castine, Maine, spending "whole blue and golden Maine days in my bedroom with a ghastly utility bedside lamp on, my pajamas oily with sweat, and I have six poems started."[2] "Skunk Hour"—perhaps Lowell's single most celebrated poem, which he dedicated to Bishop and that he acknowledged was heavily indebted to her "Armadillo"—was one of these six. So were the very beautiful "Sailing Home from Rapallo" about bringing his mother's corpse home from Italy and the superb "My Last Afternoon with Uncle Devereux Winslow" about the shadow that his uncle's early death cast over his childhood.

These poems were not only among the finest Lowell ever wrote, but they were also abruptly unlike anything he had written before. At age forty Lowell had silenced what Bishop called "the old trumpet blast" of his early style. "Distant, symbol-ridden, and willfully difficult," Lowell appraised in retrospect his first two volumes, *Lord Weary's Castle* (1946) and *The Mills of the Kavanaughs* (1951), "my own poems seemed like prehistoric monsters dragged down into the bog and death by their ponderous armor."[3]

In *Life Studies,* Lowell pried off the armor. In poems that were as clear and tense and jarring as midnight conversation, Lowell exposed his parents' unbalanced marriage, his own guilt and fury and baffled helplessness as a son and husband and father, and his recurring collapses into madness. "He made family life acceptable as a subject for American poetry," said Robert Haas.[4] Casually, seemingly haphazardly, he planted the poems with the ephemera of his time and place—Rogers Peet's boys' store, the Tauchnitz classics, Jehovah's Witnesses, *panetone* and tin foil, McLean's Hospital for the mentally ill, Miltown tranquilizers, L. L. Bean—and let the meanings blow up like mines. Each new explosion comes as a surprise: The aging "Mayflower screwballs" at McLean's have "ossified young"; the unseen and all-seeing child observer is "Agrippina in the Golden House of Nero"; "red fire" flames in the eyes of moonstruck skunks. *Life Studies* gave poetry the emotional urgency and historical specificity of the best fiction: Like Tolstoy, Lowell scrutinized a miserable family caught in the vortex of its culture. *Life Studies* was the landmark book of what became known as confessional poetry and the critical turning point of Lowell's career.

The fact that Lowell was working furiously at these poems just a few weeks after a visit from Elizabeth Bishop is not coincidental. Bishop did not inspire *Life Studies* nor are any of the poems directly "about" her—yet she released some vital creative spring in Lowell's mind that allowed him to find his subject and his voice. Lowell acknowledged this frankly and generously. "I was reading Elizabeth Bishop's poems very carefully at the time and imitating the loose formality of her style," he told an interviewer a few years after the book appeared.[5] "Rereading her suggested a way of breaking through the shell of my old manner," he wrote in a little essay on "Skunk Hour." "Her rhythms, idiom, images, and stanza structure seemed to belong to a later century."[6]

Bishop's influence was not limited to her poetry. Her friendship, her conversation, her presence in Castine that summer were as essential to the breakthrough of *Life Studies* as Hawthorne's friendship and conversation and presence were essential to *Moby-Dick*. The fact that Lowell had nearly proposed marriage to Bishop when they were last together in Maine, nine years before, was also swirling through his mind on those blue and golden days. Bishop stimulated Lowell in every sense. In imitating Bishop's poetry, Lowell was in a sense trying to live inside her and see through her eyes. It was a way of possessing *her*. "I am as much in his skin as he is himself," Henry James once wrote to Edith Wharton of his feelings for Morton Fullerton, "and . . . my idea of a proper affection for my friends is to *be* to that degree in their skins."[7] In *Life Studies*, especially in "Skunk Hour" (the first poem written in the new style), Lowell came as close as he ever would to being inside Bishop's skin.

Years later, Lowell groped through numerous versions of a sonnet about Bishop until he hit at last upon the defining final image: "unerring Muse who makes the casual perfect." Unerring and often unwilling muse, Bishop instinctively resisted Lowell's desires to exalt and absorb her. One of the many ironies of this tense and intense friendship was that Bishop should have served as muse to the breakthrough volume of confessional poetry, a style that "in general, I deplore" as she later wrote to Lowell.[8] "The tendency [of confessional poets] is to overdo the morbidity," she told a reporter from *Time* in a much-quoted interview of 1967. "You just wish they'd keep some of these things to themselves."[9]

Keeping things to herself was one of Bishop's most sacred codes. In the 276 pages of her complete poems one may find glimmers of autobiographical detail—mentions of aunts and uncles and grandparents; parlors and kitchens that seem cozy but for the eerie absence of parents; veiled references to drinking, grieving, abandonment; scenery and homes she admired, lived in, or passed through. But Bishop bars the door against the naked revelations of the confessional poets. Lines like "My mind's not right" or "I myself am hell"—the climactic revelations of "Skunk Hour"—are inconceivable in Bishop. "The enormous power of reticence—that is the great lesson of the poetry of Elizabeth Bishop,"[10] Octavio Paz wrote of her. It was a lesson that Robert Lowell, no matter how much he admired her, never learned and never really wanted to learn.

Given their tremendous differences, it's extraordinary that Bishop and Lowell were friends at all—and such good friends for so long. In poetry and in person, they stood at the antipodes of temperament, style, manner: Lowell exposed where Bishop concealed; he dominated where she subverted; he ravened where she sustained. Lowell was forever in thrall to Hawthorne's and Melville's "power of blackness" while Bishop needed to see the world as "awful but cheerful" and insisted, however ironically, that "somebody loves us all." Lowell's self-obsession verged on megalomania; Bishop's modesty verged on self-delusion. It was a true instance of the attraction of opposites.

"Lowell was really a very simple person," remembers the poet Richard Tillinghast, who knew him well in the last decade of his life. "The primal drive to power was the most important part of his personality."[11] And yet Tillinghast adds, "He was a very loyal friend, a great conversationalist, a sweet person." "He had a horror of being commonplace, of not being distinguished amongst the best," Peter Taylor, perhaps Lowell's closest male friend since college, told an interviewer. "He imagined that all life was made up of compartments and that he would go into each of them and learn everything about them and finally pull the whole thing together."[12] The critic Helen Vendler, another friend, speaks of the intellectual excitement Lowell generated: "He was a charming companion and the most brilliant talker I've ever known. Nothing was sacred, everything was funny. Lowell had an exceptionally good memory. He talked fast and he had these odd flights of ideas. There were no compartments in his mind—law, music—it all sloshed together in a stream of consciousness."[13]

The poet Frank Bidart also recalls the vortex of excitement Lowell created: "He was an extremely thrilling person to be around. Life seemed faster and more intense when he was around. Everything was at a higher level of intensity. Life seemed bigger with him, and Bishop certainly responded to this."[14] But there was a dark side too. "You were a trying man, God knows," Philip

Booth, a friend and neighbor from Castine, wrote in his elegy for Lowell.

> Over drinks, or after, your wit mauled,
> twice life sized: like your heroic mattress-chest.
> Manic, you were brutal . . .
> . . . Sane
> you almost seemed God's gentlest creature.[15]

"There was both cruelty and gentleness in Lowell's nature," Richard Wilbur, yet another close poet friend, commented on these lines, "and they alternated at blinding speed."[16]

Lowell's primal drive to power seemed as much a physical as an emotional trait. He was a large, enormously strong and dominating man. His head was big and, in his youth, his features had almost an imperial Roman cast—severe, classic, chiseled rapidly from marble. Terribly myopic, he wore thick black-framed glasses and peered out at the world through eyes that looked like shattered blue glass. His voice was disconcertingly soft and whispery and his accent vaguely southern—derived, perhaps, from his apprenticeship to southern poets Allen Tate and John Crowe Ransom or maybe a borrowing from Elizabeth Hardwick, his Kentucky-born second wife. Lowell fought a losing battle nearly his entire adult life with mental illness, succumbing almost yearly (usually between Thanksgiving and Christmas) to psychosis. Even when sane, he appeared to be in pain, as if haunted by his illness. There was no mistaking Lowell for anything but a poet.

Again, quite the opposite was true for Elizabeth Bishop. Rather small of stature, cropped-haired, neatly tailored, this paralyzingly shy, flat-voiced, demure woman looked more like an office worker taking the day off than a poet, which suited her to a tee. "Prim, impeccably coiffured, and smoking, . . . [she was] disappointingly normal," her former student Dana Gioia wrote of her in a reminiscence called "Studying with Miss Bishop."[17] Her close friend James Merrill, in a memorial piece, spoke of Bishop's "instinctive, modest, lifelong impersonations of an ordinary woman, someone who during the day did errands, went to the beach, would perhaps that evening jot a phrase or two inside the nightclub matchbook, before returning to the dance floor." It is the characterization that her friends like best—and Bishop would no doubt have appreciated it too. "She was always ladylike, except when she'd had too much to drink," recalls Richard Wilbur, who knew her well from the mid-1940s on. "She was given to polite understatement—the very reverse of a show-off."[18] Unlike Lowell's mauling wit, Bishop's sense of humor was wry and satirical and often most wicked when directed at herself ("what I liked to be called now is *poetress*," she once wrote Lowell, recounting how a Brazilian woman proudly produced the word at a dinner party. "I think it's a nice mixture of poet and mistress").[19]

"I give the impression of mysterious ease," Bishop's Giant Snail says in the prose poem "Rainy Season; Sub-Tropics," "but it is only with the greatest effort of my will that I can rise above the smallest stones and sticks. And I must not let myself be distracted by those rough spears of grass. Don't touch them. Draw back. Withdrawal is always best."[20] Lloyd Schwartz, a poet and friend of Bishop's, acknowledges that the strange creatures in "Rainy Season" are Bishop's alter egos.[21] Her Giant Toad complains of seeing too much, even though there isn't much in its field of vision; her Strayed Crab prefers "the indirect approach" and conceals its feelings. Withdrawal; painfully acute vision; precision and elegance; reticence and obliquity: These traits compose a kind of map to Bishop's inner geography. "You can never have enough defenses," she supposedly said to a friend.[22] And yet she made such beautiful use of her own.

Bishop and Lowell met in 1947, shortly after both their first books of poems were published. Lowell at age thirty (six years younger than Bishop) was a newly minted celebrity, having just won the Pulitzer Prize for *Lord Weary's Castle,* as well as a Guggenheim Fellowship and a grant from the American Academy of Arts and Letters. The popular press was lionizing him as the oracular scion of an old distinguished Boston family, and his handsome profile in *Life* magazine caught the eye of a movie producer, who wanted him to come to Hollywood for a screen test (Bishop always loved this story). Since prep school, Lowell had sought the company and friendship of the greatest writers (as a Harvard student he visited Robert Frost and pressed on him a lengthy epic poem about the first Crusade), and by the time he met Bishop he knew (or would soon meet) just about everyone who mattered on the poetry scene, including Eliot, Tate, Pound, Williams, Ransom, Randall Jarrell, and Robert Penn Warren. Despite his fame, his enormous ambition, his growing literary power, his ever-widening circle of distinguished friends, Lowell from the very start made a special place in his life for Bishop. "She could do no wrong as far as Cal [Lowell's prep school nickname, from the mad Roman emperor Caligula, that stuck with him all his life] was concerned," recalls Stanley Kunitz. "She was sainted."[23]

Bishop, though too much the agnostic to return the favor of canonization, found Lowell's attentions irresistible. She was powerfully attracted to him, to his verse, and to his admiration of her verse. Unlikely as it seemed, the friendship clicked into place at once: It was a true literary friendship, flowing from a shared admiration for each other's work into a passionate devotion to each other. Their differences, if anything, seemed to cement the bond. Over the years, they came to rely on the bracing blasts of their contrary winds.

By 1957, Bishop and Lowell had been friends for a decade, but their paths had rarely crossed. Bishop, as passionate a traveler as Edith Wharton and even more adventurous in her choice of destinations, seldom spent two seasons running in the same latitude (until she settled in Brazil). Lowell was also much on the move in these years, serving as Consultant in Poetry to the Library of Congress during 1947 and 1948, then moving on to Yaddo, traveling in the Midwest, marrying the novelist and essayist Elizabeth Hardwick (his second wife), and then, in 1950, traveling with her to Europe for two years. Meetings between the friends became even less likely after 1951, when Bishop stopped off in Brazil on an intended voyage through the Strait of Magellan and ended up settling there for the next fifteen years. While in Rio she suffered a severe allergic reaction to the fruit of the cashew tree and she was nursed back to health by Lota de Macedo Soares, a Brazilian woman she had befriended some years earlier in New York. Bishop fell in love with Lota (the use of first names is universal in Brazil) and with Brazil, and when Lota asked her to share the new home she was building in the mountain resort of Petrópolis, Bishop gratefully accepted. The Brazilian years proved to be the longest stretch of settled happiness in an extremely unsettled and unhappy life.

Bishop and Lota arrived in New York in April 1957, intending to remain for six months. It was Bishop's first prolonged absence from Brazil and the first time she had seen Lowell since 1950, when she came to the Manhattan dock to toast him and Elizabeth Hardwick off to Europe. The journey north was funded in part by an Amy Lowell Traveling Fellowship (Bishop was never quite sure whether Lowell had a hand in arranging this—Amy, after all, was his distant cousin, and Lowell was always more than generous about throwing prizes and grants her way—but she thanked him just in case). The fellowship money allowed her and Lota to set up in some style. They sublet an apartment on East Sixty-seventh Street, and Bishop made the best of a city she had never liked. She saw her old friend Marianne Moore and plunged, somewhat reluctantly, into the swing of New York intellectual life ("I had a very good time [with Mary McCarthy, Hannah Arendt, and Philip Rahv, editor of the influential *Partisan Review*]," she wrote Lowell, "although afraid to open my mouth among such BRAINS").[24] Irritating publishing matters consumed a good deal of time, but there were also several visits to friends' houses in the country.

Bishop and Lowell, who was now living rather grandly on his inheritance in Boston, traded notes professing how much they were dying to see each other. But when they did get together briefly after Lowell returned from a grueling poetry reading tour of the West Coast, the encounter was not altogether happy. It's not clear exactly what happened between them—probably Lowell made some sort of romantic declaration to her in front of Lota or suggested that they run away together.[25] In a letter of apology, Lowell explained that he had been "in a very foolish, exalted and exhausted state" after the reading tour, and he promised he would never again behave like "some sort of centaur fusion of" rooster and pig (the beasts are allusions to two of Bishop's poems, "Roosters" and "The Prodigal," in which the "light-lashed, self-righteous" pigs plaster their sty with "glass-smooth dung"). "Honor bright, I'm not rowdy," he swore Boy Scout fashion. "Perhaps you both will reconsider staying with us" during the summer in Castine.[26]

His offense, whatever it was, did not drive off Bishop and Lota, but it raised a red flag that more trouble lay ahead. The terms he used to excuse his lapse—"foolish, exalted and exhausted"— were part of the vocabulary of Lowell's madness, a sign that he was spiraling once again into the "tireless, madly sanguine, menaced, and menacing" state that preceded his descents into "the kingdom of the mad."[27] Lowell's illness was eventually diagnosed as manic depression, and his breakdowns followed a fairly predictable pattern of overexcitement, sleeplessness, and oppressive energy leading to violently delusional behavior and then a collapse into despair and lethargy.

Scientists still don't know exactly what triggers a manic episode. In Lowell's case, some of the serious breakdowns correlated with stressful external events—his mother's death, President Kennedy's assassination, the crash following a burst of creativity; many occurred during the bleak months of late autumn and early winter, but others seemed to tumble on him out of the blue. "You could never pinpoint with certainty what caused a breakdown," Hardwick insists, though she became expert at recognizing the signs that one was on the way.[28] The warning signs of incipient mania were hard to ignore that spring and summer. Hardwick denies that Bishop "overexcited" Lowell, but the letters and drafts of poems he wrote after seeing her suggest otherwise. At the very least, she keyed him up. Seeing her again rekindled his old obsession with her and with their relationship.

Lowell initially envisioned the visit to Castine as a lengthy one, but the time got whittled down to just a week as the date approached. A flurry of nervous letters preceded Bishop and Lota's arrival in early August. "We are between two rivers and face a thousand islands," Lowell wrote enticingly of the local scenery. "Everyone who has come has wanted to buy a house or at least a barn."[29]

Castine is indeed lovely—a classic New England harbor town of elms, Colonial white clapboard, fluted Greek Revival columns, wooden church towers, and well-scrubbed yachts at anchor in the harbor. Lowell's white clapboard house, which he first borrowed and later inherited from his beloved cousin Harriet Winslow (actually his mother's cousin), stands at one corner of Castine's fine old town common—"a cover for *The American Boy*" as he once described it. The house and the town appear often in Lowell's verse. "Skunk Hour" draws a kind of map of the town—the harbor islands, the hill "where the graveyard shelves on the town," the "chalk-dry and spar spire" of the white Trinitarian Church rising above Main Street. But the poem's atmosphere of sinister decay is pure Lowell: The actual Castine slumbers in serene picturesque propriety, carefully protected by several generations of old Boston money.

Bishop had never been to Castine before, but she knew and loved the Maine coast and returned to it again and again throughout her life (years later she wrote to Lowell that the Maine island where she was summering was "approximately my idea of heaven").[30] Maine appealed to her deeply because it reminded her of the happiest years of her childhood in rural Nova Scotia. The weathered fish houses, the chill clinging fogs, the "dignified tall firs" and deep peacock-colored spruce, the song sparrows and daisies that she makes so vivid in her Nova Scotia poems are also part of Maine's landscape. "When you cross a certain point in Maine, you smell Nova Scotia," said Bishop friend's John Malcolm Brinnin, who also grew up there.[31] It's not clear whether the smell of Nova Scotia reached Bishop in Castine, but it seems unlikely. Bishop generally preferred dumpier, shabbier, *dirtier* places—rundown fishing villages, littered harbors, baroque Brazilian mountain towns—and Castine might have been too proper for her.

In any case, she and Lota made the best of it. Lowell installed the women in the house on the shore next door to his "work barn" and played the assiduous host, driving them up to Bar Harbor, taking Bishop fishing in Castine Harbor, introducing her to some of the literati summering in the area, walking her to the lighthouse at Dyce's Head. Together they stood outside Lowell's house one night and watched a family of skunks go through the garbage—the actual "skunk hour" was a moment they shared. Though Lowell had written to her beforehand that he hadn't had a drink in a week and was planning to remain sober for "a good year,"[32] he seems to have fallen off the wagon in honor of her visit. It's uncertain whether or not Bishop fell off with him—but if she did, the consequences would have been far more serious for her than for him. Lowell by all accounts was a frequent heavy drinker but not an alcoholic. Bishop, on the other hand, was a serious alcoholic and had been for at least a decade. Like most alcoholics, she found it far easier to abstain altogether than to limit herself to a few drinks. What started as social drinking often ended in a binge.

It's not clear whether it was the drinking, the tension of overanticipation, or the intensity of being together again—but *something* happened to spoil the visit. Ian Hamilton, Lowell's biographer, quotes an unidentified friend of theirs as saying that Bishop felt "Cal was getting sick and part of it was getting very amorous with her. There was this reawakened interest in her as someone he was in love with."[33] He might have gotten "rowdy" again and made a pass at her or he might have launched into some embarrassing monologue about the kinship of their souls. Friends have said that Lowell's frankness was "alarming" when he was sane; drunk, amorous, and spinning into mania, he was capable of anything. Bishop was upset enough by his behavior to discuss it privately with Hardwick, even though the two were never very fond of each other. And she decided to end the visit early. Lowell drove Bishop and Lota to the Bangor airport and returned to Castine where, restabilized on the tranquilizer Sparine, he threw himself into the composition of the great poems of *Life Studies*.

"I see clearly now that for the last few days I have been living in a state of increasing mania—almost off the rails at the end," Lowell wrote to Bishop right after she left. "It almost seems as if I couldn't be with you any length of time without acting with abysmal myopia and lack of consideration. My disease, alas, gives one (during its seizures) a headless heart." But he added that he has already begun to calm down: "Gracelessly, like a standing child trying to sit down, like a cat or a coon coming down a tree, I'm getting down my ladder to the moon. I am part of my family again, I love my lovely family again. . . . I see what an ass I have been."[34]

Bishop replied in her "awful but cheerful" mode that his letter made her feel both terribly sad and extremely optimistic. "You weren't 'inconsiderate,' Cal! You were a wonderful host, and we had such a nice time with you, really." But she went on to suggest, very gently, that if he *did* come visit them in Brazil, maybe it would be better if he brought Hardwick and their baby instead of coming alone, as originally planned (the Lowell family did finally make this trip in 1962). And she set about trying to find him the name of a Boston psychiatrist who might be able to help him. "There *are* many hopeful things, too, you know," she concluded in what Marianne Moore called her "*brave* Elizabeth" manner. "Sobriety & gayety & patience & toughness will do the trick. Or so I hope for myself and hope & pray for you, too."[35]

Bishop obviously was trying to put some distance between herself and Lowell. But Lowell could not—or would not—shake off his obsession with her. A second and far longer letter followed the apology of August 9, and this time he spoke openly of their past—how he had fallen in love with her nine years earlier when they were together in Stonington, Maine, how he had "assumed that [it] would be just a matter of time before I proposed and I half believed that you would accept. . . . But asking you is *the* might have been for me, the one towering change, the other life that might have been had. . . . It was deeply buried, and this spring and summer (really before your arrival) it boiled to the surface."[36] The "other life" was boiling to the surface in his verse as well. On the back of a draft of what eventually became "Sailing Home from Rapallo," he typed "The Two Weeks' Vacation—For E. B." about the single day in 1948 when "we were alone / And together at last/More or less hand in hand/On the rocks at Stonington." In the various versions of a poem he called "For Elizabeth Bishop" or "Lines for Elizabeth Bishop," he wrote of their parting at the Bangor airport:

> . . . ten years later I saw you to your plane in Bangor.
> You are thirty pounds lighter,
> Your uncertain finger floated to your lips,
> And you kiss them to me, and our fellowship
> Resumes its old transcendence like a star . . .

In one version, Lowell made Bishop herself speak the lines:

> Wholly Atlantic, though half fugitive
> From Nova Scotia, I have tried to live
> Our country's egotistical sublime.
> I raised the great sail, there came a time
> Unanchored and unmoored to any hope—
> My total memory lashed me fast with rope . . .[37]

There are pages and pages of these drafts—more than a dozen versions among his papers. Lowell circles and circles around a cluster of images: Bishop kissing her hand in farewell, the lost anchor (associated variously with her imagination, her giant memory, her lack of hope), the "whole Atlantic seaboard" from Yarmouth to Rio that she "combed . . . for room to live," the gold locket watch embossed with an eagle, the sole keepsake from her mother (which Bishop confesses losing in "One Art"). Sea, flight, memory, entrapment and escape, quest and loss, home and dislocation: Lowell has the pattern of a poem, but he can't quite find the sharp compelling voice that would make the images gel.

Bishop saw Lowell once more, very briefly in Boston in September, before she and Lota returned to Brazil in October, and Lowell excitedly showed her his new works in progress, including the fragments he had written about her. All that autumn he barraged her with his communications, worrying finally that she would feel "inundated to death with letters, gifts, manuscripts etc. from me."[38] Bishop kept uncharacteristically silent. She telegraphed him in November—POEMS LOVELY HAVEN'T FORGOTTEN YOU—but sent him no other word between September and December. It was one of the longest gaps in her side of their correspondence. When she finally did write to Lowell, on December 11 and 14, she elaborated magnificently on what she meant by "poems lovely."

"I am delighted with the reception your poems have been getting," she writes, "in fact the whole phenomena of your quick recovery and simultaneous productivity seems to me in looking back to be the real marvel of my summer." "Skunk Hour" is her favorite and she is "charmed" to have it dedicated to her.

But Lowell's successful productivity brings her sharply around to her own prodigality: "The one poem I've done anything with since I've been back is a long one I started two years ago, to you and Marianne [Moore], called 'Letter to Two Friends,' or something like that. . . . It is rather light, though. Oh heavens, when does one begin to write the *real* poems? I certainly feel as if I never had. But of course I don't feel that way about yours—they all seem real as real—and getting more so—

"I find I have here surely a whole new book of poems, don't I? I think the family group—some of them I hadn't seen in Boston—are really superb, Cal . . . they make a wonderful and impressive drama, and I think in them you've found the new rhythm you wanted, without any hitches." She singles out "Commander Lowell," "Terminal Days at Beverly Farms," "My Last Afternoon with Uncle Devereux Winslow," and "Sailing from Rapallo" ("which is almost two awful to read, but a fine poem"). "They all also have that sure feeling, as if you'd been in a stretch (I've felt that way for very short stretches once in a long while) when everything and anything suddenly seemed material for poetry—or not material, seemed to *be* poetry, and all the past was illuminated in long shafts here and there, like a long-waited for sunrise. If only one could see everything that way all the time! It seems to me it's the whole purpose of art, to the artist (not to the audience)—that rare feeling of control, illumination—life *is* all right, for the time being. Anyway, when I read such an extended display of imagination as this, I feel it *for* you. . . ."[39]

This, surely, is one of the most beautiful and lucid hymns to poetic inspiration ever penned. Bishop makes one *see* those "long shafts" illuminating the past, makes one feel how, in such a stretch of inspiration, the poems all but write themselves. She really was inside Lowell's skin: When she writes "I feel it *for* you," she means it literally.

Three days later, Bishop picks up the thread of her admiration in another letter:

> . . . here I must confess (and I imagine most of our contemporaries would confess the same thing) that I am green with envy of your kind of assurance. I feel that I could write in as much detail about my Uncle Artie, say—but what would be the significance? Nothing at all. He became a drunkard, fought with his wife, and spent most of his time fishing . . . and was ignorant as sin. It is sad; slightly more interesting than having an uncle practising law in Schenectady maybe, but that's all. Whereas all you have to do is put down the names! And the fact that it seems significant, illustrative, American, etc., gives you, I think, the confidence you display about tackling any idea or theme, *seriously,* in both writing and conversation. In some ways you are the luckiest poet I know!—in some ways not so lucky, either, of course. But it is hell to realize one has wasted one's talent through timidity that probably could have been overcome if anyone in one's family had had a few grains of sense or education. . . . Well, maybe it's not too late!
>
> I'm not really complaining and of course am not really "jealous" in any deep sense at all—I've felt almost as wonderful a sense of relief since I first saw some of these poems in Boston as if I'd written them myself and I've thought of them at odd times and places with the greatest pleasure every single day since.[40]

Bishop's modesty in these letters is astounding, really almost shocking. She turns Lowell's success—his breakthrough in *Life Studies,* his stature in the literary world, his family's stature in American history—into a personal reproach. His greatness diminishes her. His wealth impoverishes her. His assurance and seriousness make her painfully conscious of her own timidity, frivolousness, and insignificance. She cedes him dominion over the whole American tradition by right of birth ("all you have to do is put down the names!"): Being a Lowell from Boston gives him a claim on meaning that a Bishop from Worcester and Nova Scotia could never attain (whether Bishop ever wanted to sound "significant, illustrative, American, etc." is another matter).

Lowell's triumph very nearly paralyzes Bishop. In a funny way, what rescues her is her envy. Confessing, comically, that she is "green with envy" gives her some distance from Lowell. It offers her an escape. Bishop's envy was a form of self-protection, and so was her modesty, as James Merrill points out: "If you admit you're hot stuff, wicked things can follow. Her modesty was a piece of great good fortune."[41]

Bishop's December letters are most fascinating for the way they show her in the act of grappling with Lowell, assigning him a safe place in her life. She fends him off, but not too far. On several other occasions, she wrote him that she must stop reading his poems because they get into her head and make it impossible for her to write her own verse. The same was true about his friendship. Too much Lowell would crush or wither her. Draw back. Withdrawal is always best.

Bishop draws back most of all from the intense personal emotions that boiled to the surface during her visit. A single qualifying clause—"in some ways not so lucky, either"—is as close as she comes to his madness, his "rowdiness" toward her, and the marriage proposal he never made. Characteristically, she lets her silence speak for itself.

Lowell's blaze of creativity had already burned itself out by the time Bishop sent these letters. "I've really exploded my powder writing and feel I have no force left," he wrote her in early December.[42] The breakdown he had narrowly avoided during the summer caught up with him now. It was one of the worst he had yet suffered. As Lowell's biographer Ian Hamilton reports, Lowell became increasingly violent as December wore on and finally Hardwick called the police, who escorted him to Boston Psychopathic Hospital. Discharged after about a week, he returned home still manic, protesting his love for a girl named Ann Adden, and "thoroughly adrift," as Hamilton puts it. At the end of January, Lowell was committed again—this time to the locked ward of McLean Hospital near Boston. It was spring before he got out.[43]

When Bishop learned of the breakdown, she wrote to Lowell "but you do have that wonderful group of poems on hand now to console you, and we can all be grateful for them."[44] Lowell's prolonged, terrifying descent into the "kingdom of the mad" yielded two more wonderful poems—"Waking in the Blue," about his three-month confinement in the "house for the 'mentally ill,'" and "Home After Three Months Away," about resuming "normal" life "frizzled, stale and small" on Marlborough Street. These poems are like a nightmare coda to the family portraits of *Life Studies*. After the privileged childhood, after Mattapoisett, St. Mark's, Harvard, Beverly Farms, Lowell winds up among the "thoroughbred mental cases" of McLean's, staring at his bloated face in a metal shaving mirror and clutching a locked razor. It was Lowell's genius to give this progression the inevitability of tragedy.

Life Studies was published in the spring of 1959. Fittingly, Bishop contributed a lengthy blurb for the jacket, which reads in part:

> This new book begins on Robert Lowell's now-familiar trumpet-notes . . . then with the autobiographical group the tone changes. . . . A poem like "My Last Afternoon with Uncle Devereux Winslow," or "Skunk Hour," can tell us as much about the state of society as a volume of Henry James at his best.
>
> . . . . Somehow or other, by fair means or foul, and in the middle of our worst century so far, we have produced a magnificent poet.[45]

It is the perfect epilogue to this complicated chapter in Lowell's life—and in their lives together.

The *Life Studies* breakthrough and its consequences in the lives of Lowell and Bishop are central to their friendship. During the months that Lowell found his new style and wrote the new poems, the tensions and passions of this relationship came to a head. Inspiration, envy, mania, admiration verging on obsession, comradeship, confession, rivalry, self-destruction, desire and remorse, pursuit and withdrawal: These were the essential elements of the thirty-year friendship between Lowell and Bishop—and they all surfaced at once during the composition of *Life Studies*. The twisting together of these tough strands—the binding of inspiration to madness, madness to desire, desire to envy, envy to inspiration—made this friendship especially strange and intense. Like the far briefer relationship between Melville and Hawthorne, theirs was a true literary friendship, a bond that altered the course of both life and art, a connection in which life and art actually merged into each other.

Painful, embarrassing, emotionally fraught as it was, the encounter in Castine in 1957 was one of the shining moments in the friendship between Lowell and Bishop. It makes a kind of touchstone on which to test what preceded and what followed it. Their friendship's "meaning," if one can wrest this word from art to life, flows out of what happened that summer when their "fellowship resume[d] its old transcendence like a star." And this meaning recurs again and again through the course of their radiant fellowship.

EIGHTEEN

Stonington, Maine, 1948: "The Other Life That Might Have Been"

> By the sea, lying
> blue as a mackerel,
> our boarding house was streaked
> as though it had been crying.
>
> —ELIZABETH BISHOP, "A Summer's Dream"

> In the end
> the water was too cold for us.
>
> —ROBERT LOWELL, "Water"

THIRTY YEARS after she met Robert Lowell at the New York apartment of their common friend Randall Jarrell, Elizabeth Bishop recollected the occasion quite clearly in an interview: "I had just published my first book, and Robert Lowell had just published his first book. Randall had known him at Kenyon College. Randall invited me to dinner to meet him and we got along immediately. I'd read *Lord Weary's Castle*, but that wasn't it. For some reason we just hit it off very well. By chance we'd been to see the same art exhibits that afternoon and we talked about those."[1]

"We just hit it off very well"—the mysterious, spontaneous combustion of friendship. The same unbidden spark of sympathy, shared interests, immediate emotional and intellectual attunement sprang up between Hawthorne and Melville on Monument Mountain during a summer thunderstorm, between James and Wharton over a winter's lunch in London, between Porter and Welty on a hot July evening in Baton Rouge. Bishop supplies even more details in a letter to Lowell correcting *his* memories of the occasion: "What I remember about that meeting is your dishevelment, your lovely curly hair, and how we talked about a Picasso show then on in N.Y., and we agreed about the Antibes pictures of fishing, etc—and how much I liked you, after having been almost too scared to go—and how Randall and his wife threw sofa pillows at each other. . . . You were also rather dirty, which I rather liked, too."[2]

A written correspondence sprang up at once and within a few months they were exchanging poems and comments on them. During the summer, Lowell published an extremely perceptive and influential review of Bishop's book in the *Sewanee Review*. With a young man's bravado and a brilliant poet's insight Lowell struck right to the heart of Bishop's poetic vision:

> There are two opposing factors. The first is something in motion, weary but persisting, almost always failing and on the point of disintegrating, and yet, for the most part, stoically maintained. This is morality, memory, the weed that grows to divide, and the dawn that advances, illuminates, and calls to work, the monument "that wants to be a monument," the waves rolling in on the shore, breaking, and being replaced. . . . The second factor is a terminus: rest, sleep, fulfillment, or death. This is the imaginary iceberg, the moon which the Man-moth thinks is a small clean hole through which he must thrust his head; it is sleeping on the top of a mast, and the peaceful ceiling: "But oh, that we could sleep up there."[3]

Bishop was both grateful and a bit awed when she read the review. "I was quite overwhelmed by [it]," she wrote him from Nova Scotia, where she was spending the summer. "It is the first review I've had that attempted to find any general drift of consistency in the individual poems and I was beginning to feel there probably wasn't any at all. . . . It seems to me you spoke out my worst fears as well as some of my ambitions."[4]

Bishop's modesty and candor about her work are very appealing, and Lowell adopted a similar tone in his letters. "I'm a fisherman myself," he wrote her after reading her poem "At the Fishhouses," "but all my fish become symbols, alas!"[5] Though both poets could be quite competitive with their colleagues, they spared each other all but the gentlest combat. Precise praise, reverence for the other's work, deference to the other's opinions, and a polite respect for privacy were to remain the "notes" of their correspondence for the next thirty years.

The friendship came at a time when both of them were ripe for new ties, new endeavors, new sources of inspiration. Lowell, despite his newfound celebrity and his Pulitzer Prize, was rather at loose ends. His marriage to the writer Jean Stafford was over, but the divorce had not yet gone through, and he was living a grubby bachelor's existence in a depressing basement flat under the Third Avenue el in New York City (this is the grim setting for his poem "Thanksgiving's Over" in which a dead insane woman appears to her husband in a dream and begs for her freedom). The fires of his conversion to Catholicism that burned so fiercely in "Colloquy in Black Rock" and "The Quaker Graveyard in Nantucket" had subsided, at least for the moment. Ahead of him loomed the post of Consultant in Poetry to the Library of Congress, a tribute to his new status in the poetry world; a protracted wrestling match with his long, strange, overwrought poem "The Mills of the Kavanaughs"; his father's death; his first serious psychotic episode. But for now Lowell was luffing.

Bishop, too, had reached a turning point, but it was a more troubled, more perplexing time for her than for Lowell, and with fewer happy prospects. Six years older than Lowell, Bishop had by 1947 been on the literary scene for twelve years, ever since Marianne Moore had arranged to have a few of her poems published in an anthology called *Trial Balances* (1935). Bishop's version of the literary life was to travel without ceasing, like Shelley's leaves "from an enchanter fleeing." After graduating from Vassar in 1934, she settled for a spell in New York, and then went abroad, living mostly in Paris and traveling around the Continent and to Morocco and Ireland. In 1938 she returned to the States and established herself in Key West, where she eventually bought an old wood-frame house surrounded by an untamed patch of jungly fruit trees on White Street. Key West and a tiny apartment in Greenwich Village were the poles of her life for the next nine years, though she took a lengthy trip to Mexico in 1943 and shorter ones over the years to Cuba, Haiti, and Nova Scotia.

"I guess I have liked to travel as much as I have because I have always felt isolated & have known so few of my 'contemporaries' and nothing of 'intellectual' life in New York or anywhere," she wrote Lowell shortly after they met.[6] "Actually it may be all to the good." "Her compulsive travelling . . . seemed a kind of curse," wrote her friend Lloyd Schwartz; "like some modern Wandering Jew, she felt doomed never to rest."[7] Curse or blessing, compulsion or indulgence, travel was always at the center of Bishop's life, far more even than such tireless globetrotters as Edith Wharton, Henry James, or Katherine Anne Porter. Questions of travel, as she called her third book of poems, occupied her life and her work.

By 1947, Bishop's Key West period was winding up, she was confirmed in her dislike of New York, and the dreadful question *What next?* yawned before her. Bishop was not in good shape physically or emotionally. Her asthma, which had afflicted her since childhood during periods of stress, was severe during these years. She was drinking a lot and becoming increasingly alarmed by it. She was sick of being so unanchored to any place, so rudderless in her wanderings. Though *North & South* had received mostly favorable reviews, she was tired of her old poems and, as always, dubious about the quality of the new ones.

One of these new ones, the magnificent "Over 2000 Illustrations and a Complete Concordance," reveals her intense skepticism about the value and the coherence of her peripatetic life. She compares the "serious, engravable" scenes depicted in the old family Bible of her childhood to her own adult travels, which she distills into a random catalog of increasingly unsettling impressions: Goats bleat "among the fog-soaked weeds" at St. Johns, Newfoundland; at St. Peter's the sun shone "madly"; there was a dead man lying in a blue arcade in Mexico; naked prostitutes flung themselves at her knees in Marrakesh; and out in some nearby nameless pink desert "I saw what frightened me most of all:" an empty "holy grave . . ./yellowed/as scattered cattle-teeth." Her travels have given her all of these disturbing images, but what does it all add up to? "Everything only connected by 'and' and 'and.' " Disillusioned, unnerved, perhaps even disgusted by the chaotic frivolity of her many journeys, she remains nonetheless in the grip of the mania to see more—to see everything. "Open the heavy book," Bishop commands herself at the end of the poem. "Why couldn't we have seen/this old Nativity while we were at it?" It is the question of a greedy, disappointed child. The "heavy book" itself compels her to set out yet again in search of images as "serious, engravable" as those depicted on its gilt-edged pages.

The "I" of "2000 Illustrations" craves solidity, purpose, direction, weightiness—or feels she *should* crave them—all qualities that Lowell seemed to have in abundance in 1947. He was, as Bishop knew even before meeting him, a "real" poet; and, as she learned the instant they met, he was dead serious about the art of poetry. Lowell excited Bishop as he excited Jarrell, John Berryman, and later Philip Booth, Richard Tillinghast, and Seamus Heaney, with the totality, the obsessiveness of his commitment to poetry. The fact that Lowell, of all poets, admired her so much was immensely flattering to Bishop just then. It was also immensely sobering. Lowell's exalted (and at times tormented) sense of vocation and professionalism made Bishop acutely self-conscious about her own unproductive dilettantism. Almost from the first, she adopted a kind of self-deprecating guilt-ridden tone in her letters to him.

"I am very sick of sounding so quiet," she complains when she sends him "2000 Illustrations," obviously daunted by what she called the "trumpet blast" of Lowell's style.[8] "I take your remarks about writing a lot *now* very much to heart," she writes in response to his report of sailing ahead with the pages and pages of "The Mills of the Kavanaughs," "and I'd like to look forward to a long stretch of nothing but work. . . ."[9] And again, after seeing him in Washington in the spring of 1948, she confesses, "I feel quite jerked up again to the proper table-level of poetry for the summer, off which I guess one does gradually slip unless there are a few people like you to talk to—except I guess there aren't more than two or three—."[10]

David Kalstone is right in pointing to an element of posturing in these letters. "Bishop liked to represent herself as wayward to other poets," he writes, "especially men."[11] Years later, Bishop told an interviewer, "I know I wish I had written a great deal more. Sometimes I think if I had been born a man I probably would have written more. Dare more, or been able to spend more time at it. I've wasted a great deal of time."[12] (Katherine Anne Porter made exactly the same complaint. She, like Bishop, refused to join forces with women's libbers.) Lowell could well have been the man Bishop had in mind as this model of daring, profusion, commitment. "For Bishop, Lowell must have stood for what it was possible for a *man* to do, given sensitiveness and talent," James

Merrill comments.[13] "She thought of him as *the* poet to measure herself against," according to Frank Bidart, who knew them both well. "The comparison always existed in her mind."[14] Kalstone believes that in these early years of her relationship with Lowell, Bishop was "testing herself against his apparent self-discipline. . . . She began to feel her very waywardness as a matter for nourishing poetic investigation—an instinct, still shadowed, about an imagined weakness that was yet to be unmasked as a strength."[15]

The ambivalences of Bishop's responses to Lowell came to a head in "The Prodigal," the poem of hers that owes the most to him. With its harsh imagery, muscular verbs and enjambments ("the sty/was plastered halfway up with glass-smooth dung"; "the sunrise glazed the barnyard mud with red;" "The pigs stuck out their little feet and snored"), "The Prodigal" *sounds* like a Lowell poem. And the stance of staring fixedly at what most pains and appalls is also right out of Lowell—what Kalstone calls his "grimmer imaginings."[16] But Bishop borrows Lowell's techniques to wrestle with Lowell. If she is a truant next to his bookworm, if she is ashamed and disgusted by her truancy, she is still not ready to renounce "exile." Nor is she really sure that she should. Will "shuddering insights" still descend when the prodigal Bishop is "jerked up to the proper table-level of poetry"? Or do they require dung and pigs and drunkenness and isolation? Bishop is torn. A hesitant, qualifying "but" keeps cropping up at the start of sentences, including most memorably the last: "But it took him a long time/finally to make his mind up to go home."

Bishop did not *want to* make her mind up to go home. Home, wherever that may be, was not where she got her work done. The "pleasant eroding daily damnation" of prodigality, as Kalstone calls it, had its rewards—and its safety. "I shall try to profit by your stern example," Bishop vowed to Lowell. "The Prodigal" is a record of her attempt and her uneasy, perhaps relieved, failure in this endeavor. She earned far bigger profits, as she was yet to discover, in exile.

The friendship that sprang up so quickly between Bishop and Lowell was complicated by the question of sex. Though Bishop was a lesbian, and certainly knew it by 1947, she had also had several affairs with men. Lowell was exclusively and powerfully heterosexual, and he carried on numerous affairs between and during his three marriages. But at the time he met Bishop, he was becoming increasingly obsessed with sexual purity, a kind of last gasp of his Catholicism and a symptom of his impending mania. He didn't swear off sex altogether, but he punished himself for succumbing to his desires and resented his partners for enticing him into sin. Bishop and Lowell were attracted to each other—physically as well as emotionally and intellectually. The possibility of a sexual relationship was by no means out of the question, but given the peculiarities of their characters and situations, the possibility was fraught with tension. These tensions became acute during the two weeks that Lowell spent with Bishop in Maine during the summer of 1948.

The vacation arrangements were snarled by the fact that Lowell was now romantically involved with an older, rather wealthy, twice-divorced woman named Carley Dawson. Lowell had met her in Washington, where he had moved in October 1947 to assume his post as Consultant in Poetry to the Library of Congress, and though he was still technically married to Jean Stafford (their divorce was not finalized until April 1948) and entangled with Gertrude Buckman (a New York book reviewer and an ex-wife of Delmore Schwartz), he promptly proposed marriage to Dawson. It was not a promising match. Dawson was a worldly and conventional person, a polished Washington hostess who enjoyed mixing with the literary elite. Her chief attraction for Lowell seemed to be that she had been the mistress of the French poet St.-John Perse. While professing his love for Dawson, Lowell subjected her to a series of tests to discover whether her taste in poetry and painting was sufficiently high brow. Lowell's biographer Ian Hamilton describes the six-month affair as "singularly joyless."[17] Strangely enough, Bishop, who had met Dawson in Washington, seemed to be fonder of her than Lowell was.

Bishop preceded Lowell and Dawson to Maine, establishing herself in the fishing village of Stonington. Built on a rocky, knobby hill that drops steeply down to the sea, Stonington, then as now, was a working town—not pretty, but ramshackle, weather-beaten, remote, stark, and utterly *authentic*. The men go out on the water to fish for lobster; and in those days, they still rowed out in dories every morning to work the last few granite quarries on the surrounding islands. Stonington's harbor, like the Key West Bight, is an untidy jumble of fishing boats, pilings, sea birds, strong smells, and gear. The rickety wooden houses stand on thick blocks of granite. Flowers in ragged garden patches glow in the white sea light. Bishop loved it.

She settled into a Victorian boarding house near the shore and in mid-August, Lowell and Dawson joined her there. The complex emotional ménage à trois held up for the better part of two tense and rather drunken weeks, and then it snapped. Dawson later told Hamilton that, before she left, she and Lowell stayed up all night talking and she realized that "something was very wrong with Robert."[18] The truth was that Lowell had come to despise Dawson after seeing her next to Bishop and he was dying to get rid of her. The next morning, Bishop had a friend drive Dawson to the station, and that was the end of her. She and Lowell never met again. Lowell and Bishop were, as he later wrote, "alone and together—at last"—for a single day.

The two spent most of the day on the water. They went fishing on their landlord's lobster boat, and later, they picked their way through the rocks to stand waist deep in the frigid Maine water. Bishop, years later, recalled that Lowell "inadvertently posed against a tree trunk, and looked just like Saint S [Sebastian] for a moment!"[19] They talked incessantly, even in the water, and exchanged more confidences than they ever had before. All day they had before them the cool blue distances of Maine, the islands with streaks of water glittering between, the broken shoreline, the working harbor. They ate dinner together and then returned to their separate rooms in the boardinghouse. The next day, Lowell left for Boston. Bishop stayed on in Stonington through the early autumn.

That was all that "happened" between them—and yet it marked a critical moment in their relationship, a moment that Lowell, especially, returned to again and again, in memory, in imagination, in his verse. It is tempting to write that Lowell and Bishop were in love after Stonington and that circumstance kept them apart, but it was not as simple as that. Lowell, indeed, left Stonington convinced he was going to marry Bishop and promptly began broadcasting the news to his friends. Yet he made no declaration of love in his letters to her and, according to an unidentified friend quoted in the Hamilton biography, he never proposed to her.[20] Bishop's friend Joseph Summers, however, distinctly recalls her saying that Lowell *did* propose and that she turned him down.[21]

Whatever the truth, the idea of a Lowell–Bishop marriage got out and circulated quickly through the literary community. When the two of them attended the famous Bard College Poetry weekend in early November, everyone assumed they were an established couple. The rising generation of poets and critics was out in force that weekend—Richard Wilbur, James Merrill, Kenneth Rexroth, Richard Eberhart, Joseph Summers—along with such distinguished members of the older generation as William Carlos Williams and Louise Bogan. Bishop, characteristically, was paralyzed by shyness, and when her turn came to read her work, she asked Lowell to read "The Fish" for her. "My wife and I were aware of Cal's talking about Elizabeth," Richard Wilbur recalled forty-five years later, "and I thought it seemed like a plausible match. We felt close—really almost intimate—with Elizabeth, and we talked with her about it. Of course, the concept of lesbianism was not clear at that time. People did not talk openly about these things then. My wife said to Elizabeth, 'You're fond of Cal and he's fond of you—why don't you just marry him. Dare to do it.' Elizabeth was amused. 'It won't work, it won't work, it won't work,' she kept saying."[22] Long afterward, when Bishop was involved with Lota, she told Joe Summers, "I love Cal more than anyone in the world, except Lota, but I never could have married him. He's so violent he'd destroy me."[23]

Other friends remember Bishop joking, or half joking, that she didn't really want to marry Lowell but she would have had his baby if she hadn't been so worried about the possibility of insanity, which ran in both their families. Frank Bidart says she would have slept with Lowell had he made a sexual advance, but he never did.[24] Lowell blew his opportunity on the Bard weekend by drinking himself into a stupor. Years later Bishop described to James Merrill how she and Elizabeth Hardwick, who was also present that weekend, carried Lowell back to his dormitory room one night and put him to bed. It was on this occasion that Hardwick, after loosening Lowell's tie and opening his shirt, supposedly murmured, "Why, he's an Adonis."[25] "Elizabeth realized then that Elizabeth Hardwick was going to be the next Mrs. Lowell," Merrill recounts. " 'This is the outcome of Cal's helplessness,' I remember her saying. 'Someone will move in and take him over.' Maybe she reacted to this because she had a fear of being taken over herself."[26]

Bishop, looking back, chose to distance herself from the

situation with Lowell and to treat the possibility of a sexual relationship between them with amused irony. But Lowell's feelings about their day in Stonington only became more intense with the passage of time, reaching a peak, as described above, when Bishop visited him in Castine nine years later. After Bishop and Lota left Castine, Lowell wrote her a letter in which he revealed for the first time everything he had failed to say to her after Stonington. The August ninth letter, by far the longest Lowell ever wrote to Bishop, is the fullest account of what happened that day in Stonington—at least what happened to *him*. Reading the letter side by side with the drafts of poems he was composing simultaneously is like looking into the refining fires of Lowell's imagination.

In the letter, Lowell rambles on for several pages about a hilarious drunken poets' boating party before he gets to the heart of the matter:

> My frenzied behavior during your visit has a history and there is one fact that I want to disengage from all its harsh frenzy. There's one last bit of the past that I would like to get off my chest and then I think all we [sic] be easy with us.
>
> Do you remember how at the end of that long swimming and sunning Stonington day after Carlie's removal by Tommy, we went up to, I think, the relatively removed upper Gross house and had one of those real fried New England dinners, probably awful. And we were talking about this and that about ourselves and I was feeling the infected hollowness of the Carlie business draining out of my heart, and you said rather humorously yet it was truly meant, "When you write my epitaph, you must say I was the loneliest person who ever lived." Probably you forget, and anyway all that is mercifully changed and all has come right since you found Lota. But at the time everything, I guess (I don't want to overdramatize) our relations seemed to have reached a new place. I assumed that [it] would be just a matter of time before I proposed and I half believed that you would accept. Yet I wanted it all to have the right build-up. Well, I didn't say anything then. And of course the Eberharts in-laws wasn't the right stage-setting, and then there was that poetry conference at Bard and I remmember [sic] one evening presided over by Mary McCarthy and my Elizabeth was there, and going home to the Bard poets' dormitory, I was so drunk my hands turned cold and I

felt half-dying and held your hand. And nothing was said, and
like a loon that needs sixty feet, I believe, to take off from the
water, I wanted time and space, and went on assuming, and
when I was to have joined you in Key West I was determined
to ask you. Really for so callous (I fear) a man, I was fearfully
shy and scared of spoiling things and distrustful of being
steady enough to be the least good. Then of course the Yaddo
explosion came and all was over. Yet there were a few months.
I suppose we might almost claim something like apparantly
[sic] Strachey and Virginea Wolf [sic]. And of course there was
always the other side, the fact that our friendship really wasn't
a courting, was really disinterested (Bad phrase) really led to
no encroachments. So it is. . . . But asking you is *the* might
have been for me, the one towering change, the other life that
might have been had. It was that way for these nine years or
so that intervened. It was deeply buried, and this spring and
summer (really before your arrival) it boiled to the surface.
Now it won't happen again, though of course I always feel a
great blytheness and easiness with you. It won't happen, I'm
really underneath utterly *in* love and sold on my Elizabeth and
it's great solace to me that you are with Lota, and I am sure it
is the will of the heavens that all is as it is.[27]

Here is how Lowell treated the same memories in one of the
versions of "The Two Weeks' Vacation":

"You and I, I and you,"
The old stuck ballad record repeating
My Darling Elizabeth, we were alone
And together at last
More or less hand in hand
On the rocks at Stonington,
For thirteen days we had been three . . .
My old flame, Mrs. X—never left us,
Each morning she met us with another
Crushing ensemble,
Her British voice, her Madame du Barry
Black and gold eyebrows,
She survived a whole day of hand-lining
Deep sea for polock [sic], skate and skulpin [sic],
Made us bait her hooks,

And wear her blue silk "ski-suit,"
Blouse, trousers, cape and even gloves matched!
All this—for me! . . .

I came down the corridor in pajamas
No doubt arousing false hopes
And said . . . Well, who cares . . .

We sat. You talked of Marianne Moore
Taking her water cress sandwiches
To feed the Bronx Zoo "denizens."
. . .

Dear Elizabeth,
Half New Englander, half fugitive,
Nova Scotian, wholly Atlantic sea-board,
Unable to settle anywhere, or live
Our usual roaring sublime,
And once two years out of Vassar, there was a time
Unanchored, unsecured by any home—
Your giant memory whipped you with a rope. . . ,[28]

It's curious that the best lines in "The Two Weeks' Vacation" are about Dawson, not Bishop. Lowell takes off at a gallop when he hits "Madame X"—her voice, her clothing, her eyebrows, her squeamishness, and vanity have the stinging clarity of the *Life Studies* poems (in one version he calls her "the elfin, blue-blooded/Psychotic blue-stocking"—she belongs with the "thoroughbred mental cases" in "Waking in the Blue"). Lowell turns Dawson into one of the shrill, overbearing, disappointed females he eviscerated so expertly—his mother, Anne Kavanaugh, Clytemnestra in *History* (who is really his mother in Greek drag), Elizabeth Hardwick in *The Dolphin*.

The poem goes slack when Bishop enters. When he does finally manage to get her alone, they barely connect—only "more or less hand in hand." Trying to "capture" her in verse after she left Castine, Lowell remains as awkward and abashed as he was in Stonington nine years earlier. It's as if his imagination seizes up when he tries to bring her into focus.

Five years after Castine, Lowell did eventually finish a poem about their day in Stonington, but "Water," as he called the poem, bears only a ghostly resemblance to "The Two Weeks' Vacation."

To begin with, Dawson has been removed and even Bishop's presence been distilled to a vague, hovering, disembodied "you." Instead of the tense, farcical drama of an unraveling ménage à trois, Lowell has written a hushed descriptive poem, very much in Bishop's manner, in which the emotion has soaked into the scenery. A mood of mournful resignation replaces the "infected hollowness" of the earlier poem. Lowell sets "Water" in the distant past, as if evoking a self he can never be again and a place he can return to only in fond misty memory. "Remember?" he asks halfway through the poem. "We sat on a slab of rock./From this distance in time,/it seems the color of iris,/rotting, and turning purpler,//but it was only/ the usual gray rock . . ."[29] The overall effect is reminiscent of Matthew Arnold's "Dover Beach," a poem Lowell loved and from which he took the epigraph for "The Mills of the Kavanaughs."

Lowell admitted when he sent Bishop the poem that the effect is "more romantic and gray than the whole truth, for all has been sunny between us . . . better than life allows really."[30]

But the depths of "Water" conceal still other, and darker, questions between the friends. The dream of a "mermaid clinging to a wharf-pile" that Lowell attributes to the "you" at the end of the poem is in fact lifted almost intact from a depressed and depressing letter that Bishop wrote him shortly after he left Stonington: "I've just been indulging myself in a nightmare of finding a gasping mermaid under one of the exposed docks—you know, trying to tear the mussels off the piles for something to eat,—horrors." The real horror is how closely this stranded nightmare mermaid resembles Bishop herself: flung out of her proper element, famished, gasping for air, just as Bishop gasped for air during her attacks of asthma. It was utterly characteristic of Lowell to have remembered the letter, fourteen years after receiving it, and to have zeroed in on its most horrifying passage. (Mermaids were to resurface in his work far more conspicuously a decade later in *The Dolphin*). Though Bishop let him "have" her mermaid without protest, his habit of poetic appropriation was to become a serious bone of contention between them later.

That single day on the rocks in Stonington lived on and on and down and down in their friendship—Lowell probing, exposing, reinventing the "whole truth"; Bishop resisting, correcting, parrying Lowell's thrusts but absenting herself emotionally. It encapsulated the entire story of their friendship and what each of them chose to make of it.

There is no question that marriage would have been a catastrophe for Lowell and Bishop.[31] Bishop was predominantly lesbian. Lowell was skidding into psychosis. Bishop's drinking bouts were becoming more frequent and more debilitating. Both of them required a great deal of care. Neither had the strength or the stamina to cope with the other's crises. At some deeply sane instinctive level, they must have understood this. Their friendship might have survived a brief affair, but marriage would have destroyed it—and might well have destroyed both of them. As Bishop's friend U. T. Summers puts it, "Had they married, we would have had two fewer poets."[32] "The other life that might have been had" remained forever submerged between them to resurface in fantasy, memory, and art. "Remember?" Lowell asks her in "Water" about that day so distant in time. Remembering, through verse, was what suited them best. Distance was their happiest medium. Poetry, always poetry, sustained their friendship.

NINETEEN

The Unbroken Draught of Poison: Madness and Alcoholism

> *In this world, our world, deviation is a prison.*
>
> —ROBERT LOWELL, *Notebook*

> *He does not dare look out the window,*
> *for the third rail, the unbroken draught of poison,*
> *runs there beside him. He regards it as a disease*
> *he has inherited the susceptibility to.*
>
> —ELIZABETH BISHOP, *"The Man-Moth"*

INCURABLE DISEASES—madness and alcoholism—shadowed the friendship between Lowell and Bishop. Lowell suffered recurrent episodes of violent mania followed by paralyzing depression requiring prolonged hospitalization, sometimes in padded cells. Bishop was a secret binge drinker who periodically drank and drank until she literally collapsed. Lowell's madness and Bishop's alcoholism would have made a marriage between them disastrous, but in a strange covert way, illness intensified their friendship. The shadow of disease was something they endured in common. It connected them.

But the connection remained largely unacknowledged. In their long correspondence only rarely and reluctantly did they bring up their "conditions." They spared each other both questions and confessions. As Lowell wrote Bishop after one of his worst breakdowns in 1954, "I have been sick again, and somehow even with you I shrink both from mentioning and not mentioning."[1] Bishop also shrank from the embarrassment of "mentioning and not mentioning." Sharing illness made the friends delicate with each other. They agreed, tacitly, considerately, to draw the curtains against the shadows and make the friendship a bright safe haven from disease. There was also the fact that after the summer and fall of 1948, they were seldom together. They didn't *have to* encounter each other in illness. "Distance," as David Kalstone puts it, "gave [the friendship] a certain immunity."[2] And yet by a strange sort of alchemy, the shadows massed all the thicker for being ignored.

Lowell's biographer Ian Hamilton covers every one of his breakdowns, hospitalizations, and recoveries in unsparing clinical detail, and there is no need to repeat this gruesome record here. What is most striking in Hamilton's account is the *pattern* of Lowell's disease, its terrifying regularity, its rigid consistency over the course of his life. From childhood Lowell had been violent, "excitable," bullying. "[T]he school's most cruel monitor," Philip Booth wrote of the young Lowell in his elegy, "you wrenched skin, or twisted arms, as if/Caligula were just. Of those who never made/a team, you were Captain . . ."[3]

His parents were a Freudian nightmare. His mother, the former Charlotte Winslow, was a shrill, selfish, domineering society matron who openly flirted with her son and scorned her husband ("Oh Bobby, it's such a comfort to have a man in the house," she gushes to her sullen son in "91 Revere Street"). His father, Robert Traill Spence Lowell III, was, despite his distinguished Boston lineage, a weak, vague, blithering dullard. Lowell described him as "deep—not with profundity, but with the dumb depth of one who trusted in statistics and was dubious of personal experience. In his forties, Father's soul went underground."[4] A career officer in the navy, Commander Lowell had a character that faded steadily, like the Cheshire cat, until only his smile remained. Lowell was criticized for his harsh portraits of his parents in *Life Studies,* but Blair Clark, a boyhood friend who knew the family well, insists that Lowell actually "spared them, and thus perhaps himself, in his accounts of their behavior."[5]

Lowell's first full-scale psychotic episode hit in 1949, just seven months after the two weeks' vacation with Bishop in Stonington. In retrospect, one can see that Lowell was speeding up even in Maine—his erratic behavior toward Carley Dawson, his sudden passion for Bishop, the bizarre announcement to friends (but not to Bishop) of his plans to marry her were all signs of incipient mania. He grew more and more wound up through the fall and winter. Lowell was at Yaddo during the winter of 1948–49, and it was then that he launched his notorious assault on Elizabeth Ames, the artists' colony director of many years, accusing her of being a Communist agent and demanding her resignation. Flannery O'Connor and Alfred Kazin, both of whom were in residence at Yaddo at the time, describe in letters and memoirs the uproar Lowell caused.[6] His attack on Ames polarized the literary community. Elizabeth Hardwick, who had become deeply involved with Lowell that winter, backed him up. Eleanor Clark rallied the opposition party, enlisting the support of John Cheever, Alfred Kazin, Delmore Schwartz, and Katherine Anne Porter among others. (Bishop, who went to Yaddo a short time later, seems to have stayed out of the fray.) Ames ultimately retained her post, but the incident festered as one of the uglier flare-ups of McCarthyism.

Few of those involved in the Yaddo business realized that Lowell's vehemence against Ames was fueled, at least in part, by mental illness. During the spring of 1949, when the Ames affair came to a head, Lowell was wild with manic energy, talking constantly, staying up night after night, firing off telegrams and phoning everyone he knew, buttonholing strangers in the street. In April he traveled to the Midwest, blazing like a comet. When he became violent he was finally overpowered by the police in Bloomington, Indiana, where he was visiting Peter Taylor. His mother took him back to Boston and had him committed to Baldpate Hospital near Georgetown, Massachusetts. At Baldpate he was placed in a padded cell and given electric shock treatment. Lowell proposed to Hardwick while he was still in the hospital, and they were married on July 28, 1949, just weeks after his release. (Friends who had been informed the previous fall that he was going to marry Bishop were rather startled, as was Bishop.)

Hardwick, like Lowell's other two wives, was a writer. She had the further merit in Lowell's eyes of being southern—born and raised in Kentucky and a friend of his old mentor Allen Tate and his wife, Caroline Gordon. Though she had been on the New York literary scene for some time when she met Lowell, publishing both fiction and criticism, Hardwick still spoke with a soft southern drawl and she had soft southern graces to go with it—a large-eyed open countenance, an elegant way of smoking a cigarette, and an easy mastery of the household arts. But the softness of appearance and voice were deceiving. Hardwick was a notoriously harsh critic —Katherine Anne Porter called her a "hatchet man. . . . Hatchet woman sounds too gentle for her"[7] and Peter Taylor, among many others, reeled under her verbal blows. In conversation and domestic combat, Hardwick was always a match for Lowell, and his verse gives a fair sampling of what he called "the shrill verve of [her] invective." Their marriage, the longest-lasting of Lowell's three, did not begin auspiciously. That autumn, Lowell was back in the hospital, this time Payne Whitney in New York. For the rest of his life, Lowell was lucky if twelve months passed without a breakdown.

The ensuing attacks followed the same basic pattern. "These things come on with a gruesome, vulgar, blasting surge of 'enthusiasm,' " Lowell wrote to Bishop in one of his rare allusions to his illness, "and one becomes a kind of man-aping balloon in a parade—then you subside and eat bitter coffee-grounds of dullness, guilt, etc."[8] The depression that followed the mania was, as he put it, "an incredible formless time of irresolution, forgetfulness, inertia, all the Baudelairean vices plus what he must never have known, stupidity."[9] Usually during the "surge of 'enthusiasm,' " Lowell latched on to a girl—a young and attractive and adoring woman with whom he declared himself passionately in love. Reviling Hardwick publicly, he announced his intention of ending his marriage and starting a new life with his girl. The surge of enthusiasm exploded in violence. He started fights, set his friends against each other, shouted from windows. Then Hardwick would call the police and have Lowell committed.

Treatments varied. He was put on Thorazine and sedatives, given warm baths and electric shock. In a prose account of his illness, he writes of one round of treatment, "Each morning before breakfast, I lay naked to the waist . . . and received the first of my round-the-clock injections of chloropromazene: left shoulder, right shoulder, right buttock, left buttock. My blood became like melted lead. . . . I sat gaping through Scrabble games, unable to form the simplest word."[10] Coming to consciousness after sleep was an agony: "Waking, I suspected that my whole soul and its thousands of spiritual fibers, immaterial ganglia, apprehensive antennae, psychic radar, and so on, had been bruised by a rubber hose. In the presence of persons, I was ajar."[11] After his release from the hospital, Lowell usually saw a doctor for psychotherapy, sometimes for several sessions a week. In 1967 he started taking lithium, then being hailed as a major breakthrough in the treatment of manic depression. On lithium Lowell teetered through several Decembers, when the attacks often hit, without a breakdown. But even lithium eventually failed him. In the last years of life, Lowell suffered another series of devastating attacks. Of all the horrors of his twenty-eight years of madness—nearly half his life—perhaps the most horrible of all was the knowledge that there was no cure.

Hardwick, incredibly, faced twenty years of Lowell's madness. She suffered his "indescribably cruel" betrayals and humiliating exposures. She was his jailer, his target, and his nurse. And each time, she forgave him—or at least "took him back." Friends and colleagues also showed tremendous forbearance toward Lowell. Though he lashed out savagely at people when in the grip of mania, afterward he was abject. He had no sentimental illusions about the value or nobility of his illness. "I don't think it a visitation of angels but dust in the blood," he told an interviewer.[12] "There was something movingly helpless about him," recalls the poet Anthony Hecht. "His vulnerability was touching. Cal would impose himself and demand total affection and support and forgiveness for all the bad things he had done. And yet he was severely critical of himself when he was at the bottom. His Puritanism was most merciless when he was ill."[13] "Lowell's friends stuck by him, even though they had to put up with outrageous events and horrible shaming maneuvers," Helen Vendler comments. "The fact that they didn't write him off was proof that when he was sane he was very, very sane."[14]

People forgave, they sympathized, but they also came to dread him. "All persons chronically diseased are egotists, whether the disease be of the mind or body," Hawthorne wrote in his creepy story "Egotism; or, The Bosom Serpent." Lowell was certainly no exception to this leaden rule. His egotism, like his disease, was severe, and could be very, very wearing.

Bishop was especially sensitive to, and wary of, Lowell's madness, because of her own early exposure to mental illness. Her mother, Gertrude Bulmer Bishop, suffered a nervous breakdown after her husband died of Bright's disease at age thirty-nine, just eight months after the birth of their only child. The couple had been living in Worcester, Massachusetts, where William Thomas Bishop worked as an executive in his father's prosperous building business; but after her husband's death, Gertrude Bishop moved back to her childhood home in Great Village, Nova Scotia, leaving her baby in the care of her parents. Gertrude's condition was serious enough to require hospitalization, first, according to Bishop, in McLean's sanatorium outside Boston (where Lowell was treated a number of times) and later in a mental hospital outside Dartmouth, Nova Scotia (the Bishop family tried to get her back into McLean's, but this proved to be impossible since she had lost her American citizenship after her husband's death). Gertrude's visits home were brief and traumatic for all concerned, especially her daughter. In 1916, when Elizabeth was five, the visits stopped altogether. In that year, Gertrude Bishop was confined permanently to the Dartmouth mental hospital. Elizabeth never saw her mother again. Gertrude died in the hospital in 1934.

Bishop, on one occasion, pointed out to Lowell the coincidence of McLean's figuring in both their lives (strangely, the hospital has no record of her mother's stay). Writing to him during one of his sojourns at the sanatorium, she confided that "my mother stayed [at McLean's] once for a long time. I even have some snapshots of her in very chic clothes of around 1917, taking a walk by a pond there (?) However, I hope you don't have to stay very long—the people in such places are so fascinating I think one begins to find the usual world a bit dull by comparison. . . . You know there are several of our contemporary poets who always live in sanatoriums, feeling they're the only sensible place for a poet to live these days. . . . "[15] This is a rare breach of her silence on the subject.

She was just as reticent in her work. "In the Village" is the single occasion when Bishop published a piece dealing explicitly with her mother's madness. Though she called it fiction, she didn't make any of it up: "it was all the way it happened," Bishop told her friends Joe and U. T. Summers. And yet even here the crucial fact is left unstated—indeed, it becomes all the more terrifying for being unmentionable.

The story flashes a series of incredibly vivid sense impressions—translucent colors, echoing sounds, pungent smells, baffling scraps of overheard conversations—through the consciousness of a little girl who, like Bishop, has been brought to her grandparents' house in Nova Scotia and left there to wonder about the mysterious comings and goings of her ill mother. "A scream, the echo of a scream, hangs over that Nova Scotian village," she begins. "No one hears it; it hangs there forever, a slight stain in those pure blue skies. . . . It was not even loud to begin with, perhaps. It just came there to live, forever—not loud, just alive forever. Its pitch would be the pitch of my village. Flick the lightning rod on top of the church steeple with your fingernail and you will hear it."[16] The scream itself—her mother's piercing cry of panic on succumbing once more to madness—is rendered as an abstraction, hovering between sound and color, smoke and ash, event and memory. But everything else in the story is fresh and immediate and absolutely clear: the color and texture of the clothes her mother wears; the cow ambling off to the meadow, "drooling glass strings" and leaving dung piles behind her—"Smack. Smack. Smack. Smack."; the welcoming, sheltering gloom of the blacksmith shop where "horseshoes sail through the dark like bloody little moons and follow each other like bloody little moons to drown in the black water, hissing, protesting." Always, just beneath the vibrant surface, is the tension of whether the mother will scream again.

Joe Summers believes that "the child's capacity for meticulous attention serves as . . . a method of escaping from intolerable pain"—and that this strategy is the key to Bishop's poetry.[17] Without ever naming the cause or nature of her mother's illness, Bishop conjures up the fraught atmosphere of a family coping with insanity. "In the Village" is a masterpiece, one of those stories that live on in the imagination so powerfully that they become indistinguishable, over time, from one's own life and experience—like a dream one suddenly recollects in minute detail years after dreaming it.

Lowell adored the story and praised it in a letter to Bishop as "a great ruminating Dutch landscape full of goneness."[18] He loved it so much, in fact, that he decided to "translate" the twenty-four-page story into a forty-line poem. But Lowell's "The Scream" is as inert, crude, and forced as "In the Village" is delicate, luminous, and effortless. Lowell appended a note to the beginning of *For the Union Dead,* the volume in which he published the poem, explaining that " 'The Scream' owes everything to Elizabeth Bishop's beautiful, calm story, *In the Village.*" This was not false modesty for with the exception of two lines—" 'But you can't love everyone,/your heart won't let you!' " supposedly said by his young daughter, Harriet—every phrase and image in the poem comes directly out of the story. Yet Lowell makes the whole thing a shrill cartoon. He put in seven exclamation marks as if punctuation can somehow supply the emotion he has siphoned off.[19]

"The Scream" is a strange, awkward poem, but the strangest part of all is that Lowell should have attempted it in the first place. He might have intended it as a form of homage, but it comes off as an act of butchery. This was not an isolated act. The impulse to stamp the work of others with his own image grew on Lowell through the 1960s and 1970s. "His style manages to make even quotations and historical fact a personal possession," Randall Jarrell once commented of Lowell.[20] Why he needed so many personal possessions is another question. Madness might well have fanned Lowell's greed and competitiveness into a raging megalomania but this lay some years ahead. With "In the Village," he felt entitled to a personal stake in the story because he had madness in common with Bishop's mother. It was his "beat" and thus fair game for the Lowell treatment. In his mind, "versing" the story into a poem was another expression of his fellowship with Bishop.

Bishop let him off the hook gently. "The Scream really works well, doesn't it," she wrote him from Brazil when she read the poem, "the story is far enough behind me so I can see it as a poem now. . . . It builds up beautifully, and everything of importance is there. But I was very surprised."[21] Joe Summers questions the sincerity of her praise. He believes that Bishop was scared of offending Lowell because she knew he was "delicately balanced" and because she valued the friendship too much to jeopardize it. So she let him "have" "In the Village."

But there were limits to her leniency. In one of the poems he was writing about Bishop after she left Castine in 1957, Lowell has Gertrude Bishop say to her four-year-old daughter, "All I want/To do is kill you!"[22] Bishop read the drafts before she left the States, and she protested later from Brazil: "If you ever do anything with the poem about me—would you change the remark my mother was supposed to have made? She never did make it; in fact I don't remember any direct threats, except the usual maternal ones—her danger for me was just implied in the things I overheard the grown-ups say before and after her disappearance. Poor thing, I don't want to have it any worse than it was."[23] She could stomach "The

Scream"—perhaps because her story was so far behind her—but Lowell's invention of a violent new script for her past was really going too far. He had touched a very sensitive nerve.

Bishop had serious enough qualms about using her mother's madness herself without Lowell's seizing and distorting it. "I am feeling fearfully rich," she wrote a friend after selling "In the Village" to *The New Yorker* for a handsome fee (about $1,700), "and of course having fearful doubts about whether I should ever have written 'In the Village' at all or not."[24] Profiting from her mother's insanity was almost as bad as exposing it. Eudora Welty had the same misgivings after using her mother's family stories and her illness and death in *The Optimist's Daughter*. Both of these intensely private women worried whether it was right to betray the mothers who had betrayed them—by going mad, by dying. Both feared they would somehow be punished for their breach of silence, even from beyond the grave (like the shrinking, pathetic sisters in Katherine Mansfield's "The Daughters of the Late Colonel" who live in dread that their dead father will rage at them for burying him).

Bishop had some help in allaying her "fearful doubts" about writing "In the Village" from alcohol and a massive dose of cortisone, which she was taking for her asthma. Like Katherine Anne Porter, she was a notoriously slow worker, sometimes perfecting poems for a decade before publishing them, but she wrote "In the Village" in a great two-night rush of inspiration. Long afterward, she told an interviewer, "The story came from a combination of cortisone and the gin and tonic I drank in the middle of the night. I wrote it in two nights."[25] Part of this is modesty—as if the gin and cortisone magically wrote the story *for* her or *through* her. But being high might have freed up the content of the story even more than its rapid composition. Friends point out that only when she was drunk could Bishop acknowledge the pain and darkness of her life—the early loss of her parents, her abiding loneliness, the very fact that she was an alcoholic. "Getting drunk was a way of allowing despair into her conscious mind," notes Frank Bidart. "She allowed herself to get depressed when she was drunk. Otherwise she did not confront or verbalize her negative emotions."[26] Bishop once told Anne Stevenson, an early critic of her work, "Although I think I have a prize 'unhappy childhood,' almost good enough for the text-books—please don't think I dote on it."[27] She *didn't* dote on it except when she was drunk. And then she doted on it to distraction. Bishop was obviously not blind drunk when she wrote "In the Village," but she was high enough to shed the "awful but cheerful" mask and look dead on at the origin of her misery.

Like many alcoholics, Bishop came from a family of problem drinkers. David Kalstone reports that her father, her grandfather, and three of her uncles had to quit drinking.[28] Her uncle Arthur was the village drunk of Great Village (or "one of them," as Bishop wryly put it), and she describes his sad decline in her story "Memories of Uncle Neddy" (which, aside from the alteration of names, is as true to facts as "In the Village"): "Finally phrases like 'not himself,' 'taken too much,' 'three seas over,' sank into my consciousness and I looked at my poor uncle with new eyes, expectantly. . . . He is operated on, but won't stop, can't stop drinking—or so I am told. It has taken the form of periodic bouts and an aunt tells me (I'm old enough to be confided in) that 'Everyone knows' and that 'It will kill him.' However, when he dies it is of something quite different."[29] Uncle Neddy's symptoms and history were alarmingly similar to Bishop's own, as she knew perfectly well. Indeed, the heritability of alcoholism may well be a concealed meaning of these lines from "The Man-Moth," one of her early masterpieces:

> He does not dare look out the window,
> for the third rail, the unbroken draught of poison,
> runs there beside him. He regards it as a disease
> he has inherited the susceptibility to.[30]

Bishop's drinking was reaching crisis level when she met Lowell in the late 1940s. Heavy drinking was de rigueur in literary circles in those days, and Bishop's thirst did not stand out at parties or dinners. The real problem was that once she got drunk she would keep on drinking. "It was always when something went wrong or I got upset about something that I thought of it first," she wrote, "and *then*, of course, I couldn't stop."[31] Alone and miserable, she drank for days on end, consuming all the alcohol she could put her hands on until she physically could not continue.[32] "She would drink until she literally fell down at your feet in the middle of the afternoon," remembers Elizabeth Hardwick. "It was very sad."[33] Her "periodic bouts" were frequently so bad that she had to be hospitalized. In a sense, each binge was a suicide attempt for when she drank, Bishop seemed determined to drink herself to death. Joe Summers tells a harrowing story of Bishop's mental state in the late 1940s: "The only time I saw her drunk was in a Greenwich Village restaurant. She hit every other rail on the banister as she came downstairs. At the end of the meal there was some talk about whether Loren [MacIver—a painter and close friend of Bishop's] should take her home. Elizabeth turned to me and said, 'What should I do?' I said, 'Go home with Loren.' But she said, 'No—I mean, should I kill myself?' "[34]

In the late 1940s, Bishop came under the care of a New York physician named Anny Baumann, and she remained in close touch with Baumann for the rest of her life. Baumann, to whom "A Cold Spring" is dedicated, became Bishop's confessor. The letters she wrote to her over thirty years are a stark diary of her "terrible fight" with alcohol. "I . . . know I'll go insane if I keep it up," she wrote in 1950. "I *cannot* drink and I know it. . . . I will *not* Drink."[35] And yet a few months later she had to admit that she has disgraced herself with another binge. "What has me so very upset is knowing that everyone knows and that I am 'no good,' etc. etc."[36] Looking back on this awful period of her life a few years later, Bishop told Baumann that she had been "losing the power to concentrate for any good long stretches of time" because of the drinking. And her blood ran cold when she contemplated the "gruesome and unnecessary fates and old ages of various friends and acquaintances" who were heavy drinkers.[37] Bishop knew that alcohol was destroying her, but that knowledge did not make it any easier to quit.

Compounding Bishop's problem with alcohol was her asthma, which began during the miserable year when she was removed at age six from her mother's parents' home in Nova Scotia and installed in the home of her father's wealthy parents in Worcester, Massachusetts (she wrote, much later, that she was "on the same terms in the house" as the family's Boston bull terrier).[38] Asthma also afflicted Lowell during trying moments of his childhood and Edith Wharton suffered from asthmatic attacks brought on by stress and marital discord. Asthma plagued Bishop from age six until her death, becoming acute when she was tense or depressed or drinking heavily. During the aimless, fraught years of the 1940s, her asthma was constant.

U. T. Summers believes that Bishop's move to Brazil—a coffee-drinking culture—really saved her life: "It was miraculous that she seemed to straighten out in Brazil."[39] With Lota's help, Bishop stayed on the wagon for most of the seventeen years she lived there—succumbing to temptation only "one evening once or twice a month," as she wrote Baumann, and stopping "before it gets really bad."[40] She controlled her drinking for long stretches after she moved back to the States, but she never mastered it. Friends who knew her in Cambridge in the 1970s describe how shocked they were by the difference between Bishop sober and Bishop drunk. "Sober, she was a tremendously unconventional, original, alive, present person," Bidart remarks. "There was nothing received about any of her opinions or responses. It was a delight to be with her. But she was not fun or brilliant when she drank. She became repetitive—she became not herself. Drinking cut off or short-circuited her brilliant side." Drinking also dissolved her habitual reserve. When she drank, she confessed how miserably humiliating her binges were. And she drowned in guilt, blaming herself for "ruining" the lives of friends and lovers. She admitted that the accidents that plagued her late in life—the broken shoulder, the falls down the stairs—happened when she was drunk. "She talked about her drinking with great remorse," says Bidart. "She wished she was in control."[41]

Toward the end of her life, Bishop developed an intolerance for alcohol and a single drink would make her drunk. Even social drinking became impossible. Friends worried that another binge would kill her. But, like Uncle Neddy, when she died it was "of something quite different."

Lowell was also a heavy drinker—heavy enough that he went on Antabuse (which he called antibooze), a drug that makes one feel ill after drinking, during the 1970s when his doctors forbade him to mix alcohol with lithium. Vows to go on the wagon crop up regularly in this correspondence, and he did succeed in abstaining for months at a time. But, like Bishop, who also spent years on Antabuse, he never quit altogether and never really wanted to. "You know it's hard, I seemed to connect almost unstopping composition with drinking," he wrote Hardwick in the late 1960s when he was turning out unrhymed sonnets at a furious pace. "Nothing was written drunk, at least nothing was perfected and finished, but I have looked forward to whatever one gets from drinking, a stirring and a blurring? I'll really try as a child might say, but even the Trinity can't make the crooked stick straight—or young again."[42]

Yet for all his enjoyment of alcohol's "stirring and blurring," Lowell was not an alcoholic, at least in the opinion of those who knew him well, and certainly not a binge drinker in the way Bishop was. He often drank a lot socially—"that sociable drop," as he described it to Bishop, "that makes us all one species, in warmth, weakness and talkativeness"[43]—but when the occasion ended, he went to bed and slept it off. He could also hold his liquor, part of his Boston Brahmin inheritance. The only time he got into serious trouble with alcohol was when he was spiraling toward another breakdown. "When he got manic, he'd start drinking a lot," Joe Summers remembers. "Then he'd grab on to some girl." The poet Richard Tillinghast says at some point during his lithium treatment, Lowell started cheating by drinking again. "It produced a middle state between sanity and insanity—a kind of semi-sanity. This was not a good development at all. His judgment was seriously skewed."[44]

Bishop also saw a connection between Lowell's madness and his drinking. She wrote in alarm to Baumann, now Lowell's physician as well, in 1967, "*Of course* I know that my drinking & Cal's (& that of most of my N Y friends) are not in the least alike and that his is only a small part, maybe, of the problem." But even she, with her "pattern" of heavy drinking, feels stunned by the quantity of alcohol Lowell is consuming—"2 or 3 big vodkas and a bottle of wine, alone, for lunch"—and she asks Baumann to intervene before he gets out of control.[45]

Considering how much both Bishop and Lowell loved to drink, it is hardly surprising that alcohol figured in their relationship. Theirs was not a "drinking companionship" according to Elizabeth Hardwick, but they did drink a lot when they were together, especially in the early days of their friendship. Lowell, as we've seen, was so drunk at the 1948 Bard College poetry weekend that he felt "half-dying" (James Merrill, who was present, remembers Bishop and Lowell "delightedly drinking each other in" at a party).[46] A few weeks later, Bishop had to be hospitalized for five days after a binge that started in Carley Dawson's Washington apartment, where Bishop was staying by herself. It was probably not a coincidence that she started drinking shortly after she had seen Lowell at a poets' party and right before she was supposed to meet him and W. H. Auden for lunch.[47]

Kalstone may well be right when he associates the friends' excessive drinking in those early days with their "evasion of intimacy." Neither of them could handle being together sober. They started drinking to ease the tension or simply to celebrate the occasion, but then one or both of them ended up half dead, overexcited, passed out, or in the hospital. The pattern persisted for years. Bishop and Lowell both fell off the wagon during her brief visit to Castine with Lota in 1957. And five years later, when Lowell and Hardwick visited Bishop in Brazil, Lowell kicked into a manic attack by drinking heavily—six double vodka martinis before lunch, according to the government official traveling with him.[48] Bishop also got drunk on one occasion during this visit, recalls Hardwick, and went around "denouncing everything."[49] To say that Bishop made Lowell manic and Lowell made Bishop drink would be to turn a complex relationship into a soap opera, but there is a kernel of truth here. When Bishop and Lowell were together, their self-destructiveness boiled to the surface. Madness and alcohol might have been one reason why their friendship worked best as a correspondence.

Sickness killed countless hours of work time for both poets. Lowell sometimes tried to work in the hospital—once during the 1950s he spent "a mad month or more rewriting *everything* in my three books"—but when he was himself again he realized "it was mostly waste."[50] During the long "nursing" periods after his release, he was too stale and depressed to do anything but translate poems from other languages. The eight-year gap between *The Mills of the Kavanaughs* and *Life Studies* was due, at least in part, to the series of severe breakdowns he suffered in the 1950s. But Lowell compensated for some of his loss by making mental illness a subject and a metaphor in his poetry. Illness impelled and deepened his work. Some of the best poems in *Life Studies*—"Man and Wife," "Skunk Hour," "Waking in the Blue," "Home after Three Months Away"—document the phases of manic depression. The desperation of insanity spills over into *For the Union Dead* as well, especially in "Eye and Tooth," "Night Sweat," "Caligula," and "The Drinker." "I am tired. Everyone's tired of my turmoil," Lowell says at the end of "Eye and Tooth."[51] And yet the revelations of his turmoil were precisely what made his poetry seem so new, so important, and so eerily in tune with his times. As the English critic A. Alvarez puts it, "When he wrote nominally about his own crack-ups he seemed in the process to be describing the symptoms of crack-up in the society around him."[52]

Though alcohol, as we've seen, freed Bishop to write "In the Village," far more often it incapacitated. Helen Vendler speculates that drinking might have been "one of the many things that she could blame for having less of an output than she desired"—self-blame being a constant note in her life, something that plagued her well beyond the time she wrote "The Prodigal."[53] Unlike Lowell, Bishop was far too private to make her illness the subject of her work. A sharp-eyed reader can comb out allusions to drinking from a number of her poems—the "hang-over moons" implored to "wane" in "Love Lies Sleeping"; the fireflies in "A Cold Spring" "drifting simultaneously to the same height,/—exactly like the bubbles in champagne"; the Prodigal's stashed pint bottles; the Brazilian *cachaça* (a strong, rough sugarcane spirit) consumed by the riverman and the wounded black beggar in "Going to the Bakery"; Crusoe's home brew, "the awful, fizzy, stinging stuff/that went straight to my head"; and the unnamed "he" who "took to drink" in "The Moose." But these stray references can hardly be taken as a poetic reckoning with alcoholism. If anything, they throw up a kind of smoke screen since, as the poet and critic Lorrie Goldensohn notes, all the drinkers in the poems, as in the stories, are male.[54]

The only time a woman "takes to drink" in Bishop's verse is when the presumably female narrator of "The End of March" imagines having "a *grog à l'américaine*" nightcap in her "proto-dream-house": "I'd blaze it with a kitchen match/and lovely diaphanous blue flame/would waver, doubled in the window."[55] In finally, if rather quietly, acknowledging her taste for alcohol, Bishop is careful to extract its sting. In this fantasy, alcohol is cozy and quaintly domestic: Unlike the wounded beggar's lethal *cachaça* vapors that "knock me over" in "Going to the Bakery" or the hallucinatory fumes of the early story "The Sea and Its Shore," the grog is an innocent spirit that feeds the flame of the household gods.

"The End of March," which first appeared four years before Bishop's death, allays many of the anxieties of "The Sea and

Its Shore," published in 1937 at the start of her career. Story and poem circle the same ring of images: a fantasy seaside shack ("a child's perfect playhouse, or an adult's ideal house," she calls it in the story), fire, and alcohol. In the story, Edwin Boomer (who shares his creator's monogram) is condemned like a Kafka character to a bizarre marginality—a nighttime existence of drinking, collecting wastepaper along the beach, reading it and then burning it. Alcohol is both his escape and his worst danger. After only a couple of drinks Boomer feels "isolated and self-important" and in this mood he occasionally tries his hand at art ("a little rough modelling" out of soaked newspaper); but when he is most drunk he becomes terrified that the "brilliant, oily, and explosive" sea "might ignite and destroy his only means of making a living."[56] Alcohol was the "gasoline, terribly dangerous" of Bishop's life. In "The End of March," she finally imagines a way to quell the danger. Boomer's explosive bonfire becomes a lovely comforting blue flame that shimmers in its doubleness between the warm interior and the mysterious black outside, between the magic and the real. And besides, in the poem Bishop allows herself only *a* grog—not enough to ignite a binge. This was a fantasy that satisfied a range of needs.

As Kalstone and Goldensohn discuss, fire and drinking are also the central images of "A Drunkard," a poem Bishop worked on in the early 1960s but left unfinished. The fragment opens with a childhood memory of being awakened by a nighttime fire (an event that also figures in "In the Village"). The frightened and thirsty child stands in her crib calling for her mother, but her cries are ignored. The next day, walking with her mother on the beach to inspect the still-smoldering blaze, the child picks up a charred stocking, but her mother tells her "sharply":

> *Put that down!* I remember clearly, clearly—
> But since that day, that reprimand
> that night that day that reprimand
> I have had a suffered from abnormal thirst—
> I swear it's true—and by the age
> of twenty or twenty-one I had begun
> to drink & drink—I can't get enough
> and, as you must have noticed,
> I'm half-drunk now . . .[57]

The echoes to "The Sea and Its Shore" and "The End of March" are striking. In "A Drunkard," Bishop supplies the crucial missing link—the childhood trauma of being ignored and reprimanded by her mother—between fire and "abnormal thirst." The fragment, as Kalstone points out, is an "explanation" of her alcoholism, really almost a confession in the *Life Studies* mode. It is hardly surprising that Bishop left it buried.

Kalstone speculates that Bishop's "A Drunkard" might have been written in response to Lowell's "The Drinker." Bishop was indeed fascinated with that poem about a drunk condemned to "killing time" after he has killed his last fifth of bourbon. She wrote Lowell after she read a draft of it: "Oh—I think your drunkeness [sic] poem is going to be superb! It started me off on mine again—mine is more personal and yet a bit more abstract, I think."[58] And later, when she read the finished poem in *Partisan Review,* she told Lowell that she found it "even more horrendous" and she offered a deeply sensitive appreciation: "The most awful line for me is 'even corroded metal . . .', and the cops at the end are beautiful, of course—with a sense of release that only the poem, or another fifth of Bourbon, could produce." She noted with alarm that she had used some of the same images—the galvanized bucket and the phrase "dead metal"—in a draft of a poem, but not her "Drunkard" one, which, she insisted, has "nothing to do with" Lowell's poem.[59]

Behind Bishop's comments on "The Drinker" is a kind of unspoken admission that she and Lowell are "fellow sufferers." The misery of disease—the dead time, the "galvanized color" of despair, the wretchedness of waking up to yet another day with "no help"—was something they understood intimately about each other, though they seldom alluded to it. Only once in their long correspondence did Bishop write openly of the bond they shared in sickness. The letter refers to Lowell's breakdown during the disastrous South American trip: "I, too, have 'spells' (very rarely, thank God). They are a lot like yours, on a modest scale, I think—in origin and result, even—But you have to do everything on the grand scale! I learned a great deal—."[60] Bishop's drunken binges were her "modest" version of Lowell's madness. During their spells both Bishop and Lowell plunged into what Henry James called "black darkness and sheer abysses." At the bottom of the deepest abyss, the shadows of their illnesses interlaced—madness brushing alcoholism, fear gripping fear, horror touching horror—

and bound the friends more tightly, more sympathetically together.

"In sickness, the mind and body make a marriage,"[61] Lowell wrote in his *Notebook*. Both friends suffered again and again the humiliations of this merciless solitary marriage. Since they lived for most of the friendship on different continents, they couldn't provide each other much solace, and in fact the tension of their rare encounters might have made each of their sicknesses worse. But chronic incurable illness set them on parallel tracks. Sickness deepened their friendship even as it darkened both their lives. Together they shared the bitter knowledge that flows through the veins like a poison.

TWENTY

Another Inscrutable House

> Great ash and sun of freedom, give
> us this day the warmth to live,
> and face the household fire. We turn
> our backs, and feel the whiskey burn.
>
> —ROBERT LOWELL, "Fourth of July in Maine"

> I threw off my blanket, sweating;
> I even tore off my shirt.
> I got out of my hammock
> and went through the window naked.
>
> —ELIZABETH BISHOP, "The Riverman"

ANOTHER SIGN of the parallelism of Bishop's and Lowell's lives was that they began and ended their most enduring sexual relationships within a few years of each other. Lowell, as mentioned above, married the novelist and critic Elizabeth Hardwick in 1949, and the marriage survived two decades of psychotic breakdowns, infidelities, and painful public exposures, along with all the usual stresses and strains of modern marriage. Bishop's relationship with Lota de Macedo Soares (which both women considered a marriage) lasted from 1951, when Bishop arrived in Brazil, until Lota's death in 1967 (though there was a good deal of tension between them toward the end).

Both of the poets relied tremendously on the stability of

these relationships, and both found joy, comfort, and inspiration in the trappings of settled domesticity. Lowell fathered a daughter. Bishop happily played godmother to the children of Lota's relatives and servants. A good deal of their best work—Lowell's *Life Studies, For the Union Dead,* and *Near the Ocean;* Bishop's *Questions of Travel,* her translation from the Portuguese of Alice Brant's diary, and "In the Village"—dates from this period in their lives. Yet for both Lowell and Bishop, the routines of stable relationships also stirred up a kind of countervailing inner storm.

Much as they cherished the idea of home, both had trouble dealing with the daily realities of domestic life, as Melville, Wharton, James, and Porter did in their own ways. Each had the impulse to throw off the heavy quilt of marriage. As Peter Taylor said of Lowell, "He wanted his wife and children around him in an old fashioned household, and yet he wanted to be free and on the town. Who wouldn't wish for all that, of course? But he *would* have both. He wanted it so intensely that he became very sick at times."[1] Bishop also in her own way craved the thrill of "freelancing out along the razor's edge" and the stimulus of the strange even as she needed the solidity of an old-fashioned household.

As their marriages wore on and wore thin, both found relief from the oppressive responsibilities of domesticity in love affairs, travel, and work. And in each other. The period of Bishop's exile in Brazil was in many ways the time when the friends were closest and when each was most influenced by the other's work. Throughout their years apart, they never ceased to speak—or rather write— the same language. Bishop's letters to Lowell from Brazil, some of the most beautiful she ever wrote, could fill a small volume. Part of the grammar of their common language was the ambivalence both of them felt about settling down. "Both Bishop and Lowell were waifs and strays who were lucky enough to find people to take care of them," Helen Vendler remarks acutely.[2]

Waifs and strays require more care than "normal" people—but even with the best care they remain unreliable. They have a way of wandering back into the night. The tension between the urge to wander, whether physically or emotionally, and the need for home was something Bishop and Lowell understood intuitively about each other. Like being mad and alcoholic, being waifs and strays put them on the same wavelength. It was their version of Hawthorne and Melville's fire worship.

●

"I am extremely happy, for the first time in my life," Bishop wrote to Lowell two years into her residence in Brazil. "I arrived to visit Lota just at the point where she really wanted someone to stay with her in the new house she was building. . . ."[3]

It was also just at the point of utter desperation in her own life. Bishop had slipped even deeper into alcoholism and depression after Lowell's marriage. Professionally, she had let herself be swept along in his wake, taking up residence in Yaddo and, in 1949, accepting the post of Consultant in Poetry to the Library of Congress (Lowell had helped engineer the appointment and convinced her to take it). Both endeavors failed her. Unlike Lowell, who had reveled in the prestige of the consultantship, Bishop hated the requisite public appearances, detested Washington, and resented the interruptions to her work. In her diary, with characteristic precision, she labeled the year 1950 "just about my worst, so far."[4] The "so far" glances, terrified, at the future. "After that dismal year in Washington and that dismaler winter at Yaddo . . . I thought my days were numbered and there was nothing to be done about it," she later confessed to Lowell from the safety of her new life in Brazil.[5] Like Melville beweeping his outcast fate to Hawthorne in 1856, Bishop had "pretty much made up [her] mind to be annihilated."

The story of Bishop's "rescue" by Lota and Brazil has by now been told several times, most notably by David Kalstone and Lorrie Goldensohn. The haphazard embarkation on the S.S. *Bowplate* bound for the Strait of Magellan, the intended brief layover in Rio, the severe allergic reaction to the fruit of the cashew, the incredible good fortune of finding Lota again (the two had met years before in New York), Lota's nursing her back to health, the falling in love, and the decision to remain in Brazil and move into Lota's new house—all of these events have become part of the mythology of modern literature. There is no need to repeat the full story here. It's enough to say that stumbling upon Brazil was the best thing that ever happened to Bishop. Though her first brush with the country nearly killed her, ultimately Brazil and Lota together really did save her life.

Lota—Maria Carlota Costellat de Macedo Soares to give her full name—was a formidable and fortunate person for Bishop to have fallen in with. Born into an old and distinguished Rio family (a family as finely pedigreed and culturally prominent as the Lowells), Lota was a funny blend of aristocrat and bulldog, a "rather unbalancing combination of the proper and the misfit," as Elizabeth Hardwick put it. "Masterful in some ways, but helpless too."[6] With her glasses, her short-cropped dark hair, her mannish clothing, and her piercing, almost combative gaze, she looked like a scrappy Latin intellectual. Lota had never been to university, but she had the passionate instinctive enthusiasms of the self-taught, and she knew just about everyone who "mattered" in Brazilian arts, politics, and society (her father, from whom she had been estranged for some time, owned the *Diario Carioca,* one of the leading newspapers in Rio).

"Warm and lively, brimming with tempestuous energy, Lota believed that in Brazil she could provide Elizabeth with the stable tranquility and domestic peace she needed for her work and well-being," writes Pearl Bell in her memoir of Bishop in Brazil. "They became lovers, even if Lota more often acted the mother to Elizabeth the child."[7] Lota immediately took charge of Elizabeth's health, her drinking, her social life, her work habits—and Elizabeth at age forty-two surrendered happily to the mothering she had scarcely known in childhood. "I still feel I must have died and gone to heaven without deserving to," she wrote to Dr. Baumann, "but I am getting a little more used to it."[8] Hawthorne also used the language of paradise to describe the bliss of being happily married after thirty-eight years of lonely bachelorhood.

The greatest gift Lota gave her lover was a home. Actually two homes. When Bishop came to Brazil, Lota had a small apartment in Rio on the Copacabana beach; but Bishop infinitely preferred the new country house Lota was building near the upper-class resort town of Petrópolis, the former summer residence of Brazil's emperors, outside of Rio. In an early letter to Lowell, Bishop breezily described the place as "an ultra-modern house up on the side of a black granite mountain, with a waterfall at one end, clouds coming into the living room . . . etc." The "etc." belies the depth of love Bishop felt for Sitio da Alcobaçinha, as the house on the Samambaia property was called. She loved most of all the separate studio Lota built for her "away up in the air behind the house, overlooking the waterfall," as she wrote Baumann,[9] where she could work in roaring (or trickling, depending on the season) peace.

The short walk to the studio took her past a bricked terrace set with potted palms, along garden paths lined with flowers, and up the hillside to a perch that afforded a huge view of the lush extravagant mountains that "look like the hulls of capsized ships, slime-hung and barnacled," as she described them in "Questions of Travel." While working, Bishop turned her back on the big view (she had asked the architect to place no window on that side), and faced instead a more intimate patch of bamboo near at hand. For company she hung up photographs of Lowell, Marianne Moore, and Baudelaire. "I am so overcome I dream about it every night," she wrote to Pearl Bell of her studio. "I'm sure I'll just sit in it weeping with joy for weeks and not write a line."[10] But in fact, she got a tremendous amount of work done there over the next fifteen years. It was the longest stretch she ever spent at the same address.

At the end of nearly two years in Brazil, Bishop reported to Lowell that she had stopped drinking "almost entirely" and that she had lost twenty pounds.[11] "It is a little hard to get used to being happy after forty-two years . . . of being almost consistently unhappy," she said in amazed contentment to Pearl Bell.[12] And to Dr. Baumann, she reported her delighted surrender to disorientation in the Southern Hemisphere: "My Anglo-Saxon blood is gradually relinquishing its seasonal cycle and I'm quite content to live in complete confusion, about seasons, fruits, languages, geography, everything."[13]

One consequence of her unaccustomed happiness was that for the first time she allowed herself to draw directly on memories of her childhood. In 1953, two years into her Brazilian exile, she wrote both "In the Village" and "Gwendolyn," another story set in the Nova Scotia of her youth. During the same period she was engaged in the long and difficult task of translating *Minha Vida de Menina* ("My Life as a Young Girl"), the actual diary of a young girl growing up in the remote Brazilian mining town of Diamantina in the 1890s. Bishop's translation—*The Diary of "Helena Morley"* (the pseudonym of Alice Brant)—appeared in 1957. In her introduction, Bishop notes that "the scenes and events [the diary] described were odd, remote, and long ago, and yet fresh, sad, funny, and eternally true"[14]—and the same could be said of the scenes and events of Bishop's own early years.

Childhood, which Howard Moss called "a sacred period in [Bishop's] life,"[15] was very fresh in her imagination during her first years in Brazil. In a strange way, Brazil gave her back the beauty, the innocence, and the comforting village life of her "odd, remote, and long ago" childhood in Nova Scotia. At Samambaia, as at Great Village, she was surrounded by trees and flowers, animals and children, and she was once again part of a large family, even if it was now a rather unconventional family. Long afterward she wrote Lowell that in Brazil she was fashioning a "sort of deluxe Nova Scotia," but now she was her own grand-mother.[16] Immersing herself in the "fresh as paint" world of Alice Brant's childhood, Bishop finally felt safe, secure, and happy enough to write about her own.

In the Nova Scotia poems and stories she wrote in her waterfall studio during the 1950s, Bishop shows an extraordinary gift for capturing not only *what* a child perceives but also *how*. Her child narrators and protagonists are not sheltered from pain and loss and mystery, but from their causes and the connections among them. Things happen *to* these children, but they don't know why or what they mean or what will happen next. They simply take everything in and wait for the next thing to happen. When the pain becomes unbearable, they blot it out by taking in something, *anything*, else. As Lloyd Schwartz notes, Bishop's sub-ject in the childhood stories is "the mysterious intimacy children have with the physical world, their peculiar acceptance of the suffering that surrounds them, their capacity to be 'fearfully ob-servant.' "[17]

At the heart of all of these stories and poems is the paradox of home: Home is both shelter from unbearable pain and the place where that pain originates. In "In the Village," as we've seen, the mother's cry of madness pierces the drapery and embroidery of the domestic scene. The narrator of "Gwendolyn" (who shares Bishop's background and family situation) recounts how as a child she play-acted the funeral of a little friend who died of diabetes. In laying out a precious doll for burial, the narrator domesticates the mystery of death just as she and her grandfather domesticate the family plots in the village graveyard—"one of the prettiest in the world"—by scything the grass and picking teaberries from among the headstones. In the poem "First Death in Nova Scotia" the corpse of the narrator's little cousin lies chilling in the parlor. The fact that death is part of the home decor makes it more familiar but no less baffling and no less terrifying.

In "The Moose," written some years later, Bishop describes how she lulled herself on a long bus ride with the memories of the nighttime voices of her grandparents murmuring of: "deaths, deaths and sickness . . ./She died in childbirth . . ./He took to drink. Yes./She went to the bad./When Amos began to pray/even in the store and/finally the family had/to put him away." These were the conversations weaving through the rooms of her childhood—hardly the topics to reassure a child. When the moose looms suddenly in the night, Bishop calls it "safe as houses," but as Frank Bidart points out, how safe *are* houses in Bishop's memories? These strange, cherished, mysterious houses in which a cousin's coffin sits displayed in the parlor like "a little frosted cake," in which a mother briefly returns to fret and scream and then vanishes forever, houses in which grandparents murmur through the night of deaths, madness, and alcoholism, in which the absence of parents is never commented on, in which the grandmother rocks and moans to herself "Nobody knows ... *nobody knows* ..."

In the "Sestina" she published in 1956, Bishop conjures up a scene of rustic domestic harmony—the snug country kitchen, the wise old grandmother, the old-fashioned almanac, the cozy Marvel Stove—and then quietly, delicately, rips holes through it. The old grandmother sits in the kitchen "laughing and talking to hide her tears"; the Marvel Stove pronounces cryptically, *"It was to be";* the almanac weeps little moons; and the parentless child, baffled by the unmentionable griefs and deprivations of her life, draws "another inscrutable house." Bishop desperately wants to remember her childhood house as a safe refuge, but she is forced to admit that the shelter also encloses madness and death, fear and misery. The real brilliance of the Nova Scotia stories and poems is that they catch the child in the act of discovering that her house is inscrutable—mysterious, perishable, unyielding to her perplexity.

Eudora Welty came to the same realization of the flimsiness of houses against tragedy when her father suddenly died just a few years after building a grand new Tudor house for his family; the death both catalyzed her writing career and sealed her fate as the daughter who would remain at home to care for her mother. In her work, Welty uses houses alternately as metaphors for tradition and imprisonment, just as Edith Wharton had done two generations earlier and Nathaniel Hawthorne had done before her. Wharton once compared a woman's mind to the rooms of a house, and in her story "Madame de Treymes" she wrote of the "almost human consciousness" of an old aristocratic hotel in Paris: Her houses are the repositories of memory, family secrets, beautiful objects, and tormenting emotions while Hawthorne's houses enshroud ancient crimes and locked chambers black with sin. "We may build almost immortal habitations, it is true," Hawthorne writes in *The Marble Faun,* "but we cannot keep them from growing old, musty, unwholesome, dreary, full of death scents, ghosts, and murder stains."[18] For Hawthorne, Wharton, and Welty, as for Bishop, the phrase "safe as houses" was fraught with irony.

The house is a central image not only in the Nova Scotia pieces, but also in the poems Bishop was writing during the same period about Brazil. If anything, her Brazilian houses are even more inscrutable than her childhood house in Great Village. As Helen Vendler points out, in Bishop's work there is a "continuing vibration . . . between two frequencies—the domestic and the strange . . . the strange can occur even in the bosom of the familiar, even, most unnervingly, at the domestic hearth. . . . The fact that one's house always *is* inscrutable, that nothing is more enigmatic than the heart of the domestic scene, offers Bishop one of her recurrent subjects."[19]

In the Brazilian sequence of the volume *Questions of Travel,* this vibration reaches its highest pitch. The eleven Brazilian poems were written over the course of a decade, but when Bishop gathered them into a book, she arranged them not chronologically but thematically to form a kind of breaking wave of restlessness and desperation. In the course of the sequence, she (or her persona) sails into Santos harbor, penetrates the Brazilian "interior," rejoices at finding a "cherished" house, imagines its destruction by time, fire, and water, jumps through the window naked, fantasizes a new magical dwelling at the bottom of the Amazon, and finally ends up identifying with the millions of displaced shanty dwellers who "come to Rio/And can't go home again." As she moves from poem to poem Bishop transforms herself (or her protagonist) from a demanding unsatisfied tourist to an ambivalent but addicted traveler, to a peevish landowner, to a wistful lover, to an Amazon witch doctor, to a criminal. The series begins and ends with the lone figure homeless and adrift at the ocean's edge.

The question Bishop asks at the close of the poem "Questions of Travel"—*"Should we have stayed at home,/wherever that may be?"*—reverberates through all eleven poems in the sequence. The answer she arrives at in various forms is that even if we *should* have stayed at home, we *cannot,* because home, wherever that may be, keeps dissolving around us. Our homes, like the shanties that the millions of Rio poor build "out of nothing at all, or air," are illusions. Not only *can't* we move in permanently; ultimately, we really don't *want* to. As the poet Mark Strand puts it, "There's always the possibility of [Bishop's] finding a place for herself, travels will end and she will settle down. But that of course is illusory. If our whole identity is predicated on movement, home is best as an ideal."[20]

Perhaps Bishop's clearest distillation of this idea is the poem "Song for the Rainy Season." This poem, which she explicitly situates at Sitio da Alcobaçinha, Fazenda Samambaia, Petrópolis, is the point of stasis in the Brazil sequence, the still moment when the forces that bind her to Lota's house and pry her out of it embrace in perfect equilibrium.

> Hidden, oh hidden
> in the high fog
> the house we live in,
> beneath the magnetic rock,
> rain-, rainbow-ridden,
> where blood-black
> bromelias, lichens,
> owls, and the lint
> of the waterfalls cling,
> familiar, unbidden.

All the water that flows through the volume—the "too many waterfalls" of "Questions of Travel," the thunderstorm that soaks the "specklike girl and boy" in "Squatter's Children," the wisps of fog that twine around Manuelzinho, the pelting drops of "Electrical Storm"—gathers around this "rain-, rainbow-ridden" house. Water sings, roars, envelops, hides, softens, and nourishes, surrounding and invading the house, pressing it into the fecund life of giant fern and fat frogs "shrilling for love." But the water that holds the house lovingly "in a private cloud" also works secretly to destroy it: Mildew draws its "ignorant map" on the wall; moths, silverfish, bookworms, and mice creep in with the damp; even the warm moist breath of its human residents leaves the house "darkened and tarnished." The house's very openness to the elements exposes it to ruin; its fleeting beauty is inscribed with its decay; love itself stains. Rejoice now, Bishop commands herself and the house, "For a later/era will differ./(O difference that kills,/or intimidates, much/of all our small shadowy/life!)" (Lowell echoed this idea in *For Lizzie and Harriet,* when he wrote of his unraveling marriage to Hardwick: "If we have loved, it's not returnable;/this room will dim and die as we dim and die,/its many secrets change to others' things."[21])

Bishop ends "Song for the Rainy Season" in mournful recognition that the rainy season must one day end and the "waterfalls shrivel/in the steady sun." Like the dried up waterfalls, the house—and its loving residents—will succumb in time to the "difference that kills." To quote Vendler once more, "Domestication is followed, almost inevitably, by that dismantling which is, in its acute form, disaster. . . ."[22] "Song for the Rainy Season" is Bishop's eerie shiver of premonition of the dismantling of her life with Lota at Samambaia. Though she did not yet know what form the end would take, she was dead certain, even as she rejoiced, of its arrival. Such dismantlings, such vanishings were, she knew, a condition of her life.

A couple of years into her Brazilian residence, Bishop wrote to Pearl Bell about her plans for a series of prose pieces on Brazil, admonishing herself to forge ahead quickly, "before I know too much and would feel I had to get 'serious,' also before things have stopped striking me as strange, which they're already beginning to do."[23] Strangeness and "unseriousness" were requirements of Bishop's life and work. Without them she shriveled, like the waterfalls under the steady sun. Familiarity was perhaps the "difference that kills" most surely of all.

"I get just as excited now over a jeep trip to buy kerosene in the next village as I did in November at the thought of my trip around the Horn," Bishop wrote Lowell in her first flush of enthusiasm for her new life with Lota. But later, when the excitement of strangeness wore off, she began to grow restless for more exotic journeys, especially trips into the primitive regions up the Amazon. Her passion to keep moving ran very deep, as deep as the displacements of her childhood. To the extent that she pictured herself as at home anywhere, it was always in a far flimsier arrangement than Samambaia—a seaside shack, a "fairy palace," like "Jeronimo's House" in her first volume, "of chewed-up paper/glued with spit . . ./my shelter from/the hurricane." Or, in other moods, she saw her true home as utter solitude. As she wrote Lowell in 1960, "I've always had a day dream of being a light-house keeper, absolutely alone, with no one to interrupt my reading or just sitting."[24] Much as she adored Lota and the life they shared in Petrópolis, Bishop came to feel hemmed in by their "private cloud," especially in the mid-1960s when Lota turned pathologically suspicious and controlling. Already, in the Brazil sequence of *Questions of Travels,* Bishop was imagining her escape. When the time came, she would follow the riverman through the window naked and travel "fast as a wish." And then, bereft but unencumbered, she would be free to draw another inscrutable house.

"We seem attached to each other by some stiff piece of wire, so that each time one moves, the other moves in another direction," Lowell wrote to Bishop in 1954.[25] "We should call a halt to that." It's true that the friends usually had a continent or an ocean between them. Lowell and Hardwick had sailed for Europe a year before Bishop embarked for Brazil (both husband and wife earnestly, improbably, invited Bishop to join them), and they spent about three years abroad, living first in Italy (where they visited Bernard Berenson in his villa, I Tatti, outside Florence, as Berenson's friends Henry James and Edith Wharton had done half a century earlier), then traveling rather frantically around the Mediterranean countries, and after that settling down for a long, rather dull and unproductive stretch in Amsterdam. When they returned to the States, Lowell took up a teaching position at the University of Iowa Writers' Workshop, where he had taught for a term before leaving for Europe. The following year his mother died, and Lowell, as if emerging from some spell of enchantment, promptly returned "home" to roost in Boston—the city of his birth that he had left in 1937 after quarreling violently with his parents over his engagement to a girl named Anne Dick.

A friend described the move as "their first attempt to be the Boston Lowells."[26] After shuttling for a few months between a large house in the suburb of Duxbury and an apartment on Commonwealth Avenue in Boston, Lowell and Hardwick bought a nineteenth-century town house at 239 Marlborough Street in Back Bay, a block from where he had grown up. He proudly described the house to Bishop as "rather Parisian . . . [with] white, neat, dainty Italian fireplaces, a lovely foyer, a sort of stream-lined Victorian."[27] Hardwick, in her memoir/novel *Sleepless Nights* recounted how she and Lowell set up like grandees, furnishing the house with old china and silver, Italian mirrors, fine rugs and curtains, antiques—rather like Edith Wharton (his social peer) decorating one of her beloved mansions. Flush with inherited funds, the new Lowells of Boston were determined to establish their claim on the family title.

"We are very pretentious and sociable, sort of Poobahs," Lowell gently mocked himself in a letter to Bishop. Yet the Boston splendor was not an act. In a funny way, Lowell's habits and passions were far more typical of his class and background than he cared to admit: the town house in Boston, the country house in Maine, the distinguished relatives, the trust fund, the sail boats and tennis matches, the gin-soaked evenings, the extramarital affairs, the penitential confessions. It's surprising how often the same conventional elements crop up in his poetry.

For all the edgy violence and howling Melvillean blackness of his verse, the situations Lowell wrote about were not very different from those of John Cheever or John Updike (or Edith Wharton, for that matter)—adultery, divorce, the bitterness between parents and children, Puritan guilt, the mutual strangulation of sexual and religious impulses, the alienation of the male from the family he loves and supports, the strangeness of leading a passionate life in a consumer culture. As Bishop put it, he made "family, paternity, marriage, painfully acute and real."[28]

Once one has cleared one's eyes of the smoke of Lowell's pyrotechnics—the Catholic contortions of *Lord Weary's Castle*, the existential gloom of prison cells and mental wards, the apocalyptic threat of nuclear holocaust—one sees the truth of this comment. The home, the family was the main arena of Lowell's imagination. As Hardwick wrote, "Marriage. We would often argue over *interpretation,* so fruitful of conjecture is the text of the family."[29] Lowell always took the fact of home far more for granted than Bishop. It was the *given,* the place where the argument began and ended. Bishop, on the other hand, though she cherished domesticity, never ceased to be amazed by it.

Of course, Lowell was hardly the model of the family man. In madness, he again and again ripped the "text of the family" to shreds, denouncing his marriage, physically threatening his wife and child, pouncing on some new woman as his ticket to freedom and true love. Yet even when sane and gentle, Lowell frequently gasped for air. He desperately needed contacts outside of marriage—friends, lovers, students, work, new ideas, new passions, and eventually a new wife and new family. New places mattered to him far less.

Perhaps because his eyesight was so poor, Lowell lived much more inside his own mind than Bishop did: He scarcely noticed his surroundings or cared very much where he was so long as he was someplace where he could work and talk. "Change I earth or sky I am the same," he writes in *The Dolphin*,[30] echoing Horace. As Helen Vendler remarks, "Everything he knew was from reading and talking. He lacked Elizabeth's sensual perceptiveness."[31] Bishop found Lowell and Hardwick well matched in this regard. "They aren't interested in things or places much," she confided wearily to a friend after entertaining them for several weeks in Brazil in 1962, "just people and books. . . ."[32]

The tension between wanting to take shelter and to flee it (Melville's vacillation between land dreams and sea dreams) figures in Lowell's work, as it does in Bishop's, but, as one might expect, his approach differs radically from hers. Lowell shoves his ambivalence toward home and family right onto center stage. From the late 1950s on, Lowell drew house after inscrutable house at a furious clip. Never content to let the houses stand intact, he tore open the curtains on the intimate action within.

Lowell ranks with Tolstoy in the intensity with which he scrutinized his marriages and the ruthlessness with which he exposed them to the public. Like Tolstoy, Lowell entered into marriage with impossibly high ideals and a huge appetite for disappointment. As he wrote toward the end of his married life with Hardwick, "when we joined in the sublime blindness of courtship,/ loving lost all its vice with half its virtue."[33] Lowell took the marriage vows as a license to be as frank and unsparing about his wife as he always had been about himself. Hardwick occasionally floats into his verse as a celestial being "clearest of all God's creatures, still all air and nerve"; but mostly she takes a far heavier—and louder—shape, as a prickly hedgehog, a monster, a sharp-tongued harpy, a turtle, a tortoise, and finally as the exhausted, ranting, middle-aged woman forsaken for the beautiful new bride "all muscle, youth, intention." Combat and warfare are Lowell's dominant images for marriage. In the poem "Man and Wife" home is a powder keg about to explode. Husband and wife are wild animals, drugged, caged, and panting in the hot morning light. Their joint property—"our magnolia"—is a joke, since it lasts but five murderous days. Married love is a suspicious truce, a grudging dole of consolation that will dry up when the partners run out of patience. By the poem's end, the wife has turned her back on the man. In a funny way, "Man and Wife" harks back to the vicious marital contest that Melville describes in "I and My Chimney," only Lowell, characteristically, burns Melville's whimsy to ash.

It was Lowell's willingness to "hit bottom" in describing his marriage that makes reading the poems in *Life Studies* and *For the Union Dead* feel like having one's face slapped. Thirty years later, his recklessness, his shamelessness still stun. Family and privacy meant nothing to Lowell next to his urge to "lay bare." Despite his Brahmin blood, his inherited wealth, his plush conventional abodes, he always had one foot dangling in the void. Anyone who can describe himself and his wife as "two walking cobwebs" is clearly operating at a level of alienation well beyond the niceties of "hardly passionate Marlborough Street."

In their way, Lowell's *Life Studies* and *For the Union Dead* were as piercing declarations of American anguish as Allen Ginsberg's "Howl," which was published around the same time. Set Ginsberg's opening incantation—"I saw the best minds of my generation destroyed by madness, starving hysterical naked"—beside Lowell's cutting ironic query: "These are the tranquillized *Fifties,/* and I am forty. Ought I to regret my seedtime?" For all their differences in manners and breeding, Lowell and Ginsberg were kin in writing about the psychic damage our society inflicts on its "best minds." (Ginsberg and a few fellow beats once came to call on Lowell at Marlborough Street; Lowell wrote Bishop a report of the visit, rolling his eyes over the bizarre juxtaposition of angel-headed hipsters and dainty family heirlooms—and yet he and Ginsberg respected each other and carried on a wary correspondence of their own.)

Poetically, Lowell managed to be simultaneously heir and outcast—perhaps most desperately outcast when the trappings of inheritance massed around him most luxuriously, as in "Memories of West Street and Lepke." It was typical of Lowell that "hogging" a whole house in a posh neighborhood should summon up memories of his imprisonment during the war for being a "fire-breathing Catholic C.O." The forty-year-old poet, in shaky remission from psychosis, feels as out of place in Boston's Back Bay "where even the man/scavenging filth in the back alley trash cans,/has two children, a beach wagon, a helpmate,/and is a 'young Republican' " as the twenty-six-year-old Catholic C.O. felt among the odd assortment of pimps, hoods, and pacifists in the West Street jail. "When I look back," he wrote in "The Withdrawal" in his final volume, *Day by Day,* "I see a collapsing/accordion of my receding houses." Lowell would always be a ghost haunting his own life.

•

Bishop and Lowell intuitively understood each other's ambivalence toward domesticity and dispossession. One can feel them vibrating along the same wavelength in "The Armadillo" and "Skunk Hour," the poems of theirs that are most commonly linked and that they dedicated to each other. For Lowell the existential dilemma at the end of "Skunk Hour" is whether or not to enter the house; the dilemma for Bishop in "The Armadillo" is whether or not the house will still be there. For both poets, the house implies the existence of a spouse or family: Lowell in "Skunk Hour" returns to stand on "our back steps" and Bishop writes in "The Armadillo" that "we saw" the owls flee the fire and notes "our surprise" at the baby rabbit's short ears. Yet these shadowy partners are powerless to allay the narrator's solitary panic. Bishop breaks off from the "we" at the poem's end to cry out alone over the "falling fire" that threatens the house. Lowell, with the fires of hell burning within, stalls before the prospect of rejoining his family. "Skunk Hour" and "The Armadillo" both take place at night. For waifs and strays, night is the only real home.

Eudora Welty, in Harold Bloom's view, "emerges" from *Huckleberry Finn:* Her "obsessive American concern is Huck's: the freedom of a solitary joy, intimately allied to a superstitious fear of solitude." Elizabeth Bishop also "emerges" from these deep swift-flowing waters. Like Huck and Welty, Bishop loved rivers, loved to drift with the current, observing life along the riverbanks, imagining what it would be like to lead one of those lives, occasionally pulling up to try it. "That golden evening I really wanted to go no farther," she writes of a Brazilian river journey in "Santarém," one of the last poems she published; "more than anything else I wanted to stay awhile/in that conflux of two great rivers, Tapajós, Amazon,/grandly, silently flowing, flowing east." But of course she doesn't stay, even "awhile." Like Huck, she had been launched into the world at a tender age, a victim of a failed home, and she never really ceased her flight and her pursuit.

Bishop is even closer kin to Huck than to Welty in her childlike temperament—in her choice of children or childish grown-ups as narrators or protagonists; in her literal mindedness; in what Lloyd Schwartz calls the "fairy-tale vividness and coloring-book clarity" of her images;[34] in her greed to see new places and her illusion that they would really seem new; in her unquenchable awe and her instinctive passivity. Bishop is constantly eavesdropping on adult arrangements that she is powerless to fully comprehend or to change. Events befall her in her poems and stories—fires burn; mother returns home, screams, and vanishes for good; friends die; houses are given and taken away; new continents, cities, countries, societies revolve before her eyes. Like her sandpiper in the poem of that name who sees the immediate with stunning acuity ("no detail too small") but who "couldn't tell you" whether the tide is higher or lower, Bishop remains ignorant—deliberately—of the "big picture": the mysterious motives and worries of the grown-ups; the question of who owns the house; the irksome practical matter of how to manage.

Mary McCarthy put her finger on something very basic to Bishop's nature when she wrote in *The New York Times Book Review*: "I envy the mind hiding in her words, like an 'I' counting up to a hundred waiting to be found. . . . I would like to have had her quiddity, her way of seeing that was like a big pocket magnifying glass. *Of course* it would have hurt to have to use it for ordinary looking: that would have been the forfeit."[35] Bishop had a child's genius for the best hiding places. Her trouble was that when night fell and the game ended and the other children went home, she couldn't stop playing.

If Bishop is a child, then Lowell is an eternal adolescent, an unruly spiritual descendant of Melville, forever demanding retribution from a universe whose cruelty never ceases to amaze him. The plight of the adolescent is to remain stuck at home against his will: He has the power to light out on his own but he can't quite bring himself to do it yet. Much as he hates to admit it, he still needs his parents. The war between dependence and breaking loose was endlessly frustrating, infuriating, fascinating to Lowell. "No end to the adolescence we attained/by overworking," he writes in *The Dolphin* sonnet "Death and the Maiden," "then struggled to release—."

In "The Withdrawal" he recalls his first flush of manhood spent "moving from house to house,/still seeking a boy's license/to see the countryside without arrival." Arrival means growing up, taking charge of one fixed house, surrendering his "license" to roam. And in "During Fever": "Mother, Mother!/as a gemlike undergraduate,/part criminal and yet a Phi Bete,/I used to barge home late. . . . " As a husband and father twenty years later, he was still barging home late, still confronting and resenting and colluding with the female guardian of the hearth. "Terrible that old life of decency," he writes of his parents' Edwardian courtship in "During Fever." Terrible *any* life of decency as far as Lowell was concerned. Most terrible of all, however, was his terrible need for it. Inside him, there was never any peace between the criminal and the Phi Bete.

In Lowell's mind, one of the great beauties of his friendship with Bishop was that it was exempt from this terrible life of decency. She lived for his imagination not by the hearth but outside, in the night. Bishop stood with Lowell on the back steps in Castine on the night the skunks crept out to swill the garbage pail. Her presence transfigured the experience. "We've talked over a lot of things together I've never mentioned to Elizabeth [Hardwick]," he wrote to Bishop in Brazil three months later, when the creative explosion of "Skunk Hour" and the other *Life Studies* poems was over and another serious psychotic episode was closing in on him. "If you ever feel like writing me privately (I don't mean anything by this) you can address the letter c/o the Dept. of English, Boston University."[36] "I don't mean anything by this," he insisted—but, in fact, given his life, his marriage, and the depth of his reverence for Bishop, he meant everything.

TWENTY-ONE

Pity the Planet:
1960s Politics

> We live in the fire and burn-outness of some political
> or religious movement.
>
> —ROBERT LOWELL *letter to Elizabeth Bishop,*
> *March 10, 1963*

> Modern revolutions, I've learned, are funny—every-
> thing goes but the telephone, because it's automatic
> —so everyone sits in the dark, unwashed, etc. and
> telephones their friends all day and all night.
>
> —ELIZABETH BISHOP *to Robert Lowell,*
> *April 4, 1964*

BISHOP AND LOWELL had a history of charged encounters, but his visit with her in Brazil in the summer of 1962 was their worst. The whole debacle might have been scripted by Graham Greene: There was political intrigue, too much alcohol, thwarted lust, bumbling petty officials, vitriolic Latino generals, red tape, and insanity—all played out against a damp, brooding, tropical backdrop. The friends, and the friendship, survived, but it was not an experience either of them cared to repeat. After 1962, they limited themselves to brief visits at long intervals. The Brazilian fiasco marked the beginning of a divergence for Lowell and Bishop. Their correspondence continued with unabated intensity, but over the next decade, their lives and their work grew further and further apart until, in 1973, they came perilously close to a split.

Lowell had hatched the idea of going to Brazil back in 1957, during Bishop and Lota's trip to the States. After the blow-up in Castine that summer, Bishop, foreseeing a repeat performance, very gently tried to scotch the plan, but Lowell was determined and eventually he prevailed. What really clinched the trip was that Lowell, through his connections in the Kennedy administration, had gotten himself appointed to the Congress for Cultural Freedom, and so his expenses would be paid (Lowell claimed to be shocked and outraged when he learned that the money actually came from the CIA, which was funding the Congress for Cultural Freedom).[1] His official duties were rather vague: He was supposed to deliver some poetry readings, hold press conferences, mingle with South American intellectuals and writers, and generally make a good impression on behalf of the United States and American literature.

United States government money flowed freely in those days, and Lowell arranged to take along Hardwick and Harriet, then five, and Harriet's nanny. The party flew to Brazil in early June and traveled south down the coast by way of Recife and Bahia before establishing themselves at Rio's Copacabana Palace Hotel, near Lota's Leme beachfront apartment. The Congress for Cultural Freedom assigned Lowell an official escort named Keith Botsford, "an old Iowa acquaintance of mine," as Lowell wrote Bishop, "and now in charge of the Freedom Congress things in Rio. . . . He's quite attractive in a slightly too sharp and shiny way."[2] Botsford, as it turned out, was to play a kind of Rozencrantz–Guildenstern role to Lowell's Hamlet in the ensuing drama.

The Lowells stayed in Rio for more than a month, and while Bishop was racking her brains for what to do next with her party of intellectuals, Lowell began to unravel. He was drinking heavily, arguing a lot, pursuing an attractive younger woman, spinning wild political theories, insulting anyone who came into range—all the familiar signs of a manic attack. Bishop kept a kind of shorthand log of Lowell's descent into madness, which she later sent on to Hardwick. The document, preserved with her papers, makes for harrowing reading:

> Aug. 20th—E [Hardwick] went to Brasilia for the day; C [Cal] to dinner. Pretty hysterical.

Aug. 21st . . . C pretty hysterical and drinking . . .
Aug. 23 Roberto's party—for the L's, I think but am not sure.
E didn't go. C drinking wine.

And so it went for several more frantic days. While Lowell
is out dining with Clarice (the intended amour of this breakdown),
Hardwick spends the evening with Bishop and Lota talking for
two hours about Lowell's last attack. On August 25, Bishop notes
that Lowell is becoming "more hysterical every day." By August
29, she concludes that he is "absolutely off his rocker." On the
31st, they all go to dinner and there is a "general fight"—"all
exhausted—I *cried* for 1st time." On September 1, Hardwick and
Harriet sail for New York, according to their original plan, leaving
Lowell in the care of Botsford. (Hardwick, as Bishop notes,
"MUST have known [Cal's] state when she left," so why did she
ditch him in Rio? It's possible she was just too exhausted or too
angry to pick up the pieces yet again.)

The day after Hardwick left, Bishop takes to her bed, probably to sleep off the effects of a binge (she doesn't mention her own
drinking in the log, but Hardwick recalls that Bishop got very
drunk toward the end of her stay). Bishop tries to persuade Lowell
to fly back to New York, but she makes "no impression on him."
On September 3, there is another awful dinner out. "Obviously off
his rocker—that awful laugh," Bishop writes. "Interrupting constantly; comparing his father to Eisenhower, etc.—etc—wild political ideas."

Bishop breaks off the log here to consider her own role in
the situation:

> I begged him not to come here until the P M each day—but he
> came and stayed, in the A M, many times—said it was 'sooth-
> ing,' like his doctor, only 'That's *all* about *me*. .' etc.—(as if I
> had intruded my own personality too much.) Endless protes-
> tations of love and eternal friendship, etc. . . . I felt he knew he
> was getting sick but didn't want to stop the process, some-
> how—Absolutely wouldn't listen to me and began being rude
> to me, finally—saying I was "*wrong*" not to like all the same
> things he likes, etc. Yet I felt he was depending on me, just the
> way he said he was, and rarely had the heart to send him
> away.[3]

This was exactly what had started to happen in Castine five years before—the "endless protestations of love," the awful mixture of dependence and abuse, the belligerent insistence that she adopt his tastes and opinions. Lowell had been able to avert a crisis in Castine because Bishop left and Hardwick dragged him down to earth. But this time, stuck in an alien environment and without his family, Lowell went all the way.

Bishop, as it turned out, was not present for the denouement. On Tuesday, September 3 or 4, Lowell and Botsford left for Buenos Aires, again according to the original itinerary, and it was there Lowell went completely off the deep end. Botsford reported that upon arrival Lowell drank six double vodka martinis and then went to lunch at the presidential palace, where he insulted an important general, told the American cultural attaché that he was illiterate, and then took off on a tour of the city, disrobing and mounting equestrian statues. Lowell insisted that Botsford, who was not a drinking man, keep up with his own alcohol intake, and he accused him of being homosexual. Lowell had thrown away all his pills, and he started spending money "like water," as Bishop put it, buying expensive presents for everyone in sight, though of course it was all CIA money (Botsford kept cabling for more). After a couple of days of this, Botsford got fed up and returned to Rio, leaving Lowell by himself in Buenos Aires.

Bishop hit the roof when she discovered what had happened: "I asked him what the HELL he thought he was doing," she wrote Hardwick; "didn't he know Cal's history? (he did); WHY hadn't he called me before; WHAT was he doing in Rio, anyway, and WHY had he left Cal alone and sick in B.A.?" Terribly worried that Lowell would get beaten up or thrown in jail, Bishop ordered Botsford to return and rescue Lowell.[4] (She later wrote sheepishly to Lowell that she had "toyed" with going down herself "but I didn't think I'd be of much help, somehow . . . and members of my sex are particularly at a disadvantage in emergencies here . . ."[5]) Finally, a group of men helped Botsford overpower Lowell, get him into a straitjacket, and take him to the Clinica Bethlehem, where he was kept tied down with leather straps and given Thorazine. Bishop wrote him a rather strained get-well-soon note from Rio: "I hope the Clinica is comfortable and the doctor nice, etc."[6] (In the same letter she commented, mostly positively, on the just-published *Ship of Fools,* which Lowell, who loved the book, had brought down for her.) Lowell spent several weeks in the clinic under heavy sedation before his old friend Blair Clark came to accompany him back to New York. Hardwick committed him to a psychiatric hospital in Hartford, Connecticut, and he remained there until November.[7]

The whole South American disaster reveals a great deal both about their friendship and about the state of each of their lives at that moment in time. Bishop, who had previously been spared a full-fledged manic attack, was clearly horrified at witnessing Lowell go "off his rocker." She didn't have "the heart" to send him away when he was plaguing her in Rio, but she didn't have the nerve to bail him out when he cracked up in Buenos Aires. She just couldn't—or wouldn't—handle it.

Lowell, whatever his other failings, was not the type to blame Bishop. In fact, he was acutely embarrassed afterward that he had exposed her to his mania. "I guess I was beginning to go off during the last two weeks in Brazil," he wrote her in December, after his release from the Hartford hospital, "and this must have been painful for you to watch or at least sense. When I got to Buenos Aires, my state zoomed sky-high and I am glad you didn't see it. It's hard for the controlled man to look back on the moment of chaos and calm. I shan't try, but it was all me, and I am sorry you were touched by it."[8]

By the following summer, Lowell was able to reminisce fondly about the visit: "I kept thinking of you and Rio, and realize that there were never better moments."[9] He mentioned their day on the beach on several other occasions as a high point of their friendship. Lowell continued, all his life, to idolize Bishop. But the South American episode marked the last gasp of the romantic fantasies he had been nursing since their day in Stonington in 1948. Never again, sane or mad, would he pursue her with his "endless protestations of love." "The other life that might have been" was laid to rest in Rio.[10]

The South American trip was increasingly typical of Lowell's life during the 1960s: The frantic pace, the long evenings out, the entanglements with politics and political figures, the tense public appearances, the violent mental collapses—all escalated in the course of the decade. Lowell was now a celebrity—famous not only in literary circles, but also in the New York intellectual scene, in the antiwar movement, the student movement, and eventually in England. Almost despite himself, Lowell got swept into the central arena of the circus of 1960s politics. Norman Mailer gave him a leading role in *Armies of the Night,* his account of the celebrity-studded October 1967 march on the Department of Justice and the Pentagon. And in 1968, Lowell joined Eugene McCarthy's campaign for the Democratic nomination, stumping for votes in New Hampshire, Wisconsin, and California.

Fame and politics radically altered his life and his work, and, inevitably, his friendship with Bishop as well. Bishop, in Brazil, also became far more involved in politics during the 1960s than she ever had been before; but unlike Lowell, she was not a political player but a political victim. Politics, more than anything else, wrecked her life in Brazil and poisoned her happiness with Lota. By the decade's end, politics had thrust Bishop and Lowell into very different worlds. Bishop grew suspicious of Lowell's power and envious of his prestige, just as Melville a century before had envied Hawthorne's political clout (and monetary profits) during the Pierce administration. Lowell's behavior, both in print and in person, offended her sense of decorum. Their friendship suffered and almost died.

"Cal the public figure—he knew what he was doing," commented Lowell's friend Blair Clark. "I'm sure there were people who were terribly envious of his ability to manipulate himself as a public figure. He did it without any pomposity—but he definitely believed that he *was* a public figure."[11]

Lowell's prominence might not have made him pompous, but it did steadily swell the size of his ego. More and more during the 1960s, he wrote out of the assumption that the poems were important *because* they had happened to Robert Lowell. "All you have to do is put down the [family] names," Bishop had written him about *Life Studies* in 1957, for the poems to seem "significant, illustrative, American." Now all he had to put down was his *own* name. An early symptom of this poetic arrogance was *Imitations,* the volume of extremely free translations from world poetry through the ages that he published in 1961. Lowell explained his intent and his method in the volume's brief introduction: "This book is partly self-sufficient and separate from its sources, and should be first read as a sequence, one voice running through many personalities, contrasts and repetitions. . . . I have been reckless with literal meaning, and labored hard to get the tone. . . . I have dropped lines, moved lines, moved stanzas, changed images and altered meter and intent."[12] Essentially, Lowell had rounded up his favorite poems by Homer, François Villon, Heine, Baudelaire, Eugenio Montale, and Pasternak, among others, and branded them with his own unmistakable voice and style. However one judges the results—and critical reception was decidedly mixed—this was clearly an extremely nervy undertaking. Stanley Kunitz feels that *Imitations*, like *History*, was a product of Lowell's megalomania, "the worst of all his extreme passions."[13] Anthony Hecht sees it as a product of his "limitless ambition": "He set out to rewrite and improve everyone else. There is something that smacks of arrogance about that." Joe Summers teased Lowell that *Imitations* was the most original thing he had ever written. (Lowell was not amused.)

Bishop voiced her own serious reservations about the book (the only volume that Lowell dedicated to her) in a long rambling letter dated March 1, 1961. Though she handles him, as always, rather delicately, it's plain that she was appalled by what he had done. It wasn't just the poetry that upset her, but the whole tangle of art, politics, personal influence, power games, and literary careerism that was beginning to complicate both their lives. In that March first letter we can see the source of the strong currents that would carry them so far, and so far apart, during the next ten years.

Before she gets to *Imitations*, Bishop mentions how envious she is that Lowell attended the Kennedy inauguration, and then she promptly qualifies it: "But I don't like that Roman Empire grandeur—the reviewing stand [which she'd seen in newsreels], for example, looks quite triumphal—of course Mrs K's hat looks Byzantine. . . . I wish K[ennedy] weren't so damned RICH. It all turns my stomach, slightly." Next she recounts some startling political news of her own. Due to the latest upheaval in Brazilian politics, Lota's old friend Carlos Lacerda, a newspaper editor and politician and "*the* head of the opposition for years," has just been appointed governor of the newly created state of Guanabara (which includes Rio). Carlos rewarded Lota for her friendship with a very special piece of patronage: "He has put Lota in charge of a huge new 'fill' along the Rio bay—about 2 miles of it—4 lane highways, etc.—and enough land besides to build restaurants, parks, playgrounds, outdoor cafes.—It is just the kind of thing Lota has been really preparing herself for for years and of course it is about time her poor country made some use of her brains."

Lota is, suddenly, no longer an idle, opinionated aristocrat,

but a government official—the "Chief Co-ordinatress of the Fill"—
charged with an explosively difficult mission. Already Bishop reports that she and Lota have been back and forth to Rio every
week for two months, the last time to stand in 105° heat amid
over- and underpasses, "sewers and dumps and scows and steam-
shovels—accompanied by a dozen melting engineers, mostly in
white linen." "My work (ha ha) has suffered badly, of course," she
adds sourly. There would be a good deal more about "the fill" and
its debilitating effects on Lota and on their relationship in the
coming years. As Lota got more and more entangled in the snarls
of Brazilian politics, she became increasingly difficult to live
with—or to love. Bishop found herself relegated to the sidelines, a
frustrated observer with too much time on her hands. Politics
drove a painful wedge between them. In the end it was the fill,
more than anything else, that dried up the "private cloud" of
Samambaia.

Having raised an eyebrow over the new political prominence of both Lowell and Lota, Bishop turns to the translations,
but politics enter in here too. "Your star is so very high now . . .
and to publish things open to misunderstanding might produce a
lot of foolish jealous haggling and criticism that you could easily
avoid. . . . I don't want you to be attacked." The overt intent of
her "corrections" is to protect Lowell's reputation from the assault
of petty-minded enemies. But despite her protests and hand wringing ("I feel I am running an awful risk and I am suffering, writing
this"), she makes it fairly clear that the spirit of Lowell's translations turns her stomach, "slightly," as much as the "Roman Empire grandeur" of the Kennedy inauguration—and for much the
same reasons.

Bishop limits her critique to the French translations ("the
only ones I can judge at all"), going through the poems line by line
to point out Lowell's "changes that *sound* like *mistakes*," his dis-
tortions of tone, color, meaning, and literal fact—what his attackers lumped together as "howlers."[14]

In terms of the future of their friendship, the key words in
this prodigious letter are "envy," "reputation," and "workmanship." These were to be the grounds of Bishop's growing disaffec-
tion with Lowell and his work. Though she thanked him
handsomely for dedicating *Imitations* to her ("of course [it] made
me shed tears"), she never understood why he had done it. The
book marks a turning point in their fellowship, a subtle lapse of

sympathy. A friend remembers her commenting tartly that in *Imitations* Lowell was not satisfied with being the best poet in America; he wanted to be the best poet in the world—in fact, he wanted to be *all* the poets in the world (she made the friend promise never to breathe a word of this to Lowell).[15] The impulse behind the translations, the association with the Kennedys, the ascendancy of Lowell's "star," the widening circle of his connections and influence, his occasional insensitivity to her feelings: All of these made Bishop uneasy with Lowell in a way she never had been before. She continued to love and admire him, despite the catastrophe of his 1962 visit to Brazil, but more and more he disappointed her. The friendship was growing strained.

Part of the problem was that Lowell's entry into the "great world" corresponded with the dwindling of Bishop's happiness in Brazil. Even before Lota got involved with the fill, Bishop was becoming restless, questioning her "purpose" in staying on, wondering what this prolonged exile was doing to her work and to her own reputation.[16] And she told other friends around the same time, "The novelty has worn off. I never would stay for a week if it weren't for Lota."[17] As time went on, Bishop grew more painfully aware of her low status in Brazil as an expatriate "lady poet": "I know almost no one literary and almost no one knows of me—and I think they think if I were any good I'd be at home anyway. . . . Here a lady-poet is a male poet's mistress, as a rule, and he writes her poems for her."[18]

Bishop's anxieties and her need to escape them became drastic once Lota got caught up in the political whirlpool of the fill. Lota had accepted the post on the condition that she receive no pay, a wise move politically but extremely unfortunate financially as inflation drained the value of her and Bishop's inheritances. Even more unfortunate was the toll the project took on Lota's physical and mental health. As regimes rose and fell, Lota was thrust into or out of power. She fought with former political allies and was attacked by enemies new and old. Eventually, Parque do Flamengo, as the fill was christened, was a triumphant success, and Lota became a celebrity in Rio, but the project consumed her.

Bishop revealed far more intimately to Anny Baumann than to Lowell the horrible transformation that Lota underwent between 1961 and 1967. "Unfortunately," she wrote Baumann in 1961, "there are Departments of Parks and Gardens and Departments of Transportation, and brigadier-generals, and many, many entrenched bureaucrats to deal with, and jealousies, politics, and the Position of Woman here!"[19] All of this became infinitely more difficult when Carlos Lacerda fell from power and the new regime gave the fill only tepid support.

As the pressure mounted, Lota turned tyrannical, bullying everyone around her, including Bishop, swinging between rage and despair, seeing conspiracies and betrayals everywhere. Bishop, feeling "rather useless and despondent," traveled more and more by herself. "I feel guilty at abandoning her," Bishop wrote Lowell in 1965 during a two-month stay in the baroque town of Ouro Prêto, "but I wasn't being much help, really moping around the apartment in the heat, and trying to work, very unsuccessfully, while she copes with politicians and crooks and journalists 18 hours a day."[20] That same year Bishop bought an early eighteenth-century house in Ouro Prêto and began to fix it up for herself. "Buying and restoring the house there was entirely her own project," notes the poet Lloyd Schwartz, a good friend of hers, "an attempt at independence."[21] She also began a love affair with a woman in Ouro Prêto.

But she really needed to get away from Lota, and Brazil, altogether. In the winter of 1965, the University of Washington in Seattle approached her about taking over the teaching position left vacant when Theodore Roethke died, and in desperation she agreed. Bishop's relationship with Lota never really recovered from the semester in Seattle. With distance, she realized she had reached the end of her rope in Brazil. "I can't stand it anymore," she wrote to Baumann of Lota's bossing.[22]

Things were worse when Bishop returned. She reported to Baumann in September that Lota had become obsessed with her drinking and was telling everyone that she had really gone to Seattle so she could drink and that she had spent her time there on a six-month binge. Bishop wanted to quit taking Antabuse, which she blamed for her despondent moods, but Lota forced her to continue with it. Lota was opening her mail. "She doesn't seem to realize that I have perhaps grown up a lot (!—about time) in the past 15 years," she wrote Baumann, "and can really manage pretty well on my own, and stay sober about 98 percent of the time—I know I can, because I DID."[23] But she confessed sheepishly that she was drinking again, especially when she was around Lota. To complicate matters even more, while she was in Seattle, Bishop had become involved with a young American woman who happened to be several months pregnant when they met.

The last year of Bishop's life in Brazil was hellish. At the end of September, Lota had a nervous breakdown and was hospitalized. Bishop checked into the same clinic for a month for emotional exhaustion and also, probably, to dry out. In January 1967, she wrote to Baumann that the doctors had ordered her not to see Lota for six months. "All her obsessions have fixed on me—first love; then hate. . . . I haven't a home any more—actually nothing but 2 suitcases and a box of old papers, all the wrong ones." She hated to leave Lota but "it seems almost as if it were a question of saving my own life or sanity, too, now."[24]

In July, Bishop fled to New York, and Lota followed her in September. The night of her arrival, Lota took an overdose of Valium and she died, five days later, in St. Vincent's Hospital. She was fifty-seven years old. Bishop sent a note to a friend in Ouro Prêto repeating over and over, "It's not my fault. It's not my fault. It's not my fault."[25] But she told Baumann in October, "I can't stop blaming myself for all the things I know I did wrong—in the past, and probably, without realizing it, on that Sunday." In the same letter, she insisted that she had intended to return to Brazil with Lota after leaving New York.[26]

Lota's death sealed Bishop's fate with Brazil. Though she went back, shortly afterward, to collect her possessions, to attend to her affairs (Lota's sister had instigated a lawsuit against Bishop, accusing her of stealing the family jewels, among other things), and to look after the house in Ouro Prêto, she never really felt at home there again. Lota's family and most of their friends in Rio and Petrópolis blamed Bishop for Lota's death. People she had been close to for sixteen years wouldn't speak to her.

Over the next few years, Bishop and her American lover and her lover's baby spent a good deal of time in Ouro Prêto, but the situation there became increasingly stressful. The townspeople gossiped about the American lesbian couple. Workmen and servants cheated her. Neighbors threw stones at Bishop's lover and emptied their garbage cans in the garden. From Ouro Prêto Bishop wrote to Lowell in bitter frustration, "Now I feel her [Lota's] country really killed her—and is capable of killing anyone who is honest and has high standards and wants to do something good . . . and my one desire is to get out."[27]

●

There is a terrible irony in the fact that politics wrecked Bishop's relationship with Lota and killed her happiness in Brazil for she had always had a kind of instinctive aversion to political involvement. ("I was always opposed to political thinking as such for writers," she once told an interviewer.[28]) Yet it would be wrong to call Bishop apolitical. Though she seldom tackled politics head on in her verse, the way Lowell did in the 1960s, her sympathies and her subjects have clear political implications. Hers was the politics of the victim, the hapless, helpless individual crushed by huge impersonal social forces—poverty, ignorance, government corruption, the spread of mass culture. "The dying out of local cultures seems to me one of the most tragic things in this century—and it is true everywhere," she wrote to Lowell in disgust at the relentless march of Coca-Cola and television into the jungles of Brazil and the villages of Nova Scotia.[29]

Unlike Lowell, she did not "pity the planet," but rather its individual inhabitants—the squatter's children who have rights only "in rooms of falling rain"; the uprooted poor of Rio who spread "a fearful stain" over its "fair green hills"; the beggar in the park of "Anaphora" in her first book who "weary, without lamp or book/prepares stupendous studies." "The economic disparity and the relation between rich and poor was always a subject in her work," said Frank Bidart. "But it heightened all those issues—it made them more savage. She obviously through her life . . . identified with outcasts."[30]

That identification rises to a fever pitch in the poem "Pink Dog," published the year of Bishop's death (but probably written in 1964, when her troubles with Lota and Brazilian politics were getting bad).

> The sun is blazing and the sky is blue.
> Umbrellas clothe the beach in every hue.
> Naked, you trot across the avenue.
>
> Oh, never have I seen a dog so bare!
> Naked and pink, without a single hair . . .
> Startled, the passersby draw back and stare.

The depilated dog becomes a horrifying symbol, at once pathetic and laughable, of the plight of the Brazil poor as she trots around town, begging and living by her wits. But in this nightmare carnival city, begging is a perilous profession, for "they" (the authorities?) have begun "dealing" with beggars and other "parasites" by drowning them—and if "they" do this to beggars, "what would they do to sick, four-legged dogs?"

What is "the practical, the sensible solution" to the dog's dilemma? To cover her nakedness with a *"fantasia"*—a carnival costume—and dance the samba. "Dress up! Dress up and dance at Carnival!" this furious, funny poem ends. Like Henry James in his last short stories, Bishop allows herself in "Pink Dog" the relief of howling. The poem resounds with what Lloyd Schwartz calls "the laughter of despair."[31]

Schwartz also notes that "Pink Dog" is a poem about being female,[32] and it certainly lends itself to a feminist reading. The "poor bitch" with her hanging teats and hidden babies suffers the burdens and disgraces of her sex: Being female and poor puts her on a par with "idiots, paralytics, parasites." The "practical solution" to the dog's problems is like a sick joke of the standard advice to troubled women—shut up and buy a new dress. In a patriarchal society, to use the jargon, no one takes a poor bitch seriously (one recalls Bishop's complaints to Lowell about the disadvantages of "my sex" in Brazil and the disrespect shown there to a "lady-poet"). Feminine "wiles" are both a humiliation and a defensive strategy. Dressing up may turn the bitch into a clown, but for the disenfranchised, disguise offers at least some protection.

Strangely enough, Bishop would have been the first to disavow a feminist interpretation of her poem. Despite the fact that her life embodied certain feminist ideals—sexual and economic independence, a rewarding career, freedom of thought and movement—Bishop firmly dissociated herself from "women's libbers," something she had in common with Wharton, Porter, and Welty. She hated being grouped with other female poets (Lowell was often guilty of this—and she rebuked him once in a letter: "I'd rather be called *'the 16th poet'* with no reference to my sex, than one of 4 women—even if the other 3 are pretty good . . .").[33]

She steadfastly refused to let her work appear in anthologies of women's poetry ("I prefer my sexes mixed," she told Joe Summers), and she was faintly horrified when feminists adopted her "Roosters" as a "feminist tract" in the 1970s.[34] "A HUGE anthology just came for me—SISTERHOOD IS POWERFUL," she wrote derisively to Lowell in 1970. "('Women's Lib'). Oh dear. A list of 'Resistances to Consciousness': <u>Thinking that individual solutions are possible.</u> I suppose that's me. It is all so right—& yet I have always felt it beneath me to complain (Like the aristocrats beheaded because they wouldn't kick and scream.) Finding things funny is a great handicap for the Higher Life, I'm afraid."[35] Katherine Anne Porter and Eudora Welty could not have agreed more.

James Merrill remembers Bishop's exasperation when readers commented with surprise that she had begun to incorporate political themes into her Brazilian poems. "Do they think I'm blind?" she demanded. Yet it remains true that, like the pink dog, she needed to disguise her politics, to dress them up in symbols. In her early Kafkaesque story "In Prison," Bishop wrote that being a rebel in prison is "entirely a different thing from being a 'rebel' outside the prison; it is to be unconventional, rebellious perhaps, but in shades and shadows."[36] "Rebellious perhaps, but in shades and shadows" is an apt description of Bishop's own political stance. She was temperamentally unsuited for bold political activism. Unlike Lowell, she never mounted a platform in her life or her art. Quietly subversive, "naturally perverse" as she once described herself to an interviewer,[37] she viewed politics as a crude invasion into life's privacy. She would have avoided politics altogether had she not fallen victim to its vagaries.

Bishop never recovered from Lota's death and the last awful stretch of public and private torment that precipitated it. It's little wonder that she had some trouble relating to Lowell and his work when she returned to the States in 1967. Fallout from the explosions of the late 1960s was to create a good deal more serious trouble between them in the years to come.

TWENTY-TWO

"What We're Really Like in 1972": The Rift over <u>The Dolphin</u>

> Should revelation be sealed like private letters,
> till all the beneficiaries are dead,
> and our proper names become improper Lives?
>
> —ROBERT LOWELL, "Draw"

> When we came to Hustler Hill,
> he said that the mare was tired,
> so we all got down and walked,
> as our good manners required.
>
> —ELIZABETH BISHOP, "Manners"

WHEN BISHOP REENTERED the American poetry scene in 1967, the Age of Lowell was at its height. She felt like a footnote. Bishop knew in Brazil that Lowell's star had been rising steadily higher through the 1960s. But it wasn't until she resumed residence in the States, for at least part of the year, that she fully comprehended his status—and what his status meant for her own. Frank Bidart remembers Bishop browsing through his books and pulling a collection of essays about contemporary American poets off the shelf. There were pieces about John Berryman, Sylvia Plath, Lowell—but nothing on her. "It's like being buried alive," she said morosely. "She was not Olympian and above all this," notes Bidart. "It was a source of pain that her work was not in fashion when

Lowell was at the height of his fame. A touchiness about her reputation was part of her."[1]

Lowell's preeminence was particularly demoralizing to Bishop because of her long habit of measuring herself against him. "Lowell was the figure that she was always arguing with in her own mind," as Lloyd Schwartz puts it. "He challenged her."[2] The challenge became more immediate when Bishop was hired by Harvard to take over Lowell's teaching spot in the fall of 1970. Although Lowell had gotten her the job, which she needed and clung to, Bishop hated laboring in his shadow. "At Harvard she was surrounded by people who knew Lowell and had a high estimation of his work," says Bidart, who remained close to both friends during this strained period and acted as a kind of go-between for them. "There were far fewer people who liked her work. Being a 'poet's poet's poet' as [John] Ashbery called her was different from having undergraduates know and idolize you. She felt drowned by the way that Lowell dominated the literary world. His fame and popularity became a source of tension between them. It wrecked their relationship."

An even more serious source of tension was Bishop's dislike of Lowell's new work—not just individual poems or lines, but the very impulse behind the work. As we've seen, the presumption and apparent sloppiness of *Imitations* gave her trouble in 1961. She had even more trouble with the unrhymed sonnets that Lowell began turning out at a furious clip starting in 1967, often a sonnet a day dashed off in the gaps between rallies, classes, and long drunken evenings. "The sonnets were coming very quickly, and he let them come," remembers Bidart. "Clumps of lines came banging through his head."[3] Lowell had lit on the new form as his answer to Ezra Pound's cantos and Berryman's "Dream Songs," and he literally poured himself into it, writing his life as he lived it and vice versa.

Bishop was alarmed when she observed Lowell's frenzied work style in the fall of 1967, and she was puzzled when she saw the results two years later. "I really don't know what to say at all," she wrote him from San Francisco after reading the galleys of his first version of *Notebook* (a second, revised and expanded, edition appeared in 1970). "I am overcome by their sheer volume partly, but also by the range, the infinite fascinating detail, the richness, and everything else. I shall have to read them many more times through to get it all."[4] A few years later she wrote him that the "jump from thought to thought . . . bothers me . . . [there are] individual images that I see & understand—then a leap in thought I can't understand the reason for . . ."[5]

An immersion in the sonnets quickly reveals why they reduced Bishop to inarticulate stammering. Their sheer volume is indeed daunting—two versions of *Notebook,* which Lowell proceeded to recast into *History* (the "public" sonnets) and *For Lizzie and Harriet* (the private), and the new sonnets that he gathered in *The Dolphin,* the last three books published together in 1973. As Helen Vendler remarks, reading the sonnets for the first time is "like being pelted with hard stones. You feel the smart more than you take in the object."[6] But quite aside from their bulk, the sonnets are, as Bishop indicates, hard to "get." Each volume has its own principle of construction—the *Notebook*s follow the cycle of the year and the cycle of Lowell's sexual adventures; *History* moves more or less chronologically through western civilization from Adam and Eve to the Manhattan winter sunset Lowell is observing at the moment of composition; *For Lizzie and Harriet* and *The Dolphin* trace the wanderings of Lowell's heart—but individual sonnets often seem scattershot, arbitrary, and disjointed to the point of incoherence. "Accident threw up subjects," Lowell wrote in his "Afterthought" to *Notebook,* "and the plot swallowed them—famished for human chances."

Lowell's range of allusion is breathtaking—in *History* he leaps from Bernard Berenson to the Columbia University riots, from Emerson to Don Giovanni, Robespierre to Harpo Marx, Al Capone to Julius Caesar, Che Guevara to Marie Antoinette, Attila to Rimbaud, sometimes all in the same fourteen lines. Historical figures and events take on substance and meaning through Lowell's personal experience of them: Napoleon appears as a facet of his boyhood obsession; his last trip to the dentist takes its place beside an elegy for Robert Kennedy; the 1930s sonnets are a record of battles with his parents, summer vacations, encounters with Ford Madox Ford and Allen Tate. Past and present, historic and private references, the global and the intimate blur together in a vibrating collage of the world according to Lowell. As one critic describes the guiding principle, "In Lowell's poems the self is the pivot. There is always his romantic, mythic self moving through his words."[7]

History also became a catchall for anything that "fit"— sonnetized versions of poems from previous volumes, translations, family reminiscences, tributes to friends, overheard snatches of conversation. Richard Wilbur remarks that when Lowell was writing the sonnets, "his ego was in a runaway condition. He had gone into orbit at an altitude beyond criticism. He dropped every conceivable name. If he had met an eminent scholar once at lunch, he would turn up the next day in a fourteen-liner."[8] This is rather snide, but there is something to it.

One of Lowell's ambitions in the sonnets was to catch consciousness on the wing: "I want words meat-hooked from the living steer" is the famous manifesto of his aesthetic in "The Nihilist as Hero." Thus everything that touched him, everything he had ever thought or done or known was fair game. He deliberately left the poems ragged, open-ended, studded with non sequiturs and great swoops of association because that's the way his mind worked. "One of the disarming features of Lowell's work is that it does not pretend to aspire to the condition of an absolute art," writes Stanley Kunitz. "He makes us excruciatingly aware of the thrashing of the self behind the lines; of the intense fragility of the psyche trying to get a foothold in an 'air of lost connections,' struggling to stay human and alive. . . . What we get from these poems is the sense of a life . . . a life that has been turned into a style."[9] "The well-made poem seemed too neat for the processes of modern consciousness," as Vendler aptly puts it. "The sonnets did not have finality. They were rough, slap-dash. And he kept changing them, shifting them around." Being "exempt from the tyranny of the well-made" makes individual sonnets seem sloppy, but they make their strongest impression in the aggregate.[10]

Bishop, who strove for the very opposite qualities in her own verse—clarity, closure, understatement, perfect balance, lightness of touch, a high and yet seemingly natural "finish"—was ill disposed to Lowell's sonnets by temperament. "Workmanship" was her term for what the sonnets lacked but she also had a serious personal grievance against the poems. In putting together his revised *Notebook* in 1970, Lowell reworked the poems he had written for and about Bishop over the years. He trimmed "Water," from *For the Union Dead*, down to sonnet size; he dug up the drafts of the poems he had written after she left Castine in 1957 and extracted a sonnet from them; and he completed a new sonnet, originally titled "Calling," about her artistic method and sensibility. The poem beautifully crystallizes what Bishop meant to and for him as friend and artist. He concludes:

Have you seen an inchworm crawl on a leaf,
cling to the very end, revolve in air,
feeling for something to reach to something? Do
you still hang your words in air, ten years
unfinished, glued to your notice board, with gaps
or empties for the unimaginable phrase—
unerring Muse who makes the casual perfect?[11]

Lowell dispatched the three poems to Bishop at Ouro Prêto for comment in February and she promptly wrote back that she loved the poems, "of course." "Oh, thank you; thank you very much—you can really never know how much this has cheered me up and made me feel a bit like myself again." Bishop was acutely in need of cheering at this particular moment, when she felt that all the accumulated miseries and frustrations and brutalities of her life in Brazil were crashing down on her head.

"Well, you are right to worry about me, only please DON'T," the letter continued, "—I am pretty worried about myself. I have somehow got into the worst situation I have ever had to cope with and I can't see the way out. . . ." And she told "a terrible tale of woe" about her attempt to sell the house while continuing the renovation, about the racket and thefts, and the misery of trying to cope with Brazil without Lota. She ended with a kind of epic simile for her wretchedness: "Have you ever gone through caves?—I did once, in Mexico, and hated it so I've never gone through the famous ones right near here. Finally, after hours of stumbling along, one sees daylight ahead—faint blue glimmer— and it never looked so wonderful before. That's what I feel as though I were waiting for now—just the faintest glimmer that I'm going to get out of this somehow, alive. Meanwhile—your letter has helped tremendously—like being handed a lantern, or a spiked walking stick. . . ."[12]

Lowell's response to this cry of anguish—perhaps the most emotionally naked letter Bishop ever wrote him—was to extract the darkest passages and "verse" them into one of his fourteen-liners. In *History,* he added "Letter with Poems for Letter with Poems" to the three sonnets he had sent Bishop for comment:

You are right to worry, only please DON'T,
though I'm pretty worried myself. I've somehow got
into the worst situation I've ever

had to cope with. I can't see the way out.
Cal, have you ever gone through caves?
I did in Mexico, and hated them.
I haven't done the famous one near here. . . .
Finally after hours of stumbling along,
you see daylight ahead, a faint blue glimmer;
air never looked so beautiful before.
That is what I feel I'm waiting for:
a faintest glimmer I am going to get out
somehow alive from this. Your last letter helped,
like being mailed a lantern or a spiked stick.[13]

Bishop was furious and terribly hurt when she read the new sonnet. "I fear I may owe you an apology for versing one of your letters into my poems on you in Notebook," Lowell wrote her in sheepish anticipation of her reaction. "When Lamb blew up at Coleridge for calling him 'Frolicsom Lamb,' C. said it was necessary for the balance of his composition. I won't say that, but what could be as real as your own words, and then there's only a picture that does you honor. Still, too intimate maybe, and if so I humbly ask pardon."[14] Lowell's apology was an empty gesture since he went ahead and published the poem anyway. But in any case, he failed to perceive the depth of the injury he had inflicted. His lame supposition that the poem is "too intimate maybe" is trifling beside the fact that he has taken *her* words, *her* pain, *her* crisis and absorbed them into *his* art. She forgave him a decade earlier for versing "In the Village" into "The Scream"—but this was worse, far worse, for now he was invading not the sanctity of her art, but the privacy of her life.

The rift that "Letter with Poems for Letter with Poems" opened between the friends grew wider and deeper in the course of the early 1970s. There was never an outright break—both Bishop and Lowell were too loyal to the past, too devoted to each other to let that happen—but for three or four years a good deal of bitterness and suspicion festered between them, especially on Bishop's part. Personal and professional circumstances exacerbated their artistic conflict. Bishop felt—rightly—that she was at Harvard by the grace of Lowell, but her economic dependence on him made her anxious. She assumed her employment was contingent upon his absence (Lowell went to teach in England in 1970) and she lived in dread that he would one day reclaim his Harvard appointment and cast her out naked into the world.

Bishop's lowly status within the university, positively wormlike compared with Lowell's near divinity, was also a trial to her. Lowell, who rather enjoyed teaching, was immensely popular with students and highly respected by faculty. In his classes he appeared the very image of the Great Poet—wild-haired, moody, distracted, and brilliant. With his large hands swimming through the air before him, he exhaled great clouds of cigarette smoke and terse cryptic remarks—"disconnected sentences that were more musings than messages," as Helen Vendler puts it. The poets whose work he discussed—Browning, Wordsworth, Crane, Hopkins—loomed in the classroom as living presences, Lowell's beloved colleagues, really his friends whose lines he tackled and wrestled with as if they had been written that morning. In class, "he gave the sense," notes Vendler, "so absent from textbook headnotes, of a life, a spirit, a mind, and a set of occasions from which writing issues."[15] His office hours became a local institution, a gathering of gifted poets in the know not only from Harvard but also from all over the Boston area—Richard Tillinghast, Frank Bidart, Lloyd Schwartz, Helen Chasin, Jean Valentine, Grey Gowrie, Courtenay Graham. Lowell was a galvanizing force at the university, a kind of vortex of poetic energy.

Bishop, on the other hand, loathed teaching and it showed. (She told James Merrill that she only took the job for the health insurance.) In class, she was, as Dana Gioia writes in his reminiscence, "Studying with Miss Bishop," "politely formal, shy, and undramatic. . . . She wanted no worshipful circle of students, and got none." Bishop, unfashionably, stressed memorization (ten lines a week) and told her class to use the dictionary ("It's better than the critics"). Extremely dubious that poetry could really be *taught,* she tried at least to make her students get the literal meaning of every word, image, fact, and reference in a poem. When her class read Lowell, she sent the undergraduates in search of the local places mentioned in the poems—the Boston Common, 91 Revere Street, the public garden, hardly passionate Marlborough Street. A student asked about the song "Love, O Careless Love" in "Skunk Hour," and Bishop, dismayed that such a hit should have been forgotten, sang it to the class (the same song plays on the hamburger joint nickelodeon in Eudora Welty's "The Hitchhikers").

Bishop was as unenthusiastic about her students as most of them were about her. "They are DULL," she wrote Lowell about her first crop. "Their poems are competent, and so DULL. I think I'll issue dexedrine, or pot . . ."[16] To make matters worse, the Harvard English Department treated her quite shabbily. "She was a distinguished and remarkable poet," comments Lloyd Schwartz, "and at Harvard they gave her a classroom in the basement of Kirkland House. It was damp and dim and she would have asthma attacks. She was sick a lot and missed classes." Her drinking was also getting bad again. Though she taught Lowell's verse to her students, she found it painful to talk about him outside of class. "The biggest problem was that she felt neglected by him and left out and left behind," recalls Schwartz. "There was a great deal of distance between them."[17]

The distance increased with new upheavals in Lowell's personal life. Just before Bishop's first term at Harvard, Lowell (who was in England on a visiting professorship at All Souls, Oxford) wrote her a tight-lipped letter from London in which he dropped the explosive news that "Lizzie and I have more or less separated . . . good-naturedly . . . I have someone else."[18] The next month he disclosed that his "someone" was Lady Caroline Blackwood, a thirty-eight-year-old writer and a member of the Anglo-Irish aristocracy (her father was the fourth marquis of Dufferin and Ava, and her mother was a Guinness, the immensely wealthy stout-brewing family). Blackwood, like Lowell, had been married twice before: Her first husband was the English painter Lucien Freud (Sigmund Freud's grandson) and her second was the musician Israel Citkovitz, with whom she had had three children, all girls. "She is very beautiful and saw me through the chafes and embarrassments of my sickness with wonderful kindness," Lowell gushed to Bishop. "I suppose I shouldn't forget Harriet and Lizzie, anyway I can't. Guilt clouds the morning, and though things are not embattled, nothing is settled."[19] Bishop replied acidly, "I am glad the lady is beautiful; that really cheers one a lot."[20]

It certainly cheered Lowell a lot. In *The Dolphin* he conjures up an image of Blackwood as a kind of goddess-muse-enchantress-restorer-of-lost-youth. Above all, as a marvelous beauty: "fair-face, ball eyes, profile of a child," he describes her in one poem, and in another, "Alice-in-Wonderland straight gold hair,/fair-featured, curve and bone from crown to socks."[21] With her hard slender graceful body ("all muscle, youth, intention") and her delicately hollowed pre-Raphaelite face, Blackwood was as striking as a movie star or model (which in fact she once had been). Lowell's love for her consumed him. "To Cal, it seemed an alliance made in heaven," says Stanley Kunitz. "Caroline had literary power, social power, money power. She was a fit culmination of his romantic history."[22] Richard Tillinghast remembers that Lowell had an almost mystical faith that Blackwood could keep him sane: "Part of their relationship revolved around the notion that their love could keep him from going off on a breakdown."[23] Lowell moved into her London apartment on the same night they attended a publishing party together (they had actually become acquainted a few years before in New York).

Friends were struck by how alike Lowell and Blackwood were in their moodiness, their abstraction, their impracticality, their huge thirst for alcohol, their utter obliviousness of everything except the intensities of their own internal states. Lowell was notorious for descending on friends, drinking and monologuing deep into the night, leaving a trail of cigarette ash and smoldering holes behind him. Now he had Caroline at his side, boozing and burning holes in sofas right along with him. "They seemed to be two of a kind," says Kunitz. "Spontaneous, feckless, dangerous. When I visited them in England, it seemed like the most reckless and haphazard household." "They existed in a state of destruction," recalls John Malcolm Brinnin. "The amenities and proprieties of life did not exist for them."[24]

Bishop instinctively sided with Hardwick. Though the two women had never been fond of each other—a mutual friend remembers hearing Hardwick refer to Bishop as a witch and Bishop felt pretty much the same way about her[25]—Bishop was nonetheless horrified at the way Lowell had unceremoniously disposed of his wife of two decades. The whole thing smacked of a vulgar midlife crisis—the great man facing old age; the glamorous sexy younger woman; the abandoned grief-stricken wife.

If Lowell's divorce and swift remarriage offended Bishop, the poems he wrote about this life passage appalled her. Lowell had outlined his dominant theme in his October letter to Bishop: "Guilt clouds the morning, and though things are not embattled, nothing is settled." "One man, two women—" as he wrote in one of the new sonnets, "the common novel plot." The "plot" might have been common, but the way he had chosen to handle it was certainly not. Lowell was taking passages from Hardwick's most anguished letters and conversations and versing them into sonnets, just as he had done with Bishop's Ouro Prêto letter. Bishop was angry enough when she had been Lowell's victim, but that was a single letter, and at least Lowell had been discreet enough to omit any revealing details about *why* she had gotten herself into such an awful situation. But in *The Dolphin* Hardwick's words are naked, desperate, furious, and all too clearly the actual words of a rejected, miserable wife.

The situation has strange parallels to the plot of Edith Wharton's short novel *The Touchstone* in which a man finances his marriage by selling the passionate love letters that a deceased woman writer sent him, only Lowell was raising artistic, not actual, capital from Hardwick's letters—and of course Hardwick was not dead. "What a record year, even for us—" she sails into him in "Voices," the first of her letters. "That new creature/when I hear her name, I have to laugh./You left two houses and two thousand books,/a workbarn by the ocean, and two slaves/to kneel and wait upon you hand and foot—/tell us why in the name of Jesus." *"Don't you dare mail us the love your life denies,"* she rages in "Exorcism"; *"do you really* know *what you have done?"*[26] And so on. It is the searing voice of guilt incarnate.

When Lowell sent Bishop the manuscript for comment, she responded with what can only be termed a tirade. "It's hell to write this," she prepares him for the assault in her first paragraph, "so please first do believe I think DOLPHIN is magnificent poetry. It is also honest poetry—*almost.* You probably know already what my reactions are. I have one tremendous and awful BUT. If you were any other poet I can think of I certainly wouldn't attempt to say anything at all; I wouldn't think it was worth it. But because it is you, and a great poem (I've never used the word 'great' before, that I remember), and I love you a lot—I feel I must tell you what I really think."

Bishop proceeds to hammer at Lowell in three and a half pages of close-packed type for invading Hardwick's privacy, for irresponsibly mixing fact and fiction, and for inflicting needless pain both on his family and his readers by publishing these letters. In *The Dolphin* she felt Lowell's artistic predation had crossed the line from the intrusive to the indecent. The book, in her view, was practically obscene.

The first [of Lizzie's letters], page 10, is so shocking—well, I don't know what to say. . . . One can use one's life as material—one does, anyway—but these letters—aren't you violating a trust? IF you were given permission—IF you hadn't changed them . . . etc. *But art just isn't worth that much.* I keep remembering [Gerard Manley] Hopkins' marvellous letter to [Robert] Bridges about the idea of a "gentleman" being the highest thing ever conceived—higher than a "Christian" even, certainly than a poet. It is not being "gentle" to use personal, tragic, anguished letters that way—it's cruel.

Then she veers off into a more sweeping condemnation of the whole confessional school of poetry:

In general, I deplore the "confessional"—however, when you wrote LIFE STUDIES perhaps it was a necessary movement, and it helped make poetry more real, fresh and immediate. But now—ye god—anything goes, and I am so sick of poems about the students' mother & fathers and sex-lives and so on. All that *can* be done—but at the same time one surely should have a feeling that one can trust the writer—not to distort, tell lies, etc.

The letters, as you have used them, present fearful problems: what's true, what isn't; how one can bear to witness such suffering and yet not know how much of it one *needn't* suffer with, how much has been "made up," and so on.

I don't give a damn what someone like [Norman] Mailer writes about his wives & marriages—I just hate the level we seem to live and think and feel on at present—but I DO give a damn what you write! . . . This counts and I can't bear to have anything you write tell—perhaps—what we're really like in 1972 . . . perhaps it's as simple as that. But are we? Well—I mustn't ramble on any more.[27]

It was the most damning blast Bishop ever ventured in their thirty years of correspondence, and it pained her enormously to send it.

Lowell found Bishop's letter "a kind of masterpiece of criticism," as he told Bidart, "though her extreme paranoia (for God's sake don't repeat this) about revelations gives it a wildness."[28]

And he wrote to Bishop several times to defend and explain himself: "I did not see them [the letters] as slander, but as sympathetic, tho necessarily awful for her to read. She is the poignance of the book, tho that hardly makes it kinder to her. . . . I combed out abuse, hysteria, repetition. The trouble is the letters make the book, I think; at least they make Lizzie real beyond my invention. . . . It's oddly enough a technical problem as well as a gentleman's problem. How can the story be told at all without the letters. I'll put my heart to it. I can't bear not to publish Dolphin in good form."[29] And later: "Let me rephrase for myself your moral objections. It's the revelation (with documents?) of a wife wanting her husband not to leave her, and who does leave her. That's the trouble, not the mixture of truth and fiction. Fiction—no one would object if I said Lizzie was wearing a purple and red dress, when it was yellow. Actually my versions of her letters are true enough, only softer and drastically cut. The original is heartbreaking, but interminable."[30]

In a fiercely personal way, Lowell and Bishop were debating issues that continue to reverberate through the worlds of art and literature: What materials or documents rightfully "belong" to the artist? What makes a work of art indecent? Is there any justification for cruelty in art? Where does one draw the line between fiction and nonfiction? Does art justify invasion of privacy? These are vexed and complicated questions, and Bishop's and Lowell's contrary answers to them are worth examining in some detail.

Lowell is persuasive when he insists that mixing fiction with fact is unobjectionable so long as the resulting versions are "true." His example of altering the color of Hardwick's dress from yellow to purple and red makes Bishop's obsession with literal accuracy look like an idiosyncrasy (actually, she too altered names, dates, and circumstances in her poems and stories; she was, in Marianne Moore's phrase borrowed from Yeats, a "literalist of the imagination"—but only when it suited her aesthetically).

But Lowell's strongest defense on the fact and fiction issue is in the poems themselves, where he goes well beyond Bishop's quibbling over "what's true, what isn't" to consider the very capacity of words to "say what happened." "Which is truer—" he asks in "No Telling," "the uncomfortable full dress of words for print,/or wordless conscious not even no one ever sees?" In "Heavy Breathing" he confesses, "Conscience incurable/convinces me I am not writing my life;/life never assures which part of ourself is life/ . . . what is true or false tomorrow when surgeons/let out the pus, and crowd the circus to see us/disembowelled for our afterlife?" And in "Rival," he asks, "Is there an ur-dream better than words, an almost/work of art I commonplace in retelling/ through the fearfullness of memory,/my perfunctory, all-service rhythms?"[31]

How does one tell the truth in any form? Lowell asks over and over again in *The Dolphin*. How does one separate art from life? How does one catch the experience of "everything on the run" in static words? How does one "fix" truth so that time does not unwind it? In probing the nature of fact and fiction, truth and falsehood in writing, Lowell was anticipating our own doubts about the "purity" of *any* narrative—memoirs, biography, even history, as Simon Schama plays with in his historical novel *Dead Certainties*. The urgency and the complexity with which Lowell addresses this issue in *The Dolphin* give the poems a shimmering intellectual rigor that many critics missed.

It's fair to say that Lowell acquitted himself on the issue of fact and fiction—or maybe it would be truer to say that our literary culture has come to embrace his position. That leaves the question of whether art is worth the pain Lowell inflicted by publishing Hardwick's letters. In weighing the morality of *The Dolphin,* it is essential to consider the book in its historical and personal moment. In cutting up his ex-wife's letters into five-beat lines and publishing them as his fourteen-liners, Lowell was acting very much in the spirit of the late 1960s: It was an assaulting, desperate, hyper-self-conscious act conceived at a time when artists in all media were trashing the norms of form and content, taste and custom, political and social values. In their very different ways, Lowell, Mailer, Ginsberg, Sexton, the Living Theater, Warhol, Rauschenberg were all operating under the assumption that if the artist strips off convention, decorum, decency and stands, naked and shivering, in the blast of experience, then truth, TRUTH *must* inevitably, radiantly shine forth.

The Dolphin was the culmination of Lowell's aesthetic of self-exposure. It carried the ultimate 1960s justification: Why not? Which is not to suggest that Lowell acted lightly or instinctively on the impulse to offend. Astoundingly erudite, "ruthlessly serious" as a colleague dubbed him, Lowell was every inch the poet-scholar who bore the full weight of the western tradition on his back.

Lowell slapped the decency inherent in the tradition with grave deliberation. Hence his refusal to paraphrase or disguise Hardwick's letters. (Richard Tillinghast suggests that Lowell might also have been motivated by a desire to bite the hand that had fed him for so long. "Hardwick was a mother to him," he notes, "and had cared for him through all his breakdowns. He got fed up with her."[32]) Despite the conventionality of its "common novel plot," *The Dolphin* is extremist art, and *épater les bourgeois* is part of its point. Offensiveness is meaning.

But in Bishop's view, such meaning fouls the very wellsprings of art. As she winds up her attack, she admits that Lowell might have seized on a facet of reality—"what we're really like in 1972"—but she cannot accept that reality of that sort has a place in art. By violating a sacred human trust, by inflicting pain on his family, himself, and his readers, Lowell is dragging all of us down to the abysmal modern "level" of cruelty, hype, and exhibitionism that Bishop, like Henry James and Edith Wharton before her, hated so much. As Bishop's friend John Malcolm Brinnin puts it, "She was no prude but she did have a congenital reserve about intimate matters. She inherited a ladylike sense of propriety, which she maintained along with a sense of outrageous knowledge."[33]

In essence, Bishop and Lowell were arguing about the relationship between life and art. For Lowell, "anything goes" as Bishop said. Art—*his art*—took precedence over everything and everyone, because, as the poet Gregory Orr puts it, "to Lowell, writing *is* life—life isn't real until he transfers it to writing. He only lived, it seemed to him, to turn his experiences into poems." It was the same for Henry James, who wrote in a famous letter to H. G. Wells, "It is art that *makes* life, makes interest, makes importance," though James and Lowell had vastly different conceptions of what *makes* art. For Lowell, telling "what we're really like in 1972"—really experiencing it by writing it—was his reason for living. "He lived for art in a way that few people do or would understand," says Tillinghast.[34] On these grounds, the revelations, the letters, the humiliations were not only worth it; they were also necessary.

This was emphatically not the case for Bishop, who had grave doubts about publishing "In the Village" even after her mother had been dead for years and who suppressed her story "Memories of Uncle Neddy" until not only her uncle Arthur but also his wife were both safely in the grave. For Bishop, as for Eudora Welty, privacy was an essential condition of art.

Stanley Kunitz, who felt the same way as Bishop about *The Dolphin*, wrote Lowell after reading the manuscript: "There are details which seem to me monstrously heartless . . . passages I can scarcely bear to read: they are too ugly, for being too cruel, too intimately cruel."[35] Twenty years later, when Kunitz was asked if his feelings about the issues raised by *The Dolphin* had changed, he replied, "In general I try to do everything possible not to injure other persons in my work. That seems to me part of my human and social responsibility. I don't think that one's art can be an excuse for trespassing on one's friendships or one's loves."[36] Bishop would have agreed wholeheartedly.

Bishop was accurate in her prediction that the people "just waiting in the wings" would fall on *The Dolphin* with knives unsheathed. Reviews were mixed, but the negative notices were far more impassioned than the positive ones. Adrienne Rich, a former student and friend of Lowell's, branded it "a cruel and shallow book" in a stinging piece in the *American Poetry Review*: "The inclusion of the letter poems stands as one of the most vindictive and mean-spirited acts in the history of poetry, one for which I can think of no precedent." Marjorie Perloff advised Lowell in *The New Republic* that he should have kept his "revelations, sometimes embarrassingly personal, sometimes boring" to himself. Stephen Yenser writing in *Poetry* sniffed that the book was "more gossip (fact, data, raw material) than gospel (parable, pattern, truth)."[37] A fellow poet accused Lowell of living his life solely "in order to provide material for poems; one sees with horror the cannibal-poet who dines off portions of his own body, and the bodies of his family."[38]

And yet despite the furious reviews and the outcry in literary circles—Auden refused to speak to Lowell, Mary McCarthy was horrified, Richard Wilbur was repelled—Lowell got away with it. *The Dolphin* went on to win the Pulitzer Prize. Bishop, Kunitz, Wilbur, Tillinghast, and other disapproving friends remained loyal. Even Elizabeth Hardwick, though she was understandably devastated when the book appeared (Lowell feared she was on the verge of suicide; and Hardwick told Bishop that "somehow it has hurt me as much as anything in my life"[39]), ultimately forgave Lowell. When asked how she feels about *The Dolphin* now, Hardwick refused to comment on the grounds that to do so would be a self-inflicted invasion of her own privacy—in itself a rebuff to Lowell's confessional, art-above-anything stance. Richard Wilbur recalls her saying, "If Cal was going to break all the rules, I wish the poems were better,"[40] which is just the kind of "loving, rapid, merciless" remark that Lowell attributes to her in his verse. In a letter thanking Bishop for her sympathy when the book appeared, Hardwick deplored the parts of the work relating to her and Harriet as "inane, empty, unnecessary" and wondered how Lowell could have spent so much time on the verse and still left in "so many fatuities, indiscretions, bad lines. . . . That breaks my heart, for all of us."[41]

In public, Hardwick has refrained from making use of her ample opportunities for literary revenge, whether out of discretion, weariness, forbearance, or self-protection. Those who know her speak of her incredible tolerance of Lowell while he was alive and her continued respect for him. "In something she wrote, she called Lowell 'an unaccountable person,'" notes Tillinghast, "by which I think she meant not only that you just couldn't predict what he'd do, but that he wasn't responsible in the normal way. In my view she's the real heroine of this episode. I've heard people say—and I believe it—that she stood by Lowell because she is generous and because she cares that much about literature."[42]

And because she cares, still, that much about him. "She knew she was marrying a difficult man who was a great writer," says Wilbur. "The seed of ultimate forgiveness was present in their relationship from the beginning."

Bishop softened her stance on *The Dolphin,* at least in her subsequent letters to Lowell, but the episode rankled her for a long time. The poems coupled with her jealousy of his fame and the sticky situation at Harvard came very close to killing their friendship. "This was the low point of their relationship," recalls Bidart, "the time of greatest tension between them."[43] Other shared friends remember having to choose sides, as one would do in a divorce.

Years before their rift over *The Dolphin,* Lowell mused in a letter to Bishop about the perils of literary friendships: "Aren't people difficult? I think, perhaps I have almost more warm intellectual friends than anyone, and have lost none except Delmore

Schwartz. But it's like walking on eggs. All of them have to be humored, flattered, drawn out, allowed to say very petulant things to you. I'm sure they have to bear the same things from me—however, I don't feel the need to be diplomatic with you and Peter Taylor."[44]

After the *The Dolphin,* Lowell clearly *did* feel the need to be diplomatic with Bishop. The old easiness was gone, and the friends never fully recovered it. Yet the core of feeling between them remained intact, too deeply lodged by time and habit to be disturbed. Each was still *the* poet for the other. And each continued, albeit more warily, to learn from the other's art. As horrified as Bishop was by the cruelty of Lowell's revelations, she couldn't help admiring the serious daring of his desire for total honesty. And Lowell, having reached the edge of the precipice with *History* and *The Dolphin,* was ready to pull back, to find a quieter and more sheltéred path to the interior—and he let Bishop show him the way. In their final poems, their voices harmonized as they had never done before.

TWENTY-THREE

Unerring Muse, Sad Friend

> Christ,
> may I die at night
> with a semblance of my senses
> like the full moon that fails.
>
> —ROBERT LOWELL, *unpublished fragment*

> Freed—the broken
> thermometer's mercury
> running away . . .
>
> —ELIZABETH BISHOP, *"Sonnet"*

"IF I HAVE SPOKEN to you in less than my old admiring and loving voice, forgive me," Lowell wrote Bishop late in 1972. "We (you and I) are together till life's end." He was particularly eager just then to shore up the damage in their friendship for he was feeling shorn and flayed by the "barracuda settlement" he and Hardwick had finally arrived at. "I lose everything inherited, all trust interest, New York apartment, Maine house and barn," he told Bishop in the same letter. Harriet "has been stolen from me like the dozen silver spoons."[1] In need of funds, Lowell was making noises about resuming his Harvard teaching post the following fall (1973). Bishop, on receiving this mixed bag of news in Cambridge, was far more agitated about the repercussions on her own future than about the terms of his divorce. She was keenly aware of her low status in the Harvard English Department (whose chairman, according to her, hated both women and poets),[2] and she assumed all along that Lowell's return would terminate her job. She felt, with some justification, as if her fate dangled on the vagaries of Lowell's domestic situation. And it made her quite peevish.[3]

But, as always, Bishop valued the friendship too much to allow what she called "this academic stuff" to come between them, and she wrote Lowell of her hope that they would remain friends "for the rest of our lives."[4] In the event, Harvard kept them both on the faculty and let them alternate terms for several years. Lowell was only too happy to put the "academic stuff" and all the other recent strains on their friendship behind him. We are "airily and happily beyond the days of our clouds," he wrote her in relief after they met in Cambridge that winter for a "lovely long night of drinks, gossip, memories, everything."[5] In another token of reconciliation, Lowell asked Bishop to be godmother for his and Caroline's son, Robert Sheridan Lowell. "If it is an unconsecrated, informal, Bohemian-type godmother you are after—" Bishop replied, "I'd be delighted."[6]

In his subsequent letters to Bishop, Lowell continued to celebrate, almost to eulogize, the resumption of their fellowship. Their long history together—twenty-five years of friendship—was much on his mind these days. "Talking with you in Cambridge was somehow like the old days in Stonington—a lovely warmth (1948)," he wrote her in the spring of 1974. "No need to stop talking, and always when the talk stops it starts."[7]

The wistful nostalgia was a new note for Lowell. He approached his sixtieth birthday—on March 1, 1977—with "twinges of mortality," acutely aware that his father had died at that age. Friends remember that Lowell almost took it for granted that he would die that year, and he was right: He outlived his sixtieth birthday by only two seasons. In the last years of his life, Lowell needed as never before to commemorate the "old days," to summon up the shades of his youth and trace his experiences back to their origins.

Bishop's feelings toward Lowell softened during the mid-1970s, partly because her own situation had improved considerably. Having finally sold the Ouro Prêto house, Bishop was free of her painful entanglement with Brazil and, as Kalstone writes, she was now able to concentrate on "her own 'American' life: prizes,

judgeships, a circuit of readings about which she was always reluctant. She became visible in ways she had never been when she
was the mysterious talented writer who lived in Brazil."[8] Bishop
was also involved in a stable, sustaining relationship with a young
woman named Alice Methfessel. They met at Kirkland House,
where Methfessel was working as the house secretary and where
Bishop lived when she first came to Cambridge. As disparate as
they were in age and interests (Methfessel, who was twenty-six in
1970, later enrolled in a business school MBA program), the
women shared a love for the outdoors and a passion for travel.
Together, they journeyed to the Galápagos Islands, Scandinavia,
Russia, the Greek islands, and Yugoslavia. And starting in 1974,
they began spending part of every summer at a rented house on
North Haven, an island in Maine's Penobscot Bay (due west of
Stonington and due south of Castine). With Methfessel, Bishop
had the calmest, happiest years she had known since Lota's death.

In the spring of 1973 Bishop sealed her commitment to
Boston and to Methfessel by buying an apartment in an 1838
granite warehouse building on Lewis Wharf, part of the city's
waterfront renovation. The harbor view from her fourth-floor balcony was pure Bishop: tankers and pleasure boats cruising past on
the dirty water; the Bunker Hill Monument and the spire of Old
North Church; a scraggly distant shoreline; a wedge of parking
lot. When she finally moved in (after much financial lamentation)
in the fall of 1974, Bishop adored having a place to unpack her
books, to hang her cherished paintings (including two by Loren
MacIver and the twin childhood portraits of her mother and her
uncle Arthur that she describes in "Memories of Uncle Neddy"),
and to arrange her life's collection of odd furniture and fascinating
objects (a friend called the apartment a "veritable museum of
Brazil artifacts"). Though less exotic or inspiring than her Casa
Mariana in Ouro Prêto, the Lewis Wharf apartment was far more
practical and comfortable. A home of her own at last. It also suited
Bishop to live at one remove from the bruising academic fray at
Harvard.

Settled, stable, and relatively prosperous, Bishop was also
writing some of the finest and most original poetry of her career.
Geography III, her final volume, and the uncollected poems that
followed it, mark both a departure and a culmination for Bishop.
Her voice in wonderful poems like "Crusoe in England," "In the
Waiting Room," "The Moose," and "Santarém" is at once more

relaxed and more immediate than it had ever been before: Clearly, simply, seemingly without artifice, Bishop *narrates.* She tells stories, recounts incidents and scraps of family and personal history, she argues "cases"—and yet at the same time, without apparent effort or rhetorical embellishment, she manages to extend and deepen her range of emotion. These last poems put one in mind of Yeats's "Words for Music Perhaps," Shakespeare's romances, and Beethoven's last quartets—transcendently assured works of art whose utter clarity permits us to see down to the lowest depths.

It is tempting to attribute Bishop's openness in these last poems to the influence of Lowell's confessional mode, as indeed several critics have done. "In the Waiting Room," like Lowell's "My Last Afternoon with Uncle Devereux Winslow," describes a vivid emotional crisis of early life. "The Moose," like "Dunbarton" and "Grandparents" from *Life Studies,* summons up the shades of departed grandparents—their "altogether otherworldly" lives and customs, and the "narrow provinces" in which the child lovingly encountered them. "One Art," a strict villanelle that reads like a lucid discourse on "the art of losing," is, in fact, as Frank Bidart points out, "a confessional poem about a painful time when Alice (Methfessel) seemed to be leaving her."

Did Lowell's work inspire or challenge Bishop into autobiography? It's impossible to answer definitively. "She admired his honesty and openness about his life," says Lloyd Schwartz. "It scared her but it also encouraged her to open up toward the end of her life." Bidart agrees that there is a "tremendous directness and openness about *Geography III,* a loosening and warmth. The book has the inner nakedness and intimacy of Lowell's work, but Bishop did not necessarily get this from Lowell. George Herbert [Bishop's favorite poet since college] also has these qualities."[9] Whatever the source or inspiration for the impulse, Bishop achieved spectacular results by letting down some of her defenses. Having mastered the art of losing (family, memories, places, love) and looked disaster in the face, Bishop finally allowed herself to dispense with disguise—or to choose more transparent disguises. Perhaps it would be most accurate to say that Lowell, for all the dangerous excesses of his sonnets, showed her the value of being herself.

"Crusoe in England," although the most highly disguised of the longer later poems, is also perhaps the most deeply and personally revealing. Begun in 1964 and first published in 1971, it is a poem that "sums up everything," as Helen Vendler puts it.

Most urgently, it sums up Bishop's feelings about her exile in Brazil and her return from that exile. Bishop's Crusoe, an old man wearily resettled in England, conjures up "his" island as a nightmare Eden of shifting perspectives and exotic phantasmagoria—maddening but fascinating in its isolation, exasperating in its inane strangeness. The saddest lines come near the poem's end, when Bishop's Crusoe gazes at the knife that kept him alive for so many years on the island and now sits untouched upon a shelf: "Now it won't look at me at all./The living soul has dribbled away./My eyes rest on it and pass on." The magical mute exchange between object and observer is over for good. Crusoe's despondency is reminiscent of Wordsworth's in "Intimations of Immortality from Recollections of Early Childhood":

> It is not now as it hath been of yore;—
> Turn wheresoe'er I may,
> By night or day,
> The things which I have seen I now can
> see no more. . . .
>
> Whither is fled the visionary gleam?
> Where is it now, the glory and the dream?

"Crusoe in England" is like a catalog of the central themes and preoccupations of Bishop's life—home and homelessness, the equivocal attitude toward solitude ("Just when I thought I couldn't stand it another minute longer, Friday came"), drinking ("the awful, fizzy, stinging" home brew that "went straight to my head"), homosexuality ("Friday was nice . . . he had a pretty body"). The mask of Crusoe fit very closely on the face of Bishop.

In his blurb for the jacket of her *Complete Poems* published in 1969, Lowell spoke of Bishop's "own tone" as one of "large, grave tenderness and sorrowing amusement." In "Crusoe," the sorrow is tinged with despair, the amusement with alarm. Lowell admired "Crusoe" tremendously: It "may be your very best poem," he wrote Bishop, "an analogue to your life, or an 'Ode to Dejection.' Nothing you've written has such a mix of humor and desperation."[10] ("Dejection: An Ode" is Coleridge's version of "Intimations of Immortality": "All this long eve, so balmy and serene,/Have I been gazing on the western sky,/And its peculiar tint of yellow green:/And still I gaze—and with how blank an eye!. . ./I see, not feel, how beautiful they are!")

The wonderful poems kept coming after Bishop published *Geography III* in 1976—"Santarém" and "North Haven," her elegy for Lowell, appeared in 1978, "Pink Dog" and "Sonnet" in 1979. Each was a masterpiece, each, as Goldensohn writes, had "its own brilliant consistency of style, tone, and theme."[11] Schwartz believes that at the time of her death in October 1979, "She was writing her best work, her public readings were better than ever, warmer and more conversational. She was becoming more and more confident and less and less shy."[12] She was also coming into her own with critics, poetry award givers, and with a (slightly) larger audience. In 1976 she won the Books Abroad/Neustadt International Prize for Literature, the first American and the first woman to win this award; and *Geography III* won the National Book Critics' Circle Poetry Award in 1977. Having complained of being "buried alive" in the early 1970s, Bishop burst forth trailing clouds of glory in the last years of her life.

Lowell's life was considerably more troubled in its last years. The relationship with Blackwood began to sour rather quickly, and his manic attacks returned with renewed ferocity. Tillinghast remembers Lowell as a rather pathetic lost figure in this dwindling time of his life: "Blackwood used Lowell—she used him up. He had moved to England and cut his ties with the U.S. for her, but then he felt stranded and isolated. Living there depressed and demoralized him."[13]

Lowell had always needed a lot of care, but Blackwood could not or would not provide it. When he suffered a serious breakdown in November 1975, "it knocked the magic out of the affair," as Tillinghast puts it. When another came the next year, right before he was supposed to begin the fall semester at Harvard, Blackwood fled with Sheridan. "I'm no use to him in these attacks," she told Ian Hamilton. "They destroy me. I'm really better if I'm away if he has one."[14] Then in January Lowell suffered congestive heart failure and spent ten days at Massachusetts General Hospital.

Later that winter, Blackwood sold Milgate, the country house in Kent that she and Lowell had lived in for much of their relationship, and moved with her daughters and their son to an apartment in one of the Guinness family mansions at Castleton, near Dublin. Lowell visited her there over Easter (1977) and it was then that they agreed to end their marriage. Blackwood couldn't bear the prospect of living through another of his manic attacks. Lowell knew he would not be able to endure the isolation and pomposity of Castleton. And besides, Hardwick was back in the picture.

She and Lowell had become reconciled a few years after *The Dolphin* and they were in close touch during this period, "on the most affectionate and old-shoe sort of terms," as a friend put it.[15] Upon his return to America, Lowell decided to go back to her, and they spent the summer together in Castine. That September, Lowell traveled once again to Ireland to see Blackwood and Sheridan. Blackwood wanted to resume their marriage; Lowell writhed in vacillation. He telephoned Hardwick in New York to tell her he was ending the visit early because being with Blackwood was "sheer torture." Lowell flew back to New York from Dublin and he died on September 12, 1977 in the taxi that was taking him from Kennedy Airport to the West Sixty-seventh Street apartment that he and Hardwick had shared for the better part of a decade.

Happily, Lowell's last few meetings with Bishop were pleasant ones. Though she still became annoyed at his "antics" and at his way of turning conversations into emotionally naked encounters ("fearlessly holding back nothing from a friend," he says of his own conversational style in "Unwanted"), she was more willing than she had been a few years earlier to forgive him, to ignore his lapses. With *The Dolphin* behind them, the friends were easier with each other, more relaxed together. "They had a good time together; they had fun," remembers Lloyd Schwartz. "There was some instinctive connection that was very deep and that never ended."[16]

Bishop went to visit Lowell and Blackwood in England in June of 1976. Though she found Blackwood hard to take, Bishop was, of course, cordial, as her good manners required. The friends were both at Harvard during the spring term of 1977. She attended his last birthday party at Frank Bidart's apartment in Cambridge, and guests recall how the two of them convulsed the gathering by one-upping each other with outrageous tales of the allegedly sadistic dentist they shared. That summer there was talk of Lowell's and Mary McCarthy's ferrying to North Haven to visit

Bishop, but sadly, she called it off. She had been entertaining all of July and now, at the start of August, could not bear the idea of more guests. "I've been feeling so sick I really haven't been able to do anything except read and—with the seven guests—cook. . . . I hope you'll understand when I say I *must* work and not break off for a while (I haven't written anything for over a year)."[17] This was the final letter that passed between them.

The poems Lowell was writing in these years were markedly different from the fourteen-liners. Looser, longer, gentler, purged of history and politics and aggressive literary allusion, more meditative and more weary, they are an old man's poems, a poetry of "ache and twilight," in Helen Vendler's phrase.[18] *Day by Day*, the elegiac final volume in which he gathered these poems, is a book of leave-taking and final reckoning. Lowell retraces all the steps of his journey through life. There are poems to, for, or about all three of his wives; poems for Peter Taylor, John Berryman, Robert Penn Warren; poems about his parents, his children, and his own wretched childhood. He follows his dazed wanderings in and out of hospitals and describes the break-up of his marriage with Blackwood as well as her mental breakdown. There are many poems about mental and physical illness, old age, the ravages of chronic incurable suffering. "It's not death I fear,/but unspecified, unlimited pain," he writes in "Death of a Critic," yet death is omnipresent in the volume—both his own death and the deaths of friends and relatives. In Yeats and Auden, this premature preoccupation with old age and death was a poetic conceit for they both outlived their morbid lines by many years; but Lowell's sense of finality in *Day by Day* proved to be prophetic. Anthony Hecht calls the book "as warm as any that Lowell wrote, a moving, gentle book tinged with a sense of his own pain and the pain he gave to others."[19]

Twenty years earlier, when he found a radically new voice in "Skunk Hour," Lowell had very deliberately set out to assimilate Bishop's style, her "rhythms, idiom, images, and stanza structure" as he catalogued it in his essay on the poem. In *Day by Day*, Bishop's influence is less willed, less consciously striven for, but perhaps even more pervasive. It's nothing so concrete as rhythms or images—but rather the manner and stance of the poems, his preoccupation with the humble facts of dailiness, his absorption in life's routines and in what was going on outside the window

(Bishop remarked on how much weather there is in the late poems). As Helen Vendler puts it, "In *Day by Day* Lowell slows down to a ruminativeness, a meditativeness. One can see his life as a struggle between the influence of Bishop to 'catch the moment on the wing,' (as in 'Arrival at Santos') and the monumentality of Tate. In *History* he Tatized the *Notebooks,* took them out of the Elizabeth mode. *Day by Day* is the final victory for the Elizabeth mode. It is the closest to her work of any of his volumes."[20]

Again, one can't assert flatly that the quietness and seeming casualness of *Day by Day* come out of Bishop any more than one can say that the openness and intimacy of *Geography III* come out of Lowell. In comparing the books it may be more useful to speak of correspondences and resonances than of influences. The two volumes set off a marvelous vibration when read together. "Crusoe" and "Ulysses and Circe" are companion pieces—both poems of bitter homecoming in old age. Lowell writes: "I have grown bleak-boned with survival—/I who hoped to leave the earth/younger than I came./Age is the bilge/we cannot shake from the mop." And Bishop: "I'm old./I'm bored, too, drinking my real tea,/surrounded by uninteresting lumber."

Bishop's "Poem" ("About the size of an old-style dollar bill") and "Five Flights Up" are, like Lowell's "Epilogue," meditations on art and truth, memory and experience, the lifelong work of turning the "art of the eye" into words: "Which is which?" she asks in "Poem" as she moves in her mind back and forth between a painting her uncle did of a Nova Scotia landscape and her own vivid memory of the scene. "Life and the memory of it cramped/dim, on a piece of Bristol board,/dim, but how live, how touching in detail/—the little that we get for free/the little of our earth trust. Not much." She, too, at the poem's end prays for what Lowell calls the "grace of accuracy" to "give each figure . . . his living name": "the munching cows,/the iris, crisp and shivering, the water/still standing from spring freshets,/the yet-to-be-dismantled elms, the geese." It is typical that the "figures" in Bishop's scene are plants and animals and that her prevailing metaphor is painting while Lowell's medium in "Epilogue" is photography and his "figures" presumably human. Typical, also, that Bishop lets the certainty of death and destruction steal in on tiptoe in the "Not much" and the "yet-to-be-dismantled elms."

Despite their fascinating echoes, *Geography III* and *Day by Day* do hold fundamentally different places in their authors' careers. Lowell's book marks a retraction and a withdrawal while Bishop's shows a remarkable extension of range. After charting the history of western civilization and vaulting into the political arena, Lowell falls back in *Day by Day* to the small world of the immediate—his houses, his rituals, his family, his memories. "I decamp from window to window/to catch the sun," he writes in "Logan Airport, Boston." "I am blind with seeing." Space collapses in on Lowell in these final poems, light shrinks, vision narrows. In poem after poem he sounds the same note—a heavy sigh of fretful exhaustion. The volume is moving but monotonous. "I am too weak to strain to remember" sadly confesses the once muscular poet who wrestled Christ to the ground in *Lord Weary's Castle* and unscrewed the doors from their jambs in *Life Studies*. A sense of defeat pervades *Day by Day:* It's as if Lowell were writing about the end of writing.

Bishop, on the other hand, opens out in *Geography III* to embrace new forms, new personae, new tones. The wry prose poem "12 O'Clock News" in which she describes her desk from the perspective of a Lilliputian television newscaster is about guerrilla warfare. In "Night City," about an airplane descending into an urban airport, she records her horror of the blighted landscape of capitalism ("The city burns guilt./—For guilt-disposal/the central heat/must be this intense"). "In the Waiting Room" and "The Moose" are both long narratives of personal initiation or illumination. "By the time she published *Geography III*," says James Merrill, "it seemed to me there was nothing she could not write about directly or imply."[21] Unlike Lowell's gravely meditated leave-takings in *Day by Day,* Bishop's performances in *Geography III* seem to proclaim buoyantly that the show has just begun.

Though *Day by Day* is strewn with the names of Lowell's friends, wives, mentors, children, fellow poets, he makes no mention of Bishop and dedicates no poem to her (he probably didn't dare to after "Letter with Poem"). But from their correspondence, we know that "Thanks-Offering for Recovery," placed next to last in *Day by Day*, is about a Brazilian carved balsa-wood head that Bishop sent him as a present.

In the poem, Lowell gives thanks that the "wooden winter shadow" of illness has been taken off and that he is once more free to work: "I give thanks, thanks—/thanks too for this small/Brazilian *ex voto*, this primitive head/sent me across the Atlantic by my friend . . ." As the poem progresses, he ponders the nature and meaning of the "primitive head" (for of course Bishop *must* have meant something by it), and he begins, inevitably, to see himself in its rough misshapen form:

> Free of the unshakable terror that made me write . . .
> I pick it up, a head holy and unholy,
> tonsured or damaged,
> with gross black charcoaled brows and stern eyes
> frowning as if they had seen the splendor
> times past counting . . .
> It is all childcraft, especially
> its shallow, unchiseled ears,
> crudely healed scars lumped out
> to listen to itself, perhaps, not knowing
> it was made to be given up.

Lowell turns the head into a totemic symbol of his own "damaged" head and even makes it self-obsessed like himself.

The word "free" is crucial to the poem, and each time Lowell uses it he twists its meaning in a different direction. "I am the *homme sensuel,* free/to turn my back on the lamp, and work," he writes near the beginning. He is free of illness and pain, everyman at liberty in his own body and his home. But this freedom feels rather hollow if in order to work he must turn his back on illumination. The word "free" crops up next in the line "Free of the unshakable terror that made me write . . . ," the line on which the poem pivots. Is the "unshakable terror" a terror of death? or terror of another descent into madness? Is the writing that was impelled by the unshakable terror a different kind of writing from the "work" he now pursues with his back to the lamp?

The line is elusive, but the feeling it conveys is one of relief tinged with suspicion that the relief may be, after all, only a temporary evasion of terror not a permanent shaking off. This freedom may be an escape from pain, but it also involves a falling away from the harsh compulsions of art. One can sense a link between the unshakable terror and "the splendor" that the head's eyes appear to have seen "times past counting." Freedom is thus loss as well as gain, a dimming as well as a brightening. The *"homme sensuel"* is a less heroic figure than the mad artist writing for his life. There is an echo of Coleridge's "Dejection: An Ode" here, though it is fainter than the resonance in "Crusoe in England."

Bishop's gift is also free, as all gifts are, and doubly free since "it was made to be given up"—given to be given away again. Light (a "corkweight thing"), unpossessible, the head costs nothing—but does that mean it is also worthless? just a toy? Would it do him any good if he took it to church? Would church do any good? Bishop plays with these same meanings of "free" in "Poem." Her uncle's painting is "useless and free"; it "never earned any money in its life"—but it represents something enormously valuable; "the little that we get for free,/the little of our earthly trust."

"Goodbye nothing," Lowell bids farewell to the head at the poem's end with the same words he used to dismiss his "winter shadow" at the beginning. "Blockhead,/I would take you to church,/if any church would take you . . ./This winter, I thought/I was created to be given away." The return to winter at the end of the poem seals his identification with the head: A winter death would have made him a free empty nothing like the blockhead. Though the word "recovery" in the title and the use of the past tense in the final lines declare that the worry is over and that *now* he is fine, the whole movement of the poem, and especially the revolving meanings of the word "free," suggests otherwise. The "thanks" in "Thanks-Offering for Recovery" are bleak and dim and weakened by terror. The kind gesture of the friend "across the Atlantic" is no match for the wooden winter shadow. The next time the shadow falls might really be the time past counting.

In "Thanks-Offering for Recovery," as in most of the poems in *Day by Day*, Lowell looks death in the eye. At the brink of the abyss, he still has the grace to turn around and thank his old friend. And to say good-bye.

Bishop was famous among her friends for her eccentric genius for gift giving ("one ached for a present from Elizabeth," recalls Schwartz), and the Brazilian balsa-wood head was certainly an apt choice for Lowell. But Lowell did not live to receive Bishop's finest present to him. "North Haven," the elegy she composed for him the summer after his death (and the summer before her own), ranks as a literary gift with Melville's "Hawthorne and His Mosses" and his dedication of *Moby-Dick* to Hawthorne, Porter's introduction to Welty's first collection of stories, and Welty's essay "The Eye of the Story" about Porter's work.

Years before, Bishop had dedicated "The Armadillo" to Lowell and she supplied a marvelous blurb for *Life Studies;* but "North Haven" is the only poem she ever addressed to him. It is a token of belated acknowledgment of the series of dedications, essays, and poems Lowell wrote to and for her over the thirty years of their friendship (beginning in 1947 with his brilliant review of *North & South* and running through "Skunk Hour," "Water," *Imitations,* the Elizabeth Bishop poems in *Notebook* and *History,* the blurb for her *The Complete Poems,* and ending with "Thanks-Offering"). "North Haven" is a gesture of thanks as well for Lowell's unflagging loyalty and for the assistance he lavished on her (often without her knowledge) in securing awards, appointments, prizes, and fellowships.

"North Haven," a formal pastoral elegy, is a distant descendant of Milton's "Lycidas" (one of Lowell's favorite poems); but Bishop refrains here, as everywhere, from hoisting what Lowell called the great sail. This is a deceptively simple poem, luminous and inviting, that dazzles on the surface but conceals its depths, like sun-struck water. The season is high summer. The mood is melancholy, resigned but not despairing. Bishop filters her sadness through the bright and soothing sensory impressions that surrounded her on the island—colors, flowers, sweet smells, birdsong, brimming water.

She opens with a Whitmanesque boast about the acuity of her "famous eye":

> I can make out the rigging of a schooner
> a mile off; I can count
> the new cones of the spruce. It is so still
> the pale bay wears a milky skin, the sky
> no clouds, except for one long, carded horse's-tail.

But unlike Whitman, who boasts of his powers to expand himself infinitely in time and space ("I contain multitudes," "I am with you, you men and women of a generation, or ever so many generations hence,/Just as you feel . . . so I felt"), Bishop boasts of her power of minute, supernaturally sharp perception of the here and now. It's a kind of invocation of her Muse, a gently Bardic declaration of her place in the scheme of things and the condition of her art.

She continues beautifully in the next stanza:

The islands haven't shifted since last summer,
even if I like to pretend they have
—drifting, in a dreamy sort of way,
a little north, a little south or sidewise,
and that they're free within the blue frontiers of bay.

The echoes to "The Map," the first poem in her first volume, are very strong: In both poems Bishop studies the shapes that land makes in water and in both she plays with the notion that geography has a secret, sentient life of its own ("Are they assigned, or can the countries pick their colors?"). It is the quintessential Bishop stance: the keen-eyed observer, intent on scrupulous, meticulous accuracy (*counting* cones on the spruce, finding the perfect words for a single cloud) and yet indulging in a childish game as she *pretends* (the child's word for "imagine") that the islands are free to drift like toy boats "within the blue frontiers of bay." The imaginary shifting of the islands—"a little north, a little south or sidewise"—follows the course of Bishop's own lifelong migration ("wholly Atlantic,/you combed this seaboard north and south/for room to live," Lowell wrote of her in one of his versions of "Flying to Rio"; in other versions he used the words "drift," "anchor," "rock," and "star," all of which turn up in Bishop's elegy. Bishop read the drafts in 1957, and, blessed with what Lowell called a "giant memory," she might well have remembered them).

The tensions that she sets up in the second stanza between freedom and fixity, stasis and drift, permanence and change run right through the poem. In one of her characteristic qualifying asides, Bishop acknowledges that the seemingly eternal returns of nature are not exact repetitions: "The Goldfinches are back, or others like them." Some of last year's flock have probably died, but their offspring have returned in their places. Nature is thus ever new, yet at the same time unfailing, unchanging in her essence.

The elegiac note swells ever so gently as the poem continues. Sorrow steals over the landscape with the "five-note song" of the white-throated sparrow: The "pleading and pleading, brings tears to the eyes" (one thinks of "the sandpipers' heart-broken cries," in "Twelfth Morning," which Richard Wilbur took "for a sign that grief is a radical presence in the world").[22] Bishop weeps for the aching beauty of nature, for Lowell's inability to come back, for man's separateness from the endless cycles of the pastoral.

With the shedding of tears, Bishop steps back to moralize on the scene she has painted: "Nature repeats herself, or almost does:/*repeat, repeat, repeat; revise, revise, revise.*" Herein lies the link between man and nature, or rather between poet and nature. The repetitions of nature, the annual returns of birds and flowers to the fixed islands ignite the poet's obsession to keep writing and rewriting until he has gotten it right. In the word "revise" Bishop reaches down to the Latin root—to look back at, to see again. This is the poet's place in the landscape: to return, to see again, to see freshly, to seek again, to rewrite.

But of course "revise, revise, revise" was also the iron law that Lowell, even more than most poets, imposed on himself. The word reminds Bishop of the "sad occasion dear" that compels her to write. Only in the final two stanzas of the poem does she introduce Lowell into this lovely, highly charged, fallen Eden:

> Years ago, you told me it was here
> (in 1932?) you first "discovered *girls*"
> and learned to sail, and learned to kiss.
> You had "such fun," you said, that classic summer.
> ("Fun"—it always seemed to leave you at a loss . . .)
>
> You left North Haven, anchored in its rock,
> afloat in mystic blue . . . And now—you've left
> for good. You can't derange, or re-arrange,
> your poems again. (But the Sparrows can their song.)
> The words won't change again. Sad friend, you can-
>   not change.

The bits of intimate revelation about Lowell—the glimpses of him sailing and kissing as a teenager, the jump to his tragic "deranged" maturity, the image of the tortured, overly serious poet compulsively revising his poems—are immensely affecting. (It's interesting, in looking at the drafts of the poem, to see how much trouble the perfect line " 'Fun'—it always seemed to leave you at a loss" gave her. She started off with the clumsy, " 'Fun,' the elemental good you often later seemed to miss" and only after much groping did she find the phrase "leave you at a loss," which clicked the line into place.) In death, Bishop sadly acknowledges, Lowell has merged with changeless nature: He is one with the island "anchored in its rock,/afloat in mystic blue"—a line that beautifully enfolds and resolves fixity and freedom. As Merrill writes, Bishop finds in nature "a poignant and oddly appropriate image, whereby [Lowell's] lifelong recyclings of earlier work come to seem not so much tortured as instinctive, part of a serene Arcadian world."[23] But there is still a stab of grief in admitting that her sad friend has fallen silent. Nature will continue, year after year, to paint the meadows with delight but Lowell has left for good. He has achieved completeness only by surrendering his life.

Milton, Keats, Spenser, Shakespeare, Herbert, a fleeting shadow of Whitman are "behind" "North Haven," and so are the mingled feelings of Bishop's thirty-year friendship with Lowell—the love and exasperation; the admiration and anxiety; the pleasure she took in his strapping, virile, handsome youth (she once likened the young Lowell to James Dean); and her fear of his madness. The word "derange" in the last stanza comes as a slap in the face: Writing "derange" where she could have put "revise" is her way of linking Lowell's endless tinkerings and irresponsible poetic appropriations to his incurable insanity. Madness compelled him to make his poems as deranged as his mind, until death cried halt and fixed the words for all time. "And now—you've left/for good" in the final stanza breathes a sigh of relief, a kind of benediction for the blessed rest granted even mad poets in the end.

"North Haven" plays a thin, serene, heart-catching northern music—"sure-as-a-hymn" as Bishop once said of "Skunk Hour." It was just the living sound that Lowell loved best of anything on earth.

In "Ulysses and Circe" Lowell writes of how insects die "instantly as one would ask of a friend." Lowell himself died this way, and perhaps he interceded for Bishop from beyond the grave for she, too, was granted an instant death when a brain aneurysm killed her on the evening of October 6, 1979. "Elizabeth was morbidly afraid of failing mental powers, of feebleness and lingering illness," remarks Lloyd Schwartz. "She would have been a lot happier if she had known she was to die suddenly." She was sixty-eight years old.

Though Bishop and Lowell spent most of their friendship with an ocean between them, they were nearly always in close touch. Their love for each other survived madness, alcoholism, a brush with marriage, and a variety of personal and professional squabbles. Both mentioned in letters their habit of addressing the other mentally, conducting silent imaginary conversations with the other, composing interior letters that were never written down. Each lived with a daily sense of the other near at hand, looking over the shoulder as a new line got written and scratched out, sharing a laugh at the infelicities in a colleague's book, gossiping, comparing reviews, awards, reputations. They defined for each other what it meant to be a poet. Theirs was a true literary friendship in which affection and admiration were inseparable. In their three decades together, they shared and exchanged all that friends, all that writer friends, can hope for.

And so, who was the better poet, as Lowell (at least the intensely competitive younger Lowell) would have demanded? There is no question that Bishop's stock is very high today and that Lowell's continues to fall, especially among their fellow poets. Lowell's rhetoric seems dated. His turmoil strikes us as somewhat irrelevant now that he is no longer around to generate it. "The age burns in me," he wrote in "Death of a Critic"—and this was both his strength and his weakness. Now that "his" age is passing, the fire has lost some of its warmth.

The poet and critic Anne Stevenson tersely sums up the prevailing judgment when she asserts that Bishop is "finer than Lowell, though of course more limited."[24] Strangely, Bishop's very limitations now strike us as virtues. Her cool skeptical restraint accords better with our played-out anti-idealistic sensibility. We have become fed up with large gestures. Rather than pity the planet, we'd prefer to *see* the planet with new eyes, "infant sight," as Bishop lets us do. Her vision is irresistible: Once we have seen her make the casual perfect, we can never see it any other way. A house in Key West has "a veranda/of wooden lace" ("Jeronimo's House"); "Greenish-white dogwood infiltrated the wood,/each petal burned, apparently, by a cigarette-butt" ("A Cold Spring"); "The beach hisses like fat" ("Sandpiper"); the feet of a dead mouse "curled into little balls like young fern-plants" ("The Hanging of the Mouse"); "the iris, crisp and shivering" ("Poem"); Crusoe's flute is "Home-made, home-made! But aren't we all?" ("Crusoe in England"). These are miracles of language that will surely go on being miraculous, and her poetry is full of them. Almost all of her poems still *feel* just right, still look "fresh as paint." Without ever hoisting the "great sail," she catches everything—except history. One would have to study her verse through a microscope to know that she lived through the Depression, the Second World War, the tranquilized fifties, the wild sixties. We must turn to Lowell for the confluence of the significant and American, as Bishop pointed out.

"There is something cautious, careful and modest about Bishop's stake-out," comments Anthony Hecht. "Everything she does she does superbly well. But she wrote as the outsider, the young girl, the Canadian, someone who was in exile a long time. Lowell, on the other hand, staked out his claim right in the middle. You could not be unaware of Lowell—the name alone gave him importance, just as it did to Eliot. Lowell intended to be mainstream—the poems resonate with echoes of Thoreau, Melville, Emerson. He stepped into the shoes of the major American tradition. *History* covers all of civilization. You don't catch Elizabeth writing stuff like that. Lowell aimed so high it's easy for him to disappoint."[25]

Lowell would have been the first to admit the truth of this. "I don't know the value of what I've written," he told Frank Bidart near the end of his life, "but I know that I changed the game." Changing the game (with the emphasis on *the*) was his ambition, and also the terms on which he will be judged. Bishop never even tried to play. "Somebody loves us all" she ends the poem "Filling Station," which begins "Oh, but it is dirty!" She admitted the dirt together with the love: They don't cancel each other out; they are simultaneously welcome and irreconcilable. Even with the irony, or *because* of the irony, we find this an immensely appealing stance. It seems to fit the way things are just now. Just now. But who knows what will come up next on "fortune's wheel"?

Despite his fall from fashion, Lowell, by virtue of what Hecht calls his stake-out at the center of the major American tradition, draws together all the various strands of this group portrait. He stands as the culmination of the tradition, the conscious heir, in his life and his work, of all who came before him. He had close social, family, and literary ties with the other six friends—his ancestor James Russell Lowell was a friend of both Hawthorne and James; he was born into the same exalted social sphere as Melville and Wharton; his apprenticeship in the South connected him to Porter and Welty. Lowell wrote about every one of the friends considered here (with the exception of Eudora Welty)—adapting Melville's "Benito Cereno" and Hawthorne's "My Kinsman, Major Molineux" into his play *The Old Glory;* astutely comparing Katherine Anne Porter to Edith Wharton; tossing off brilliant assessments of Hawthorne, Melville, and James in his unfinished essay "New England and Further" (Hawthorne "an ironic allegorist, therefore shady and suspect as a moralist . . . he knew how to dislike, not the lawless and ungodly, but the simple, the tedious, the absurd. . . . [His] best prose has the red-claret glow and iron of a villagery saturation, not always at the command of that unsatisfied and much greater friend, Melville." On James: "Two Jameses: one is Proust's tender, idealized narrator yearning for truth, kindness, eternity; the other is Baron Charlus, a whale in society, overbearing behind the scenes and conspiring. Oh, mountainous Henry James!").[26]

Lowell was mountainous himself. He lived an incredibly full, almost supernaturally intense life. He was a teacher, a husband and father, a public figure, an antiwar activist, a tireless wooer of young women, a friend of the major writers and intellectuals of his day, an incurable madman. He wrote eleven volumes of poetry and a play, he translated from most of the major languages of the West, and wrote enough criticism and essays to fill a substantial volume. He lived in elegant town houses and country estates as well as shabby basement apartments, mental hospitals, and jails.

Viewed in this way, Lowell steps forth as almost a mythic figure, a kind of Ahab of contemporary American poetry. America burned in him. As the poet Derek Walcott remarks, Lowell was "continually trying to get into the core of what it was to be American."[27] In this too he focused in himself and magnified the life work of all the writers in this book, indeed of all American writers.

"Please never stop writing me letters," Bishop begged Lowell thirteen years into their friendship, "—they always manage to make me feel like my higher self (I've been re-reading Emerson) for several days."[28] All the writers in this book made their friends feel like their higher selves (at least occasionally). Perhaps what is most uniquely American in these friendships is the assumption that spiritual elevation is of the essence of friendship.

Friendship is born of hope, thrives on free and open exchange, withers with suspicion and mistrust. Sadly, most friendships vanish when the friends die: Packets of letters get stowed in old trunks, descendants puzzle over strange faces in old photos, fond stories tarnish or blur with time. For good or ill, we live in a time when artists are exempt from such oblivion: We deem their lives worthy of saving, and we sift the details of their existences for clues about the meaning of our own. Writers by the very nature of their profession make such sifting easy for us. It is our privilege that these eight American writers left records of their great friendships—their high ideals and immodest demands—for us to wonder at.

Notes

Introduction

1. Henry James, *Hawthorne* (London: Macmillan, 1967), p. 45.
2. Edith Wharton, "Henry James in His Letters," *Quarterly Review*, July 1920, p. 195.
3. Ralph Waldo Emerson, "Friendship," in Stephen E. Whicher, ed., *Selections from Ralph Waldo Emerson* (Boston: Houghton Mifflin, 1957), p. 134.
4. Eudora Welty, "The House of Willa Cather," in Eudora Welty, *The Eye of the Story: Selected Essays and Reviews* (New York: Vintage, 1979), p. 48.
5. ———, introduction in Eudora Welty and Ronald A. Sharp, eds., *The Norton Book of Friendship* (New York: W. W. Norton, 1991), p. 40.
6. Edith Wharton, "Henry James in His Letters," in *Quarterly Review*, July 1920, p. 195.
7. Henry David Thoreau, *A Week on the Concord and Merrimack Rivers*, excerpt in Welty and Sharp, eds., *The Norton Book of Friendship*, p. 519.

ONE: *Turkey and Thunder*

1. Quoted in Luther Stearns Mansfield, "Melville and Hawthorne in the Berkshires," in Howard P. Vincent, ed., *Melville and Hawthorne in the Berkshires* (Kent, Ohio: Kent State University Press, 1968), p. 12.
2. Quoted in Jay Leyda, *The Melville Log*, Vol. 1 (New York: Harcourt Brace, 1951), p. 384.

3. Quoted in Harrison Hayford, "Melville's 'Monody': Really for Hawthorne?" (Evanston, Ill.: Northwestern University Press, 1990), p. 11.

4. Herman Melville letter to Nathaniel Hawthorne, June 1?, 1851, quoted in Merrell R. Davis and William H. Gilman, eds., *The Letters of Herman Melville* (New Haven: Yale University Press, 1960), p. 129.

5. Edwin Haviland Miller, *Salem Is My Dwelling Place* (Iowa City, Ia.: University of Iowa Press, 1991), p. 27.

6. Quoted in James. R. Mellow, *Nathaniel Hawthorne in His Times* (Boston: Houghton Mifflin, 1980), p. 37.

7. Quoted in Miller, *Salem Is My Dwelling Place*, p. 121.

8. Nathaniel Hawthorne, preface to *The Snow Image and Other Twice-Told Tales* in Hyatt H. Waggoner, ed., *Nathaniel Hawthorne: Selected Tales and Sketches* (New York: Holt, Rinehart & Winston, 1970), p. 591.

9. Nathaniel Hawthorne, *The Scarlet Letter* (Boston: Houghton Mifflin, 1960), p. 67.

10. Quoted in Miller, *Salem Is My Dwelling Place*, p. 7.

11. Quoted in Henry James, *Henry James Autobiography (Notes of a Son and Brother)* (Princeton, N.J.: Princeton University Press, 1983), pp. 360–61.

12. Henry James, *Hawthorne* (London: Macmillan, 1967), p. 42.

13. Philip Rahv, "The Dark Lady of Salem," reprinted in Philip Rahv, *Essays on Literature and Politics 1932–1972* (Boston: Houghton Mifflin, 1978), pp. 25–42.

14. James, *Hawthorne*, p. 29.

15. Philip Young, *Hawthorne's Secret: An Untold Tale* (Boston: Godine, 1984), p. 30.

16. Quoted in Mellow, *Nathaniel Hawthorne in His Times*, p. 296.

17. James, *Hawthorne*, p. 109.

18. Nathaniel Hawthorne, "The Custom-House" introduction to *The Scarlet Letter*, p. 15.

19. Hawthorne, "The Custom-House," pp. 44–45.

20. Quoted in James Playsted Wood, *The Unpardonable Sin: A Life of Nathaniel Hawthorne* (New York: Pantheon Books, 1970), p. 100.

21. Quoted in Leyda, *The Melville Log*, Vol. 1, p. 207.

22. Edith Wharton, *A Backward Glance* (New York: Scribner's, 1962), pp. 10, 68.

23. Harrison Hayford, Hershel Parker, and G. Thomas Tanselle, "Historical Note" to *Moby-Dick* in Harrison Hayford, Hershel Parker, and G. Thomas Tanselle, eds., *The Writings of Herman Melville*, Vol. 6 (Evanston and Chicago, Ill.: Northwestern University Press and the Newberry Library, 1988), p. 588.

24. John Updike, "Melville's Withdrawal," *The New Yorker*, May 10, 1982, p. 146.
25. Herman Melville, *White-Jacket* (New York: Library of America, 1983), p. 529.
26. Harry Levin, *The Power of Blackness* (New York: Knopf, 1958), p. 170.
27. Herman Melville, "I and My Chimney," in Herman Melville, *Herman Melville: Uncollected Prose* (New York: Library of America, 1984), p. 1325.
28. Davis and Gilman, eds., *The Letters of Herman Melville*, pp. 91–92.
29. Ibid., p. 108.
30. Updike, "Melville's Withdrawal," p. 120.

TWO: *Fire Worship*

1. Herman Melville, *Moby-Dick* (New York: Library of America, 1983), p. 848.
2. Ibid., p. 849.
3. Harrison Hayford, Hershel Parker, and G. Thomas Tanselle, "Historical Note" to *Moby-Dick* in Harrison Hanford, Hershel Parker, and G. Thomas Tinselle, eds., *The Writings of Herman Melville*, Vol. 6 (Evanston and Chicago, Ill.: Northwestern University Press and the Newberry Library, 1988), p. 612.
4. The details about his desk come from a letter written to Duyckinck on August 16, 1850, quoted in Davis and Gilman, eds., *The Letters of Herman Melville* (New Haven: Yale University Press, 1960), p. 111. Jay Leyda states without question that Melville began "Hawthorne and His Mosses" on August 11, 1850, but the editors of Melville's letters write that "the evidence is conflicting as to whether Melville wrote the essay before or after he met Hawthorne." Though Melville's fictionalized Virginian narrator claims, "I never saw the man" (meaning Hawthorne), the warmly affectionate tone would suggest otherwise.
5. Herman Melville, "Hawthorne and His Mosses," in Herman Melville, *Herman Melville: Uncollected Prose* (New York: Library of America, 1984), p. 1159.
6. Ibid., p. 1170.
7. Ibid., p. 1167.
8. Melville, *Moby-Dick*, p. 1239.
9. Quoted in Leyda, *The Melville Log*, Vol. 1 (New York: Harcourt Brace, 1951), pp. 391–92.
10. Quoted in ibid, p. 391.
11. Sophia Hawthorne to her mother, quoted in Eleanor Melville Met-

calf, *Herman Melville: Cycle and Epicycle* (Westport, Conn.: Greenwood Press, 1950), pp. 92–93.

12. Undated and unaddressed letter, September ? 1850 from Sophia Hawthorne quoted in ibid., pp. 91–92.

13. For the record, dogs, but emphatically not children, also figured in the friendship between James and Wharton: Wharton and her husband, Teddy, adored their Pekingeses far more than they adored each other, and James commiserated elaborately with her every time one of the little darlings died. James had a Dachshund named Max, "the best and gentlest and most reasonable and well-mannered as well as most beautiful, small animal of his kind to be easily come across," as he once wrote. James dampened Max's fur with his tears when he had to leave him behind at Lamb House during his year-long sojourn in America in 1904–5. Elizabeth Bishop, allergic to dogs, kept cats and immortalized one of them—Tobias—in her poem "Electrical Storm." Lowell's daughter, Harriet, had hamsters, which likewise creep into several poems. Porter was also a cat fancier. Welty seems to have been petless, preferring to garden.

14. Harrison Hayford, Hershel Parker, and G. Thomas Tanselle, "Historical Note" to *Moby-Dick* in Harrison Hayford, Hershel Parker, and G. Thomas Tanselle, eds., *The Writings of Herman Melville,* Vol. 6, p. 615.

15. Harry Levin, *The Power of Blackness* (New York: Knopf, 1958), pp. 169–70.

16. Henry A. Murray, introduction to *Pierre,* reprinted in Edwin S. Shneidman, ed., *Endeavors in Psychology* (New York: Harper & Row, 1981), p. 423.

17. Herman Melville, *White-Jacket* (New York: Library of America, 1983), p. 396.

18. Melville, *Moby-Dick*, p. 1239.

19. Ibid., p. 906.

20. Herman Melville, *Pierre* (New York: Library of America, 1984), p. 214.

21. John Updike, "Melville's Withdrawal," *The New Yorker,* May 10, 1982, p. 136.

22. Herman Melville, "I and My Chimney," in Herman Melville, *Herman Melville: Uncollected Prose* (New York: Library of America, 1984), p. 1316.

23. Quoted in Melville, "Hawthorne and His Mosses," p. 1157.

24. Melville, *Moby-Dick*, p. 1333.

25. Quoted in Edwin Haviland Miller, *Salem Is My Dwelling Place* (Iowa City, Ia.: University of Iowa Press, 1991), p. 43.

26. Levin, *The Power of Blackness*, p. 100.

27. Nathaniel Hawthorne, "Fire Worship," in Hyatt H. Waggoner, ed., *Nathaniel Hawthorne: Selected Tales and Sketches* (New York: Holt, Rinehart & Winston, 1970), p. 494.
28. Melville, *Pierre*, p. 27.
29. Lyall H. Powers, ed., *Henry James and Edith Wharton Letters: 1900–1915* (New York: Scribner's, 1990), p. 268.

THREE: *Infinite Fraternity and the Negatives of Flesh*

1. James R. Mellow, *Nathaniel Hawthorne in His Times* (Boston: Houghton Mifflin, 1980), p. 341.
2. Jay Leyda, *The Melville Log*, Vol. 1 (New York: Harcourt Brace, 1951), p. 403.
3. Ibid., p. 406.
4. Ibid., p. 407.
5. Merrell R. Davis and William H. Gilman, eds., *The Letters of Herman Melville* (New Haven: Yale University Press, 1960), p. 119.
6. Leyda, *The Melville Log*, Vol. 1, p. 408.
7. Ibid., p. 410.
8. Davis and Gilman, eds., *The Letters of Herman Melville*, p. 119.
9. Leyda, *The Melville Log*, Vol. 1, p. 419.
10. Ibid., p. 422.
11. Ibid., pp. 422–23.
12. Sophia Hawthorne to her sister, Elizabeth Peabody, quoted in Edwin Haviland Miller, *Melville: A Biography* (New York: George Braziller, 1975), pp. 42–43.
13. Davis and Gilman, eds., *The Letters of Herman Melville*, p. 124.
14. Ibid., p. 125.
15. Ibid., p. 127.
16. Ibid., p. 128.
17. Ibid., p. 129.
18. Ibid., p. 130.
19. Ibid., p. 119.
20. Ibid., p. 128.
21. Miller, *Melville: A Biography*, pp. 34–36.
22. Davis and Gilman, eds., *The Letters of Herman Melville*, p. 135.
23. Ibid., pp. 132–33.
24. Ibid., p. 142.
25. Edwin Haviland Miller, *Salem Is My Dwelling Place: A Life of Nathaniel Hawthorne* (Iowa City, Ia.: University of Iowa Press, 1991), p. 363.

26. Leon Howard, *Herman Melville* (Berkeley: University of California Press, 1951), p. 300.

27. Harrison Hayford, "Melville's 'Monody': Really for Hawthorne?" (Evanston, Ill.: Northwestern University Press, 1990), passim.

28. Ibid., p. 16.

29. John Bryant, ed., *A Companion to Melville Studies* (New York: Greenwood Press, 1986), p. xxi.

30. Herman Melville, *Clarel*, in Hennig Cohen, ed., *Selected Poems of Herman Melville* (New York: Fordham University Press, 1991), p. 71.

31. See Paul Fussell, *The Great War and Modern Memory* (London: Oxford University Press, 1975), pp. 270–309.

32. Leslie Fielder, *Love and Death in the American Novel*, in Hershel Parker and Harrison Hayford, eds., *Moby-Dick as Doubloon* (New York: W. W. Norton, 1970), p. 270.

FOUR: *The Downlook*

1. Harrison Hayford, "Melville's 'Monody': Really for Hawthorne?" (Evanston, Ill.: Northwestern University Press, 1990), p. 10.

2. Quoted in James R. Mellow, *Nathaniel Hawthorne in His Times* (Boston: Houghton Mifflin, 1980), p. 377.

3. Quoted in Edwin Haviland Miller, *Salem Is My Dwelling Place* (Iowa City, Ia.: University of Iowa Press, 1991), p. 305.

4. Ibid., pp. 346–47.

5. John Updike, "Melville's Withdrawal," *The New Yorker*, May 10, 1982, p. 135.

6. Nathaniel Hawthorne, *The Marble Faun* (New York: New American Library, 1961), p. 208.

7. Merrell R. Davis and William H. Gilman, eds., *The Letters of Herman Melville* (New Haven: Yale University Press, 1960), p. 146.

8. Jay Leyda, *The Melville Log*, Vol. 1 (New York: Harcourt Brace, 1951), p. 438.

9. Davis and Gilman, eds., *The Letters of Herman Melville*, p. 162.

10. Leyda, *The Melville Log*, Vol. 1, pp. 430, 438, 439.

11. Davis and Gilman, eds., *The Letters of Herman Melville*, p. 129.

12. Ibid., pp. 152–53.

13. Mellow, *Nathaniel Hawthorne in His Times*, p. 402.

14. Henry James, *Hawthorne* (London: Macmillan, 1967), p. 125.

15. Quoted in Mellow, *Nathaniel Hawthorne in His Times*, pp. 402–3.

16. Leyda, *The Melville Log*, Vol. 1, pp. 455, 456, 462, 463.

17. Herman Melville, *Pierre* (New York: Library of America, 1984), p. 341.

18. Henry A. Murray, introduction to *Pierre*, reprinted in Edwin S. Shneidman, ed., *Endeavors in Psychology* (New York: Harper & Row, 1981), p. 462.
19. Melville, *Pierre*, p. 253.
20. Edwin Haviland Miller, *Melville: A Biography* (New York: George Braziller, 1975), p. 237.
21. Nathaniel Hawthorne, *The Blithedale Romance* (New York: W. W. Norton, 1958), pp. 149, 151.
22. Henry A. Murray, introduction to *Pierre*, reprinted in Shneidman, ed., *Endeavors in Psychology*, p. 462.
23. James, *Hawthorne*, p. 132.
24. Philip Young, *Hawthorne's Secret: An Untold Tale* (Boston: Godine, 1984), p. 40.
25. Mellow, *Nathaniel Hawthorne in His Times*, p. 415.
26. Quoted in Eleanor Melville Metcalf, *Herman Melville: Cycle and Epicycle* (Westport, Conn.: Greenwood Press, 1950), p. 147.
27. Metcalf, *Herman Melville: Cycle and Epicycle*, p. 133.
28. Leyda, *The Melville Log*, Vol. 2, (New York: Harcourt Brace, 1951), p. 527.
29. Ibid., pp. 527–28.
30. Ibid., p. 528.
31. Ibid., p. 529.
32. Ibid.
33. Ibid., p. 531.
34. Ibid.
35. Davis and Gilman, eds., *The Letters of Herman Melville*, p. 125.
36. Leyda, *The Melville Log*, Vol. 2, p. 528.
37. Quoted in Henry A. Murray, introduction to *Pierre*, reprinted in Edwin S. Shneidman, ed., *Endeavors in Psychology*, p. 516.
38. Herman Melville, "Monody," in Hennig Cohen, ed., *Selected Poems of Herman Melville* (New York: Fordham University Press, 1991), p. 141.

INTERGENERATIONAL: *Hawthorne and Melville to James and Wharton*

1. Henry James, *Hawthorne* (London: Macmillan, 1967), pp. 22–23.
2. Harold Bloom, introduction to Harold Bloom, ed., *Modern Critical Views: Nathaniel Hawthorne* (New York: Chelsea House, 1986), p. 1.
3. James, *Hawthorne*, p. 55.
4. Nathaniel Hawthorne, *The Marble Faun* (New York: New American Library, 1961), p. vi.

5. Philip Rahv, "The Dark Lady of Salem," reprinted in Philip Rahv, *Essays on Literature and Politics 1932–1972* (Boston: Houghton Mifflin, 1978), p. 36.
6. Henry James, *Notes of a Son and Brother* in *Henry James Autobiography* (Princeton, N.J.: Princeton University Press, 1983), p. 478.
7. R.W.B. Lewis and Nancy Lewis, eds., *The Letters of Edith Wharton* (New York: Macmillan, 1988), p. 238.
8. Cynthia Griffin Wolff, *A Feast of Words: The Triumph of Edith Wharton* (New York: Oxford University Press, 1977), p. 163.

FIVE: *On the Road*

1. Henry James letter to Howard Sturgis, July 20, 1912, in Leon Edel, ed., *Henry James Letters,* Vol. IV (Cambridge, Mass.: Harvard University Press, 1984), p. 620.
2. Edith Wharton, *A Backward Glance* (New York: Scribner's, 1962), p. 172.
3. Quoted in Louis Auchincloss, *Edith Wharton: A Woman in Her Time* (New York: Viking, 1971), p. 13.
4. Letters quoted in R.W.B. Lewis, *Edith Wharton: A Biography* (New York: Fromm International, 1985), p. 128.
5. Wharton, *A Backward Glance*, p. 173.
6. Henry James letter to Mary Cadwalader Jones, quoted in Lewis, *Edith Wharton*, p. 166.
7. Henry James, "Venice," originally published in 1882, reprinted in *Italian Hours* (1909) and in *Henry James on Italy* (New York: Weidenfeld & Nicolson, 1988), p. 13.
8. Wharton, *A Backward Glance*, pp. 187–89.
9. Edith Wharton, "Henry James in His Letters," *Quarterly Review*, July 1920, p. 190.
10. Henry James letter to Edmund Gosse, October 27, 1904, in Edel, ed., *Henry James Letters*, Vol. IV, p. 332.
11. Henry James letter to Jessie Allen, October 22, 1904, in ibid., pp. 329–30.
12. Henry James, *The American Scene* (New York: St. Martin's, 1987), p. 29.
13. Lyall H. Powers, ed., *Henry James and Edith Wharton Letters: 1900–1915* (New York: Scribner's, 1990), p. 168.
14. Henry James letter to Howard Sturgis, October 17, 1904, in Edel, *Henry James Letters*, Vol. IV, p. 325.
15. Edith Wharton, *A Motor-Flight Through France* (New York: Scribner's, 1909).
16. Quoted in Lewis, *Edith Wharton*, p. 120.

17. Nathaniel Hawthorne, *The Marble Faun* (New York: New American Library, 1961), p. 236.
18. Ibid., p. 330.
19. Quoted in Tony Tanner's introduction to Henry James, *Hawthorne* (London: Macmillan, 1967), p. 1.
20. Quoted in Edwin Haviland Miller, *Melville* (New York: George Braziller, 1975), p. 290.
21. Herman Melville, *Pierre* (New York: Library of America, 1984), p. 255.
22. Quoted in Steven Gould Axelrod, *Robert Lowell: Life and Art* (Princeton, N.J.: Princeton University Press, 1978), p. 214.
23. Quoted in Millicent Bell, *Edith Wharton and Henry James: The Story of Their Friendship* (New York: George Braziller, 1965), p. 140.
24. Henry James, "The Velvet Glove," in Leon Edel, ed., *The Complete Tales of Henry James*, Vol. 12 (Philadelphia: Lippincott, 1964), pp. 233–66.
25. Wharton, *A Backward Glance*, p. 308.

SIX: *Sex and Money*

1. Henry James, *The Outcry* (New York: Scribner's, 1911), pp. 82, 67.
2. Leon Edel, introduction to *Henry James Letters*, Vol. IV (Cambridge, Mass.: Harvard University Press, 1984), p. xxiii.
3. Cynthia Griffin Wolff, preface to Edith Wharton, *The Touchstone* (New York: Harper, 1991), p. 21; see also Wolff's critical biography, *A Feast of Words: The Triumph of Edith Wharton* (New York: Oxford University Press, 1977).
4. Wolff, preface to *The Touchstone*, p. 18.
5. R.W.B. Lewis, *Edith Wharton: A Biography* (New York: Fromm International, 1985), p. 326.
6. Lyall H. Powers gives this as the period when Wharton took James into her confidence in *Henry James and Edith Wharton Letters: 1900–1915* (New York: Scribner's, 1990), p. 84, but the internal evidence from the letters is by no means totally clear. He might not have known the truth until the following years.
7. Leon Edel, *Henry James: A Life* (New York: Harper & Row, 1985), p. 374.
8. Ibid., p. 224.
9. Henry James letter to Morton Fullerton, October 2, 1900, in Leon Edel, ed., *Henry James Letters*, Vol. IV, pp. 169–70.
10. Edel, introduction to *Henry James Letters*, Vol. IV, p. xix.
11. Ibid., p. xiv.

12. Henry James, *The Wings of the Dove* (Harmondsworth, Eng.: Penguin Books, 1972), p. 347.

13. Powers, ed., *Henry James and Edith Wharton Letters*, p. 200.

14. Marion Mainwaring, in the *Times Literary Supplement*, December 16-22, 1988, p. 1405, reveals that R. W. B. Lewis indulged in some fabrication in his biography of Wharton. Mainwaring, then living in Paris, assisted Lewis in researching the Fullerton–Wharton affair; but she was shocked on reading the book to discover that he had invented a name for Fullerton's vengeful lover—Henrietta Mirecourt—and used the address of *The Times* Paris office as the location of the apartment building that they supposedly both lived in. She also insists that Fullerton was never *The Times* correspondent in Paris although "heartbreaker, satyr and con man . . . he contrived to make his friends think he was."

15. Lewis, *Edith Wharton*, p. 210.

16. Ibid., pp. 218–19.

17. Edith Wharton, "The Letters," in Anita Brookner, ed., *The Stories of Edith Wharton*, Vol. 1 (New York: Carroll & Graf, 1988), p. 98.

18. R.W.B. Lewis and Nancy Lewis, eds., *The Letters of Edith Wharton* (New York: Collier Books, 1988), p. 162.

19. Ibid., p. 144.

20. Ibid., pp. 134–35.

21. Ibid., p. 135.

22. Ibid., pp. 138–39.

23. Edith Wharton, "The Pretext," in R. W. B. Lewis, ed., *The Collected Short Stories of Edith Wharton* (New York: Scribner's, 1968), p. 646.

24. Lewis and Lewis, eds., introduction to *The Letters of Edith Wharton*, p. 8.

25. Lewis, *Edith Wharton*, p. 219.

26. Henry James letter to Edith Wharton, October 13, 1908, in Powers, ed., *Henry James and Edith Wharton Letters*, p. 101.

27. Letter to Gaillard Lapsley, quoted in Millicent Bell, *Edith Wharton and Henry James: The Story of Their Friendship* (New York: George Braziller, 1965), p. 153.

28. Henry James letter to Edith Wharton, May 9, 1909, in Powers, ed., *Henry James and Edith Wharton Letters*, pp. 112–13.

29. Edith Wharton letter to Sara Norton, March 12, 1901, in Lewis and Lewis, eds., *The Letters of Edith Wharton*, p. 45.

30. Quoted in Lewis, *Edith Wharton*, p. 259.

31. Lewis and Lewis, eds. *The Letters of Edith Wharton*, p. 189.

32. Mainwaring, *Times Literary Supplement*, p. 1405, and a letter to Lyall H. Powers, cited in Powers, ed., *Henry James and Edith Wharton Letters*, p. 16.

33. Lewis, *Edith Wharton*, p. 263.
34. Powers, ed., *Henry James and Edith Wharton Letters*, p. 115.
35. Ibid., pp. 117–18.
36. Lewis and Lewis, eds., *The Letters of Edith Wharton*, p. 207.
37. Ibid., p. 248.
38. Quoted in Lewis, *Edith Wharton*, p. 304.
39. Powers, ed., *Henry James and Edith Wharton Letters*, p. 182.
40. Ibid., p. 246.
41. Henry James letter to Percy Lubbock, May 3, 1913, quoted in Bell, *Edith Wharton and Henry James*, p. 188.
42. Edith Wharton, *The House of Mirth* (New York: Scribner's, 1905), p. 41.
43. Louis Auchincloss, *Edith Wharton: A Woman in Her Time* (New York: Viking, 1971), p. 96.
44. Edith Wharton, "Autres Temps . . ." in Anita Brookner, ed., *The Stories of Edith Wharton*, Vol. 1, p. 141.
45. Statistics from U.S. Bureau of the Census, *U.S. Census Population 1950* and *1960*, U.S. Summary, National Center for Health Statistics, *Vital Statistics of the United States*, 1950, Vol. I and 1960, Vol. III; 1988 statistics from the National Center for Health Statistics, *Advanced Report of Final Divorce Statistics, Monthly Vital Statistics Report Series.*
46. Glenda Riley, *Divorce: An American Tradition* (New York: Oxford University Press, 1991), p. 125.
47. Edith Wharton, *A Backward Glance* (New York: Scribner's, 1962), p. 6.
48. Auchincloss, *Edith Wharton*, p. 12.
49. R.W.B. Lewis, *The Jameses: A Family Narrative* (New York: Farrar, Straus & Giroux, 1991), p. 30.
50. Wharton, *A Backward Glance*, pp. 55–56.
51. Powers, ed., *Henry James and Edith Wharton Letters*, p. 144.
52. Ibid., p. 203.
53. Lewis, *The Jameses*, p. 30.
54. Henry James, "The Jolly Corner," in Leon Edel, ed., *The Complete Tales of Henry James*, Vol. 12 (Philadelphia: Lippincott, 1964), pp. 193–232.
55. Lewis, *Edith Wharton*, pp. 47–48.
56. Powers, ed., *Henry James and Edith Wharton Letters*, p. 144.
57. Leon Edel, *Henry James: The Master* (Philadelphia: Lippincott, 1972), p. 207.
58. Henry James letter to Gaillard Lapsley, January 1, 1910, quoted in Bell, *Edith Wharton and Henry James*, p. 162.
59. Lewis and Lewis, eds., *The Letters of Edith Wharton*, p. 205.
60. Powers, ed., *Henry James and Edith Wharton Letters*, pp. 143, 145.

61. Scribner and James quoted in Lewis and Lewis, eds., *The Letters of Edith Wharton*, p. 300.
62. Lewis and Lewis, eds., *The Letters of Edith Wharton*, p. 286.
63. Edith Wharton letter to Gaillard Lapsley, April 2, 1913, quoted in Lewis and Lewis, eds., *The Letters of Edith Wharton*, p. 290. James's telegram and letter to Billy quoted on p. 291.
64. Lewis and Lewis, eds., *The Letters of Edith Wharton*, p. 293.
65. Wharton, *A Backward Glance*, pp. 243–44.
66. Edel, *Henry James: The Master*, pp. 206–8.
67. Henry James letter to Howard Sturgis, August 9, 1912, quoted in Bell, *Edith Wharton and Henry James*, p. 184.
68. Powers, ed., *Henry James and Edith Wharton Letters*, p. 147.

SEVEN: *Literary Rough and Tumbles*

1. R.W.B. Lewis and Nancy Lewis, eds., *The Letters of Edith Wharton* (New York: Collier Books, 1988), p. 88.
2. Leon Edel, *Henry James: The Master* (Philadelphia: Lippincott, 1972), p. 301.
3. Edith Wharton, *A Backward Glance* (New York: Scribner's, 1962), pp. 190–91.
4. Ibid., pp. 191–92.
5. William Crary Brownell, "Henry James," in *The Atlantic*, April 1905, p. 496.
6. Reviews quoted in Millicent Bell, *Edith Wharton and Henry James* (New York: George Braziller, 1965), pp. 217–18.
7. Wharton, *A Backward Glance*, p. 176.
8. Lyall H. Powers, ed., *Henry James and Edith Wharton Letters: 1900–1915* (New York: Scribner's, 1990), pp. 32–33.
9. Wharton, *A Backward Glance*, p. 181.
10. Ibid., p. 183.
11. Leon Edel, ed., *Henry James Letters*, Vol. IV (Cambridge Mass.: Harvard University Press, 1984), p. 208.
12. Powers, ed., *Henry James and Edith Wharton Letters*, p. 34.
13. Edel, ed., *Henry James Letters*, Vol. IV, pp. 237–38.
14. Powers, ed., *Henry James and Edith Wharton's Letters*, p. 33.
15. Wharton, *A Backward Glance*, pp. 182–83.
16. Powers, ed., *Henry James and Edith Wharton Letters*, pp. 239–40.
17. Edith Wharton, *The Reef* (New York: Macmillan, 1987), pp. 83, 89.
18. R.W.B. Lewis, *Edith Wharton: A Biography* (New York: Fromm International, 1985), p. 326.
19. Wharton, *The Reef*, p. 307.
20. Lewis and Lewis, eds., *The Letters of Edith Wharton*, p. 284.

21. Lewis, *Edith Wharton*, p. 327.
22. Edith Wharton letters to Edward L. Burlingame, February 12, 1908, and March 27, 1908, quoted in Bell, *Edith Wharton and Henry James*, p. 271.
23. Powers, ed., *Henry James and Edith Wharton Letters*, p. 111.
24. Ibid., p. 74.
25. Quoted in Bell, *Edith Wharton and Henry James*, p. 258.
26. Powers, ed., *Henry James and Edith Wharton Letters*, pp. 77–78.
27. Henry James, "The New Novel," reprinted in *Notes on Novelists* (New York: Biblo and Tannen, 1969), p. 356.
28. Bell, *Edith Wharton and Henry James*, p. 282.

EIGHT: *Little Old New York*

1. Edith Wharton, *A Backward Glance* (New York: Scribner's, 1962), p. 175.
2. Leon Edel, introduction to *Henry James Letters*, Vol. IV (Cambridge, Mass.: Harvard University Press, 1984), p. xxi.
3. Wharton, *A Backward Glance*, p. 94.
4. Henry James, *The American Scene* (New York: St. Martin's, 1987), p. 56.
5. Quoted in Leon Edel, *Henry James: The Master* (Philadelphia: Lippincott, 1972), p. 293.
6. Henry James, *Washington Square,* in Leon Edel, ed., *Henry James: Selected Fiction* (New York: Dutton, 1964), p. 95.
7. Henry James, *A Small Boy and Others,* in Frederick W. Dupee, ed., *Henry James Autobiography* (Princeton, N.J.: Princeton University Press, 1983), pp. 16, 42.
8. Robert A. M. Stern, et al., *New York 1900* (New York: Rizzoli, 1983), pp. 12, 280.
9. Edel, ed., *Henry James Letters*, Vol. IV, p. 222.
10. James, *The American Scene*, p. 55.
11. Quoted in Stern, *New York 1900*, p. 145.
12. James, *The American Scene*, p. 60.
13. Ibid., p. 61.
14. James, *A Small Boy and Others*, p. 57.
15. Wharton, *A Backward Glance*, pp. 54–55.
16. Ibid, pp. 5–6.
17. Louis Auchincloss, introduction to *A Backward Glance*, pp. x–xi.
18. Edith Wharton, *The Age of Innocence* (Harmondsworth, Eng.: Penguin Books, 1974), pp. 11, 39.
19. Ibid., p. 42.
20. Ibid., pp. 286–301.

21. Cynthia Griffin Wolff, *A Feast of Words: The Triumph of Edith Wharton* (New York: Oxford University Press, 1977), pp. 312, 313.
22. Quoted in ibid., p. 40.
23. Wharton, *The Age of Innocence*, p. 280.
24. Edith Wharton, *The Old Maid* (New York: Appleton, 1924), pp. 14–15.
25. Wolff, *A Feast of Words*, p. 309.
26. R.W.B. Lewis, introduction to R.W.B. Lewis, ed., *The Collected Short Stories of Edith Wharton* (New York: Scribner's, 1968), p. xi.
27. Edith Wharton, *The Mother's Recompense* (New York: Scribner's, 1986), p. 58.
28. Ibid., p. 140.
29. Robert Lowell interview with Albert Alvarez, in Jeffrey Meyers, ed., *Robert Lowell: Interviews and Memoirs* (Ann Arbor, Mi.: University of Michigan Press, 1988), pp. 442–43.
30. Leon Edel, introduction to Leon Edel, ed., *The Complete Tales of Henry James*, Vol. 12 (Philadelphia: Lippincott, 1964), p. 7.
31. Henry James, "The Jolly Corner," in ibid., p. 547.
32. Wharton, *The Age of Innocence*, p. 67.
33. Quoted in Millicent Bell, *Edith Wharton and Henry James: The Story of Their Friendship* (New York: George Braziller, 1965), p. 52.
34. Edel, introduction to Edel, ed., *Henry James Letters*, Vol. IV, p. xxviii.
35. Henry James, "Crapy Cornelia," in Edel, ed., *The Complete Tales of Henry James*, Vol. 12, p. 348.
36. Henry James, *The Ambassadors* (Boston: Houghton Mifflin, 1960), pp. 137–38.
37. Bell, *Edith Wharton and Henry James*, pp. 309–10.

NINE: *"This Crash of Our Civilization"*

1. Lyall H. Powers, ed., *Henry James and Edith Wharton Letters: 1900–1915* (New York: Scribner's, 1990), p. 289.
2. Quoted in Leon Edel, *Henry James: The Master* (Philadelphia: Lippincott, 1972), p. 512.
3. Powers, ed., *Henry James and Edith Wharton Letters*, p. 342.
4. Edith Wharton, "Henry James in His Letters," *Quarterly Review*, July 1920, p. 194.
5. Edith Wharton, *A Backward Glance* (New York: Scribner's, 1962), p. 367.
6. Powers, ed., *Henry James and Edith Wharton Letters*, p. 293.
7. R.W.B. Lewis, *Edith Wharton: A Biography* (New York: Fromm International, 1985), pp. 371, 378.

8. Edel, *Henry James: The Master*, p. 516.
9. Edith Wharton to Gaillard Lapsley, Nov. 8, 1914, Beinecke Library, Yale University.
10. Powers, ed., *Henry James and Edith Wharton Letters*, p. 293.
11. Ibid., p. 324.
12. Ibid., pp. 324–25.
13. Ibid., p. 326.
14. Ibid., p. 328.
15. Ibid., pp. 341–42.
16. Lewis, *Edith Wharton*, p. 380.
17. Quoted in Ian Hamilton, *Robert Lowell* (New York: Random House, 1982), pp. 88–89.
18. Quoted in Edel, *Henry James: The Master*, p. 530.
19. Quoted in ibid., p. 531.
20. Quoted in Lewis, *Edith Wharton*, p. 381.
21. R.W.B. Lewis and Nancy Lewis, eds., *The Letters of Edith Wharton* (New York: Collier Books, 1988), p. 373.
22. Wharton, *A Backward Glance*, p. 367.
23. Ibid., p. 365.
24. Lewis and Lewis, eds., *The Letters of Edith Wharton*, p. 202.
25. Powers, ed., *Henry James and Edith Wharton Letters*, p. 267.
26. Lewis and Lewis, eds., *The Letters of Edith Wharton*, p. 369.
27. Powers, ed., *Henry James and Edith Wharton Letters*, pp. 376–77.
28. Edel, *Henry James: The Master*, p. 557.
29. Powers, ed., *Henry James and Edith Wharton Letters*, p. 383.
30. Ibid., p. 391.
31. Wharton, *A Backward Glance*, pp. 366–67.
32. Lewis and Lewis, eds., *The Letters of Edith Wharton*, p. 365.
33. Quoted in Lewis, *Edith Wharton*, p. 383.
34. Wharton, "Henry James in His Letters," p. 194.
35. Wharton, *A Backward Glance*, p. 249.
36. Powers, ed., *Henry James and Edith Wharton Letters*, p. 316.
37. Henry James letter to Rhoda Broughton, August 10, 1914, in Leon Edel, ed., *Henry James Letters*, Vol. IV (Cambridge, Mass.: Harvard University Press, 1984), p. 713.
38. Wharton, *A Backward Glance*, p. 368.

INTERGENERATIONAL: James and Wharton to Porter and Welty

1. Katherine Anne Porter letter to Flannery O'Connor, October 20, 1963, quoted in Isabel Bayley, ed., *Letters of Katherine Anne Porter* (New York: Atlantic Monthly Press, 1990), p. 623.

2. Katherine Anne Porter letter to Paul Porter, March 31, 1943, quoted in ibid., pp. 261–62.
3. Quoted in Joan Givner, ed., *Katherine Anne Porter: Conversations* (Jackson, Miss.: University Press of Mississippi, 1987), p. 73.
4. Katherine Anne Porter, "The Days Before," in *The Collected Essays and Occasional Writings of Katherine Anne Porter* (New York: Delacorte, 1970), p. 242.
5. Author telephone interview with David Diamond in Rochester, New York, on November 5, 1990.
6. R.W.B. Lewis, *The American Adam* (Chicago: University of Chicago Press, 1955), p. 151.

TEN: *The Most Unburdensome Friendship*

1. Eudora Welty interview, in Calvin Skaggs, prod., *Katherine Anne Porter: The Eye of Memory* film documentary, New York, Lumiere Productions, 1986.
2. Author interview with Cleanth Brooks, New Haven, Connecticut, June 19, 1990.
3. Katherine Anne Porter, introduction to Eudora Welty, *A Curtain of Green and Other Stories* (San Diego: Harcourt Brace, 1979), p. xii.
4. Eudora Welty, *One Writer's Beginnings* (New York: Warner Books, 1983), p. 90.
5. Eudora Welty letter to Katherine Anne Porter, November 23, 1943, McKeldin Library, University of Maryland.
6. Welty, *One Writer's Beginnings*, pp. 102–3.
7. Ibid., p. 114.
8. Peggy Whitman Prenshaw, ed., *Conversations with Eudora Welty* (Jackson, Miss.: University Press of Mississippi, 1984), p. 178.
9. Ibid., p. 208.
10. Ibid., p. 86.
11. Ibid., p. 41.
12. Eudora Welty, "My Introduction to Katherine Anne Porter," *Georgia Review*, Spring/Summer 1990, p. 14.
13. Prenshaw, *Conversations with Eudora Welty*, p. 80.
14. Joan Givner, *Katherine Anne Porter: A Life* (New York: Simon & Schuster, 1982), p. 16.
15. Joan Givner, ed., *Katherine Anne Porter: Conversations* (Jackson, Miss.: University Press of Mississippi, 1987), p. 311.
16. Glenway Wescott, "Katherine Anne Porter Personally," in Lodwick Hartley and George Core, *Katherine Anne Porter: A Critical Symposium* (Athens, Ga.: University of Georgia Press, 1969), p. 27.

17. Author interview with Marcella Winslow, Washington, D.C., May 15, 1990.
18. Katherine Anne Porter, *The Collected Essays and Occasional Writing of Katherine Anne Porter* (New York: Delacorte, 1970), p. 469.
19. Wescott, "Katherine Anne Porter Personally," p. 45.
20. Robert Penn Warren, ed., *Katherine Anne Porter: A Collection of Critical Essays* (Englewood Cliffs, N.J.: Prentice-Hall, 1979), p. 4.
21. Givner, *Katherine Anne Porter: A Life*, p. 314.
22. Author interview with Cleanth Brooks, New Haven, Connecticut, June 19, 1990.
23. Wescott, "Katherine Anne Porter Personally," p. 25.
24. Author telephone interview with David Diamond in Rochester, N.Y., November 5, 1990.
25. Caroline Gordon letter to Jean Stafford as quoted in Veronica A. Makowsky, *Caroline Gordon* (New York: Oxford University Press, 1989), p. 167.
26. Author telephone interview with Professor Daniel Aaron in Cambridge, Mass., March 12, 1990.
27. Interview with Marcella Winslow, Washington, D.C., May 15, 1990.
28. Eudora Welty, "My Introduction to Katherine Anne Porter," p. 23.
29. Elizabeth Hardwick, review of Joan Givner, *Katherine Anne Porter: A Life*, in *The New York Times Book Review*, November 7, 1982, p. 3.
30. Katherine Anne Porter letter to Eudora Welty, August 27, 1941, quoted in Welty, "My Introduction to Katherine Anne Porter," p. 25.
31. Katherine Anne Porter, introduction to Welty, *A Curtain of Green*, p. xxii.
32. Welty, *A Curtain of Green*, pp. 148–49.
33. Welty, *One Writer's Beginnings*, p. 95.
34. Eudora Welty letter to the author, May 31, 1990.
35. Prenshaw, ed., *Conversations with Eudora Welty*, p. 54.
36. Givner, ed., *Katherine Anne Porter: Conversations*, p. 156.
37. Norman McMillan, "The Closing of the Circle: The Correspondence of Katherine Anne Porter and Eudora Welty," unpublished paper presented at the University of Maryland, May 1991.

ELEVEN: *Fellow Colonists*

1. Eudora Welty letter to the author, May 31, 1990.
2. Eudora Welty letter to Katherine Anne Porter, undated, 1941, McKeldin Library, University of Maryland.
3. Katherine Anne Porter letter to Eudora Welty, March 7, 1940,

quoted in Eudora Welty, "My Introduction to Katherine Anne Porter," *Georgia Review*, Spring/Summer 1990, p. 14.

4. Ibid., p. 17.

5. Ibid.

6. Joan Givner, *Katherine Anne Porter: A Life* (New York: Simon & Schuster, 1982), p. 316.

7. Katherine Anne Porter letter to Eudora Welty, September 18, 1940, quoted in Welty, "My Introduction to Katherine Anne Porter," p. 16.

8. Eudora Welty letter to Diarmuid Russell, late May 1941, as quoted in Michael Kreyling, *Author and Agent: Eudora Welty & Diarmuid Russell* (New York: Farrar, Straus & Giroux, 1991), p. 74.

9. Ibid., p. 19.

10. Ibid., p. 19–20.

11. Peter Taylor interview, in Calvin Skaggs, prod., *Katherine Anne Porter: The Eye of Memory* film documentary, New York, Lumiere Productions, 1986.

12. Author telephone interview with Joan Givner in Regina, Canada, May 8, 1990.

13. Peggy Whitman Prenshaw, ed., *Conversations with Eudora Welty* (Jackson, Miss.: University of Mississippi Press, 1984), p. 318.

14. Eudora Welty letter to Diarmuid Russell, June 26, 1941, as quoted in Kreyling, *Author and Agent*, p. 76.

15. Author interview with the critic and English professor Ruth Vande Kieft, New York, N. Y., May 18, 1991.

16. Welty, "My Introduction to Katherine Anne Porter," p. 21.

17. Author telephone interview with Joan Givner, in Regina, Canada, May 8, 1990.

18. Welty, "My Introduction to Katherine Anne Porter," p. 21.

19. Sally Wood, ed., *The Southern Mandarins: Letters of Caroline Gordon to Sally Wood, 1924–1937* (Baton Rouge, La.: Louisiana State University Press, 1984), p. 214.

20. Welty, "My Introduction to Katherine Anne Porter," p. 23.

21. Quoted in Veronica A. Makowsky, *Caroline Gordon* (New York: Oxford University Press, 1989), p. 167.

22. Welty, "My Introduction to Katherine Anne Porter," p. 23.

23. Eudora Welty letter to Diarmuid Russell, June 26, 1941, as quoted in Kreyling, *Author and Agent*, pp. 77–78.

24. Eudora Welty letter to Katherine Anne Porter, undated, November 1941, McKeldin Library, University of Maryland.

25. Richard Ellmann, *Oscar Wilde* (New York: Vintage, 1988), p. 313.

TWELVE: *Too Much Life and Too Little*

1. Eudora Welty letter to Katherine Anne Porter, September 13, 1941, McKeldin Library, University of Maryland.
2. Author telephone interview with David Diamond in Rochester, N.Y., November 5, 1990.
3. Peggy Whitman Prenshaw, ed., *Conversations with Eudora Welty* (Jackson, Miss.: University Press of Mississippi, 1984), p. 84.
4. Carson McCullers, "The Ballad of the Sad Café," in *The Ballad of the Sad Café and Other Stories* (New York: Bantam Books, 1971), pp. 26–27.
5. Author telephone interview with David Diamond in Rochester, N.Y., November 5, 1990.
6. Virginia Spencer Carr, *The Lonely Hunter: A Biography of Carson McCullers* (Garden City, N.Y.: Doubleday, 1975), p. 175.
7. Author telephone interview with Michael Seide in New York, N.Y., October 9, 1990.
8. Carr, *The Lonely Hunter*, p. 155.
9. Ibid.
10. Author telephone interview with David Diamond in Rochester, N.Y., November 5, 1990.
11. Author telephone interview with Marcella Winslow, in Washington, D.C., May 15, 1990.
12. Author telephone interview with Joan Givner in Regina, Canada, May 8, 1990.
13. Katherine Anne Porter letter to Robert Lowell, July 26, 1952, Houghton Library, Harvard University.
14. Enrique Hank Lopez, *Conversations with Katherine Anne Porter* (Boston: Little, Brown, 1981), p. 250.
15. Author telephone interview with David Diamond in Rochester, N.Y., November 5, 1990.
16. Author telephone interview with E. Barrett Prettyman, Jr., in Washington, D.C., May 21, 1990.
17. Author interview with Marcella Winslow, Washington, D.C., May 15, 1990.
18. Author interview with Ruth Vande Kieft, New York, N.Y., May 18, 1991.
19. Author telephone interview with William Jay Smith in New York, N.Y., May 21, 1990.
20. Quoted in Maurice Dulbier, "I've Had a Good Run for My Money," reprinted in Joan Givner, ed., *Katherine Anne Porter: Conversations* (Jackson, Miss.: University Press of Mississippi, 1987), p. 77.
21. Quoted in Josephine Novak, "Katherine Anne Porter Makes a Feast of Life," reprinted in ibid., p. 137.

22. Henry Allen, quoted in "Katherine Anne Porter: The Vanity of Excellence," reprinted in ibid., p. 165.

23. Author telephone interview with David Diamond in Rochester, N.Y., November 5, 1990.

24. Eudora Welty letter to Katherine Anne Porter, February 22, 1941, McKeldin Library, University of Maryland.

25. Eudora Welty to Katherine Anne Porter, undated, Fall 1941, McKeldin Library, University of Maryland.

26. Carr, *The Lonely Hunter,* p. 156.

27. Eudora Welty letter to Katherine Anne Porter, October 1950, McKeldin Library, University of Maryland.

28. *Boston Transcript,* June 8, 1940, p. 4.

29. *The New York Times,* June 16, 1940, p. 6.

30. Author telephone interview with Michael Seide in New York, N.Y., October 9, 1990.

31. Author telephone interview with David Diamond in Rochester, N.Y., November 5, 1990.

32. Michael Kreyling, *Author and Agent: Eudora Welty & Diarmuid Russell* (New York: Farrar, Straus & Giroux, 1991), p. 111.

33. Louise Westling, *Sacred Groves and Ravaged Gardens: The Fiction of Eudora Welty, Carson McCullers, and Flannery O'Connor* (Athens, Ga.: University of Georgia Press, 1985), p. 100.

34. Eudora Welty, *One Writer's Beginnings* (New York: Warner Books, 1983), pp. 110–11.

35. Eudora Welty, *The Golden Apples* (San Diego: Harcourt Brace Jovanovich, 1977), pp. 248, 267.

36. Harold Bloom, introduction to Harold Bloom, ed., *Eudora Welty: Modern Critical Views* (New York: Chelsea House, 1986), p. 1.

37. From "Remembering Aunt Katherine," a speech delivered at Texas A&M University, cited in a letter from Paul Porter to the author, August 1990, speech reprinted in Clinton Machann and William Bedford Clark, eds., *Katherine Anne Porter and Texas: An Uneasy Relationship* (College Station, Tex.: Texas A&M University Press, 1990), p. 34.

38. Joan Givner letter to the author April 1, 1990.

THIRTEEN: *House and Garden*

1. Eudora Welty letter to Katherine Anne Porter, May 17, 1942, McKeldin Library, University of Maryland.

2. Celia Thaxter, *An Island Garden* (Boston: Houghton Mifflin, 1894), pp. 5–6.

3. Eudora Welty letter to Diarmuid Russell, August 11, 1941, quoted in

Michael Kreyling, *Author and Agent: Eudora Welty & Diarmuid Russell* (New York: Farrar, Straus & Giroux, 1991), p. 78.

4. Eudora Welty letter to Diarmuid Russell, August 28, 1941, quoted in ibid., pp. 78–79.

5. Herman Melville, *Moby-Dick* (Indianapolis, Ind.: Bobbs-Merrill, 1964), pp. 214–15.

6. Kreyling, *Author and Agent,* p. 78.

7. Peggy Whitman Prenshaw, ed., *Conversations with Eudora Welty* (Jackson, Miss.: University Press of Mississippi, 1984), p. 164.

8. Eudora Welty, "A Curtain of Green," in Eudora Welty, *A Curtain of Green and Other Stories* (San Diego: Harcourt Brace, 1979), p. 210.

9. Ibid., p. 211.

10. Ibid., p. 216.

11. Author interview with Ruth Vande Kieft, New York, N.Y., May 18, 1991.

12. Eudora Welty, "The House of Willa Cather" in *The Eye of the Story: Selected Essays and Reviews* (New York: Vintage Books, 1979), p. 48.

13. Eudora Welty letter to Katherine Anne Porter, November 23, 1943, McKeldin Library, University of Maryland.

14. Katherine Anne Porter letter to Eudora Welty, January 14, 1966, McKeldin Library, University of Maryland.

15. Katherine Anne Porter letter to Donald Elder, quoted in Isabel Bayley, ed., *Letters of Katherine Anne Porter* (New York: Atlantic Monthly Press, 1990), p. 230.

16. Katherine Anne Porter, *The Collected Essays and Occasional Writings of Katherine Anne Porter* (New York: Delacorte, 1970), p. 470.

17. Eudora Welty, "My Introduction to Katherine Anne Porter," *Georgia Review*, Spring/Summer 1990, p. 27.

18. Porter, *The Collected Essays,* p. 179.

19. Katherine Anne Porter, "Portrait: Old South," in ibid., p. 163.

20. Katherine Anne Porter, *The Collected Stories of Katherine Anne Porter* (San Diego: Harcourt Brace, 1972), p. 324.

21. Eudora Welty interview, in Calvin Skaggs, prod., *Katherine Anne Porter: The Eye of Memory* film documentary, New York, Lumiere Productions, 1986.

22. Joan Givner, *Katherine Anne Porter: A Life* (New York: Simon & Schuster, 1982), pp. 25–30.

23. Introduction to Joan Givner, ed., *Katherine Anne Porter: Conversations* (Jackson, Miss.: University Press of Mississippi, 1987), p. x.

24. Author interview with Cleanth Brooks, New Haven, Connecticut, June 19, 1990.

25. Eudora Welty letter to the author, May 31, 1990.

26. Eudora Welty interview, in Skaggs, prod., *Katherine Anne Porter.*

27. Porter, "The Old Order" in *The Collected Stories*, p. 324.
28. Ibid., p. 328.
29. Ibid., p. 359.
30. Porter, "Old Mortality" in *The Collected Stories*, p. 220.
31. Paul Porter interview, in Skaggs, prod., *Katherine Anne Porter*.
32. Eudora Welty interview, in ibid.
33. Katherine Anne Porter letter to Josephine Herbst, in Bayley, ed., *Letters of Katherine Anne Porter*, p. 151.
34. Katherine Anne Porter letter to Eudora Welty, November 4, 1961, McKeldin Library, University of Maryland.
35. Eudora Welty interview in Skaggs, prod., *Katherine Anne Porter*.
36. Author interview with Cleanth Brooks, New Haven, Connecticut, June 19, 1990.
37. Porter, "Old Mortality" in *The Collected Stories*, pp. 176, 179.
38. Ibid., p. 219.
39. Ibid., p. 221.
40. Robert Penn Warren, "Irony with a Center," reprinted in Lodwick Hartley and George Core, eds., *Katherine Anne Porter: A Critical Symposium* (Athens, Ga.: University of Georgia Press, 1969), p. 65.
41. Eudora Welty, "Katherine Anne Porter: The Eye of the Story" in *The Eye of the Story*, p. 35.
42. Author interview with Ruth Vande Kieft, New York, N.Y., May 18, 1991.
43. Katherine Anne Porter letter to Eudora Welty, January 14, 1966, McKeldin Library, University of Maryland.
44. Prenshaw, ed., *Conversations with Eudora Welty*, p. 66.
45. Ibid., pp. 66–67.
46. Eudora Welty, "Kin," in Eudora Welty, *The Bride of the Innisfallen and Other Stories* (San Diego: Harcourt Brace, 1980), p. 151.
47. Author interview with Ruth Vande Kieft, New York, N.Y., May 18, 1991.
48. Eudora Welty, "The Flavor of Jackson," in *The Eye of the Story*, p. 324.
49. Welty, "My Introduction to Katherine Anne Porter," p. 25.
50. Porter, "The Flower of Flowers," in *The Collected Essays*, p. 148.
51. Eudora Welty letter to the author, May 31, 1990.

FOURTEEN: *Drifting Apart*

1. Joan Givner, ed., *Katherine Anne Porter: Conversations* (Jackson Miss.: University Press of Mississippi, 1987), p. 84.
2. Diarmuid Russell letter to Eudora Welty, January 31, 1947, quoted

in *Author and Agent: Eudora Welty & Diarmuid Russell* (New York: Farrar, Straus & Giroux, 1991), p. 124.

3. Author telephone interview with Michael Kreyling, Nashville, Tenn., October 28, 1991.

4. Paul Porter letter to the author, June 26, 1990.

5. Joan Givner, *Katherine Anne Porter: A Life* (New York: Simon & Schuster, 1982), p. 372; see also Katherine Anne Porter letter to Paul Porter, August 2, 1949, McKeldin Library, University of Maryland, quoted in Givner, *Katherine Anne Porter: A Life*, p. 371.

6. Peggy Whitman Prenshaw, ed., *Conversations with Eudora Welty* (Jackson, Miss.: University Press of Mississippi, 1984), p. 42.

7. Paul Porter letter to the author, August 27, 1990.

8. Elinor Langer, *Josephine Herbst* (Boston: Little, Brown, 1984), pp. 252–56.

9. Givner, *Katherine Anne Porter: A Life*, p. 372.

10. Katherine Anne Porter letter to Eudora Welty, February 13, 1952, McKeldin Library, University of Maryland.

11. Ibid.

12. Author interview with Calvin Skaggs, October 1990.

13. Elizabeth Spencer letter to the author, April 18, 1990.

14. Prenshaw, ed., *Conversations with Eudora Welty*, p. 219.

15. Katherine Anne Porter letter to Eudora Welty, April 15, 1952, quoted in Isabel Bayley, ed., *Letters to Katherine Anne Porter* (New York: Atlantic Monthly Press, 1990), p. 421.

16. Notes for untitled, undated radio address by Eudora Welty delivered in Jackson, Mississippi, p. 2, McKeldin Library, University of Maryland.

17. Ibid., p. 3.

18. Ibid., p. 7.

19. Ibid., p. 6.

20. Bayley, ed., *Letters of Katherine Anne Porter*, p. 421.

21. Eudora Welty letter to Katherine Anne Porter, April 23, 1973, McKeldin Library, University of Maryland.

22. Eudora Welty, "Katherine Anne Porter: The Eye of the Story," in Eudora Welty, *The Eye of the Story: Selected Essays and Reviews* (New York: Vintage Books, 1979), pp. 30–31.

23. Ibid., p. 33.

24. Ibid., p. 34.

25. Ibid., pp. 38–40.

26. Southern Folklore Reports, Number 1, *Images of the South: Visits with Eudora Welty and Walker Evans* (Memphis, Tenn.: Center for Southern Folklore, 1977), p. 23.

27. Eudora Welty letter to Katherine Anne Porter, January 4, 1966, McKeldin Library, University of Maryland.

28. Louise Westling, *Sacred Groves and Ravaged Gardens: The Fiction of Eudora Welty, Carson McCullers, and Flannery O'Connor* (Athens, Ga.: University of Georgia Press, 1985), p. 46.

29. Interview of Eudora Welty by Hunter Cole and Seethat Srinivasen in *Eudora Welty Photographs* (Jackson, Miss.: University Press of Mississippi, 1989), p. xxvi.

30. Welty, "Must the Novelist Crusade?" in Welty, *The Eye of the Story*, p. 147.

31. Author interview with Ruth Vande Kieft, New York, N.Y., May 3, 1991.

32. Elizabeth Bishop letter to Robert Lowell, July 1948, Houghton Library, Harvard University.

33. Givner, *Katherine Anne Porter: A Life*, p. 452.

34. Herman Melville, "Benito Cereno" in *The Piazza Tales* (New York: Library of America, 1984), p. 716.

35. *Images of the South*, p. 23.

36. Eudora Welty, "Must the Novelist Crusade?," p. 153.

37. Kreyling, *Author and Agent*, p. 185.

38. Givner, *Katherine Anne Porter: A Life*, p. 444.

39. Ibid., p. 448.

40. Mark Schorer, review of *Ship of Fools*, in *The New York Times Book Review*, April 1, 1962, p. 1.

41. Theodore Solotaroff, "*Ship of Fools* and the Critics," in *Commentary*, October 24, 1962, pp. 277–86.

42. Robert Lowell letter to the editor of *Commentary*, March 1963, p. 247.

43. Robert Penn Warren, introduction to *Katherine Anne Porter: A Collection of Critical Essays* (Englewood Cliffs, N.J.: Prentice-Hall, 1979), p. 9.

44. Seymour Lawrence letter to the author, October 31, 1990.

FIFTEEN: *Battles Lost and Won*

1. Katherine Anne Porter letter to Eudora Welty, November 4, 1961, McKeldin Library, University of Maryland.

2. Michael Kreyling, *Author and Agent: Eudora Welty & Diarmuid Russell* (New York: Farrar, Straus & Giroux, 1991), p. 208.

3. Ibid., p. 204. Welty said in an interview that she wrote the novella in 1969 and revised it "a little bit when I wrote it over for a book" [Peggy Whitman Prenshaw, ed., *Conversations with Eudora Welty* (Jackson, Miss.: University Press of Mississippi, 1984), p. 115].

4. Eudora Welty letter to Katherine Anne Porter, February 21, 1972, McKeldin Library, University of Maryland.

5. Prenshaw, ed., *Conversations with Eudora Welty*, p. 72.
6. Eudora Welty, *The Optimist's Daughter* (New York: Vintage Books, 1978), p. 167.
7. Ibid., pp. 207–8.
8. Marginalia of Katherine Anne Porter in *The Optimist's Daughter*, McKeldin Library, University of Maryland.
9. Prenshaw, ed., *Conversations with Eudora Welty*, p. 116.

SIXTEEN: *The Legend of the Past*

1. Katherine Anne Porter letter to Eudora Welty, December 23, 1965, McKeldin Library, University of Maryland.
2. Paul Porter letter to the author, August 27, 1990.
3. Eudora Welty interview, in Calvin Skaggs prod., *Katherine Anne Porter: The Eye of Memory* film documentary, New York, Lumiere Productions, 1986.
4. Author telephone interview with Calvin Skaggs in New York, N.Y., October, 1, 1990.
5. Katherine Anne Porter, *The Collected Essays and Occasional Writings of Katherine Anne Porter* (New York: Delacorte, 1970), p. 248.

INTERGENERATIONAL: *Porter and Welty to Bishop and Lowell*

1. Quoted in Ian Hamilton, *Robert Lowell: A Biography* (New York: Random House, 1982), p. 49.
2. Isabel Bayley, ed., *Letters of Katherine Anne Porter* (New York: Atlantic Monthly Press, 1990), p. 151.
3. Robert Lowell, "Visiting the Tates" in Robert Giroux, ed., *Robert Lowell: Collected Prose* (New York: Farrar, Straus & Giroux, 1987), p. 60.
4. Joan Givner, ed., *Katherine Anne Porter: Conversations* (Jackson, Miss.: University Press of Mississippi, 1987), p. 119.
5. Ibid.
6. Robert Lowell letter to Katherine Anne Porter, April 29, 1960, McKeldin Library, University of Maryland.
7. Robert Lowell letter to Katherine Anne Porter, March 31, 1962, McKeldin Library, University of Maryland.
8. Katherine Anne Porter letter to Robert Penn Warren, July 22, 1963, quoted in Bayley, ed., *Letters of Katherine Anne Porter*, p. 615.
9. Katherine Anne Porter letter to Elizabeth Bishop, December 10, 1973, Vassar College Library.

10. Elizabeth Bishop letters to Robert Lowell, April 26, 1962 and September 11, 1962, Houghton Library, Harvard University.

11. Elizabeth Bishop letter to Robert Lowell, July 27, 1960, Houghton Library, Harvard University.

12. Louis Auchincloss, *Edith Wharton: A Woman in Her Time* (New York: Viking, 1971), pp. 144–45.

SEVENTEEN: *Castine, Maine, August 1957: Ten Years Later*

1. Ian Hamilton, "A Conversation with Robert Lowell," reprinted in Jeffrey Meyers, ed., *Robert Lowell: Interviews and Memoirs* (Ann Arbor: University of Michigan Press, 1988), p. 156.

2. Robert Lowell letter to Elizabeth Bishop, September 11, 1957, Vassar College Library.

3. Robert Lowell, "On 'Skunk Hour,' " in Robert Giroux, ed., *Robert Lowell: Collected Prose* (New York: Farrar, Straus & Giroux, 1987), p. 227.

4. Interview with Robert Hass, in Peter Hammer, dir., "Robert Lowell: A Mania for Phrases" segment, *Voices and Visions* television series, New York Center for Visual History, 1988.

5. A. Alvarez, "Robert Lowell in Conversation," reprinted in Meyers, ed., *Robert Lowell: Interviews and Memoirs*, pp. 80–81.

6. Giroux, ed., *Robert Lowell: Collected Prose*, p. 227.

7. Henry James letter to Edith Wharton, December 24, 1909, in Lyall H. Powers, ed., *Henry James and Edith Wharton Letters: 1900–1915* (New York: Scribner's, 1990), p. 133.

8. Elizabeth Bishop letter to Robert Lowell, March 21, 1972, Vassar College Library.

9. Elizabeth Bishop quoted in "Poets," *Time*, June 2, 1967, pp. 35–42.

10. Octavio Paz, "Elizabeth Bishop, or the Power of Reticence," reprinted in Lloyd Schwartz and Sybil P. Estess, eds., *Elizabeth Bishop and Her Art* (Ann Arbor: University of Michigan Press, 1983), p. 213.

11. Author telephone interview with Richard Tillinghast in Ann Arbor, Michigan, January 6, 1992.

12. Hubert H. McAlexander, ed., *Conversations with Peter Taylor* (Jackson, Miss.: University Press of Mississippi, 1987), p. 38.

13. Author interview with Helen Vendler in Cambridge, Mass., April 23, 1991.

14. Author interview with Frank Bidart in Cambridge, Mass., April 24, 1991.

15. Philip Booth, "This Day After Yesterday," in Philip Booth, *Before Sleep* (New York: Penguin Books, 1980), p. 52.

16. Author telephone interview with Richard Wilbur in Key West, Fl., January 9, 1992.
17. Dana Gioia, "Studying with Miss Bishop," *The New Yorker*, September 15, 1986, p. 90.
18. Author telephone interview with Richard Wilbur in Key West, Fl., January 9, 1992.
19. Elizabeth Bishop letter to Robert Lowell, December 2, 1956, Houghton Library, Harvard University.
20. Elizabeth Bishop, *The Complete Poems 1927–1979* (New York: Farrar, Straus & Giroux, 1983), p. 141.
21. Author interview with Lloyd Schwartz in Cambridge, Mass., April 23, 1991. Schwartz also quotes the prose poem in his excellent piece, "Elizabeth Bishop and Brazil," *The New Yorker*, September 30, 1991, pp. 85–97.
22. Quoted in Lorrie Goldensohn, *Elizabeth Bishop: The Biography of a Poetry* (New York: Columbia University Press, 1992), p. 59.
23. Author telephone interview with Stanley Kunitz in New York, N.Y., January 7, 1992.
24. Elizabeth Bishop letter to Robert Lowell, April 26, 1957, Houghton Library, Harvard University.
25. Author interview with Frank Bidart in Cambridge, Mass., April 24, 1991.
26. Robert Lowell letter to Elizabeth Bishop, April 29, 1957, Vassar College Library.
27. "Tireless, madly sanguine, etc." is from Lowell's essay "Near the Unbalanced Aquarium," in which he describes the breakdown that followed his mother's death in 1954, first published in Giroux, ed., *Robert Lowell: Collected Prose*, p. 350. The "kingdom of the mad" is from "Man and Wife" in Robert Lowell, *Life Studies* (New York: Noonday Press, 1964), p. 87.
28. Author telephone interview with Elizabeth Hardwick in New York, N.Y., January 13, 1992.
29. Robert Lowell letter to Elizabeth Bishop, July 26, 1957, Vassar College Library.
30. Elizabeth Bishop letter to Robert Lowell, August 1, 1975, Harry Ransom Humanities Research Center, Univ. of Texas at Austin.
31. Author telephone interview with John Malcolm Brinnin in Cambridge, Mass., August 28, 1991.
32. Robert Lowell letter to Elizabeth Bishop, July 3, 1957, Vassar College Library.
33. Ian Hamilton, *Robert Lowell: A Biography* (New York: Random House, 1982), p. 238.
34. Robert Lowell letter to Elizabeth Bishop, August 9, 1957, Vassar College Library.

35. Elizabeth Bishop letter to Robert Lowell, August 15, 1957, Houghton Library, Harvard University.
36. Robert Lowell letter to Elizabeth Bishop, August 15, 1957, Vassar College Library.
37. Unpublished Robert Lowell poetry manuscripts, Houghton Library, Harvard University.
38. Robert Lowell letter to Elizabeth Bishop, December 3, 1957, Vassar College Library.
39. Elizabeth Bishop letter to Robert Lowell, December 11, 1958, Houghton Library, Harvard University.
40. Elizabeth Bishop letter to Robert Lowell, December 14, 1958, Houghton Library, Harvard University.
41. Author telephone interview with James Merrill in New York, N.Y., February 6, 1992.
42. Robert Lowell letter to Elizabeth Bishop, December 3, 1957, Vassar College Library.
43. Hamilton, *Robert Lowell: A Biography*, pp. 239–44.
44. Elizabeth Bishop letter to Robert Lowell, January 29, 1958, Houghton Library, Harvard University.
45. Jacket blurb by Elizabeth Bishop for Robert Lowell's *Life Studies* (New York: Farrar, Straus and Cudahy, 1959).

EIGHTEEN: *Stonington, Maine, 1948: "The Other Life That Might Have Been"*

1. George Starbuck, "The Work! A Conversation with Elizabeth Bishop," reprinted in Lloyd Schwartz and Sybil P. Estess, eds., *Elizabeth Bishop and Her Art* (Ann Arbor: University of Michigan Press, 1983), p. 328.
2. Elizabeth Bishop letter to Robert Lowell, January 16, 1975, Harry Ransom Humanities Research Center, University of Texas at Austin.
3. Robert Lowell, "Elizabeth Bishop's *North & South*," reprinted in Robert Giroux, ed., *Robert Lowell: Collected Prose* (New York: Farrar, Straus and Giroux, 1987), pp. 76–77.
4. Elizabeth Bishop letter to Robert Lowell, August 14, 1947, Houghton Library, Harvard University.
5. Robert Lowell letter to Elizabeth Bishop, August 21, 1947, Vassar College Library.
6. Elizabeth Bishop letter to Robert Lowell, January 15, 1948, Houghton Library, Harvard University.
7. Lloyd Schwartz, "Elizabeth Bishop and Brazil," *The New Yorker*, September 30, 1991, p. 89.

8. Elizabeth Bishop letter to Robert Lowell, April 8, 1948, Houghton Library, Harvard University.

9. Elizabeth Bishop letters to Robert Lowell, January 1 and 15, 1948, Houghton Library, Harvard University.

10. Elizabeth Bishop letter to Robert Lowell, mid-May 1948, Houghton Library, Harvard University.

11. David Kalstone, *Becoming a Poet: Elizabeth Bishop with Marianne Moore and Robert Lowell* (New York: Farrar, Straus & Giroux, 1989), p. 115.

12. George Starbuck, "The Work! A Conversation with Elizabeth Bishop," p. 329.

13. Author telephone interview with James Merrill in New York, N.Y., January 27, 1992.

14. Author interview with Frank Bidart in Cambridge, Mass., April 24, 1991.

15. Kalstone, *Becoming a Poet*, p. 115.

16. Ibid., p. 124. My reading of "The Prodigal" owes a good deal to Kalstone's excellent interpretation of the poem and to his identification of the current of Lowell's influence. Both Kalstone and the poet Lorrie Goldensohn point to the origin of the poem's barn and farm setting in Bishop's Nova Scotia childhood and in her returns to Nova Scotia in the late 1940s. Goldensohn quotes a letter in which Bishop admits that the poem "was suggested to me when one of my aunt's stepsons offered me a drink of rum, in the pig styes, at about 9 in the morning, when I was visiting her in Nova Scotia (*Elizabeth Bishop: Biography of a Poetry* [New York: Columbia University Press, 1992], p. 172).

17. Ian Hamilton, *Robert Lowell: A Biography* (New York: Random House, 1982), p. 131.

18. Ibid., p. 134.

19. Elizabeth Bishop letter to Robert Lowell, June 25, 1961, Houghton Library, Harvard University.

20. Hamilton, *Robert Lowell: A Biography,* p. 135.

21. Author telephone interview with Joseph Summers in Rochester, N.Y., April 1, 1992. Summers speculates that the unidentified friend Hamilton quotes was Mary McCarthy and that "she spread this rumor that Cal never proposed to Elizabeth because she did not believe that anyone would turn him down." On the other hand, internal evidence from Lowell's letter about "the other life that might have been had," quoted at length here, indicates that he never found an opportunity to propose. This is not the only time that Lowell's version of the past fails to accord with Bishop's.

22. Author telephone interview with Richard Wilbur in Key West, Fl., January 9, 1992.

23. Author telephone interview with Joseph Summers in Rochester, N.Y., April 1, 1992.
24. Author interview with Frank Bidart in Cambridge, Mass., April 24, 1991.
25. Kalstone, *Becoming a Poet,* p. 146.
26. Author telephone interview with James Merrill in New York, N.Y., February 6, 1992.
27. Robert Lowell letter to Elizabeth Bishop, August 15, 1957, Vassar College Library.
28. Unpublished Robert Lowell draft, Houghton Library, Harvard University.
29. Robert Lowell, "Water," in Robert Lowell, *For the Union Dead* (New York: Noonday Press, 1964), pp. 3–4.
30. Robert Lowell letter to Elizabeth Bishop, March 10, 1962, Vassar College Library.
31. Author interview with Frank Bidart, Cambridge, Mass., April 24, 1991.
32. Author telephone interview with U. T. Summers in Rochester, N.Y., April 1, 1992.

NINETEEN: *The Unbroken Draught of Poison:*
Madness and Alcoholism

1. Robert Lowell letter to Elizabeth Bishop, November 14, 1954, Vassar College Library.
2. David Kalstone, *Becoming a Poet: Elizabeth Bishop with Marianne Moore and Robert Lowell* (New York: Farrar, Straus & Giroux, 1989), p. 135.
3. Philip Booth, "This Day After Yesterday," in Philip Booth, *Before Sleep* (New York: Penguin Books, 1980), p. 52.
4. Robert Lowell, "91 Revere Street," in Robert Lowell, *Life Studies,* (New York: Noonday Press, 1964) p. 17.
5. Blair Clark, "On Robert Lowell," in a commemorative to Robert Lowell, *Harvard Advocate*, Vol. CXIII, November 1977, p. 9.
6. See Alfred Kazin, *New York Jew* (New York: Knopf, 1978), pp. 203–4 and Sally Fitzgerald, ed., *The Habit of Being: Letters of Flannery O'Connor* (New York: Farrar, Straus & Giroux, 1979), pp. 138–52.
7. Joan Givner, ed., *Katherine Anne Porter: Conversations* (Jackson Miss.: University Press of Mississippi, 1987), p. 147.
8. Robert Lowell letter to Elizabeth Bishop, November 14, 1954, Vassar College Library.

9. Robert Lowell letter to Elizabeth Bishop, January 4, 1959, Vassar College Library.

10. Robert Lowell, "Near the Unbalanced Aquarium," in Robert Giroux, ed., *Robert Lowell: Collected Prose* (New York: Farrar, Straus & Giroux, 1987), p. 353.

11. Ibid., p. 354.

12. Jeffrey Meyers, ed., *Robert Lowell: Interviews and Memoirs* (Ann Arbor: University of Michigan Press, 1988), p. 168.

13. Author telephone interview with Anthony Hecht in Washington, D.C., March 14, 1992.

14. Author interview with Helen Vendler, Cambridge, Mass., April 23, 1991.

15. Elizabeth Bishop letter to Robert Lowell, April 1, 1958, Houghton Library, Harvard University.

16. Robert Giroux, ed., *Elizabeth Bishop, The Collected Prose* (New York: Farrar, Straus & Giroux, 1984), p. 251.

17. Joseph Summers, unpublished lecture about Elizabeth Bishop's poetry, Spring 1967, and author telephone interview with Joseph Summers in Rochester, N.Y., April 1, 1992.

18. Robert Lowell letter to Elizabeth Bishop, January 1, 1954, Vassar College Library.

19. Robert Lowell, "A Scream," in Robert Lowell, *For the Union Dead* (New York: Noonday Press, 1964), p. 8.

20. Quoted on the flap of Robert Lowell, *Notebook* (New York: Farrar, Straus & Giroux, 1969).

21. Elizabeth Bishop letter to Robert Lowell, April 4, 1962, Houghton Library, Harvard University.

22. Unpublished undated draft, Robert Lowell, Houghton Library, Harvard University.

23. Elizabeth Bishop letter to Robert Lowell, December 11, 1957, Houghton Library, Harvard University.

24. Pearl K. Bell, "Dona Elizabetchy: A Memoir of Elizabeth Bishop," *Partisan Review*, Vol. LVIII, No. 1, 1991, p. 37.

25. Interview with Elizabeth Spires, *Paris Review* (Summer 1981), p. 73, as quoted in Kalstone, *Becoming a Poet*, p. 157.

26. Author interview with Frank Bidart, Cambridge, Mass., April 24, 1991.

27. Elizabeth Bishop letter to Anne Stevenson, May 5, 1964, as quoted in Kalstone, *Becoming a Poet*, p. 25.

28. Kalstone, *Becoming a Poet*, p. 152.

29. Elizabeth Bishop, "Memories of Uncle Neddy," in Robert Giroux, ed., *Elizabeth Bishop, The Collected Prose*, pp. 247, 249.

30. Elizabeth Bishop, *The Complete Poems 1927–1979* (New York: Farrar, Straus & Giroux, 1983), p. 15.

31. Elizabeth Bishop letter to Anny Baumann, August 1, 1954, Vassar College Library.
32. Author interview with Lloyd Schwartz, Cambridge, Mass., April 23, 1991.
33. Author telephone interview with Elizabeth Hardwick, New York, N.Y., January 13, 1992.
34. Author telephone interview with Joseph Summers, Rochester, N.Y., April 1, 1992.
35. Elizabeth Bishop letter to Anny Baumann, November 10, 1950, Vassar College Library.
36. Elizabeth Bishop letter to Anny Baumann, January 17, 1951, Vassar College Library.
37. Elizabeth Bishop letter to Anny Baumann, August 1, 1954, Vassar College Library.
38. Elizabeth Bishop, "The Country Mouse," in Robert Giroux, ed., *Elizabeth Bishop, The Collected Prose*, p. 21.
39. Author interview with U. T. Summers in Rochester, N.Y., April 1, 1992.
40. Elizabeth Bishop letter to Anny Baumann, September 16, 1952, Vassar College Library.
41. Author interview with Frank Bidart, Cambridge, Mass., April 24, 1991.
42. Robert Lowell letter to Elizabeth Hardwick, January 9, 1969, quoted in Ian Hamilton, *Robert Lowell: A Biography* (New York: Random House, 1982), p. 387.
43. Robert Lowell letter to Elizabeth Bishop, August 7, 1961, Vassar College Library.
44. Author interview with Richard Tillinghast in Ann Arbor, Michigan, January 6, 1992.
45. Elizabeth Bishop letter to Anny Baumann, November 14–15, 1967, Vassar College Library.
46. James Merrill, afterword to Kalstone, *Becoming a Poet*, p. 261.
47. Kalstone, *Becoming a Poet*, pp. 146–47.
48. Hamilton, *Robert Lowell: A Biography*, p. 300.
49. Author telephone interview with Elizabeth Hardwick in New York, N.Y., January 13, 1992.
50. Quoted in Kalstone, *Becoming a Poet*, p. 202.
51. Robert Lowell, "Eye and Tooth," in Lowell, *For the Union Dead*, p. 19.
52. A. Alvarez, "Robert Lowell, 1917–1977," reprinted in Meyers, ed., *Robert Lowell: Interviews and Memoirs*, p. 216.
53. Author interview with Helen Vendler, Cambridge, Mass., April 23, 1991.

54. Lorrie Goldensohn, *Elizabeth Bishop: The Biography of a Poetry* (New York: Columbia University Press, 1992), p. 179.

55. Elizabeth Bishop, "The End of March," in Bishop, *The Complete Poems 1927–1979*, p. 180.

56. Elizabeth Bishop, "The Sea and Its Shore," in Robert Giroux, ed., *Elizabeth Bishop, The Collected Prose*, p. 174.

57. Elizabeth Bishop, "A Drunkard" unpublished draft, Vassar College Library, quoted in Kalstone, *Becoming a Poet*, p. 211.

58. Elizabeth Bishop letter to Robert Lowell, April 22, 1960, Houghton Library, Harvard University.

59. Elizabeth Bishop letter to Robert Lowell, July 27, 1960, Houghton Library, Harvard University.

60. Elizabeth Bishop letter to Robert Lowell, January 18, 1963, Houghton Library, Harvard University.

61. Robert Lowell, *Notebook* (New York: Farrar, Straus & Giroux, 1969), p. 29.

TWENTY: *Another Inscrutable House*

1. Peter Taylor, "Robert Traill Spence Lowell: 1917–1977," in *Ploughshares*, Vol. 5, No. 2, 1979, pp. 74–81.

2. Author interview with Helen Vendler, Cambridge, Mass., April 23, 1991.

3. Elizabeth Bishop letter to Robert Lowell, July 28, 1953, Vassar College Library.

4. Quoted in Lorrie Goldensohn, *Elizabeth Bishop: The Biography of a Poetry* (New York: Columbia University Press, 1992), p. 3.

5. Elizabeth Bishop letter to Robert Lowell, July 28, 1953, Vassar College Library.

6. Quoted in David Kalstone, *Becoming a Poet: Elizabeth Bishop with Marianne Moore and Robert Lowell* (New York: Farrar, Straus & Giroux, 1989), p. 150.

7. Pearl K. Bell, "Dona Elizabetchy: A Memoir of Elizabeth Bishop," *Partisan Review*, Vol. LVIII, No. 1, 1991, p. 34.

8. Elizabeth Bishop letter to Anny Baumann, September 16, 1952, Vassar College Library.

9. Elizabeth Bishop letter to Anny Baumann, October 2, 1952, Vassar College Library.

10. Bell, "Dona Elizabetchy," p. 35.

11. Elizabeth Bishop letter to Robert Lowell, December 5, 1953, Vassar College Library.

12. Bell, "Dona Elizabetchy," p. 44.

13. Elizabeth Bishop letter to Anny Baumann, July 28, 1952, Vassar College Library.

14. Elizabeth Bishop, "The Diary of 'Helena Morley': The Book & Its Author," in Robert Giroux, ed., *Elizabeth Bishop, Collected Prose,* p. 82.

15. Howard Moss interview, in Jill Janow, dir., "One Art" segment, *Voices and Visions* television series, New York Center for Visual History, 1988.

16. Elizabeth Bishop letter to Robert Lowell, June 15, 1970, Harry Ransom Humanities Research Center, the University of Texas at Austin.

17. Lloyd Schwartz, "Elizabeth Bishop and Brazil," *The New Yorker,* September 30, 1991, p. 92.

18. Nathaniel Hawthorne, *The Marble Faun* (New York: New American Library, 1961), p. 220.

19. Helen Vendler, "Domestication, Domesticity, and the Otherworldly," reprinted in Lloyd Schwartz and Sybil P. Estess, eds., *Elizabeth Bishop and Her Art* (Ann Arbor: University of Michigan Press, 1983), pp. 32–33.

20. Mark Strand interview, in Jill Janow, dir., "One Art" segment.

21. Robert Lowell, "Dear Sorrow 2," in Robert Lowell, *For Lizzie and Harriet* (New York: Farrar, Straus & Giroux, 1973), p. 26.

22. Vendler, "Domestication," p. 41.

23. Bell, "Dona Elizabetchy," p. 40.

24. Elizabeth Bishop letter to Robert Lowell, July 27, 1960, Houghton Library, Harvard University.

25. Robert Lowell letter to Elizabeth Bishop, January 1, 1954, Vassar College Library.

26. Unnamed friend quoted in C. David Heymann, *American Aristocracy: The Lives and Times of James Russell, Amy and Robert Lowell* (New York: Dodd, Mead, 1980), p. 388.

27. Robert Lowell letter to Elizabeth Bishop, July 16, 1955, Vassar College Library.

28. Elizabeth Bishop letter to Robert Lowell, August 28, 1958, Houghton Library, Harvard University.

29. Elizabeth Hardwick, *Sleepless Nights* (New York: Random House, 1979), p. 107.

30. Robert Lowell, "America," in Robert Lowell, *The Dolphin* (New York: Farrar, Straus & Giroux, 1973), p. 66.

31. Author interview with Helen Vendler, Cambridge, Mass., April 23, 1991.

32. Quoted in Goldensohn, *Elizabeth Bishop,* p. 187.

33. Lowell, *For Lizzie and Harriet,* p. 25.

34. Schwartz, "Elizabeth Bishop and Brazil," p. 86.

35. Mary McCarthy, "Symposium: I Would Like to Have Written . . . ," *The New York Times Book Review,* December 6, 1981, p. 68.
36. Robert Lowell letter to Elizabeth Bishop, December 3, 1957, Vassar College Library.

TWENTY-ONE: *Pity the Planet: 1960s Politics*

1. C. David Heymann, *American Aristocracy* (New York: Dodd, Mead, 1980), p. 425.
2. Robert Lowell letter to Elizabeth Bishop, March 10, 1962, Vassar College Library.
3. Elizabeth Bishop typescript, undated, 1962, filed with Elizabeth Hardwick folder, Vassar College Library.
4. Elizabeth Bishop letter to Elizabeth Hardwick, September 13, 1962, Vassar College Library.
5. Elizabeth Bishop letter to Robert Lowell, October 8, 1962, Houghton Library, Harvard University.
6. Elizabeth Bishop letter to Robert Lowell, September 1, 1962 (misdated by Bishop—probably actually September 20), Houghton Library, Harvard University.
7. Details about Buenos Aires and the aftermath of the illness are from Ian Hamilton, *Robert Lowell: A Biography* (New York: Random House, 1982), pp. 300–303.
8. Robert Lowell letter to Elizabeth Bishop, December 24, 1962, Vassar College Library.
9. Robert Lowell letter to Elizabeth Bishop, July 5, 1963, Vassar College Library.
10. Author interview with Frank Bidart, Cambridge, Mass., April 24, 1991.
11. Quoted in Hamilton, *Robert Lowell: A Biography,* p. 323.
12. Robert Lowell, *Imitations* (New York: Farrar, Straus & Giroux, 1961), pp. xi–xii.
13. Author telephone interview with Stanley Kunitz in New York, N.Y., January 7, 1992.
14. Elizabeth Bishop letter to Robert Lowell, March 1, 1961, Houghton Library, Harvard University.
15. Author telephone interview with Joseph Summers in Rochester, N.Y., April 1, 1992.
16. Elizabeth Bishop letter to Robert Lowell, February 2, 1959, Houghton Library, Harvard University.
17. Quoted in Lloyd Schwartz, "Elizabeth Bishop and Brazil," *The New Yorker,* September 30, 1991, p. 94.

18. Elizabeth Bishop letter to Robert Lowell, April 26, 1962, Houghton Library, Harvard University.

19. Elizabeth Bishop letter to Anny Baumann, May 2, 1961, Vassar College Library.

20. Elizabeth Bishop letter to Robert Lowell, September 19, 1965, Houghton Library, Harvard University.

21. Schwartz, "Elizabeth Bishop and Brazil," p. 94.

22. Elizabeth Bishop letter to Anny Baumann, March 19, 1966, Vassar College Library.

23. Elizabeth Bishop letter to Anny Baumann, September 1, 1966, Vassar College Library.

24. Elizabeth Bishop letter to Anny Baumann, January 20, 1967, Vassar College Library.

25. Quoted in Schwartz, "Elizabeth Bishop and Brazil," p. 94.

26. Elizabeth Bishop letter to Anny Baumann, October 11, 1967, Vassar College Library.

27. Elizabeth Bishop letters to Robert Lowell, December 15 and 16, 1969, Houghton Library, Harvard University.

28. Ashley Brown, "An Interview with Elizabeth Bishop," reprinted in Lloyd Schwartz and Sybil P. Estess, eds., *Elizabeth Bishop and Her Art* (Ann Arbor: University of Michigan Press, 1983), p. 293.

29. Elizabeth Bishop letter to Robert Lowell, April 4, 1962, Houghton Library, Harvard University.

30. Frank Bidart interview in Jill Janow, dir., "One Art" segment, *Voices and Visions* television series, New York Center for Visual History, 1988.

31. Schwartz, "Elizabeth Bishop and Brazil," p. 97.

32. Lloyd Schwartz interview, in Jill Janow, dir., "One Art" segment.

33. Quoted in David Kalstone, *Becoming a Poet: Elizabeth Bishop with Marianne Moore and Robert Lowell* (New York: Farrar, Straus & Giroux, 1989), p. 226.

34. George Starbuck, "The Work!" interview with Elizabeth Bishop, in *Ploughshares*, Vol. 3, Nos. 3 and 4, 1977, reprinted in Schwartz and Estess, eds., *Elizabeth Bishop and Her Art*, pp. 320, 322.

35. Elizabeth Bishop letter to Robert Lowell, October 20, 1970, Harry Ransom Humanities Research Center, University of Texas at Austin.

36. Elizabeth Bishop, "In Prison," in Robert Giroux, ed., *Elizabeth Bishop, The Collected Prose* (New York: Farrar, Straus & Giroux, 1984) p. 189. The story outraged Katherine Anne Porter when it appeared in *Partisan Review*. She labeled it "filth" in a letter to her friend Josephine Herbst, presumably offended by Bishop's aesthetic handling of a sensitive political subject; see also Elinor Langer, *Josephine Herbst* (Boston: Little, Brown, 1984), p. 235.

37. Starbuck, "The Work!" interview with Elizabeth Bishop, p. 321.

TWENTY-TWO: *"What We're Really Like in 1972":*
The Rift over The Dolphin

1. Author interview with Frank Bidart in Cambridge, Mass., April 24, 1991.
2. Author interview with Lloyd Schwartz in Cambridge, Mass., April 23, 1991.
3. Frank Bidart interview, in Peter Hammer, dir. "Robert Lowell: A Mania for Phrases" video, New York Center for Visual History, 1988.
4. Elizabeth Bishop letter to Robert Lowell, April 20, 1969, Houghton Library, Harvard University.
5. Elizabeth Bishop letter to Robert Lowell, June 13, 1973, Harry Ransom Humanities Research Center, University of Texas at Austin.
6. Author interview with Helen Vendler in Cambridge, Mass., April 23, 1991.
7. Mark Rudman, *Robert Lowell: An Introduction to the Poetry* (New York: Columbia University Press, 1983), p. 158.
8. Author telephone interview with Richard Wilbur in Key West, Fl., January 9, 1992.
9. Stanley Kunitz, "The Sense of a Life," *The New York Times Book Review*, October 16, 1977, pp. 34–35.
10. Author interview with Helen Vendler, Cambridge, Mass., April 23, 1992; see also Helen Vendler, *Part of Nature, Part of Us* (Cambridge, Mass.: Harvard University Press, 1980), p. 158.
11. Robert Lowell, "For Elizabeth Bishop 4," in Robert Lowell, *History* (New York: Farrar, Straus & Giroux, 1973), p. 198.
12. Elizabeth Bishop letter to Robert Lowell, February 27, 1970, Houghton Library, Harvard University.
13. Robert Lowell "For Elizabeth Bishop 3. Letter with Poems for Letter with Poems," in Lowell, *History* p. 197.
14. Robert Lowell letter to Elizabeth Bishop, December 1970, Vassar College Library.
15. Helen Vendler, "Lowell in the Classroom," in a commemorative to Robert Lowell, *Harvard Advocate* Vol. CXIII, November 1979, pp. 22–23.
16. Elizabeth Bishop letter to Robert Lowell, October 20, 1970, Harry Ransom Humanities Research Center, University of Texas at Austin.
17. Author interview with Lloyd Schwartz, Cambridge, Mass., April 23, 1991.
18. Robert Lowell letter to Elizabeth Bishop, September 11, 1970, Vassar College Library.
19. Robert Lowell letter to Elizabeth Bishop, October 1970, Vassar College Library.

20. Elizabeth Bishop letter to Robert Lowell, October 20, 1970, Harry Ransom Humanities Research Center, University of Texas at Austin.
21. Robert Lowell, "Angling" and "Mermaid 2 and 4," in Robert Lowell, *The Dolphin* (New York: Farrar, Straus & Giroux, 1973) pp. 55, 35, 36.
22. Author telephone interview with Stanley Kunitz, New York, N.Y. January 7, 1992.
23. Author telephone interview with Richard Tillinghast in Ann Arbor, Mich., January 6, 1992.
24. Author telephone interview with John Malcolm Brinnin in Cambridge, Mass., August 28, 1991.
25. Author telephone with U. T. Summers in Rochester, N.Y., April 1, 1992.
26. Lowell, *The Dolphin*, pp. 23, 48.
27. Elizabeth Bishop letter to Robert Lowell, March 21, 1972, Harry Ransom Humanities Research Center, University of Texas at Austin.
28. Robert Lowell letter to Frank Bidart, May 15, 1972, quoted in Ian Hamilton, *Robert Lowell: A Biography* (New York: Random House, 1982), p. 425.
29. Robert Lowell letter to Elizabeth Bishop, March 28, 1972, Vassar College Library.
30. Robert Lowell letter to Elizabeth Bishop, April 14, 1972, Vassar College Library.
31. Lowell, *The Dolphin*, pp. 67, 59, 21.
32. Author telephone interview with Richard Tillinghast in Ann Arbor, Mich., January 6, 1992.
33. Author telephone interview with John Malcolm Brinnin in Cambridge, Mass., August 28, 1991.
34. Author telephone interview with Richard Tillinghast in Ann Arbor Mich., January 6, 1992.
35. Stanley Kunitz letter to Robert Lowell, April 19, 1972, as quoted in Hamilton, *Robert Lowell: A Biography*, p. 422.
36. Author telephone interview with Stanley Kunitz in New York, N.Y., January 7, 1992.
37. Reviews quoted in Hamilton, *Robert Lowell: A Biography*, pp. 432–34.
38. Unnamed poet quoted in Helen Vendler, "The Difficult Grandeur of Robert Lowell," *The Atlantic*, January 1975, p. 72.
39. Elizabeth Hardwick letter to Elizabeth Bishop, July 27, 1973, Vassar College Library.
40. Author telephone interview with Richard Wilbur in Key West, Fl., January 9, 1992.
41. Elizabeth Hardwick letter to Elizabeth Bishop, July 27, 1973, Vassar College Library.

42. Author telephone interview with Richard Tillinghast in Ann Arbor, Mich., January 6, 1992.
43. Author interview with Frank Bidart in Cambridge, Mass., April 24, 1991.
44. Robert Lowell letter to Elizabeth Bishop, April 7, 1959, Vassar College Library.

TWENTY-THREE: *Unerring Muse, Sad Friend*

1. Robert Lowell letter to Elizabeth Bishop, undated, 1972, Vassar College Library.
2. Elizabeth Bishop letter to Robert Lowell, March 13, 1974, Harry Ransom Humanities Research Center, University of Texas at Austin.
3. Elizabeth Bishop letter to Robert Lowell, October 1, 1972, Houghton Library, Harvard University.
4. Elizabeth Bishop letter to Robert Lowell, October 26, 1972, Houghton Library, Harvard University.
5. Robert Lowell letter to Elizabeth Bishop, January 24, 1973, Vassar College Library.
6. Elizabeth Bishop letter to Robert Lowell, September 20, 1972, Houghton Library, Harvard University.
7. Robert Lowell letter to Elizabeth Bishop, May 1, 1974, Vassar College Library.
8. David Kalstone, *Becoming a Poet: Elizabeth Bishop with Marianne Moore and Robert Lowell* (New York: Farrar, Straus & Giroux, 1989), p. 248.
9. Author interviews with Frank Bidart and Lloyd Schwartz, Cambridge, Mass., April 23, 24, 1991.
10. Robert Lowell letter to Elizabeth Bishop, July 3, 1973, Vassar College Library.
11. Lorrie Goldensohn, *Elizabeth Bishop: The Biography of a Poetry* (New York: Columbia University Press, 1992), p. 269.
12. Lloyd Schwartz interview, in Jill Janow, dir., "One Art" segment, *Voices and Visions* television series, New York Center for Visual History, 1988.
13. Author telephone interview with Richard Tillinghast, Ann Arbor, Mich., January 6, 1992.
14. Ian Hamilton, *Robert Lowell: A Biography* (New York: Random House, 1982), p. 456.
15. Helen Vendler as quoted in ibid., p. 462.
16. Schwartz interview, in Jill Janow, dir., "One Art" segment.
17. Elizabeth Bishop letter to Robert Lowell, August 2, 1977, Harry Ransom Humanities Research Center, University of Texas at Austin.

18. Helen Vendler, "Ulysses, Circe, Penelope," in *Part of Nature, Part of Us* (Cambridge, Mass.: Harvard University Press, 1980), p. 137.
19. Anthony Hecht interview, in Peter Hammer, dir., "Robert Lowell: A Mania for Phrases" video, *Voices and Visions* television series, New York Center for Visual History, 1988.
20. Author interview with Helen Vendler in Cambridge, Mass., April 23, 1991.
21. James Merrill interview, in Jill Janow, dir., "One Art" segment.
22. Richard Wilbur, "Elizabeth Bishop," reprinted in Lloyd Schwartz and Sybil P. Estess, eds., *Elizabeth Bishop and Her Art* (Ann Arbor: University of Michigan Press, 1983), p. 266.
23. James Merrill, "Afterword" to Kalstone, *Becoming a Poet*, p. 261.
24. Anne Stevenson, "Letters from Elizabeth Bishop," *Times Literary Supplement*, March 7, 1980, p. 262.
25. Author telephone interview with Anthony Hecht in Washington, D.C., March 14, 1992.
26. Robert Lowell, "New England and Further," in Robert Giroux, ed., *Robert Lowell: Collected Prose* (New York: Farrar, Straus & Giroux, 1987), pp. 189, 190, 200.
27. Derek Walcott interview, in Peter Hammer, dir., "Robert Lowell: A Mania for Phrases" video.
28. Elizabeth Bishop letter to Robert Lowell, July 27, 1960, Houghton Library, Harvard University.

Index